Catching Spies

PRINCIPLES
AND PRACTICES
OF COUNTERESPIONAGE

BANTAM BOOKS

NEW YORK · TORONTO · LONDON · SYDNEY · AUCKLAND

This edition contains the complete text
of the original hardcover edition.
NOT ONE WORD HAS BEEN OMITTED.

CATCHING SPIES

A Bantam Book / published by arrangement with
Paladin Press

PRINTING HISTORY
Paladin Press edition published August 1988
Bantam edition / March 1990

ISBN 0-553-28363-4

Published simultaneously in the United States and Canada

PRINTED IN THE UNITED STATES OF AMERICA

OPM   0 9 8 7 6 5 4 3 2 1

SECRETS OF THE SECRET AGENTS

They're masters of deception, experts on human nature—and they profit by human weakness. They know how to play for time—and they know when to strike, swiftly and silently.

They're not spies, they're spy *catchers:* it's their job to corner the world's deadliest spies—not for their own fame or glory, but to ensure the security of a nation.

Catching Spies brings to vivid life the treacherous world of the counterspy, revealing many of the professional insights and actual strategies used in protecting our secrets from enemy agents. If you thrill to the chase in the greatest works of espionage fiction, you'll be fascinated by the book that shows how it's really done . . .

- Defeating "spy mania," where enemy agents are perceived to be everywhere
- "Backgrounding": seeing through bogus identities
- Building and maintaining spy traps
- Exposing "moles" and other penetration agents
- Tracking the spy's "footprints" through the system
- What to do with captured spies—including putting them on public display
- And much, much more!

CATCHING SPIES

CONTENTS

Chapter 1
Introduction 1

Chapter 2
Spy Mania: Chasing Shadows,
   Losing Sight of Substance 34

Chapter 3
Backgrounding: Getting to Know You,
   Getting to Know All About You 65

Chapter 4
Spy Traps: Building and Maintaining Them 109

Chapter 5
Moles and Other Subterranean Creatures 170

Chapter 6
Footprints: Tracking the Spy Through the System 228

Chapter 7
Nailing the Trophy to the Wall 283

Chapter 8
Concluding Observations 333

Bibliography 355

Index 361

For the Little Drummer Girl

1

INTRODUCTION

All chiefs of security are, inevitably and by profession, bastards.

Geoffrey Household[1]

The definitive history of espionage has yet to be written. Even a comprehensive appreciation of espionage in our own times has still to be essayed. Perhaps, for the moment, we stand too close to the events for proper objectivity. Even those who are not in the trenches have difficulty maintaining perspective while the smoke and noise of battle sweep across the field. There can be no doubt, however, from any standpoint, that we indeed live in interesting times.

On even the most impressionistic footing, there seems to be a great deal of espionage going on everywhere. We can certainly infer that much from the tip of the iceberg we occasionally glimpse when some sensational case breaks or some spy comes in from the cold. But the true extent of the mass remaining below the waterline defies even the most professional of calculations. Indeed, it is meant to do just that. There are no easy formulas for guidance in these matters; that which is hidden varies in all its dimensions from season to season and case to case. We are left to ponder and, if we are professionally so charged, to pursue. Catching spies, in real life, may be a very down-to-earth, theoretical—philosophical even—undertaking. An occasional glance at these underpinnings helps those in the business to keep a proper sense of perspective as well as to become more proficient at the job.

There seems to be a fair measure of agreement among both academics and professionals that spying is indeed the "second oldest profession." That it has, too, a fine future is hardly a matter for doubt. Spies may come and spies may go, but the need for their services runs on forever. They may be far from universally loved or admired. They may even become a positive embarrassment to those who resort to their employment. But there is not the remotest likelihood that the spy will pass into obsolescence or even go out of style. Contrary to what some believe, the spy is far from his (or her) last gasp.

Espionage, in one form or another, pervades all our lives like a steady, background hum. Most of the time, it is quite unobtrusive—a little like hypertension. Only in times of heightened social or political tensions, or in the true police states, is there a real, nagging awareness of the intrusiveness of spying and its meaning for the lives of ordinary folk. Elsewhere, in what we are pleased to call the democracies, spying, rather like terrorism, is the stuff of literature, or something that happens—usually—to others. In "normal" times, there is a curious kind of complacency about espionage that eventually comes to infect even those officially required to do something about it.

In the United States today, there *are* some who suspect that Big Brother is watching over our every action,[2] but it is scarcely a matter for protest or alarm among the general population. By the same token, it is confidently supposed by many that these same forces are busily engaged in the detection and apprehension of those true enemies of the state who are undoubtedly spying in our midst. Both beliefs, while mistaken in the larger sense, reveal an interesting state of mind, collectively speaking: spying and, more particularly, doing something—anything—about it are somebody else's business, usually official business. In the United States, we have come to expect at least a little bit of spying (like the ministrations of the omnipresent computer) as a part of the price of modern living. We only complain, and then not always too loudly, when the intrusions become urgent or too pressing. Espionage, at its best, passes unnoticed by most of us, as it should. That there are spies constantly among us is now taken for granted by many, though few would be prepared to say what they do or how they do it. The harm spies are capable of doing does not normally give rise to critical concern. Most ordinary people lack such concern because they do not feel sufficiently important to warrant the spy's particular attentions.

Every so often something occurs to disturb the blissful state of the public mind. A Howard, Pelton, Walker, Pollard, Wu Tai Chin, or even a Miller, perhaps. Then the question is raised: Should someone not have known these things were going on? Ought not somebody have been doing something about it? In short, where were our spy-catchers? It takes such cases, with their human interest angle, and a vigilant, balanced press with a sense of proportion and perspective to even raise the questions in ordinary times.

Yet, at other times, it seems, even the most free and liberal of nations enter upon a phase of spy mania. This is a truly pathological condition. Spies are seen everywhere, quite often where they are not.[3] This is a highly contagious social disease, one that is capable of rapid advancement. Suspicion, once sown, ripens quickly to conviction, giving an extraordinary and not always healthy impetus to the art and practice of spy-catching. The authorities are impelled to act, if for no other reason than in the interests of preserving public order. Spy mania unbalances even the most sensible populace, and violence can easily follow in its wake as a kind of social catharsis. The catching and disposal of spies in an orderly, official fashion satisfies a public urge of the most primitive kind. It is all too easy for the authorities to get caught up in the general mania. All states need to be properly equipped to face such crises of suspicion and alarm and to react appropriately.

Spy mania and what it develops into have a good deal in common with witch-hunting. Irrational in origin and direction, it is rarely productive. Ugly forces surface and carry, for a while, all before them. It is a time of the amateurs, of the self-appointed, of opportunists, and of charlatans. Spy mania not only brings out the worst in society, it is also totally ineffective in terms of engendering the conditions for true prophylaxis. Spy scares and the resulting measures help rather than hinder the real spies. They serve as a useful smokescreen. Worse yet, the posturing that goes with them, often political, substitutes for the professionalism necessary for the task of catching spies. Patience and persistence are the hallmarks of the professional spy-catcher, not posturing or pandering to misplaced public anxiety. Unlike the phantoms of spy mania, real spies and the harm of which they are capable are not occasional phenomena. McCarthyism does not unmask spies, much less create the atmosphere in which their detection might be assured or even facilitated. Spy-catching is not a part-time pastime; it is a game for all seasons.

Just as spies are ever with us, so, too, must be the mechanisms for their detection and apprehension. Such machinery cannot usefully be created ad hoc, nor can it be easily or effectively recreated once it has been dismantled. All too often the splendid security apparatus developed for use in time of war or some similar state of emergency is, in the democracies, too quickly disassembled on civil libertarian or economic grounds once the immediate need for it appears to have subsided. This is a dangerous tendency against which this book earnestly counsels and one which constantly accompanies its central theme. Like Sisyphus (the legendary king who was condemned to roll a heavy rock up a hill, only to have it roll down again as it neared the top), there can be no resting from the labors for the serious spy-catcher.

Espionage, in all its diverse forms, is essentially a people business. Moreover, despite the extraordinary technological advances of our times, it is a highly people-intensive business. The use of people—lots of people—is inescapable. Espionage is concerned fundamentally with the clandestine acquisition and employment of secret information. It may be regarded as a very special way of doing things that cannot sensibly be done by other means. The methods, techniques, systems, and means by which these things are done are all important and, often enough, unique. But it is people power that makes the whole thing work and that constitutes both its special strengths and points of greatest vulnerability. Espionage is built around human relationships. We speak of spy planes, spy ships, spy satellites, spy cameras, and all manner of spy paraphernalia, but spies are always, and only, people—human beings who have chosen or have been chosen to do a very special kind of work in a very special kind of way. Behind all the paraphernalia, no matter how sophisticated, is to be found, as designer or operator, a living, breathing human being. People provide the flexibility, inventiveness, and dynamics of the system. Espionage without people is a contradiction in terms.

Catching spies, then, calls for a very special knowledge of human beings and their spoor—the tracks and trails they leave as they travel the pathways of life. All human beings leave such footprints, however much they try to cover or disguise their undertakings. Modern social life provides a photosensitive record of man's progress through its labyrinthine complexities. Only the properly trained and very cautious know how best to distort the image, alter the scent, and confuse the trackers. Successful spies are never really what they seem. It is the ostensible that receives social authentication and acceptance. Outwardly, the spy may be an enterprising businessman or a derelict bum; a high-ranking military officer or a lowly grunt; a minister of state or a hard-working, unrecognized secretary or clerk; a suburban housewife or a famous socialite. Each of these lifestyles is combined with a secret, hidden life dedicated to something totally different. Yet there are always seams in this intricate web, awkward joints where the patterns of the two lives meet and coincide. These are the weak spots, or fault lines, that the spy-catcher must seek out so as to be able to tear apart the veil. It is hard for even the most disciplined and professional of spies to avoid all inconsistencies of status and behavior as they pass to and from this looking glass world.

Yet, perfection itself is inconsistency. Virtually all humans have something to hide; something they are perhaps unnecessarily embarrassed about or some skeletons they would rather have remain undisturbed in their personal closets. To err, and occasionally, to be caught erring, is human; it is in itself an indication of authenticity. The spy-catcher must look, then, for the inappropriate errors of his quarry. This is the point of reference the spy-catcher must seek, where he must station himself and his traps to descry his prey.

Espionage is posited upon access. To be able to do what is required of him, the spy must be able to get to whatever it is that is to be obtained, appropriated, or influenced in some way. From this perspective, spies may be divided into two broad categories for study: those who enjoy access as a right or privilege, and those who must gain it illicitly. The first category is comprised of those who are in place or who can lawfully so position themselves. They licitly enjoy access because of who they are or because of what they do. In essence, they are corrupted or are corruptible on the job. Their identity as a spy is concealed behind a persona or curtain of regularity. They are properly, often unimpeachably, accredited to be in the place that enables them to undertake their espionage activities, and they operate under a cloak of authenticity that has to be thrust aside if their true, nefarious purposes are to be revealed. For such persons, espionage involves not the manufacture of a false identity, but an abuse of trust and functions.

The other category is comprised of those who are impostors, fake from the outset. While their purposes may be identical with those of the first category, they have to approach their task from a totally different direction from the start. They must create from scratch a being endowed with the requisite attributes to be recognized as genuine and thus allowed the desired access on the mistaken premise of authenticity. There is thus a deceptive superficiality about both types; the true malevolence is concealed within. The one is genuine in origin, but has an interior that has been perverted from its true path, while the other is genuinely bad, through and through, the essential falsity being covered up with a diversionary veneer.

The two categories present distinct operational problems for the spy-catcher in the matter of detection and identification. The tracks of the spy, the depth and definition of their impressions, are characteristically different in each case, and exclusion and apprehension have to be essayed by different means. Only the most minute examination of the life and habits of the individual under suspicion will reveal the inconsistencies between appearance and reality. This task goes to the very heart of the spy-catcher's work. How it all translates into a blend of prevention and cure is a matter of systematic organization of tactics and techniques. The spy aims at concealment of purpose or person, sometimes both. The spy-catcher's light must illuminate not only the observable surfaces, but also the hidden interior. The question *who is this person?* takes on a very special meaning for those whose task is the unmasking of spies. Nothing can be taken for granted. The spy-catcher must be the quintessential skeptic and remain so. Everything and everyone who cannot be positively cleared must be suspect. The cabinet member who refuses to take a lie-detector test *may* be standing on principle, or he may be suffering from an exaggerated sense of outraged dignity. On the other hand . . . The good spy-catcher must have something of the mind of the accountant or auditor and cannot rest content until he has explained or accounted for every item affecting his subject of inquiry.

The importance of background checks as a part of this process cannot be overemphasized. The stringent background check (a rarity, alas!) is a hurdle every spy must expect to negotiate at some time or another. At some point in the past, a decision was taken which changed a dedicated, loyal subject into one whose allegiances lay elsewhere. Somewhere in the past, an impersonation was engineered, a deception was practiced, a new personality conjured up to substitute for or replace some forgotten or half-remembered other. Sometime, somewhere, somehow, something that may be likened to an exchange took place, a transaction concerning a human being who underwent a metamorphosis in his person or values. The techniques involved in bringing about such transformations have now been widely disseminated. They are practiced in our times by professionals and amateurs alike with varying degrees of skill and success. People disappear all the time and occasionally re-emerge elsewhere, having buried an inconvenient past. This birthing, or rebirthing process, however efficient and painfree it may have been, is rarely accomplished wholly in secret. Somewhere, somehow, there are those who have knowledge of what has been done, have taken part in the process, and have been witnesses to this act of creation or re-creation.

Every modern society formally records and celebrates additions to and deletions from its ranks in some way, as well as marking the appearance of strangers in its midst. Obviously, the degree of interest taken in the daily doings of ordinary people and the extent and durability of the record developed vary from society to society. However, only in the most isolated and primitive of societies does the birth of any human being now take place entirely unnoticed. In most communities it is at least celebrated by some small remembrance, however seemingly insignificant. All communities have a need to protect themselves and their patrimony against deception and pretense. The laws concerning property and inheritance alone demand such vigilance. In more sophisticated societies, the event is daily witnessed and recorded for posterity. This starting point to a journey through life can be located with precision years into the future and by total strangers to the event.

From the birth-certification process flows a host of other documentation with which the fledgling must be equipped as the demands of modern living pile up. Few can avoid these accretions. Yet their very multitude and complexity contain the seeds of their undoing. The deceptions, against which the processes are supposed to guard, are invited in by the system itself. When simplicity and directness are lost, verification, especially over time and at a distance, becomes difficult. Documentation is easier to manufacture than human beings are. There is an essential artificiality about all these processes so that the human being has no necessary or enduring correspondence with the sterile record concerning him that has come to enjoy a contemporary existence of its own.

Records can be altered and those pertaining to one person can, often without too much difficulty, be adapted so as to refer to another in his stead. There is rarely anything very procrustean about this. Spies, like many others in our fast-paced, modern world, go through these transformations painlessly on a more or less regular basis. It is difficult at times to avoid carelessness. To take advantage of such carelessness, the spy-catcher needs much patience and the most detailed knowledge of the processes used to establish an identity in the time and place in which his work is undertaken.

Catching spies is a serious, unforgiving business. Mistakes can be costly; small details that have been overlooked, inadequately evaluated, or glossed over allow the spy to do his work and to escape. The spy-catcher must be meticulous, exercise infinite patience, and begin at the beginning. The spy-catcher wants to know not only how the journey through the life of his subject was undertaken, but who was encountered along the way and how such relationships might be pertinent to his inquiries. As we have seen, most personal identities in our society take as their starting point some sort of birth record. Such certification attests not only to the human existence of the individual in question, but to an indispensable and indisputable beginning to the paper chase of life.

It is from here that the procession of signposts proliferates. The diligent researcher can lose the trail or be cunningly thrown off the scent, only to find himself back on a new road he has mistaken for the old. So many of these pathways can nowadays be made to look alike. The persistent investigator must, then, not only find his way back to the right beginning, but must follow the right path from that point to his own present. In the case of the manufactured identity, there are sure to be many suspect gaps along the route, many unrelia-

ble signs and doubtful markings on the road map. The spy-
catcher must have the means to make frequent, accurate
checks of his bearings. Fortunately, few lives are a complete
wilderness or a featureless landscape devoid of all means of
orientation. In the so-called developed societies, all life is a
carefully documented progress from the womb to the tomb.
A reasonably comprehensive, if not always complete or exact
account is kept; those claiming to be the subjects of record
can refer to it from time to time, as can other interested
parties. An identity is built up from such accumulations,
which find their resting place in a variety of sources that
those familiar with the process can consult.

Some form of accreditation is required for almost every
important transaction involving health, education, and wel-
fare (in the broadest sense), as well as a host of other engagements in the regular course of living. Life's progress, in all its
minute detail, is registered through actions, reactions, and
interactions that can be substantiated by those having the
will, energies, time, and resources to undertake the task. Of
course, not every human activity is recorded or even observed by others so as to be capable of recall and evaluation.
Privacy is preserved, in large part, as much by a simple lack
of recall as anything else. Here, we find ourselves amid the
frustrating, uncharted wastes that are the bane of those trying
to assemble a complete picture. From the investigator's point
of view, nevertheless, the gaps can often be filled in, if not by
others directly, then by the testimony of the subject of inquiry himself. Then the route can be traversed for confirmation.

All good background checks should begin with the taking of
a protocol from the person whose life is under review in
order to compare it with other evidence, confirming it or
revealing contradictions or inconsistencies requiring further
examination. Identities, like reputations, are built in part out
of documented or documentable achievements, and in part
out of memories, true or false, mendacious or simply mistaken.[4] Half-remembered, half-forgotten details are often
enough for the spy, the key to opening Pandora's box. The
spy-catcher must exercise inexhaustible patience and an extraordinary eye for detail if the background check is to be
truly revealing.

To the gaze of the inquiring other, the life of a human
being resembles something of a mosaic viewed from an ob-

lique, rather fixed angle. A long and rich life extends into the distance where its far reaches are but dimly perceived and are distorted by the viewing angle. In parts, such a mosaic will be faded so that its surface pattern is difficult, if not impossible, for the viewer to make out unaided. There may be substantial gaps where the small, individual components of the mosaic have been eroded by time and wear or from which whole segments have been deliberately removed or obliterated. In yet other cases, restoration or alterations have taken place so that the mosaic has become something of a palimpsest. The mosaic that is the spy's life has often been written over many times, but vestiges of the original tablet nearly always remain, however disguised their form or texture.

The appreciation of such tapestries of life is never a value-free exercise. Perspective and subjectivity play their part in confusing the senses; things are interpreted differently according to the viewpoint, background, experiences, temperament, and predispositions. The White Horse of Uffington looks like a dragon to some, while the great Nazca lines in southern Peru that have been interpreted as a gigantic calendar of the ancients or a landing field for vehicles from outer space cannot be seen from ground level at all. Those who are too close to the mosaic can hardly make out the full picture it represents.

The spy-catcher is all too often in an even more curious and handicapped viewing position. He has to mentally reconstruct the mosaic without an accurate frame of reference or dimensions, and with only a handful of assorted pieces, in poor condition, that might have come from any part of the picture.[5] He is denied even a glance at a representation of the completed tableau such as that ordinarily allowed the solver of jigsaw puzzles. The undisciplined imagination can easily run riot. An idée fixe, incorrectly entertained, can frustrate the entire endeavor. Every part of the mosaic is important, but, as in the case of ordinary jigsaw puzzles, some parts are more important than others. By their shape, texture, or other quality they suggest the appearance of contiguous pieces. In turn, these patiently assembled *gestalten* are used to further the reconstruction of other segments of the grand design. As the blank spaces become fewer, the outlines of the missing pieces become clearer until at last a reasonably exact picture of the whole emerges.

The restorer of such real-life mosaics must have a special kind of eye for the task, a retentive memory, a certain intuitive flair, and an unusual sense of form. As experience is acquired in the solving of these puzzles, the knowledge gained is capable of being usefully applied to the solution of others of a like nature. Surely, few things can be so exciting and rewarding as seeing the hidden picture of the spy emerge from within the mosaic of quite another life altogether.

Espionage is a highly political and politicized activity, often, in the present context, in relatively unconsidered senses of those terms. Here we introduce the expression "politics of the job" in that most useful sense in which it has been employed by Marylyn Moats Kennedy,[6] as meaning a part of the process by which the job gets done. As Kennedy points out, ". . . there is no such thing as a politically sterile environment. There never can be when two or more people work together."[7] Very special political problems arise when people—often enough, people who have no liking for each other—have to work together under great stress.[8] Espionage can, quite properly, be regarded as a hazardous occupation per se; it can certainly be very dangerous to the health of those working at it. The inherent dangers are extraordinarily augmented because the politics of the job is chronically and sometimes acutely infected with an almost total lack of trust.

The spy is not allowed the luxury of a retreat from the dangers represented by this contagious environment. It has become axiomatic that spies, in our day and age, cannot work entirely alone. They work with and for others—often enough, unknown others who, impersonally and with cold detachment, rule their lives and destinies with their requirements. However many attempts may be made organizationally to compartmentalize the operation, contact with others who know what the spy is and something of what he does—if not who he is—is inevitable. The spy simply cannot do his work in a social vacuum. For the spy, there is peril in every working relationship with others. Every such contact becomes, of necessity, part of the grand mosaic.

Moreover, all these contacts have political implications in the sense that the term is used here. Politics is power in action and spying is peculiarly prone to power plays by those who engage in it. Espionage tends to attract persons with large egos, often accompanied by an exaggerated sense of their own worth;[9] it has more than its share of prima donnas. Espionage also attracts risk-takers, both by the nature of the work and the need to get it done. However cautious and self-protective the particular individual may be, he has little armor against the risk-taking of others with whom he must, perforce, associate. Many a highly successful spy has been laid low by the politics of the job; by those who have casually or deliberately shunted their own carelessness onto others; or, in the worst case, by calculated betrayals fashioned out of revenge, disillusionment, or pure personal dislike. Among the Soviet "Grand Masters," Richard Sorge, "Abel," and "Lonsdale" all fell victim to variants of politics in the workplace. No spy is safe, regardless of state or station. Perhaps the least secure of all are those not in the field but in headquarters. However, those in the field are also not immune to the fallout from "office politics" in these high places. The spy-catcher needs to learn the practical politics of the organizations with which he is confronted as much as their respective "orders of battle." This is, paralleling a tendency in the conventional world of business, quite often a much neglected area of study. The values, quirks, culture, and practical politics of those who employ spies are at least as important to those whose business it is to catch spies as the more formal aspects of their organization, methods, and resources. It is as well to remember that politics is a volatile, unstable business at best. Those who are "in" today may be "out" tomorrow.[10] The spy-catcher needs a good nose for the changing aromas. Some of the best catches are to be taken when the subtle scent of decay perfumes the breeze.

Spying, in our times, has become an institutional rather than an individual endeavor. In some capacity or another, the spy works for others; he is never, in even the most limited sense, his own master. Espionage organizations, while ostensibly on the same side, are often pitted against one another so as to produce a distinctive, tribalized mosaic, meaningful to the well informed. The spy becomes impressed, almost from the very outset, with the mold and characteristics of the organization he serves; in a sense he is defined professionally by his organization rather than his attributes as an individual. This is a factor that is often of great value for the spy-catcher. Here, we need to observe that the spy's relationship to the organization and other personnel of which it is comprised at all levels is, therefore, most important in the matter of his recognition, identification, and apprehension. In the context we are addressing, the politics of the job affects the spy's every action from his engagement to his eventual disposition.

How settled the spy is and how committed he is to those he serves are important considerations in any plan to detach him from that environment. Once he has been discovered, can he be coaxed or lured, or must he be taken (or taken out) by main force?[11] How the spy fits in, how he gets along with those with whom he must interact, how well he is appreciated, and how that appreciation is conveyed are all important "political" questions.

The question is posed not as to whether he is happy in his job, but whether he is content with those with whom and for whom he works. Yet happiness is very much a two-way street. Are his employers happy with him? Is he seen as an important asset or a growing liability? In the overall scheme of things, the spy is rarely as important to those he serves as he tends to think he is; he is usually but a cog in a very large wheel. Indeed, it is more than ordinarily difficult for the spy to evaluate objectively where he stands in relation to his masters' scheme of things. His contacts are too limited, deliberately so, to be able to generate the data he needs. Tangibles are few and speculation on other indicia can quickly lead to paranoia. The spy must fear betrayal from the moment he signs on; only strong and repeated doses of denial keep him on the job. The spy's usefulness is generally appraised in terms of productivity, the quality and quantity of the secret information he is able to procure and deliver, and the effectiveness of the influence he can bring to bear so as to cause the results desired by those who run him. His life on the job, his livelihood as a spy, indeed, his very life, depend upon keeping those who employ him happy or, at least, avoiding their displeasure. This is, in itself, a very political task. For the spy, it colors not only his thinking, but the nature and quality of his work.

Spying can be a very demanding occupation. The servitude of espionage offers little recompense to the truly independent and quickly generates dangerous antagonisms. For some, indeed, spying comes very close to enslavement.[12] The overall political climate of an espionage organization is very important to its health. Unhappy spies are not only inefficient and unproductive, they are also a menace to themselves and those they purport to serve; they are also a signal of some deeper, more widespread, organic malaise.

The discontented spy wants out—this is bad news for those who employ him, for where is out? Such a move means not only the loss of an asset and the actual or potential dividends associated with it, but the defecting spy can take with him much that is of value to the other side, tangibles as well as intangibles. At the very least, he is a piece of a larger mosaic on which someone might be working. His role and its dimensions and coloration can suggest those of others in the organization and their respective locations within it. The curbs and snaffles placed upon the spy, frustrating and painful though they may be, are necessary for the protection of the greater whole. Discipline and conformity are expected of the spy; willfullness and eccentricity must find harmless forms of expression if these are not to attract disapproval or worse. Few spies are endowed with such ideal self-control, abnegation, or even an exact understanding and acceptance of the exigencies of their profession.[13] Relief must be sought in other ways. Many succumb to the refuge of drink, drugs, and mild psychosis. These are weaknesses the spy-catcher must sniff out and exploit. It is generally easier to catch such unhealthy creatures than those who are fit and alert and have all their protective mechanisms intact. The lures and traps of the spy-catcher's arsenal are designed and constructed with these part-willing victims especially in mind.

Those whose business it is to catch spies may be characterized as hunters or trappers in regard to temperament and their techniques and artifices. Most exercise these different ways of going about their jobs as circumstances dictate, though some are, without a doubt, constitutionally and temperamentally more inclined to one than the other. Hunting techniques tend to be more aggressive and individualistic, generating a personal involvement of a very intense kind. This kind of involvement, the very antithesis of detachment, is an important stimulus. The thrill of the chase is an intoxicating sensation that provides a steady dynamic for those favoring these pursuits. Spy hunting covers the broadest spectrum. At one end of the scale, spy hunting is almost exclusively an intellectual exercise, a pitting of wits on the highest plane against a resourceful, unseen enemy with the transitory advantages of surprise, initiative, and terrain. At the other end of the scale lie those distasteful, though eminently necessary, operations of which SMERSH was the apotheosis and certainly the most notorious. Hardly work for gentlemen, but a labor that cannot be eschewed in this field.

Most countries have their SMERSH equivalents, unacknowledged and occasionally disavowed. Such organizations tend to justify their existence on the body-count principle. There are obvious dangers in this. Is easy to inflate the body count with spy look-alikes lending themselves to unsympathetic, clandestine elimination as enemies of the state. It is all too easy, especially in unsettled times, to lump terrorists, saboteurs, and others in with the spy. The time and place usually determine whether the emphasis is to be on results or accountability. Indeed, in troubled times, from the spy-catcher's point of view, the distinctions may be quite academic. What is meant by the word "spy" governs the matter, and there is obviously much elasticity in the term's definition, embracing many different kinds of activity over and above the clandestine acquisition of information. The different facets of OSS, from the gentlemanly, clandestine pursuit of secret information through the ruffianly undertakings of assassination and sabotage, could hardly be made the basis for nice distinctions by the Gestapo or *Sicherheitsdienst*. Nevertheless, the hunter of spies tends to be saddled more with the image of James Bond than with that of Sherlock Holmes. Even in the most sympathetic of cases, the hunter of spies bears little resemblance to a DA's investigator, patiently unearthing the facts of the case for subsequent presentation to a court of law. Spies *do* end up in court and, in countries where the Rule of Law prevails, are dealt with accordingly. But the work of the spy-catcher is not primarily driven by matters of disposition, regular or otherwise. The hunter is concerned with taking his prey, a difficult enough task in itself. The prey may be followed to see where else it leads; it may be used as a lure for other, bigger creatures; it may simply be left alive under the appropriate supervision and fed a false diet for the sake of appearances.

But, whatever the spy's fate, he has first to be caught. Hunting, as opposed to trapping, is just one way of bringing about that result. In a strategic sense, the hunting techniques, in all the richness of their variety, represent an active form as opposed to a passive one. The enemy is within the gates, having effected a successful penetration. He must be sought out and destroyed before he is able to accomplish his mission or do harm. Hunting is usually resorted to when time is at a premium.[14] The more patient approach, however satisfying and effective under other circumstances, is a luxury in such cases.

What we have called trapping is a much more obviously intellectual process, although it has important technical and material aspects. As espionage itself has become increasingly complex and technologically involved, so too have the methods and techniques of the spy-catcher. It is easy to become overly impressed with these spectacular advances so as to overlook the crucial fact that the human being remains behind these processes as the key to their success and understanding. Technology has greatly extended the spy's reach and provided him with a marvelous array of defenses. It has done little to enhance the spy himself and perhaps even less to cure his fundamental human weaknesses. It is human to err, and technology has greatly increased the opportunities for error. Spy-trapping is premised upon the skillful avoidance of one's own potential for error and the calculated exploitation of the propensity for error of others.

The ideal spy is one who effects his penetration without detection, accomplishes his mission, and makes his exit without having left a trace of his presence or his accomplishment. So much the better, if all this can be achieved from a distance so that no exposure is risked at all. Clearly, even in the computer age, such ideals are almost never attained. Even if the spy escapes unscathed, having successfully completed his mission, some residue of this penetration will most usually be left in the system. It is difficult to tread on the carpet, however softly and surreptitiously, without leaving some footprints or soilage. Usually, all the spy-catcher has to go upon, at least at the outset, is the condition of the carpet itself. The more open the society or the system, the greater the risk of undetected intrusions and spoliation; this is a necessary part of the price of doing business in such a fashion. Passports, visas, and inventory control may not offer the highest degree of protection, but they do enable those concerned to keep an eye on what is going on. Obviously, the efficient spy does not deliberately advertise his presence and will do as little as possible to draw attention to his true purposes. Clandestinity is the essence of espionage.

Often enough, the spy is an unseen presence, but his work, in whole or in part, becomes evident through the ordinary functioning or malfunctioning of the system in which he is operating. Vital information is abstracted, and there is a leak, or hemorrhage even, of secrets; things are going wrong, seemingly deliberately so. The spy-catcher is reacting to an occurrence, something untoward that has happened; the loss or damage is apparent while the cause, though suspected, is not. The terribly amateurish operation that terminated in what is now known as Watergate was a reaction to such systematic leakage. Much that we call trapping in the present work is essentially of a defensive nature. It has a preemptive purpose. It signals trouble in its incipient stages. The trap is thus a protective screen that alerts those responsible for its operation of an intrusion into the system. If the spy is caught, so much the better, but even if he is not, an early warning of his attempt will help in tracking his efforts and in defining his objectives. Knowing what a spy is after is very important for the spy-catcher in the elaboration of his own techniques of apprehension. Once detected, can the spy safely be allowed to "run" so that he leads to others? Is his mission so dangerous that it must be frustrated at all costs? Can the spy be tuned, or must he be put out of harm's way? These trapping devices serve as built-in alarms with tracking features that are used in conjunction with other artifices and techniques for physical entrapment.

Some environments are like a veritable mine field for the spy. If he is unwary or incautious in making his entry upon the scene, these traps will "blow" him on contact. The successful trap is one that is unsuspected by those it is intended to catch; situated so that it is difficult to evade, circumvent, or neutralize; economical in use and preferably reusable; and likely to cause minimum interference with the regular processes within which it functions. The psychological effects of spy traps are among their most profound effects. The redoubtable trapper can cause a sense of paranoia to develop in his prospective victims to the point of inducing near-total paralysis. The spy has to fear every contact and process, that which seems to go well and that which goes badly.[15] Healthy fear thus develops into a pathological condition that, far from enhancing the spy's natural defense mechanisms, weakens and eventually destroys them. The totemistic device of the spy-catcher is surely the spider.

Espionage is sometimes organized on a short-term basis while at other times the longer view is taken. On occasion, the need is immediate and only the spy can supply what is so urgently required. Short-term objectives are pursued through relatively rapid penetrations having limited aims and an abbreviated set of specific requirements. Preparation for such speedy, limited operations may have been exceedingly lengthy and profound. There is little that is shallow in the successful practice of espionage. Fools do rush in where angels fear to tread. They are sometimes successful, on occasion spectacularly so, but they are not good role models. Almost any espionage operation, however short its intended duration, takes much time in planning and preparation. Only those who have thought ahead can pull off the lightning strike at a moment's notice with reasonable prospects of success. An asset in place can be appropriately activated more quickly than introducing an entirely new element from outside. These rapid, short-term operations pose their own particular problems for the spy-catcher, leaving little time for getting organized to cope with the threat. If the mechanism for detecting the intrusion and for the identification and apprehension of the spy is not already in place and in full working order, it is likely that the penetration will be successful and the spy will be long gone before countermeasures take effect—a useless exercise indeed. In such cases, a tribunal of inquiry will be all that is necessary.

Those in the business of counterespionage, be they hunters or trappers, can never afford to rest. Letting down one's guard leads to atrophy and decay. A counterespionage service that is not vigilant and ready to respond to any threat at any time is simply not ready and not needed at all. Despite these truisms, there is a depressing tendency for counterespionage services to be stood down when the immediate need for them seems to have passed, often in the mistaken belief that they can be rapidly resuscitated in a crisis or when some obvious penetration has occurred.[16] This too often results in no more than closing the stable door after the horse has bolted. Counterespionage services are a form of insurance, a continuing necessary cost of doing business. Something like Murphy's

Law dictates that losses occur when premiums are allowed to lapse. Protection costs money and effort, but the alternative is an open invitation to thievery and worse. If you are a target for espionage at all, you need the best protection you can afford, whether trade secrets or the national security are at stake. This is not something that can be purchased or developed in a hurry or as the need arises.

Much has been made of the espionage failure of the United States before World War II, a failure that led directly and dramatically to the Japanese attack on Pearl Harbor. The complex reasons for that lack of preparedness have been well canvassed and are understandable, though hardly to be condoned. America's counterespionage shortcomings have received slighter attention, but are no less egregious. Most often, the source of the threat is misperceived; available resources are focused on the wrong target. The espionage threat can come from any direction or a number of directions simultaneously. It is deadliest when it is angled from an unsuspected source. Gentlemen *do* read each other's mail and friends *do* spy on each other. This is a painful fact that only one entirely free of all guile and cynicism would fail to recognize; Sufi wisdom has it that the rose thrown by a friend hurts more than any stone.[17] Amity offers much opportunity for the kind of treachery so common in espionage. An effective counterespionage service cannot afford to be blindsided by friendship. A spy is a spy, no matter his provenance.

Perhaps the greatest challenge for any counterespionage service is the long-term penetration of the system it is organized to protect and, most seriously of all, of its own ranks. Operations of this kind, true masterstrokes when they succeed, are as old as espionage itself.

Within recent memory,[18] it has become common to refer to spies whose task it is to burrow into and secure a situation within the very vitals of the opponent's system as "moles." Doing so has traduced an innocent, inoffensive creature whose labors, though annoying enough to lawnkeepers and greensmen, can hardly be equated with the deadly untertakings of those to whom this sobriquet has come to be applied. The insectivores of the family *talpidae* indeed labor in the darkness, but they keep close to the surface, burrow with no evil intent, and are easily trapped, for they are creatures of habit and leave highly visible trails. Not so the "mole" who inhabits the world of espionage. These creatures go deep, seeking to become indistinguishable denizens of the environment into which they have introduced themselves. They are parasitic by nature, sucking out the host's lifeblood and being paid a salary by that host into the bargain. They are among the most audacious of spies, for they have chosen or have been chosen not merely to enter the lion's den, but to masquerade, for as long as possible, as lions themselves. It is, indeed, hard to find an exact analogy in the animal kingdom for such creatures; almost every figure has its flaws. The difficulty lies in choosing one which adequately conveys the meaning of the extraordinary process of transformation that occurs over the long term. The mole usually enters close to the bottom of the heap, at a lowly rank in the hierarchy. There is an expectation on the part of his masters that this nondescript, unsuspected creature will work his way upward, increasing its stature and responsibilities until it is in a position of real authority, capable of acquiring and communicating secret information or influencing events. This is not just a growing-up process or a function of maturity. It involves a more complete and radical change than that of chrysalis to butterfly. The "mole" is certainly transformed, yet remains a mole throughout. This creature pretends to be something it is not, namely a loyal, hardworking servant of its ostensible employer. In reality, it is from the outset a foreign organism, wholly owned and operated by opponents of the system in which it functions.

Many remarkable examples of moles have come to light in our times; "Kim" Philby was certainly one; Roger Hollis may have been another. Both entered the British secret services in the lowest grades. Philby, an avowed communist and a Soviet intelligence officer throughout his long career, nearly achieved the directorship of SIS, and Hollis became, at a very critical time, director of MI5. The damage the mole Philby was able to do is well documented and remarkable by any standards. What he might have done had he reached the pinnacle of his profession is terrifying to contemplate. The failure to perceive his treasonous work, to identify his true character, and neutralize him should be carefully studied in the present context. The Hollis case is particularly instructive with regard to the spy-catcher's dilemma in dealing with one who heads a spy-catching service. While Philby was eventually unmasked, the jury is still out on Hollis and, more importantly, on the way in which the suspicions concerning him were handled over the years.[19]

Unlike his furry counterpart, the espionage mole does not work in the dark. Indeed, the exalted position he achieves if he is able to succeed in his endeavors gives him virtual oversight of all the system's operations. Knowledge is power, and knowledge of this kind is extraordinarily powerful. Not only do the real employers of the mole have access to the most secret and sensitive information concerning the thinking and operations of its opponents, but their agent is in a position to influence the decision-making process at the highest level. He can reveal the identities and operations of secret agents of his "own side" to his real masters in a singularly vicious form of betrayal. But there is yet more. The mole may achieve a position of being able to frustrate efforts to uncover his presence.[20] He can divert suspicion from himself onto others. He can destroy incriminating evidence and "lose" that which might point to his own culpability. He can alter the record so that the institutional memory is corrupted and made to reflect a different version of history. If circumstances so warrant and the inherent risks justify such a course, he can eliminate those in a position to expose him.[21] Perhaps the greatest threat to the mole's security comes from defecting intelligence officers in the employ of his true masters who may know something, however little, of his existence, situation, operational purposes, or identity. The mole may have to make strenuous efforts to get to such persons before they are able to reveal their knowledge.[22]

A semantic point is worth interpolating here. A mole is more than just a highly placed functionary of the other side who is "on the pad." Such individuals are obviously highly useful, especially if they have risen to be heads of state or senior ministers. But these are essentially individuals who have been corrupted somewhere along the line, pulled, as it were, onto a different path than that along which life and its ordinary exigencies might have directed them. These creatures have their proper place and purpose in the scheme of things and can be as useful and dangerous as any mole. The mole properly so designated is a committed servant of his real masters from the outset. He is their original creation. He obtains position and power with their encouragement and assistance. He is an investment in long-term expectations.

Here, we are concerned not with the creation and placement of moles but with their detection, entrapment, and disposition. The most usual indicator of the presence of a mole is that things are going wrong that can have no logical explanation other than this kind of insider dynamic. These are things that can *only* have happened with this special kind of inside assistance.[23] The question then is *who* is helping from the inside? Is this unknown a comparatively recent intruder? Or a long-term penetration that has lurked unsuspected within the system and has now reached a point of virtual invulnerability? These cases truly test the patience and ingenuity of spy-catchers. The duel between the mole and spy-catcher is deadly, and the outcome is vital and often decisive for both.

A more aptly named, though somewhat similar, long-term implant is the "sleeper" (this is really taking the long view of espionage). The sleeper is inserted into the medium in which he is to operate with instructions to integrate himself as completely as possible. Over a period of years, he will become a part of the fabric of the society into which he has been introduced so as to be indistinguishable from any of its regular components. He will have an ordinary, often mundane job, and will enjoy a social life designed to be satisfying, unremarkable, and inconspicuous. Ideally, he should draw little attention to himself beyond that which might be accorded a person of his type or station, and he will avoid the kind of trouble which might incapacitate him or occasion unwelcome probing. Above all, from the moment of his appearance on the scene, he will be left strictly to his own devices by those responsible for his mission. His cover having been once established, it is up to the sleeper to make himself comfortable for the duration, alone and unaided. He will not be contacted, save in the direst of emergencies, until the moment when, perhaps even ten or twenty years down the road, he is activated for service.

Extraordinary loyalty, dedication, and discipline are required of such a secret agent. Over such a lengthy period of time, there is bound to be much to divert, disappoint, disillusion, and discourage. However enthusiastic, well-trained, and committed at the outset, it is difficult for the sleeper to keep his sense of purpose unblemished during the long years of waiting alone. Patience and belief systems are tried to their limits. People change in so many ways over the years, and a pleasant, humdrum life can be very seductive and difficult to give up. Only an espionage organization with the most remarkable management capability, truly long-range view of geopolitics, and an inflexible sense of purpose can even contemplate such undertakings. The potential benefits of such operations are considerable, but the obstacles in the way of their realization are formidable. For spy-catchers, these are rare prizes indeed. True sleepers are among the most elusive of creatures, blending so perfectly with their surroundings that the conventional, telltale signs that reveal the presence of the active spy are wholly absent. This, of course, is the main object of such a costly exercise. Once the sleeper has become operational, however, he will be as vulnerable as any other kind of spy; only the protective shell he has developed over the years will serve to shield him from suspicion. Hunting down the inactive sleeper is a thankless, profitless task, and one but rarely rewarded with success.[24] Only the most remarkable luck or reliable information from a source on "the other side" is likely to lead the spy-catcher to his quarry. Again, at the risk of stating the obvious, the more open and pluralistic the society, the easier it is to introduce a sleeper among its ranks. The advantages to those who run sleepers of an enduring, sustaining ideology (such as communism) hardly need underlining.

The spy-catcher, however professional and detached in his work, is never a wholly independent technician. He has political masters and serves distinct and distinctive political aims. His success indeed is intimately linked to the strength and appropriateness of these connections. Modern history highlights the truth of this proposition. The Cold War has many intricate and interlocking facets—political, military, sociological, and economic. Preeminently it is a war of the spies. It had provided themes for countless novels, but it is nevertheless very real, very political, and never ending. There are many players, for although the sides were chosen with a certain definition long ago, there is always room for fresh participants to accommodate the ever-shifting currents of geopolitics. Each side seeks technical advantages where it can, pressing to gain ground with small, but measurable, victories.

There are countless casualties, though few spectacular engagements. In this war without end, both sides keep score meticulously. Every enemy offensive has to be countered, whether or not any real advantage has been gained. These exchanges lately have assumed an almost ritualistic character.

For the major players, the political aspects of these games often override the purely technical or practical ones. It has become almost axiomatic that the breakup of an opponent's spy ring will be followed by a retaliatory measure of a comparable kind initiated by the originally discomfited party. The ability to arrange such an event is an important and more than incidental part of the work of the modern spy-catcher.[25] Such requirements are hardly fortuitous. They involve nice policy calculations, as well as a keen understanding of the way the game is played. They call for a certain finesse, a delicacy of touch: a resort to the crude costs political points. Basically, the mechanism is very simple: these are hostage-taking games. In recent times, these games and their purposes have become quite blatant; pretense, for the most part, has been discarded. The process, too, has been considerably speeded up as this change of attitudes has taken place. Formerly, a certain genteel decorum prevailed; the necessary linkage was not directly or pointedly suggested by word or deed. An important spy would be discovered, apprehended, and brought to book. No immediate response, save perhaps the formality of a denial, would be forthcoming from the other side. Some while later, seemingly in the most natural course of events, it was to be expected that the other side would be successful in a roughly comparable counterespionage operation. Matters would not be forced. The stage would be set for an exchange, which would take place after protracted discussion and a certain, if cynical, reluctance to suggest that the one occurrence might in any way have artificially prompted the other.[26] Some thirty-odd years ago, when these matters were still in a developmental stage, the Abel/Powers exchange may be seen as marking the crossroads of the old and the new. While these associations of events were never, of course, wholly fortuitous and always had something of a contrived character, there was nevertheless a restrained attitude toward these matters—an understanding, perhaps that they could so easily get out of hand, that has since been lost. It is now predictable that the arrest of a Soviet spy in the United States or any of the major European countries will be followed, almost instantaneously, by the arrest in the USSR of a suitably chosen national of the first arresting country, who is promptly accused of espionage. Guilt or otherwise is immaterial; the ploy is what counts. The Daniloff affair should be seen in this light.[27]

To be an effective accomplice of his political masters in this regard, the spy-catcher must have a collection of measured trophies, a storehouse of suitable prospects, or the ability to contrive situations convincingly at the drop of a hat. The disposition of spies, once caught, is an important factor in the orientation of this work. If they are simply eliminated, before, after, or without trial, they cease to be an element of exchange. The spy-catcher's work is made more difficult, for he is deprived of a useful weapon in his armory. The spy-catcher can never be above politics; he must learn how to read and use political considerations to his own professional advantage. But the mixture must be right. The FBI under J. Edgar Hoover was enormously powerful politically, but its efficiency as a counterespionage agency cannot be measured by reference to that power. The KGB is the most politically driven counterintelligence agency in existence today. Its effectiveness cannot be measured by reference to political influences; its policies can.

The philosophy of disposal can have a profound effect on the work of the spy-catcher. That the spy has to be sought out and eradicated from the system he has invaded is unquestioned. What is at issue, among the competing philosophies, are the methods, vigor, and visibility with which this goal is to be pursued. Conventionally, the disposition of offenders has a number of philosophical or policy underpinnings: incapacitation, punishment, deterrence, and rehabilitation. Clearly, even in normal times, the spy who has threatened the national security cannot be treated, in terms of disposition, in the same way as other criminals caught and processed by the regular system of criminal justice. There is the immediate question whether such spies should be tried in the ordinary courts and permitted all the rights guaranteed them by the regular legal system or whether they should be processed through special tribunals and allowed only restricted rights. Nevertheless, the stated, underlying philosophical goals receive substantial recognition and expression in the disposal of the spy. Thus incapacitation is concerned with seeing that the spy is stopped in his tracks and does not get a second chance to do his work. Death is clearly the most convenient and decisive way of attaining these objectives, but it may be inexpedient, politically unwise, or unsound in some particular historical context. Lengthy incarceration may serve similar purposes and, like some vasectomies, has the merits of being reversible should circumstances dictate. Some spies are simply too dangerous to leave alive, however secure their confinement. (An Eli Cohen or a Richard Sorge can only be safely incapacitated through execution.)

Punishment may have moralistic or practical objectives; it may be admonitory or condign, instrumental or symbolic. It may be used to set an example, the Rosenberg Solution. But it is never an end in itself. Punishment, whatever form it takes, is intended to shape the future in some way, that of the punished or others like him. It is closely tied to the notion of deterrence, special and general. It need never be pretended, in the case of the spy, that punishment may be conducive to repentance. If purgation is in mind, it is performance on this earth that is required for redemption, not repentance, real or otherwise, but a solid making of amends. The spy is required to give his act of contrition some practical form if he expects to mitigate the consequences. The Walker/Whitworth[28] cases are most instructive in this regard. Rehabilitation clearly has a special meaning in these espionage cases. Reforming or curing the spy is in itself hardly a worthwhile or realistic undertaking from a cost/benefit perspective. But the spy can, if he is so inclined, most usefully agree to work his passage. While he may not secure redemption through cooperation with those who hold his fate in their hands, he can often improve his prospects and perhaps obtain commutation of a certain death sentence by agreeing to work against his erstwhile masters. While he may in the process come to see the error of his former ways, nothing in the nature of a true spiritual or ideological conversion is sought in these cases. This is an arrangement of convenience best exemplified, perhaps, by the British World War II program known as the Double Cross system.[29] While these options and alternatives may aid the spy-catcher little in his primary work of identifying and apprehending enemy agents, they are enormously important once the catch has been made. They give him the means to bargain, coerce, and strike deals. In short, they give him leverage. Cunningly employed, they are the pry bars that can open other closed worlds. They lend their own mystique to the spy-catcher's work that adds to its deterrent value. They are part of the spy-catcher's track record. Every hunter or trapper needs a good trophy room.

This book is essentially about security—a very special kind of security. In the sense in which the word is used here, it is nothing less than the comprehensive protection of the system or institution against the insidious forces working from within to encompass its change or destruction. Security is essentially a process by which things are kept safe from harm. Security, especially that which is our subject here, is a tough, unsentimental profession. It can easily descend into inhumanity. Such a degeneration is hardly surprising. Espionage, too, is strongly laced with cynicism and suspicion. It is a world of exploiters, manipulators, con artists, and ruthless betrayers of trust and confidence. It is difficult to work with pitch and remain undefiled.

The spy-catcher has to be hard through and through. A tough hide is not enough; the rhinocerous is soft and vulnerable inside. This condition, which in another context has been called "The Oyster Paradigm,"[30] lay at the heart of the problems of Sir Percy Sillitoe, a post-World War II head of Britain's MI5.[31] Such necessary toughness can often translate into a personal unpleasantness which has a propensity to sour working relations. Even the most urbane are to be distrusted, and the very superficiality itself works against them. The successful chief of security cannot expect to win any popularity contests. Who, after all, ever heard of a popular head of the Gestapo?[32] The best that can be hoped for is to be feared, dreaded even, without being actively hated. This is indeed a difficult balance to strike. Too much dread produces isolation; few like to be close to those with such enormous potential for harming them. This detachment may be good for the soul, but it is in the end very bad for the work. The spy-catcher cannot do his work effectively in a social vacuum or an ivory tower. The image of the dilettante security chief, an academic full of high-flown ideas and ideals who is removed from all corrupting contact with the world, is attractive and whimsical enough to find a place in fiction, but unrealistic and far removed from the demands of the job. The feet of the counterespionage specialist must be firmly on the ground; a head in the clouds makes for an unacceptable sense of imbalance.

The chief of security is in an extraordinarily powerful position. He is feared because of this power and the way in which it might be used or abused. He must never be allowed to become stronger than the institution he serves or to use it as a stepping-stone to total domination. Only the most effective institutional safeguards can curb the ambitions of the truly power hungry. In an authentic police state, even these safeguards may not be enough. A system that avoids the perils of descending into the nightmare of the police state as an antidote to its espionage problems must pay great attention to these matters. There must be a strong focus upon the individual in whom these extraordinary powers are vested.

On the national level, the head of counterespionage services should have security of tenure during a limited period and be responsible directly to the head of state through an appropriate reporting mechanism. Ideally, he should enjoy anonymity and be free from personal political ambition; his political masters will feel more comfortable answering for his actions if assured he has no plans to supplant them. Above all, he should have integrity and be good at his primary job; he ought not to be a political or patronage appointee. He should be capable of earning the confidence of those who work under his direction as well as those at whose behest he serves. He should know, too, when it is time to quit.[33] He who cannot contemplate his own retirement with equanimity is too dangerous for this job.

POINTS TO REMEMBER

1. Catching spies is a full-time occupation and is best accomplished out of the public eye. It requires professional dedication, patience, and persistence. The machinery, assets, and individuals necessary to detect and apprehend spies cannot be created on a temporary ad hoc basis and are difficult to recreate once dismantled. While there are questions of liberties and limitations in counterespionage, there are also serious issues concerning the security of liberty and property for the people and the nation.

2. Espionage, the clandestine acquisition and use of secret

information, is a highly people-intensive business. It is ultimately built on human relationships, and catching spies calls for a very special knowledge of human beings—their motivations, actions, and the tracks they leave as they move through social life. Catching spies involves a deep understanding of an appreciation for deception and its employment, for disloyalty and its development, for weaknesses and their uses, and for the stitches which bind together individual character and social structure.

3. Spies may be seen as being in two broad categories: those who enjoy privileged access and those who must gain access by illicit and/or deceptive means. The first involves those who have developed an authentic character and achieved a trusted social position, and who are or have been corrupted. The second category involves those who have developed a deceptive character (have been planted, i.e., a mole) and have achieved a trusted position. The two types present distinctively different operational problems for the spy-catcher.

4. Every person leaves signs of his life's passing, a biography that is personal and social. It is composed of vast quantities of footprints (birth certificates, awards, yearbooks, hidden reports, saved doodles, and recalled quirks of behavior) that have been noted by friends or recorded in photo or film. Thus, an identity can be built up from the accumulations of paper. For the spy-catcher, patient attention to the paper identity is a necessity, as is attention to the minutest details of the currently socially manufactured identity of the person(s) under scrutiny. All good background checks should begin with taking the protocol from the person whose life is under review. The protocol must be compared with other evidence, confirming what it contains or reveals about gaps and contradictions—points for further examination. Identities are built in part out of documented or documentable achievements and in part out of memories—real, embellished, and bogus. Yet all identities are social in nature and are verified by others. Patient checking of details is crucial.

5. Good spy-catchers, in setting security, should employ spy traps that are protective screens, the violation of which alerts those responsible that an intrusion has occurred. The best traps are those which are unsuspected and so situated that they are difficult to avoid or neutralize. They should be

reusable and cause minimum interference with the regular rounds of activity.

NOTES

1. *Dance of the Dwarves*, Boston: Little, Brown, 1968, page 33.

2. See *The Age of Surveillance*, Frank J. Donner, New York: Alfred A. Knopf, 1980.

3. For a good, historical example of this condition, see the account of Great Britain on the eve of World War I and during the early days of that conflict in *Her Majesty's Secret Service*, Christopher Andrew, New York: Viking Penguin, 1986, pages 34–85.

"Japan was somewhat paranoid in this period. Spy-consciousness was almost a mania. . . ." *Pearl Harbor: The Verdict of History*, Gordon Prange with Donald M. Goldstein and Katherine V. Dillon, New York: McGraw-Hill, 1986, page xvii.

4. "As is so true so often of prominent people, vignettes in a life tell more of the character of Leading Characters than do milestone markers of positions and titles." A Forbes Report on Drew Lewis, *Forbes*, 14 July 1986, page 17.

5. An excellent account of what is involved in this process is contained in a work of fiction, *Sleeper Agent*, Ib Melchior, New York: Harper & Row, 1975.

6. *Office Politics*, Chicago: Follet, 1980, page 16.

7. Ibid.

8. An interesting example is afforded by an imaginative work of fiction, *Spies*, Richard Ben Sapir, New York: Doubleday, 1984.

9. See, for example, *In Search of Enemies*, John Stockwell, New York: W.W. Norton, 1978.

10. See that engaging work, *Red Square*, Edward Topol and Fridrikh Neznansky, New York: Quarter Books, 1983.

11. For an acutely perceptive account of what is involved in both options, see that wickedly humorous work, *The Turn Around*, Vladimir Volkoff, New York: Doubleday, 1981.

12. Charles McCarry, in one of his excellent novels, writes: "An agent always works for himself. It's a mental disease. Quite incurable." *The Tears of Autumn*, New York: Saturday Review Press/E. P. Dutton, 1975, page 205.

13. Recruiters looking for perfection will not recruit many spies. The following, written in another connection, applies forcefully here: "If you wait to make friends with people you don't have to feel ambivalent about at all, you won't have many friends." Or, it might be added, much of a case load. *Help I am being held prisoner*, Donald E. Westlake, New York: M. Evans, 1974, page 213.

14. See, for example, *The Amateur*, Robert Littell, New York: Simon & Schuster, 1981.

15. The spy-catcher often projects his own fears: " . . . security people fear the world." *The Better Angels*, Charles McCarry, New York: E.P. Dutton, 1979, page 236.

16. "Stinting security is almost the worst form of miserliness, because in the end it costs the dearest." *Spy-Catcher*, Oreste Pinto, New York: Harper & Brothers, 1952, page 210.

17. Some, in high places, are more cynical and suspicious than others. " 'Xerxes had another disease common to great men,' said Zaitsev, 'He didn't trust the people around him.' " *The Defection of A.J. Lewinter*, Robert Littell, Boston: Houghton Mifflin, 1973, page 116.

18. The precise date of the emergence of this usage has so far eluded investigation. *Partridge's Dictionary of Slang and Unconventional English*, 8th Ed., 1984, shows the term to have gained currency in the late 1940s, but it only seems to have achieved widespread acceptance in the 1970s. See, too, the interesting reservations of John Le Carré in *Tinker, Tailor, Soldier, Spy*, New York: Alfred A. Knopf, 1980, page 57.

19. Chapman Pincher's seminal work should be consulted on this. See *Their Trade Is Treachery*, London: Sedgwick and Jackson, 1981, and *Too Secret Too Long*, New York: St. Martin's Press, 1984.

20. This was the theme of a singularly perceptive novel, *The Private Sector*, Joseph Hone, New York: E.P. Dutton, 1972. The denouement and hopelessness of the tragic "hero" are very real.

21. See *Wilderness of Mirrors*, Donald Seaman, New York: Harper & Row, 1984.

22. This seems to have been the case with an NKVD defector, Volkov, who approached the British in Turkey in 1946. Philby was sent out to handle the case and the defection, which might have had serious implications, for Philby

himself was frustrated. See *Mole*, William Hood, New York: W.W. Norton, 1982, page 37.

23. See *The Man Who Lost the War*, W. T. Tyler, New York: Dial Press, 1980.

24. The following observation is worth recalling. "If enough Secret Police agents were to be employed to systematically check on all members of the public, it is obvious that at some time they are bound to detect a spy, an agent, an informer, or a go-between. But in the West, spies are almost never caught by the use of a random selection of a suspect. Spies are usually unmasked either because of their own stupidity or betrayal by other spies." *Women in Espionage*, Bernard J. Hutton, New York: Macmillan, 1972, page 182.

25. "Even the knowledge that the British had boxed in an active MGB agent whom they could pick up and exchange for him if things went wrong didn't help Sullivan's peace of mind." *Operation Splinter Factor*, Stewart Steven, Philadelphia: J. B. Lippincott, 1974, page 35.

26. Thus, James B. Donovan, counsel for "Rudolf Abel," could argue: "It is possible that in the forseeable future an American of equivalent rank will be captured by Soviet Russia or an ally; at such time an exchange of prisoners through diplomatic channels could be considered to be in the best national interests of the United States." *Strangers on a Bridge*, New York: Atheneum, 1964.

27. See, among a plethora of timely offerings, *The Wall Street Journal* editorial, "The Lefortova Hostage," 4 September 1986, and "Mason Takes a Hostage," *Time*, 15 September 1986, page 22.

28. In the case of Whitworth, a curious mixture of philosophies motivated the exemplary 365-year sentence imposed as a rather obvious example to others. Incapacitation was hardly an issue (despite some clamor of a vengeful kind for the death penalty), for his career as a spy was clearly at an end with the arrest of his associates. Contrite he might have been, but there seems to have been little he could do to earn his redemption. The sentence seemed like kicking the door after the horse has bolted.

29. See *The Double Cross System*, Sir John Masterman, New York: Avon Books, 1972.

30. See "The Oyster Paradigm," H. H. A. Cooper, *Terrorism: A MultiCultural Perspective*, Washington, D.C., Defense Nuclear Agency, 1986.

31. See *Sir Percy Sillitoe*, A.W. Cockerill, London: W. H. Allen, 1975.

32. Of the head of the dreaded DINA, the Departmento de Inteligencia Nacional, Chile's counterespionage service following the overthrow of the Allende regime, it has been written: "Manuel Contreras strove always to control: people, situations, the future. He had succeeded in dominating his family, his friends, his junior officers, and had carefully orchestrated his steady, rapid rise inside the military. Two things eluded his control. On social occasions, Contreras could not govern his response to people of different classes and views. He alternated between retiring shyness and argumentative bombast. He would get carried away, excoriating communism, women's liberation, and Christian Democracy. He had also failed to master his appetite. His obesity made him angry, and he channeled his anger into the pursuit of power." *Assassination on Embassy Row*, John Dinges and Saul Landau, New York: Pantheon Books, 1980, page 121.

33. Even the most ardent admirers of J. Edgar Hoover would have to admit that he lingered too long in the post of Director of the Federal Bureau of Investigation. His detractors would surely point to the use he made of the vast stores of secret information at his disposal in order to retain his position and die in harness.

2

SPY MANIA:
Chasing Shadows,
Losing Sight of Substance

Spy mania was not, of course, universal. Most Edwardian radicals and a part of the establishment never took it seriously. Even when taken over by Northcliffe, The Times *continued to view the scares its new proprietor was promoting in the* Daily Mail *with lofty disdain as not "worthy of the serious notice of a great nation." But in the press as a whole more column inches were devoted to documenting, than to doubting, the spy menace. Even the radical* Nation *acknowledged that invasion and spy scares had created by 1909 a public mood bordering on mass hysteria: "There is in the blood of us all a primitive instinct of alarm which takes fire at the very mention of a spy."*

Christopher Andrew[1]

Paranoia, in the common sense as well as the strict clinical sense of the term, is a curious mental state capable of affecting both individuals and entire communities. Its onset may be gradual or sudden, and it is rarely (if ever) recognized or accepted by those suffering from it as a pathological condition. It has as its defining characteristic an enormously oppressive content of fear against which defenses of all kinds are erected, sometimes hastily while at other times with great forethought and deliberation. Most authorities would agree that its pathological character resides in a patent overreaction to a certain kind of stimulus, bordering at times on the irrational.[2] To those who do not suffer from this condition, there is a scheme of delusion which informs and distorts the actions of those affected. Things are blown out of proportion and are not seen in their true state. There is a distinctive overestimation of the danger, and the resultant reaction seems on the patent evidence to be socially inappropriate, often on

34

a gross scale, to the perceived threat. The dangers against which these bulwarks are raised and these ramparts steadily manned may be real or imagined; they always, however, appear to the affected subject in an exaggerated and often fantastic form. Shadows are seen as monsters; innocent writing implements become deadly and threatening weapons of a quite different kind; facial expressions on others are interpreted as gestures of hostile intent; and everywhere the forces of evil are seen to be gathering and surveilling in dogged pursuit of the affected subject. In its darkest form, paranoia, even to the lay person, is a frightening mental illness of great destructive potential. Those suffering from this diagnosed psychosis require great care in approach, for the violence that seethes within lies like a coiled spring. Sufferers are often as adept at concealing their condition from others as they are at denying it to themselves.

The terms *paranoid, paranoia*, and *paranoiac*[3] have acquired well-understood, if somewhat more elastic, conventional meanings. They have passed into common parlance with sufficient precision that an age or a people might be categorized as paranoid or paranoiac. This conveys the meaning of fear of being out of control, a distorted perception of objective reality giving rise to unnatural suspicion, and a dangerous latent propensity for striking out at the persons or things seen to be the authors of the perceived threat. It is not otiose to insist that the threat may well be real enough; only in the grossest of cases does the imagination work to produce an impression where no evidence whatsoever justifies it. It is, rather, the exaggeration, magnification, and curious distortion that belong to the realm of the abnormal. Modern living provides much fuel for the generation and development, individually and collectively, of paranoid states. Collective paranoia is especially prone to develop in times of heightened tension, such as those times immediately prior to the outbreak of hostilities and under those conditions that have come to be known as the Cold War, where a protracted standoff involves the great powers on a global basis. It is natural enough, at such times, to see the enemy everywhere and in every guise, lurking in the shadows, within as well as without the gates. When that enemy is the spy, the result is spy mania.

Mania, too, is a scientific term, which has now acquired a

somewhat large acceptance of a rather less-than-technical kind.
Mania implies excitement of a very distinctive quality, a sort
of feverishness, again excessive in character, highly disturbing in its manifestations. Mania has, in this acquired meaning, a frenzied, agitated aspect, the very opposite of calm,
rational reflection. In these frenetic conditions, good judgment is suspended; the thought process and conclusions to
which they lead have about them a wildness, a blind striking
out at that which cannot be reached or comprehended by
more orderly avenues of contemplation. Those afflicted by
mania are prone to jump to conclusions, often enough the
wrong conclusions. Mania, in the vernacular, comprises a
wide variety of disturbed mental states in which paranoia can
clearly figure.

Mania, in this popular sense, has something about it of the
craze, another related mental state where the equilibrium of
sensible discrimination is violently upset. Something of a
passion of desire rages for a while, informed by criteria that,
rationally examined, would hardly seem to enjoy the capacity
to move the human spirit to the extent manifested. In both
cases, there is an overstimulation of the system. During the
persistence of the mania or craze, behavior is distinctly abnormal. Perceptions are altered, scale distorted, judgment
warped. Yet those so afflicted are normal enough in normal
times. The condition may indeed be limited in scope so as to
leave functioning intact in all departments save that which
concerns the particular subject of reference. The object upon
which the mania or craze is fixated may be real enough;
rationally speaking, it cannot be seen as deserving the attention or quality of attention lavished upon it. The pathology of
these conditions, interesting enough in its own right, is not
what is being discussed here, nor is their etiology. What is
important here is their existence as social rather than individual phenomena, for manic conditions are capable of being
massaged, heightened, and used to advantage by those who
recognize them and understand their dynamics.

The craze is the entrepreneur's dream, but it is difficult to
know how to start one; the entrepreneur usually enters the
scene when the thing is underway and works to turn it to
account. There is usually a mysterious element to crazes and
manias in the matter of their origins. As in the case of

rumors, it is often very difficult, if not impossible, to pinpoint their genesis.[4]

Spy mania is a peculiarly social thing, a group phenomenon. It tends to affect whole bodies of people, rather than individuals, and it has an observable political tinge. In this it resembles racism, anti-Semitism, and jingoism in its structures, properties, and propensities for unscrupulous promotion and employment by those who could, in some way or another, control the destinies of those affected by this unnatural fervor. These political possibilities are what interest us in the present work, for they are very influential in determining the strength and direction of the counterespionage efforts of any particular community at any particular stage in its history. So, too, do there exist similar possibilities for misdirection and mismanagement of effort and resources. Thus, outbreaks of spy mania have more than mere historical curiosity for those interested in the study of counterespionage. They must be carefully analyzed in an endeavor to understand who and what lie behind them and the meaning of their elaborate orchestration.

Spy[5] mania is sometimes rather superficial, while at other times there lurks a deeper social sickness. For our purposes, spy mania may be defined as an episode of abnormal social excitation in which enemy agents are perceived to be everywhere, and harmless people and objects are capable of being wrongfully identified as such.

To a greater or lesser degree, all human relationships are founded upon trust. Social life (people living and working together) without such a substratum as its foundation would become practically impossible.[6] Without trust, the mere presence of others would be so threatening as to trigger primitive instincts so as to make all social transactions fruitless, if not positively dangerous.[7] As societies and their needs grow more complex and human interactions expand, strangers are inevitably drawn into the web of daily involvements that make up the ordinary routines of social intercourse. In the typical modern society, one is constantly dealing with the unknown, with persons for whom others must vouch or who, in the main, are simply to be accepted on blind faith. In the so-called "open societies," a great deal is taken upon trust: who you are, what you do, the benevolence of your intentions. One is trusted until one is shown to be unworthy of

that trust, rather than the reverse. This is the real meaning of
openness.

In recent times, our trust has suffered rude and often
shattering blows from an onslaught of those who have abused
it. We have learned, painfully, that gentlemen do read each
other's mail—regularly and with relish. It is in the nature of
some to trust readily, while others are characteristically of a
more cautious disposition. Some are slow to learn from unfortunate experiences, hanging on to trust when everything
about them screams *beware!* Meanwhile, others are all too
hasty in putting up the shutters. An entire political history
might be constructed on the basis of some sort of trust
quotient. The human rights movement in the United States is
based upon a certain kind of trust, and any encroachment
upon these hard-won positions is viewed as closing down that
trust and confidence to be extended toward our fellows of all
creeds and races. Trust is eroded by fear; we are afraid to
trust those we believe might harm us or who we suspect
might abuse our trust. The strange, the bizarre, and the alien
are all capable of arousing our mistrust; hence our unfavorable reactions to violations of dress codes and conventions of
language and behavior. The tensions of urban life are especially fear-producing; we see the mugger or rapist in any
unfamiliar figure, and the media provides ample fuel for such
conjectures.

Suspicion is the ally of fear. It promotes, suggests, and
points the finger, often in subtle, hidden ways. We fear and
we are suspicious of those who do not appear to be like
ourselves, whose ways are different and whose beliefs and
behavior we have difficulty understanding.[8] We fear and are
suspicious of those who seem to have as their objective the
taking away of something we regard as rightfully ours. We are
especially fearful of those with whom we have no satisfactory
avenue of communication and we are therefore ever suspicious of their motives and intentions. Translated into global
terms, it is not difficult to comprehend how these fears shape
the politics of war and peace.

People en masse are ever prey to fears and uncertainties.
They look to those they recognize as leaders to set a course
for them in the matter of what they should believe and how
they ought to behave. In particular, they look for signs of who
their friends and enemies really are—in short, who on the

grand scale they should trust. Someone has to point out the witches. In even the most herdlike of societies, there are those who do not toe the line, who preserve a stubborn independence in these matters. But even where nonconformism is benignly tolerated, it is hard to swim against the tide. The majority accept the word of the leader(s) as to whom they should hate, despise, and fear.[9] This is the very lifeblood of politics. It is the meaning and raison d'etre of the Weekly Radio Broadcast. While this is all very useful and necessary for social cohesion, carried to excess it has perils too obvious to warrant extended discussion here. It is not difficult to see how, given the appropriate stimulus, these facts of socio-political life can take on an ugly, pathological hue. Social paranoia and spy mania have their genesis in the same contaminated soil.

Fear is a great social contaminant to be found as an ingredient in a wide variety of ills afflicting modern living.[10] Only the very fortunate or the very insensitive remain unaffected by it in any way. In our own times, espionage and terrorism are the seams within the sociopolitical tapestry where commonly shared currents of fear converge. Both phenomena are now capable of generating fear out of all proportion to the resources expended for the purpose and the visible harm caused by these activities. Indeed, it is difficult enough to measure that harm, tangible and intangible, so as to come up with a meaningful, comprehensive damage assessment.[11] Yet even were such an assessment much easier to make and express in simple terms, it would still be hard to convincingly relate its product to the fear quotient.

That both espionage and terrorism are susceptible to massive overstatement, being blown out of all proportion, is almost self-evident; it is their very nature that makes them so appealing as subjects of fiction. Yet, they are real enough, and the harm of which they are capable of causing on many levels is also too real to be ignored. Indeed, they have not been ignored. Within the space of a decade, we have seen the emergence of what might very well be called terrorism mania by reference to the general analysis we have offered above. While the number of terrorist victims remains very small statistically and the property damage of which terrorists are capable is slight compared with that occasioned by war, crime, and national disasters, the image of the terrorist has come to occupy an extraordinarily prominent place in the popular press and on the agenda of world leaders.

All the heat in this matter has not been generated by the terrorists themselves. The coals of the terrorism mania have been fanned often enough by the opponents of terrorism. Constant reminders of the importance accorded the subject abound. Thus we see international terrorism coming to overshadow all other topics on the agenda for what was billed as the Tokyo Economic Summit in 1986.[12] We hear the utterances of the president of the United States and high officials of his administration constantly permeated with denunciations of terrorism and terrorists so as to make the subject a predominant and permanent feature of United States foreign policy. France, after harboring for years more terrorists than Syria, Libya, and South Yemen combined, found itself under ungrateful attack from the viper it had nursed to its bosom and began a frantic reversal of its erstwhile policies while appealing to the international community for support and threatening the terrorists with "punishment without pity." [13] Meanwhile, its own flirtation with an interesting and instructive mixture of espionage and terrorism in the case of the Rainbow Warrior was supposed to go unremarked.[14] The selective, politicized character of the mania is very evident in this. Even Walter Laquer, after a curious, belated, unattributed discovery of Grivas' cats, seems to have reversed himself on the futility of terrorism.[15] And when tourists, in droves, start staying away from Europe, leading to the most extraordinary inducements to lure them back,[16] it becomes clear that something in the nature of an authentic terrorism mania is in existence.

Yet, as is painfully obvious, terrorism has a vivid materiality at this point in history and has taken on a distinctive social and political significance; the ugly evidence mounts before us daily. It is our appreciation and reactions to the menace as well as the political associations with which it is colored that have the hint of paranoia, the same sense of mania we have come to expect historically in connection with espionage. The terrorist, like the spy, is the secret enemy within. Who is he? Who does he serve? What is he trying to do to us? It is all too easy to envision whole peoples in the guise of terrorists. The implications of such an undiscriminating view are frightening enough in themselves. Thus, it can be soberly written in our time that " 'Terror' and 'Palestinian' have come to be almost synonymous."[17] For there is another problem in all this worth more than passing notice. Within the family of nations, a spy must have a master, and spy mania, though rashly generated and wrongfully focused, can have a functional outlet. Responsibility can be fixed, reparations demanded, and reprisals taken among equals; state can deal with state in gentlemanly enough fashion, even on distasteful matters such as spies and spying.[18] Small group terrorism is quite different in this respect; hence, the fear has no safety valve of a comparable kind.

Who are the clandestine masters of the terrorists? How might they be reached and interdicted? A dangerous doctrine, born out of frustration, is emerging. It requires the laying of responsibility for international terrorism at the door of some nation state that can then be dealt with for its misdeeds in the appropriate fashion. Libya is the first, deservedly or otherwise, to be charged by a major power with sponsorship of terrorism—and made to pay the price. Here we catch a glimpse of the substance disappearing down the hole as we solemnly chase the shadows for political effect. What is certain is that terrorism mania does not lead to the catching of many terrorists nor is it helpful in the proper targeting of their sponsors. There is a wider lesson for us in this that ought not to be overlooked.

There is, nevertheless, something very real to fear in these matters and we must accordingly permit ourselves one more necessary excursion here, for terrorism and espionage have more than these vitalist/teleological, comparative connections. Espionage has often to make use of the tactics and techniques of terrorism so as to attain the goals set for it by those who have chosen this form of intervention. The so-called "spy of action"[19] is as close to a terrorist, from a definitional standpoint, as to be, for all practical purposes, undistinguishable. Libya is far from having started a fashion or even promoting a new way of thinking about these matters. The OGPU and *Sicherheitdhienst* assassination squads operating overseas long predated the similar efforts of SAVAK, South Korea, and Muammar el Qadafi. The secret intelligence services of great and small powers alike have long engaged in the more vicious and deadly variants of the great game so as to influence the course of history in the direction they would desire. The principles and their applications have been established at least since the time of Sun Tzu.

The impact of these secret undertakings on the course of world events can be transcendental. The assassin Gavrilo Princip, whose shots at Sarajevo in 1914 altered the course of world history, was as surely set upon his path by the spy masters of Serbia as was Mehmet Ali Agca by those acting in the name of the Soviet Union some sixty-seven years later.[20] Neither had a very clear idea of his paymaster, and the latter's frenzied efforts to point the finger led only to psychosis.

Assassination and espionage have danced a delicate minuet through the ages.[21] International disputes are generally resolved by war, negotiation, or attrition. Few human beings have the time or the patience for the latter. War usually requires a pretext, and excuse for an aggression long prepared for and decided upon, which must nevertheless be disguised from those who would otherwise suffer disillusionment or second thoughts. Few pretexts are to be found occurring in the ordinary course of events; thus they have to be manufactured.[22] The very essence of these operations is their secret, duplicitous character; the decisive hand that moves the matter to this point is kept well hidden. The secret agent (the spy by our definition) is the clandestine executor of these policies; his role and methods are the keys to success in both the operation and the deception.

The operation itself is not necessarily concealed; it is simply made to appear to be something else—or the work of someone else. Blaming someone else for these things is, perhaps, the highest of all espionage arts; convincing others of this is the supreme triumph. It is a sham, a masquerade, but it must be flawlessly executed for it to be taken for the real thing; those to be deceived have to act upon it. The protests of those who suspect the truth, or something approximating it, must be silenced or shouted down. For the Soviets or their satraps to have engineered the attempt in 1981 on the life of Pope John Paul II would have required imagination, organizational flair, and the institutional ability to cover the tracks. All these are possessed in abundance by the secret intelligence services of the Soviet Union and its satellites. To have organized and executed such an attempt so as to throw the blame *upon* the Soviets would have required all this and a remarkable touch of genius besides. Is such a thought merely fanciful? Must it be wholly discounted on the grounds of it being improbably ambitious?[23] It would not be the first time such a huge undertaking had been successfully essayed, for deception and disinformation are the lifeblood of espionage.

The success or otherwise of these enterprises rests in large measure upon the existing state of public and private belief. Belief is dramatically altered by that state we have called mania. The present terrorism mania lends itself nicely to such exercises, and the intricate patterns are fascinating to the informed, detached observers. That, unfortunately, is what so many engaged in trying to unravel the weave are not. Private skepticism does not marry easily with professional obligations that are often informed by overriding political considerations running counter to belief or even, in some cases, common sense. Counterespionage is reduced in such instances to an exercise in practical politics rather than a tour de force of the professional instincts. It is not seriously recommended here that it should be otherwise. But the choice ought always to be made on an informed basis, however cynically. The serious spy-catcher, whatever the modality of espionage engaging his professional attentions, should never allow himself to be caught up in the general mania. In these cases, he must always ask himself the question, *cui bono* (to whose advantage)? Who profits from what is seen, on all levels, to be going on? The answer or answers will often lead to a more accurate, if not always convenient, appraisal.

We must apply some of these suggestive indications to matters current in our own times. First, we must penetrate the political smoke screens that obscure much of the contemporary scene. Is it so difficult for a generation to which the Man Who Never Was, the Ultra Secret, and Operation Fortitude have been revealed to find it so hard to believe in the "Terrorist Who Never Was?" Or does our own post-Watergate generation really think it is too sophisticated, too smart to fool?

These huge enterprises of mass deception really depend upon the ability to control and manipulate the popular organs of communication. Nowadays, these are decisive in the formation of opinion and the nourishment of belief. In our times, their pervasiveness and persuasiveness have become all but absolute. Their reach and influence are extraordinary. Small wonder that the slightest incursion in the name of "free

speech" or any other euphemism for propaganda into the
denied territories of the Socialist Bloc is sternly resisted.
South Africa has moved vigorously and effectively against the
Western news media in much the same fashion and for much
the same reasons. In the present context, what is important in
our day and age is not individual belief but mass belief; it is
not for nothing that we refer colloquially to the mass media.
Those who are in a position to control the mass media, whether
or not its organs are aware of or are accomplices to the
control, are in an unassailable position to influence mass
belief.[24] In Actonian terms, those who have absolute control
over the mass media can corrupt absolutely the opinions of
those they wish to influence. The collective mind is exceedingly plastic and pliable. Anything becomes believable if it is
reiterated enough[25] and if there is no independent opposition
that might constitute an intellectual challenge to it (Madison
Avenue depends upon this). It is easy to see how such an
awesome power can encourage a widespread belief in a terrorism epidemic and move swiftly to fuel a full-fledged terrorism mania.

Spy manias have, after all, been started from a much more
slender media power base. Almost unnoticed by most people,
something very peculiar has been happening. What is to be
suggested here rests upon a number of simple propositions
about the kind of small group terrorism now so familiar to us.
First, association with it in any way is damning in the eyes of
the civilized world. Even to write about it approvingly is to
cast oneself beyond the pale. Terrorism is an evil thing,
cowardly, despicable. Consequently, it is impossible to ap-
prove, even by implication of any of those who are associated
with or suspected of being associated with, terrorism. No one
proudly admits to being a terrorist anymore; it is necessary to
indulge in obfuscation of one's business and purposes by
claiming a more tolerable identity such as "freedom fighter."
Terrorism has become a bad word in the media lexicon,
universally understood as such through deliberate usage. Those
who associate with terrorists in any way are indelibly stained
with the evil that the term connotes. Those who have the
undisputed power to designate others as terrorists have a
terrifying power indeed—one open to the clearest of abuses.
The Palestine Liberation Organization is characterized as a
terrorist entity; hence no negotiations or helpful contacts with

it are to be permitted; above all, it is never to be permitted to represent the interests of the Palestinian people. The validity of this proposition lies in the ability to get enough influential people, in the places that matter, to subscribe to it (we shall return to this point shortly). It is not difficult to see who might be the beneficiaries of the general acceptance of this proposition or where it might have originated. Second, we have seen the emergence of what we have called the "Kleenex Terrorists," those who are used for one good hard blow and are then discarded, quite dispassionately, by those who have used them.[26] These pawns, so easy to recruit from among the idealistic, hopeless, and disaffected of the world, have no useful knowledge of those who have set them in motion. The conventional security techniques of espionage are designed to ensure just that. Thus, they *may* believe themselves to be working for an organization or cause—even an identifiable human being—while, in reality, the case is otherwise. Their own beliefs are truly irrelevant in the matter of lodging real responsibility for their acts; they simply have no useful evidence to contribute to the matter.[27] If the job has been well done, what they can tell will merely reinforce the story their masters wish to propagate. Espionage has played a crucial role in the creation, manipulation, and deception involved in the events and processes that make up the Terrorist Game.[28] The secret services of Israel, Syria, Iraq, Iran, and Libya, to name but a few, have all danced, sometimes even together, to the dangerous tunes that comprise the terrorist theme. What lies behind all this is much more interesting for the counterespionage specialist than the horrifying superficialities of terrorism that make world headlines. It is a strange—and perhaps unwise—terrorist today who truly knows his own master. But the counterespionage specialist interested in these matters is not entirely bereft of the means to solve the puzzle. Much patience and persistence are necessary to move the rubble out of the path.

Let us move now from the general to the particular, applying some of these points as we proceed. Nothing that we have written should be taken as suggesting that terrorism is media fiction. Terrorism is very real and so is the mania it is capable of inspiring. But the two realities are quite different in tone and quality. The way people feel about terrorism, how they react to it, and, particularly, who they blame for it are ab-

stractions that require delicate management by highly qualified, well-placed specialists. In the nature of things, few
indeed are those who can *know* even a part of the truth
behind each event. Fewer still are those with the capability,
even in retrospect, to connect events so as to make the
correct, coherent whole. Given what we have said above, it is
easy to see how a *legend* can be built up that is self-propagating
and self-sustaining.

The terrorist, like the spy, is of necessity a man (or woman)
of mystery. The mystique is not only an important adjunct to
getting the job done; it is a vital part of the protective screen
behind which the individual is enabled to operate. The mystery helps to keep him safe. For the so-called master terrorist, like the master spy, to remain totally out of sight yet at all
times be pervasively present in the public mind is a piece of
professional ledgerdemain that only the most accomplished
can pull off to perfection. Anonymity per se is of no use to the
master terrorist; he needs a name that is on everyone's lips
and that will evoke fear. Most ages have furnished us with an
example of the master spy, working his puppets from behind
the scenes. He is out of sight, yet his works are ever present,
visible symbols of this unseen power. To the public, some,
like Gehlen, remain little more than a name, a faceless puller
of strings. Nowadays, it is the master terrorist who has captured the public imagination, who fascinates at once by tales
of his personal elusiveness and the awful, undeniable evidence of power by those who seemingly work at his behest.

The latest in a string of master terrorists to hold this awful
fascination for the general public is Sabri Khalil al-Banna, a
Palestinian, known more usually by his nom de guerre, Abu
Nidal. That there was a real human being identified as Sabri
al-Banna is well enough evidenced, as is his early association
with the PLO and his assumption of the name Abu Nidal.
There, however, hard fact ends and the realm of mystery and
speculation enter. There is little, indeed, from which to
construct a reliable mosaic of the life of *this* Abu Nidal. It is
strange and incongruous from whatever angle it is viewed. In
this twilight zone, anything is possible; anything can be averred,
and little or nothing can be verified or established with
certainty. What is certain, however, is that there *seems* to be
someone going around claiming to be Abu Nidal and remaining appropriately secretive in the process.[29] There is a care-

fully crafted design here, the object of which is to persuade
the world that the original Sabri al-Banna is alive and well,
living the life of a master terrorist in Damascus, Syria; Tripoli, Libya; or wherever else might be called for by the fancy
or the scenario of the moment. The various other counter-
theories (that Sabri al-Banna is dead, has defected, and/or is
an agent of incongruous others) only serve to deepen the
mystery and give the transfiguration an appropriate validity
and value. What is certain and scarcely open to question at all
is that from 1976, with increasing verity into our own times, a
whole slew of misguided young "Kleenex" terrorists have
done unspeakable things in the name of Abu Nidal. Yet,
there is this curious fact: There is no objectively believable
evidence that links any one of them personally with a real-
life, flesh-and-blood Abu Nidal or that they have met and
taken instructions from him. Whatever the strength of their
own convictions, these misguided "freedom fighters" might
be working for any of the world's very capable intelligence
agencies—or anyone else with the skill, organization, and
motives for duping them in this way. Who *really* directs the
activities of those who have become known as the Abu Nidal
group is a question yet to receive a convincing answer.[30]
There is even the remote possibility that it is Sabri Khalil
al-Banna. We are left to draw our own conclusions.

Before we close this object lesson in deceit, however, it is
worth making a few points that those in pursuit of master
terrorists such as Abu Nidal and what *really* lies behind them
might wish to take into account. It may be observed prelimi-
narily that there is nothing new in what is being suggested
here. Intelligence agencies have been doing much the same
thing since the earliest days of organized espionage; only the
names of the actors and the fads and fashions of the age have
changed.[31] We are dealing, therefore, with age-old, well-
tried principles, which have simply required adaptation or
modification to a somewhat novel situation. There is, then,
nothing very original about all this and it should cause little
surprise among the knowledgeable.

Given the problem posed, the chosen solution was predictable and historically prefigured. The Israeli strategy for handling the Palestinian problem and the wider Arab problem to
which it has given rise has a Machiavellian simplicity. It is
undeniably correct, effective, and strikingly obvious: divide

and conquer. These observations imply neither admiration nor approval; they merely state the evident. The Israelis have shown a remarkable understanding of the Arab character and the factors militating against Arab unity, and they have cleverly exploited the ambivalence and even hostility that the Arab regimes, of all complexions, have shown toward the Palestinian people and the establishment of a Palestinian state.

The Abu Nidal terrorist activities can be seen to have played an important role in the implementation of that strategy. It is another curious fact that the Abu Nidal attacks upon key leaders of the PLO began shortly after the Israelis found themselves proscribed from following the more direct course upon which they had embarked after the loss of their athletes at the Munich Olympic games in 1972. This is yet one more puzzling fact to remark upon in this process. The operatives of this so-called Abu Nidal group are most truly "Kleenex" terrorists, for when they are taken or reduced into custody, they are quite callously abandoned to their fate by their ostensible employers. This group stages no operations to get its members back.[32] This is totally at variance with the established practice not only of terrorist groups the world over—and especially Middle Eastern groups—but also at odds with what is done by national espionage agencies (from which these practices derive). These will go to any lengths (as witness the Zakharov incident) to get back, for well-understood reasons, their fallen comrades. Conventional armies are equally keen to repatriate prisoners of war. The failure of the Abu Nidal organization to follow these traditions clearly does not betoken an exceptional callousness in its leadership, for that would be simply counterproductive and foolish in the extreme.

Loyal servants who are abandoned, be they spies or terrorists, quickly become disloyal to save their skins, and the group that takes such a course can clearly be hurt by it. Rather does it suggest to the perceptive that the return of these expendables would be an unwelcome embarrassment. Where and to whom should they be returned? These individuals have simply served their purpose and are not reuseable, for the second time around they might start to question their role and their relationship to that which is hidden. It is a good deal easier to frame most terrorists than it is to set up a

Nicholas Daniloff, but there are limits on the gullibility of even the most foolhardy.

It is inevitable that serious questions should have been raised in recent times concerning the continued existence of the person who seems to have started out in life as Sabri Khalil al-Banna. The evidence for his being alive and directing the activities of the Abu Nidal group, as presented by a partisan expositor, is wholly unconvincing and can be answered point by point to the contrary without the recourse to specialized sources of information.[33] The case for his being alive and directing the affairs of this group rests almost entirely upon information, analysis, and interpretation from Israeli intelligence sources, which can hardly be regarded as objective in these matters. What is perhaps more suggestive is the patent Israeli desire to demonstrate that he *is* alive and engaging in terrorist activities. The counterespionage specialist whose curiosity has been sufficiently aroused will naturally inquire into why this should be so. Who is Israel trying to persuade and why?

Let us recall, here, that we are interested primarily in the relationship of terrorism mania to spy mania and its implications for our theme. These matters have to be seen in the wider context. They have global rather than merely regional implications. They have critically affected the foreign policy and national security of the United States. The point has to be stressed here that for the Israeli strategy with respect to the Palestinians to work at all, the Israeli view of terrorism and its threat to the stability of the entire Middle East must be widely shared and, in particular, it must be uncritically accepted by the United States.[34]

It is the manifestations of spy mania that are of concern to us here. It is pertinent to observe that an argument such as that now adduced here would never have been entertained in the climate then existing, nor could reason in the shape of the suggestion that the evidence was just too thin have been allowed to prevail. Mania finds its own devils, and evidence that might have exonerated the witches of Salem was permitted consideration only hundreds of years after the event. The mania served very well those who promoted these happenings. How this trick was done and the lessons it holds for the future are what must concern those having counterespionage responsibilities; the subject is deserving of a book of its own.

What is important is that it was done by friends who managed to make us see what we were half-disposed to see, while preventing us from looking elsewhere into other matters that might have caused us to question what we were seeing.

We are concerned here only with the lessons these matters convey for us within the context of our own subject area. There are extraordinary opportunities for creative espionage here. The possibilities for deception abound. Where mania prevails, many will be disposed to believe what in other, calmer circumstances might be dismissed as bizarre or a put-on. Spy mania gives a false importance to some things at the expense of others. The seriousness of what is revealed by looking at the above examples ought not to be minimized by confining them to their own, peculiar context. The substance is lost as those responsible for countermeasures go chasing after shadows. The counterintelligence specialist needs to keep a clear head at such times so as to be able to conjure with all the intriguing possibilities. Spy mania, of which terrorism mania is but a special variant, offers excellent opportunities for sending the hounds in the wrong direction. The matter assumes a special importance when the size of the pack is small and the territory it must cover large. The distractions of McCarthyism and the generalized witch-hunting that seared the lives of so many relatively harmless people absorbed precious resources and diverted attention from the real agents of the Soviet Union, then busily engaged in the acquisition of the nuclear secrets of the United States. It would have been difficult for the Soviet Union to have created McCarthyism from scratch, but once it was on a roll, only slight lubrication was needed from time to time to keep the machinery moving. The disposition to believe had simply to be gently massaged. Such errors are historically pardonable where the luxury of time allows for eventual refocusing.

We must ever remember that we live in the nuclear age, the age in which mass destruction can be called down not in days or weeks, but in minutes. The world's leaders cannot afford to be wrong in their calculations concerning these matters. They do not have much time to ponder the impact of the intelligence conveyed to them. They need clear heads and the most exact information on which to base their decisions. They must recognize the possibilities of being deliberately deceived, even by friends, who, from the best of motives, might lead them into conflict against the better interests of their own nations. The work of spies becomes critical under such circumstances. The possibilities of a nuclear war being started by accident have long been with us. The possibilities that such a conflict among the major powers might now be engineered by a small, clandestine group have also long passed beyond the realm of fiction. Small countries struggling for survival might also use similar ploys. Israel's desperation to exist is a factor that has a dangerous propensity for bringing the world to a nuclear Armageddon. The plight of the Palestinian people and their desperation to secure the justice they have been denied for nearly forty years could well provide the detonator needed to bring about the dreaded reaction. There is fear enough in these realities for an all-consuming manic expression capable of pitting friend against friend until all are sucked into the vortex of the struggle. Those who see their own prospects of survival reduced to naught care little that all may perish in the resultant Last Battle. The terrorism mania we have seen thus far is but a harbinger of what is to come if these times materialize.[35] Disinformation, deception, and the generalized fears they can engender are dangerous weapons, and the counterespionage specialist must not only understand the theory of their employment but must quickly gain a practical knowledge of whose hands are wielding them and whose interests they are really intended to serve.

Spy mania, then, causes communities, be they nations or businesses, to look in the wrong direction for the harm that might encompass them. They are blinded by the intensity of the fear generated by the evident or suspected presence of the enemy within the gates. At the same time, the fear acts as a kind of screen so that a self-defeating, masking process occurs. Spy mania is like the false cirrus cloud which covers up the cumulonimbus that really produces the thunderstorm. Those affected may well be right in their fears and correct enough in the intensity with which the emotion is experienced. What is unfortunate, from their point of view, is that what they feel should blind them to the machinations of other enemies that are just as deadly. That you are in the jungle being stalked by a hungry tiger ought not to lead you to ignore the equally deadly cobra that lies in your path. The spies of one enemy (or friend) do not preclude those of another from running their own operations against you. Most states of insecurity carry with them their own kind of tunnel vision, their own sets of blinders.

Higher states of conflict demand concentration, a special kind of focus if the struggle is to be waged effectively, but most low-intensity conflict is more diffuse. High-order enthusiasm, of which patriotism is a significant example, demands focus; it is difficult to love your country and hate too many enemies at once. The result of trying is politically enfeebling, a slow descent into xenophobia. Ultimately, such a debilitating condition is destructive of social and political cohesiveness. Spies have a very special role to play in any shooting war, but the war in which they excel is one in which the parties have yet to come to blows. Indeed, many wars are won by espionage alone. The spreading of suspicion aids in the weakening of solidarity and social trust, which in turn weakens the will to fight. The security services become the primary line of defense. The social structure has to be preserved. It may be stated as a useful rule that it is impossible to watch all the people all the time. Who, after all, would then watch the watchers?[36]

Those who catch spies are often less numerous than the spies they seek. They must, then, choose their targets with care. All targeting is selective to some degree, and selection presupposes some method that will allow the available resources to be employed to the greatest advantage. This rarely satisfies those whose paranoia runs at a high level, who fear spies everywhere, who have good reason to fear, and whose fear is rooted in the nature of fear itself.

Such a condition inevitably leads to the "police state mentality": if everybody cannot, in the nature of things, be effectively placed under some sort of surveillance, the impression must nevertheless be created that it is difficult to escape the all-seeing eye.[37] According to this theory, if enough truly believe that Big Brother is watching them, they *will* modify their behavior accordingly. Security becomes an illusion, a demonstration of the magician's art. The trick is to induce the belief, using but a little leaven to cause the dough to rise.

A variant of spy mania is induced in the community for security purposes rather like the human body is mildly intoxicated with a harmful virus so as to produce protective, immunizing agents. The chemistry depends on getting the proportions right. The community believes itself to be infested with government spies and informers and, in the most acute of cases, this has an important snowball effect; people are persuaded to act as spies for the government lest they, themselves, fall victim to the spying of their neighbors. In theory, such a system ought not only to act as a most effective system of social control, making rebellion, insurrection, or other serious antiestablishment activities at least very difficult if not impossible, but it ought to also make it very hard for hostile spies to penetrate the community without early apprehension by the authorities. Theoretically, the community so primed becomes a vast social mine field or spy trap into which hostile elements are introduced at their peril. The belief in the effectiveness of police-state methods of this kind and for these purposes dies hard. There are many places in the world today where such a climate of fear is deliberately fomented for the purposes of social control and as a vast potential spy trap. The results seem impressive enough at first glance. It is only upon a much deeper analysis that the inefficiency of such a system and its ultimate ineffectiveness become apparent.

We have expatiated upon the negative aspects of spy mania so as to give due warning of the dangers of this phenomenon to those engaged about the business of seeking out spies. This is, in a way, like warning doctors fighting the plague to avoid being contaminated by it. Superficially, it seems so obvious that any emphasis inevitably appears otiose and overdone. Those practicing the healing arts ordinarily have no cause to spread the plague and engagement in such an enterprise would properly be regarded as a violation of their professional oaths. Vaccination is a very limited and controlled process. The sickness we have called spy mania is as contagious as any plague and those who must hold it in check, the physicians of the body politic as it were, are the specialists in counterespionage. But, as we have seen, they are, often as not, engaged in wholesale propagation and spreading of the disease, sometimes at great risk to themselves and their professional integrity. They are in violation of no oath in so doing; only their safety and that which they seek to uphold is at risk. They open the floodgates with a cleansing purpose, but sometimes the waters are too strong and carry all before them. It is all too easy for those working with the disease, in laboratories or in the field, to become infected by it. The symptomatology of the disease is never in doubt: a lack of clarity of thought and an irrational fixation are among the more obvious signs of contamination.[38]

Spy mania is insidious, like miasma rising from a swamp on a warm summer's eve. Yet, as we have seen, it is as deadly as sarin (an extremely toxic chemical warfare agent) and the damage of which it is capable is not always appreciated for some time after the event. In short, spy mania as a pathological, social condition is bad. On the other hand, the fear of spies, however intense, is not bad in itself and can be turned to good account by those who perceive the distinction. Spies should be feared; they ought not be allowed to terrify. There are positive aspects of the disease that can be distilled out of it to help the spy-catcher in the pursuit of his objectives. They require a coolheaded appraisal of the dangers we have explored here in relation to specific situations and a program of calculated containment before the germs of fear are injected into any community for the purposes of social prophylaxis.

Fear, like mystery, is one of the spy-catcher's tools of the trade, but it has to be used judiciously and directed with almost surgical precision if it is to have any real value. Generalized fear is an instrument out of control, an epidemic that can affect not only those who have unleashed it upon the community but also those who would bring it in check. It is a mistake to frighten all in order to bring the message of fear home to a few. The spy-catcher needs the energetic and enthusiastic cooperation of the community. Fear needs to be discriminatingly disseminated. It is the spies who should be made to fear, not the community as a whole.[39]

The body politic should be alert and cooperative, not fearful of those who guide and serve it. In the business of spy-catching, such cooperation requires extensive educational efforts on the part of the counterespionage service. This is perhaps, at the present time, one of the most neglected areas of the counterespionage program. It requires a great deal of specialized effort. Targeting has an important part to play here. Different areas of the community have different vulnerability levels, different ranges of attractiveness for the spy. Spies do not need to operate where open sources can provide all that needs to be known.[40] Educational focus should be directed at those areas where the risk of espionage in all its forms is significant. The educational effort should be aimed at clearly defining the nature and dimensions of the problem as it is perceived by the conterespionage services, and indicating in concise, concrete terms how community cooperation can assist in securing its patrimony against the depredations of the spy. The details of such programs will differ considerably according to the needs of time and place. Broadly, however, they should encompass the creation of community awareness (reinforced through posters, pep talks, a points system); the development of diligent attitudes (clean desk policies, adherence to procedures, prompt observance of irregularities, reward of care); and fostering active cooperation with the security authorities (reporting irregularities, approaches, and the creation of an appropriate rewards and protection system). People must be taught and encouraged to cooperate out of conviction, not fear. They must learn the benefits, both to themselves and the community, of doing so. An antiespionage ethic must be promoted that is self-sustaining.[41]

Ultimately, all spy-catching comes down to this: spies spying on other spies. We must situate this from the standpoint of a somewhat trite, commonplace observation. To a spy, a counterspy is just another spy. Such a person has all the strengths and frailties of the profession.[42] There is no "good guy, bad guy" sentiment underlying this, only "them vs. us." Whatever such persons are called (informants, informers, security or police aides, or auxiliaries), they are essentially spies and function as such.[43] The spy has an understandable dread of being spied upon by others. His mission and his very life depend upon his ability to proceed about his business undetected, to not be recognized for what he is. Known hazards can be prepared for and rational preparations made to avoid them. It is the unknown, the unseen, that causes irrational fear that develops the kind of paranoia we discussed earlier. The human element introduces the truly unpredictable dimension. The spy who is paranoid does not function effectively; indeed, he may not be able to function at all. He is simply afraid to do what he has set out to do for fear of being caught. At all times, the spy inhabits a world filled with mistrust. No amount of self-confidence nor belief in a higher guidance can substitute for the lack of reliance he can afford to place on those with whom he must necessarily come in contact.

It is the task of the counterespionage services to heighten

the hostility level or, more properly, the spy's perception of
this. The spy must be made to feel, at all times, that he is in
an unfriendly environment where his own alien character and
purposes will stand out, causing him to be revealed for what
he truly is to those who would frustrate his designs. He must
feel its presence constantly and without respite. The spy lives
with the knowledge of what he is doing. He must receive the
strongest impression from those about him and with whom he
is brought in contact that others are very concerned to find
out his real business in the community, who he is, and what
he does. Only the attentions of other human beings can
convey such impressions.

For the above purposes, the spy-catcher needs a small
army of committed helpers, rather like a neighborhood crime
watch. A commitment to good security should be built into
the community, whatever its kind or ends; it is a difficult
thing to develop and introduce as an afterthought.[44] Again,
education plays a large part in the realization of such endeavors.

It is difficult for most Western democracies, at least in
peacetime, to take the spy menace seriously. There is an air
of unreality about it, a belonging, almost, to the world of
fiction. Spy mania is sometimes but a product of the desperation of those unblindered souls who simply cannot get their
fellows to recognize the problem. This is why, in such countries, a nationwide drive to improve security is unlikely to
meet with such success and may even produce scorn. It is
better to concentrate upon raising consciousness in vulnerable areas. Successes can then be publicized and even magni-
fied so that these small examples seem to be representative of
the whole. These changes in the climate become known to all
who would spy, wherever they choose to operate. The recruitment of help will proceed according to the prevailing circumstances and the character of those involved. In some cases, it
may be useful to offer bounties to those successful in exposing
spies. But all this must be done responsibly and in the most
carefully controlled manner. The spy-catcher must have a
clear appreciation of the fear-generating machinery, its value
to him, and the way it operates.

In the context we have described, fear can be most effectively generated through prudent use of the rumor mill and
its product disseminated through carefully selected agents
(using, for example, such rumors as "they're changing all the

IDs;" "they're having a snap audit this evening;" "everyone is going to be polygraphed;" and "they've arrested X over in such and such and nobody is talking about it."). The ability to undertake such campaigns, as well as their effectiveness, depends to a large extent upon the quality of the human material available for the purpose. Such agents are not only the eyes and ears of the spy-catcher, they are, when appropriate, his mouth as well. But here it must be cautioned that the long-range success of such enterprises in achieving a spy-free environment depends upon substance. The spy-catcher must beware of crying wolf too often. He needs real trophies to back his words if the fear he uses as a weapon is not to be discounted by those against whom it is directed.

Here we come to the nub and end of the affair. Fear in all its forms can be a force for good or ill in these matters, but what counts in the final result is substance, not form. Spy mania is simply a kind of energizer. Fear merely generates energy, the energy necessary to do something about the spy problem. If enough people, the right people, have their level of concern appropriately raised by the fears generated, something (maybe not the *right* thing) will be done to address the problem with which they are concerned. This may at least be considered a step in the right direction, if direction there be. For, from the spy-catcher's perspective, the secret of success lies in channeling the energies in proper fashion. If spy mania is used to elevate the energy level with the wrong target in mind, history has shown that it is virtually impossible to divert the course of the misplaced energy and to subsequently direct it at a target of substance. The energy continues to be frittered away in the pursuit of phantoms.[45] Still, it is hard to stop the chase, fruitless though it may be. The whole thing acquires an unstoppable momentum of its own. More and more justifications and rationalizations are sought and produced for the generation and expenditure of such energy, and more and more has to be displayed in the chase after those illusionary targets that have been set up to spark the original enthusiasms.

Then come the inventions, exaggerations, and patent absurdities into which spy mania inevitably descends. These are the result of actions being run by rhetoric or, worse, of rhetoric running away with the actors (this is truly an example of the mullah running after the free lamb and rice).[46]

In the case of spy mania, the locomotive has run away with the engineer. It is especially dangerous to build up a potentially uncontrollable head of steam when the train is already on the wrong track. If spy mania is consciously started, then the object of all the consequent attention should at least be correctly chosen. The spy-catcher as technician must properly identify the target uninfluenced by these intoxicating considerations. There are strategic and tactical implications to this that will be examined in their turn. If there are numerous targets, priorities will need to be ordered and the available resources deployed accordingly. The spy-catcher must identify and pursue targets of substance, real spies, not imagined ones. Targeting is a matter of technical or political choice. Spy mania does not aid in the selection process at all.

Spy mania is best seen as a distraction, the product of which, if it can be collected and directed in the proper fashion, may have some use for the spy-catcher, beyond merely serving to inflate his budget.[47] Like poison gas, it is possibly a useful thing to have around the armory, but it is unmanageable on the battlefield and gives those who resort to its use a bad reputation.

POINTS TO REMEMBER

1. Spy manias are episodes of abnormal social excitation in which enemy agents are perceived to be everywhere, and harmless people can be wrongfully identified as spies. Spy mania undermines the very social trust which, at its onset, it is designed to protect; it erodes trust in others and promotes suspicion of others' social identities. At its worst, it stereotypically promotes majority group suspicion of all minorities. Social paranoia, terrorism mania, and spy mania have their genesis in the same contaminated soil; all fundamentally alter belief.

2. Serious spy-catchers *should never* be caught in any mania, for it always gives false importance to one set of "things" at the expense of others. The question is always *cui bono*—for whose benefits are events happening? Accurate appraisals, not convenient ones, are critical. Mass deception depends upon the ability to manipulate the popular organs of communication decisive in the formulation of mass opinion and the

nourishment of mass belief. Serious spy-catchers must always be most attentive to what lies behind events.

3. Spy-catchers must beware of all information provided through liaison operations; i.e., provided by "allies," especially those who have any stake in the situation. The greater the stake they have, in general, the greater the provided information must be *critically* assessed, for friendship is in counterintelligence secondary to survival.

4. Spy-catchers must *target* those they wish to catch, even if, when the target is set, the identity or identities of the spy or spies is unknown. Selective targeting must always be related to available resources and employment of these resources to the greatest advantage for the spy-catcher(s). The careful deployment and/or employment of resources always runs counter to spy maniacs, who fear spies everywhere. Targeting is important because communities have varying vulnerability levels, and different aspects of the community are more or less attractive to the spy. Priorities must be examined, especially when there might be numerous targets, and resources deployed accordingly. Spy mania rarely aids targeting.

NOTES

1. *Her Majesty's Secret Service*, Christopher Andrew, New York: Viking Penguin, 1986, page 43.

2. For especially interesting observations on paranoid projection relevant to the present inquiry, see "Sadism and Paranoia," Anthony Starr, in *International Terrorism in the Contemporary World*, Eds. Livingstone, Kress, & Wanke, Westport, CT: Greenwood Press, 1978, pages 231–239.

3. See, for example, an interesting observation concerning contemporary French attitudes that have led to excesses in connection with French possessions in Oceania: "In this belief he is only paranoic." *The Economist*, 6 September 1986, page 14.

That delightful author, Diane Johnson, writes in *Terrorists and Novelists*, New York: Alfred Knopf, 1982, page 249: "I was interested to learn that paranoia is a civic, not just a personal characteristic."

4. *The Choking Doberman*, Jan Harold Brunvand, New

York: W.W. Norton, 1984, should be an indispensable hand-book for all intelligence officers concerned with matters of this kind.

5. The significance of the term *spy* in this context should be properly appreciated. Spy is a bad word, a term of oppro-brium. It can be facilely used, especially in our own times, to whip up a special kind of odium for the individual so labeled. It may be recalled that the United States embassy hostages in Iran were labeled "spies." On this generally, see *Making Spies*, H.H.A. Cooper and Lawrence J. Redlinger, Boulder, CO: Paladin Press, 1986, page 10.

6. See the interesting observations on these presumptions in *Crime by Computer*, Donn B. Parker, New York: Charles Scribner's, Inc., 1976, pages 165–174, and in *The Logic and Limits of Trust*, Bernard Barber, New Brunswick, NJ: Rutgers University Press, 1983.

7. For a singular study of these matters in a primitive society (that of the Jivaro Indians), of considerable value to those concerned with all aspects of security, see "Blood Re-venge and War among the Jivaro Indians," Ralph Kersten, in *Law & Warfare*, Ed. Paul Bohannan, Garden City, NY: National History Press, 1967, pages 303–325.

8. "It is more difficult for people to trust someone whose behavior tends to be unpredictable or inexplicable." *Powerbase*, Marilyn Moats Kennedy, New York: Macmillan, 1984, page 56.

9. See the perceptive observations on Soviet military lead-ership style in *Cohesion: The Human Element in Combat*, William Darryl Henderson, Washington, D.C.: National De-fense University Press, 1985, pages 134–135.

10. "Fear was as effective a screen as barbed wire." *The Defector*, Evelyn Anthony, New York: Coward, McCann, and Geogheagan, 1981, page 218.

11. Unlike white collar and organized crime, no serious attempt has yet been made to quantify the costs of terrorism. The task is simply too staggering.

12. Washington Outlook, *Business Week*, 5 May 1986, page 39, "Terrorism will be the economic summit's No. 1 topic."

13. See "The Bombs of September," *Newsweek*, 29 Sep-tember 1986, page 30. "A 10-day siege of terrorist bombings turns the City of Light into a city of fear."

14. Cooper & Redlinger, op. cit., supra note 5, pages 236–237.

15. Compare, for example, his "The Futility of Terrorism" as reproduced in *Contemporary Terrorism: Selected Readings*, Eds. John D. Elliott and Leslie K. Gibson, Gaithersburg, MD: International Association of Chiefs of Police, 1978, pages 285–292 with his "Reflections on Terrorism," *Foreign Affairs*, Fall 1986, pages 86–100.

16. Such as tea and sandwiches with the British prime minister at 10 Downing Street and a 5,200-ticket giveaway by British airways.

17. *The Master Terrorist: The True Story behind Abu Nidal*, Yossi Melman, New York: Adama Books, 1986, page 7.

18. President Reagan was caught in an awkward backlash following the resolution of the Daniloff affair when the plight of the American kidnap victims in Lebanon was equated with the case. Mr. Reagan failed to make the proper distinctions, and his credibility on the matter suffered accordingly. His handling of the associated Iranian arms deal only compounded the matter.

19. *Anatomy of Spying*, Ronald Seth, New York: E.P. Dutton, 1963, page 298.

20. While the subsequent trial of Mehmet Ali Agca has, as might have been anticipated, done little to clarify the connections that have been alleged, Claire Sterling's *The Time of the Assassins*, New York: Holt, Rinehart & Winston, 1983, remains a good starting point.

21. See, generally, *On Assassination*, H.H.A. Cooper, Boulder, CO: Paladin Press, 1984.

22. The Nazis became exceptionally adept at the creation of incidents for the purpose of providing excuses for territorial annexation, many of these being executed by Alfred Helmut Naujocks, SD. See *Nazi Conspiracy & Aggression*, Washington, D.C.: United States Government Printing Office, 1946. See also *The Spymasters*, Charles Whiting, New York: Saturday Review Press, E.P. Hutton, 1976, pages 36–37.

23. Henry Kissinger's shrewd observation is worth recalling here: "By a selective presentation of documents one can prove almost anything." *White House Years*, Boston: Little, Brown, 1979, page xxii.

24. The press in the United States does not like to labor under even the suggestion that it is being used by others. See the furor over the assertions that the Reagan administration planted disinformation in the news media in an attempt to

destabilize the regime of Muammar el Qadafi in June/July 1986. *The Wall Street Journal,* Friday, 3 October 1986, page 2. Missing the point entirely (perhaps on purpose), Secretary of State Schultz is reported as saying: "Frankly, I didn't have any problems with psychological warfare against Qadafi."

25. "If you say something enough times it becomes accepted truth." *Stranger in Two Worlds,* Jean Harris, New York: Macmillan, 1986, page 330.

26. See "Target U.S.: Terrorist Activity Inevitable," *Plano Daily Star Courier,* 29 January 1986, page 1.

27. Thus the trial of the four perpetrators of the *Achille Lauro* piracy. Though necessary to establish their individual and collective responsibility for the piracy and the resultant death of Leon Klinghoffer, the trial was quite useless in regard to extending responsibility to those who must have planned, initiated, and directed the action.

28. It has been pertinently observed that "there is a tradition of disinformation following important political crimes." *Death in Washington,* Donald Freed and Fred Landis, Westport, CT: Lawrence Hill, 1980, page 152.

29. The careful reader is invited to analyze and compare "The Evil Spirit," *Newsweek,* 13 January 1986, page 23, with "Masters of Mystery & Murder, *Time,* 13 January 1986, page 31.

30. The answer is certainly not provided by Yossi Melman, op. cit., supra note 17.

31. The noises we hear can be very confusing. As Morris West has observed, "Once the propaganda machine starts blaring, who will hear the shots in the alley?" *The Clowns of God,* New York: William Morrow, 1981, page 143.

32. Melman, op. cit., supra note 17, page 136.

33. Melman op. cit., supra note 17, pages 145–153. Melman rests his case for the Master Terrorist being alive on:

(1) *His interviews with the media.* These have no probative value whatsoever when carefully examined. They may, however, be usefully compared with the interviews given by Menachem Begin, as head of the Irgun, in pitch blackness from behind a curtain.

(2) *Content analysis of writings attributed to him.* We simply do not have material that we can positively attribute to him."He" may well have had an amanuensis all along.

(3) *If he were dead his family would have known.* No

comment is offered beyond the suggestion that this point be compared with the same point in the case of Josef Mengele.

(4) *Israeli intelligence would know*. This makes a number of extravagant assumptions, but all that need be said here is that even if the Israelis do know, they might have reasons for not telling.

(5) *The suggestion that a group becomes dormant when its leader dies, something that has not happened in the case of the Abu Nidal group*. This, of course, presumes that the group has been under control of a "real" Abu Nidal for a long period of time, since, say, 1976. And if it has not?

34. See the editorial entitled "Israel's Discord," *Dallas Morning News*, 23 September 1986.

35. See the editorial in the *Dallas Morning News*, 26 September 1986, where much the same idea is voiced.

36. "It's the oldest question of all, George. Who can spy on the spies." *Tinker, Tailor, Soldier, Spy*, John Le Carré, New York: Alfred A. Knopf, 1980, page 70.

37. For an excellent, highly detailed, well-documented account of these processes, see *Secret Police*, Thomas Plate and Andrea Darvi, Garden City, NY: Doubleday, 1981.

38. For some interesting, homegrown examples, see *Superspies*, Jules Archer, New York: Delacorte Press, 1977, passim.

39. This has been the problem with the various spy manias induced in the United States. See the heavily documented, if rather obviously biased, *The Age of Surveillance*, Frank Donnes, New York: Alfred A. Knopf, 1980. See also *Agency of Fear*, Edward Jay Epstein, New York: G.P. Putnam's Sons, 1977.

40. Particular care has to be taken with regard to the protection of secret or proprietary information where a concern operates in more than one country and its personnel are regularly transferred or travel among its various operations. Many United States secrets are leaked overseas in this way.

41. Perhaps the hardest thing to overcome is the obligation to do a friend a favor, even if it means (as it usually will) bypassing the security procedures, and the lingering feelings that it is somehow "sneaky," "cheap," "unworthy," or whatever to cooperate with management or the authorities by turning in those who attempt to evade the security net.

42. ". . . the spy is a secret weapon. The very nature of his

work forces him to be clandestine, and because the unknown is one of the most powerful actuators of fear, the spy unknown and unseen, yet undeniably present, is feared." Ronald Seth, op. cit., supra note 19, page 28.

43. For a very useful analysis, see Plate & Darvi, op. cit., supra note 42, pages 122–123.

44. For these purposes, the problem can be conveniently envisioned in terms of computer security, with the "community," whatever it may be, representing the hardware. On this, see the invaluable text of Donn B. Parker, op. cit., supra note 6, pages 282–283, which is as valid today as it was when written.

45. This was the problem with the initiatives leading up to the Huston plan, and beyond it to Watergate.

46. This percipient oriental tale was adopted by Nikita Khruschev in his autobiography, *Khruschev Remembers: The Last Testament,* Boston: Little, Brown, 1970.

47. Whatever else may be said of J. Edgar Hoover, he certainly understood the economic dimensions of spy mania and how to ensure his agency might profit from them.

3

BACKGROUNDING:
Getting to Know You,
Getting to Know
All About You

The identity of all men is buried beneath the rubble of their own histories.

Bill Granger[1]

Crooks, just like people in finance and entertainment, transact their business via phone and Telex. They travel by jet and use computers to do their bookkeeping, whereas most cops still have to count on their fingers.

Albert Spaggiari[2]

I wanted him to look like a banker, but in the small-loan department.

James B. Donovan[3]

Deprived of my red card, and my passport, I suddenly felt naked and weaponless. I'd become an ordinary person, just like that: a cipher, a nobody.

Edward Topol and Fridrikh Neznansky[4]

A man is expected to be who he says he is.

Frederick Forsyth[5]

The question "who is the person and what do we know of him?" calls for something much more than a simple identity check. To be "known," he needs to be seen in context, to be measured against the evidence of his historical progress and appreciated against his background. It is useful to pose the following question at this point: Why backgrounding? What is it, and what purpose does it serve? And why do we engage in it? Backgrounding requires from the outset a clear understanding of the distinction between the natural being and the artificial means by which we distinguish him from his fellows. Backgrounding is a process by which we seek to reconcile these two things as referring properly to a single being. Backgrounding is a kind of reality testing, a way of determining whether we are dealing with a real, identifiable person or a social fiction. It establishes the footing on which we base our relationships, from which we proceed to deal with those with whom we come in contact.

Who are you? Who are you *really?* Is this a question you have ever tried or been called upon to answer in concrete terms? Is it one you have ever seriously thought about? Would you be prepared to do so at a moment's notice? How would you set about the task?

Let us begin this chapter by imagining a scenario.[6] You are in your middle fifties when, quite by chance, you are contacted by an acquaintance from your early twenties, a time when your life and personal circumstances were quite different from what they are now. You were once very close. You meet for old times' sake. How do you reconcile what you once were with what you have now become? Is there a purpose, beyond that of mere recognition, in trying to do so? Can you recreate the past in the present? How do you span the years so as to establish some sort of continuity, if for no other reason than to guard against the embarrassment of mistaken identity? What do you include, and what do you suppress? Do you simply accept that you are now strangers and start from that premise, regardless of the nagging reminders from the past? Is the process of establishing your own identity easier if you have remained in a relatively narrow, circumscribed environment during the intervening years even though you have had no contact with your acquaintance over that time? Does the sex of the person and the degree of intimacy have anything to do with the process of reconstruction? How would the case be affected if a blood relationship were claimed?

Clearly, the enormous complexity of what we are presenting here is revealed by these and other questions that begin to suggest themselves. What to put in, what to leave out? In the way this scenario has been posited, the reconstruction is likely to be very disorderly, a very disorganized exercise. Do we know persons—or do we know what we must call their identities? For what we're asking here essentially is what are the proper ingredients of an identity? How are they assembled and presented? Is there equal validity, at least approximately, in the different permutations that are obviously possible? This draws us, ineluctably, to the central question. Is what we call identity simply a device for recognition or perhaps more exactly, recognizability? And, if so, by whom? And for what purposes?

As we have presented the matter here, identity has an important and complex historical dimension. Identity is an evanescent, developing thing; its true materiality lies in its attachment, reference, or referability to some human being. The human life, as it is lived by the individual to whom we seek to affix the identity, is itself in motion over time and space across an ever-changing landscape. The identity or what it stands for moves like a cursor on a computer screen, sometimes alone, sometimes in combination. Like that artificial representation, it is occasionally moved backward to recall or recover something of its past journeys, or it is halted momentarily for some task requiring an exercise of its properties. But we are not dealing in our inquiry with a mere point of reference. The identity has content and significance that have to be taken into account in our operations. Is it, we must ask, the same cursor with which we started out or has progress itself transformed it? Has it remained constant in its attachment to that with which it was associated at the outset of its journey? What generates its characteristics? Is it the cursor itself or the background over which it passes that confers upon it the properties we require for our purposes? Is it the machine, the hardware, the process, or the functions of the operator that produce these perceptions?

On even the most superficial of examinations, we see that all these things go into the creation and maintenance of an identity. What we should note is that, like the cursor on the computer screen, neither the human being nor his identity can be usefully lifted out of his background, isolated as it were, from his surroundings. Identity, in particular, is given position and definition against a certain backdrop. Human existence, identity, and the background against which their essential connectedness is revealed are the interwoven themes that we must proceed to examine and understand.

The Chinese have a saying that has become a part of the lore of Occidental logic, asserting that when you have a horse and a cow you have three things. The horse is one thing, the cow is a second thing, and the horse and cow together are a third thing. Applied to the matter at hand, we can see that the human being is one thing, that which we call the human identity is a second thing, and the two conjoined are a third thing, quite distinct and possessed of important properties of its own. The human being itself is endowed with the qualities and attributes of its natural existence. In the course of that existence, some human beings are altered physiologically and psychologically to a greater extent than others, but all are undeniably subject to the processes of change. The life span of some is long and rich in experience, while that of others, though long, is comparatively meager. Yet others have lives that are nasty, brutish, and short in the Hobbesian sense. The life span of yet others is so curtailed, perhaps to a matter of hours or less, that no experience of any significance is accumulated by such individuals at all. The latter are interesting cases for the purpose of our analysis. One may question whether such abbreviated lives have any place, beyond mere mention, in such a work as this. Do such lives have anything in the nature of an identity attached to them at all? To argue thus is to miss the point. It is indeed their very brevity and its significance that is so highly instructive to us here. It tells us something about the nature and quality of identity that we might miss were we to restrict our purview to those which have reached a certain maturity.

In developed communities, even the fact of birth generates the elements of identity. The community's accounting of itself is altered, often indelibly. At a very minimum, the event will produce some record of birth, often a name, the sex of the infant, an attribution of parentage, and a record of death and disposition. Some or all of these items, though, may be separately registered and archived. These elements have a uniquely pristine quality. They are unsullied by later accretions such as those produced by a more lengthy life and therein lies their peculiar usefulness. The human being has passed on, leaving a sparse but definite identity, a mark of his having been with us for however brief a moment in time that can be recognized, recalled, and evidenced. The consequences of this involuntary social legacy are profound. The usefulness of the fact depends upon the essential properties of identity; to what extent can it be preserved, authenticated, and recycled after the original human being has passed on? It is the very separateness of identity and its detachability that is illustrated and emphasized by these cases.

Our cursor, stopped for the moment so precipitously, does indeed have some content of its own, valuable to some other provided it is not recognized as having changed its attachment. Such an operation is clearly easier to effect before the dot has traveled very far across the screen. What happens in such cases is the surgical removal of the identity from the human being to whom it was briefly attached. Here, we see the horse and cow postulate in action in a most significant way. The detached identity, inchoate and unfulfilled though it may have been in a sense at the time of the death of the human being to whom it originally belonged, *is* capable of being appropriated or misappropriated by another.

All that is required, in practice, is a certain technical operation of reattachment to get the cursor moving once more.[7] Yet more than mere documentation is involved here; something of substance is actually transferred in the process. The "old" identity begins life afresh in association with a new human being. A new identity for some other is generated by this process of acquisition and assumption, and this starts to take on a "life" of its own, its former, truncated "life" continuing to enjoy a dormant, separate existence that can be exhumed and studied if the need or the oportunity arises. The socially constructed nature of identity becomes very clear by reference to such examples. They focus our attention on how an identity is manufactured and, perhaps more importantly, how it is affixed to the human being on whom it is conferred or by whom it is assumed. What also is worthy of note is that the identity itself is a living, growing thing and how it, too, becomes something quite different from what it was at its inception. Yet ultimately, identity is always dependent for its growth and vitality upon attachment to some human being.

Although easier for others to acquire and assume in their pristine state, dormant identities can be taken over at any time during their effective "shelf life."[8] Only the methods by which this is done have to be adjusted to the circumstances of the case. We must inquire here as to what happens to "old" identities? Do they decay to the point where they are of no value to others who would misappropriate them? Clearly they do.

They must in themselves have a realistic historical context. Someone in 1987 claiming to be Napoleon Bonaparte—*the* Napoleon Bonaparte—is likely to be referred for psychiatric treatment rather than given serious consideration, whatever the documentation he might adduce to authenticate his claim. A dormant identity that is heavily laden with verifiable data is dangerous to resuscitate even when it has remained in limbo for some time. It might be recognized as having belonged to its original human owner so as to call in question the entitlement of the new claimant. Feats of memory and thespian skills are called for by such transformations that are beyond the capabilities and inclinations of most who might essay the task. An *identity*, then, is a certain, finite thing having only a measured, useful life to whomsoever it might pertain. During that lifetime, however, it has considerable elasticity, allowing for much comfortable expansion. This characteristic of human identities must also be prudently taken into consideration. A live human being invests an identity with special qualities by reason of his recognized entitlement to it. Thus, acquisition of an original human identity, artificial enough in the example given above, is nevertheless a relatively controllable process. Once the identity has been taken over, it becomes progressively less manageable until a point is reached where the human individual to whom it pertains has virtually no control over the elements with which his own identity becomes invested.

There are many important consequences of what we have been examining. Thus, everyone who is ever born has some identity. But the human being, himself one and indivisible, *can* have many identities, simultaneously or in series. They are a matter of social construction and employment. He must simply avoid getting them mixed up or on the screen where they can be observed by the knowledgeable at one and the same time.[9] A human being may not be capable of being all things to all people, but he can certainly be, contemporaneously, a number of different things to many people through the use of distinct identities. Many human transactions, and much humorous as well as serious literature, depend upon this simple fact. It is rarely useful to regard identity in a fully comprehensive fashion. We should ask, rather, what identity, and what aspects of it concern us at any particular moment. As we have seen, identity is either conferred upon and/or acquired by a human being at birth or at some other time. It continues to be nourished and shaped throughout its useful life.

Its content per se, though important, does not answer our question: Who is this person? From the point of view of the spy-catcher, what is of greater importance is the attachment of the identity to a particular human being. The vital question is always to whom does this thing we have called identity really belong? How is that attachment evidenced? What if the identity has wholly synthetic origins? For it is this third thing—the horse and the cow (the human being in question *plus* his identity) that must concern the spy-catcher. In short, is he who he says he is? How can I know? What are the processes and techniques I must use to confirm or disallow the claim?

The questions we have posed above depend in large measure upon what we understand by "knowing" a person. Of what does such knowledge consist? We need to establish this before we can decide how to proceed. What, then, do we need to know in order to be able to say that we "know" some particular person? The expression "know" in such a context can have a limited or more extensive significance.

Let us offer another suggestive scenario. Suppose you are watching a television talk show when you recognize a person being interviewed. You exclaim, unhesitatingly, "I know him!" You have thus far based your recognition upon appearance, speech, mannerisms, and other characteristics as filtered through the medium. But then you are surprised. The individual you are watching is called by a name quite different from that with which you are familiar, and, as the interview unfolds, the facts elicited seem to portray a person totally different in every respect from that whom *you* "know."

Let us put a bizarre twist on this. "Your" person (the one causing you to exclaim, "I know him!") is a trash collector by occupation, whereas the person being interviewed is presented as an acknowledgeable foreign affairs expert. For a moment, you are dumbfounded. You begin to have doubts about your recognition, especially when the expert's credentials are offered in support of his opinions. Nothing emerges, however, that might be advanced as proof positive that your original impression was mistaken or, conversely, that your recognition was right on the mark from the beginning. He certainly "looks like" the person you think he is, but he also seems to behave in a thoroughly compatible fashion with the type of person he is represented as being. Yet "your" trash collector is in a context so inappropriate as to suggest that something is wrong. He seems to have the wrong *background* for the job at hand.

Is he a "lookalike," or could this be a daring hoax? There is nothing intrinsically improbable in either suggestion; such things do occur on occasion. Yet your nagging doubts persist. Is "your" trash collector really the person you see on the screen, who has seemingly quite different background qualifications and station in life? If you are fair-minded and reasonably conversant with the relevant analytical processes, you will probably recognize that your belief that you "know" the person in question is based entirely upon appearances and the conclusions you have drawn from them. There is a situational incongruity that baffles; what is *he* doing there? Why would a trash collector fulfill the requirements of the interviewee? Why would a foreign relations expert occupy himself in the collection of trash?

You are forced into a review of what you know and how well you know it. How well do you "know" the trash collector? Have you ever exchanged more than a few words with him? Have you ever even looked at him very carefully? Do you really "know" that he does *not* have a Ph.D. or some other high academic or professional qualification? You have never, of course, had occasion to inquire. You have had no reason to entertain such engaging speculations. If the doubts are strong and persistent enough, you may start to ask more seriously just who this trash collector is? Really is? *Could* he be the foreign relations expert you have seen and, if so, what is the explanation for what is admittedly a very odd juxtaposition of occupations? And suppose the two are, after all, identical? What does this do to your way of looking at the individual in question?

You need continue no further with this line of thought. However you proceed with inquiries for the purpose of satisfying your curiosity, begin from the humbling position of how little you really "know" about one you have presumed to recognize—*identify*—and label.

Yet we rely upon appearances all the time in our daily lives; people should be and do what seems appropriate to the situation and, if they do, we raise little question concerning *who* they are. But let us reverse the coin for a moment. What do we "know" about the person observed and heard described on the television screen? Suppose we had not experienced this confusion as to identity. Would we doubt the person is who he says he is or who we are told he is by the television host? What do we inject into these images to give them substance? Where does it come from? *Is not identity, then, in the last resort, a fiction at least, a social construction at best, based upon different sets of assumptions?*[10] However rigorous our procedures and investigations, regardless of the tests we apply, acceptance rests on an act of faith: he *is* who he says he is, or who we are told he is. In a very real sense, it is the identity that speaks for the human being; he *is* who his identity declares him to be, however it may be evidenced.

Identity, then, is that which serves to fix a human being for us within our universe of reference. Identity is the referent, something we accept as *standing for* the human being in question. It is that which enables us to pick *this* human being out of a crowd, even if we have never seen him before. We do not ourselves independently manufacture identities for others in order to be able to do this. We participate, more or less, in the manufacturing even if only at the consumption stage; as consumers, we process that which is fed to us with respect to identities.

We shall, in a moment, turn our attention to the ingredients of human identity. For the present, it is merely necessary to observe, somewhat tritely, that these are culled from life itself. Identity defines, and the content of identity, so far as it can be known to us, is the product of life's experiences and their impact upon a particular individual. But, returning to our earlier metaphor, it is not only the content and quality of the cursor itself which we evaluate. The background against which it is seen to move is important to our calculations concerning what it represents. When we look at a man's identity, we are seeking to define him, to give him place and purpose, against life's ever-shifting backdrop.

He has to fit into our scheme of reference for us to be able to use the process to advantage, for the purpose of identity is to give distinction, to accord meaning and content to the cursor so as to enable us to pick it out, if need be, from all the other items on the screen. *A person only has an identity for us if we can do that*. This is what we mean when we claim to identify someone, whether by pointing a finger, affixing a label, or providing a lengthy, detailed description; he has something *for us*,[11] which marks him out from the rest of mankind. What we really "know"[12] about him is this identity and its content and whether we attach it to that particular human being or another. But attachment, too, is affected by background considerations, as we have seen in the example we just examined. Recognition and what goes with it must be capable of transcending time and place; otherwise, we should only "know" a person in some places and not others.

We are ever required to test the correspondence between the human being and the identity he claims. What of the case where one who is a total stranger presents himself to us? He makes his claim to be such and such a person. We have no earlier scheme of reference to draw upon to test his claim. For the moment the human being and the identity he claims coincide so as to appear one and the same thing. We must find the means of separating them if we would test the claim rather than accept it at face value. Background assumes considerable importance in such cases; it is what enables us to undertake the process of separation. The human being is evident by his presence; his identity is not. He must have the means to manifest it, to make it materialize so as to be accorded recognition. Identity, too, needs a presence if it is to be able to transcend time and place. Yet, as we have seen, it is a complex, compendious thing at times. Who carries such evidence in complete and connected form?

In perhaps the worst case, the human being we would identify is present to us only as a disembodied voice on the telephone claiming to be such and such a person. We acknowledge these problems when, as circumstances dictate, we say to someone who so presents himself before us, "Can you show me some identification?" When this is displayed, we are then in a position to compare what we see and hear with what is produced for our inspection. We need not consider all the intricacies of the matter here. What we must observe is that the identity in which we are interested is manifested by something in the nature of a key that may, at the verifier's option, be used to try to open the Pandora's box that is the identity corresponding to the human being who claims it. Or, alternatively, it may be the key only to the link or attachment of that identity to the human being, which is what most usually concerns us in these cases. Commonly, the "key" will be some sort of document which the individual will produce to substantiate his claim to be who that item indicates the bearer to be. Possession may be nine-tenths of the law, but it does little to resolve the problems we have been considering here.

What we need to stress here is that it is easy in such cases to confuse the item of identification tendered with the identity it is supposed to evidence. He *is* who he says he is because he has an identity card that says he is that person. But an identity card does not *stand for* the human being who carries it.[13] The identity, which does, comprises much more. The card is the "key," a convenient way of transcending time and place, of conveying verifiable information in short form to strangers. We need to understand these important methods of transmission and manifestation in order to cope with the problem of carrying and displaying as required something that is not really portable. Again, all this goes to the fundamental question of what is an identity. We must pursue the matter once more from another angle.

The investment firm of Merrill Lynch recently commissioned a most attractive and thought-provoking advertisement.[14] In black and white, it depicts the face of a two-hundred-thirty-year-old timepiece surrounded by an assortment of escapements and other items of horological machinery. The caption asks: "What would time be without the clock?" Below that question is the answer: "Unmanageable. A clock gives time structure." Identity, too, and what we mean by it, is a kind of management tool. It gives meaning and structure to the essential data of life and allows it to be associated with the requirements of the society of which it is a part. Identity may be seen as a recording device, like a clock, but one capable of maintaining a permanent point of reference for those capable of and interested in seeking it out. A clock marks the passage of the hours, but does not preserve them. Unlike the clock, identity is both a mechanism and its product. A clock marks the good moments in time indifferently along with the bad, the significant together with the trivial. Were its function to record in permanent form the passage of the hours, the compilation would include without discrimination all time that had transpired. A clock, of course, makes no value judgments of any kind in performing its management functions; our identity recorder must do so.

Clearly, in the case of a normal human life span, a comprehensive, permanent record would include a great deal of dross as well as the few odd, precious nuggets worthy of preservation by any standards. The efficient management of this mass of material clearly requires much filtration and a process for archiving that which is deemed worth saving and ridding the system of that which ought to be discarded. *An identity, as an arrangement of individually and socially significant data relating to some person, is therefore a skeleton structure*, scraped clean of the unnecessary. Still, at least in some cases, this identity is capable of being augmented from stored data so as to supply something in the nature of an ongoing history. If the continuous record were a videotape, we would see that reference could be made to specific frames in order to relate some particular portion of the history to contemporary requirements. It is necessary for purposes of authentication that the identity and the person to whom it is attached have an historic correspondence. How well or how poorly the process of retrieval might be managed is largely dependent upon the completeness and maintenance of the archives. Most people do not rate the kind of personal record-keeping that would enable this exercise to be undertaken very effectively.

Identity tends to be, for most persons, a more or less old and rickety framework onto which are juxtaposed periodic updates, the last of which is regarded as the "identity" of the person to whom it is attached; identity is concerned more with who a person *is* than with who he *was*. The latter is subsumed within the current identity. A person, then, is quite properly entitled to a number of "historical identities" that may be more or less relevant to a consideration of his current identity. This is the inevitable consequence of the unfolding of history and the process by which identities are created. This is not such a strange idea as may appear at first sight. What was the identity of Baby Kissinger? Of Private Kissinger, U.S. Army? Of Dr. Kissinger of Harvard University? Of Secretary of State Kissinger? The ultimate identity, that which serves for the latest instant in time before being superseded, is not simply a composite of *all* that has gone before it. Much has been discarded as irrelevant. A great deal of the "real" Henry Kissinger, at times when we might extract those cameos to which we referred, has been buried beneath the rubble of his own history. There is constant background change, but that which we call identity must be maintained in the face of change, and change must accordingly be incorporated into it.

The child is different from the adult, yet in the progression to that later stage of development, identity has been carried along so that we should be able to say beyond a shadow of doubt, *"That* child has become *that* person." One who has known the individual as a child may not, after long absence, recognize the adult. But there has been no physical substitution. One who has not had the advantage of knowing the child needs something that has incorporated the changes so as to be able to authenticate that child and adult are one and the same, that they share the same identity. The person is a natural entity, susceptible to physical and psychological change in the ordinary course of things. That which we call an identity is a manufactured, socially constructed, artificial thing serving to distinguish some individual from all others of his species.[15]

There is an almost mystical quality about all this. We recognize the inevitability of change, yet it does not accord well with our social scheme of things here. We are ever searching for constants to assure ourselves that whatever the changes of form, the substance has not been altered. We wish to be certain that the more things change, the more they remain essentially the same. Identity is a kind of social sheet anchor for the purpose. Otherwise, how can we "know" anyone, short of the impractical task of keeping them under constant observation throughout their lives, an exercise which obviously would produce its own Heisenberg effect. Identity is a social watchdog, situating and distinguishing the person we would "know" from the rest of the flock. Yet, to accomplish this, it too must be capable of certain accommodating transformations. It is the ability to synthesize these that allows for the being of new identities and the discarding and burying of the old.

While what we have stated has implications well beyond the narrow reach of the subject matter with which we are primarily concerned in the present work, there are clearly some very profound consequences here for the counterespionage specialist. In the matter of identity, the continuity of the record is of the highest importance; all gaps give rise to suspicion. We may pose the question, Is the individual holder of the identity under review—*the ultimate identity holder*— the same person that the record, were it stopped at any point in its progress, would show to have borne that identity throughout, notwithstanding the changes that have taken place? How do we demonstrate the requisite degree of continuity? We are interested here in methods and proof, going to the very heart of the identity check. Basically, we are seeking ways of assuring ourselves that the person who started out with a certain identity has not discarded it along the way, or that the identity in question has not been wrongfully assumed by another. Any techniques for establishing the necessary correspondences between a given human being and the identity he claims for himself must pay appropriate attention to the chain of evidence and the opportunities for tampering with it. Special attention must be paid to the weak links in the chain, those moments at which the chain itself might have been refashioned or during which substitutions might have taken place.

Every life story has its lacunae; it would be a strange and suspicious thing to find one that seemingly did not. There will be many opportunities for creative interference in the case of a long chain of evidence. Each link must accordingly be expertly examined with the greatest of care; nothing can be taken for granted. A truism deserves interpolation here. The chain, however long or short, is anchored at the moment of birth of some individual. We must always begin our investigations with what we shall call the *original human identity*, that conferred upon an acknowledged human being at birth.[16] Any identity that does not have such clear origins and an acceptable chain of evidence leading from it to the *ultimate human identity* that is currently under examination must be regarded as suspect.

Every contact between human beings sets some sort of reference check in motion. Only the most incautious or abnormal respond to others without some instinctive pause, however slight, while the mechanism of recognition and sorting out grinds into gear. A stranger speaks to us. In a split instant, our reply is framed, but a wealth of material has been reviewed, consciously or unconsciously, before we give utter-

ance or withhold a response.[17] The character and profundity
of the process depend upon the circumstances of the encounter. Thus, we do not ordinarily inquire extensively into a
person's antecedents before selling him a Hershey bar. Given
the usual conditions under which such relatively informal,
commercial transactions take place, more than a perfunctory
inquiry might well be resented and cause the customer to
take his business elsewhere.

Even more to the point, there is neither the time nor the
resources to expand upon such pursuits for matters of so
slight an economic consequence; cost/benefit ratios could not
justify such indulgences that, socially speaking, border on the
bizarre. As the proposed transaction ascends in scale and
importance, however, the matter assumes quite a different
aspect. Our forms of reference are brought into play on
another, higher plane. Clearly, when more substantial interests are at stake, we need to know with whom we are dealing
before we can even assess the value to us of the transaction.
A relatively small, simple, cash purchase, such as regularly
takes place in a store or shop, rarely warrants much by way of
inquiry; the ostensible quality of the cash and his willingness
to part with it represent the customer's warranty, the requisite evidence of his ability and intention to pay for the
merchandise.

But let us dig a little deeper into the implied assumptions
here. We do not, normally, concern ourselves with the validity of the cash tendered for payment. Let us suppose, however, we have been advised that counterfeit five-dollar bills
are circulating. Might we not, then, seek to verify that the
note we have received is genuine? Again, we do not ordinarily concern ourselves with where the money comes from
as long as it appears good on the face of it. But what if we had
been advised of a recent bank robbery and had been supplied
with a list of bank-note numbers we had been asked by the
police to check? And suppose the customer were a stranger to
us or appeared to behave in a manner inconsistent with the
nature of the business being transacted?

There are, obviously, many more possibilities that suggest
themselves along the same lines. The real point is that, in a
great many cases, we simply do not care who we deal with as
long as we are paid. Payment itself, rather than the person
who makes it, is at the heart of the business. The transaction

itself is impersonal. But when personality intrudes, a degree of uncertainty or even danger is injected into the transaction, and we need to "know" with whom we are dealing.

Thus, when credit is involved, quite another set of considerations comes into play. Fundamentally, the impersonality of the transaction is impaired. In such a case, no immediate economic benefit passes to the vendor; he is persuaded to part with his goods on the instant with the prospect of future satisfaction. The important issues are whether one will get paid, and who will pay? A question of trust arises that causes us to automatically regard closely the person who proposes such a transaction to us. *Who* the person is suggesting such a deal is quite as important as the terms of the deal itself— how, when, and by whom we are to get paid. Similar considerations arise when a casual seller offers an item of property of some value. Does he have title to pass? Who is he? Can I get in touch with him if the transaction is impeached or goes sour in some way? Credit can require a degree of pure trust; the giving of some form of negotiable instrument, most usually a check drawn on a commercial bank; or payment guaranteed by a third party, such as that now commonly arranged through the use of a charge card. Each has its own distinctive backgrounding ritual in our society. Each transaction gives rise to its own historic accretions, linking the individuals concerned to what is done, the so-called "paper trail."[18] Convenience as well as economics have played a part in shaping these transactions.

Let us suppose that a relatively small purchase has been made in a commercial establishment with the use of a bank credit card. Such a purchase conventionally triggers a certain response. The process of backgrounding begins; how much or how little, and how effectively, depends upon the merchant and his agents as well as the size and character of the transaction. Most of us are familiar with the wide variations in procedure to which such a transaction may give rise. The card itself, bearing a unique number, may or may not be verified against a list to determine whether it has been canceled or reported as lost or stolen by the person to whom it was issued. Sometimes an authorization call is made to the representatives of the credit-card issuer, sometimes it is not. The ostensible holder of the credit card may be asked to provide a telephone number and an address, and he may also be asked to produce some form of identity document, most usually a driver's license.

Much of this is perfunctory and cosmetic; many otherwise quite honest persons habitually give the wrong particulars out of irritation and a feeling for the absurdity of the procedure. This charade does little to protect against credit-card fraud, and few of the particulars taken are ever satisfactorily verified at a point in time when they might have any impact on the transaction. But this is backgrounding, albeit on a limited and, for the most part, ineffective scale.

The focus upon documentation and other evidence tends to obscure the real point here. It is the individual who is the subject of inquiry, whose *bona fides* and whose right to represent himself as what he claims to be (namely, the rightful user of the credit card) are in question. The other party to the transaction is not simply taken on trust as being what he purports to be. Inquiries are made, particulars obtained. Where the matter goes from there depends upon a variety of factors, but there is a presumption behind all this that there is a *body of data* to which the documents tendered (charge card, check, and/or driver's license) or the information obtained serve as a reference point. They are to be connected to the individual claiming to be creditworthy, who asks, in effect, by his actions to be trusted. The major considerations governing backgrounding, as they emerge from such dealings, the strength and quality of the need to know the person with whom one is dealing, and the cost of finding out in relation to the value of the transaction. Such transactions as we have considered may serve as models for others to which we shall in turn proceed. We need only observe here that the circle of people most of us really "know" is quite small. The means to "know" many more are often at hand, but we rarely avail ourselves of them, for our purposes hardly demand the effort involved.

So far, we have been dealing with process, with the techniques for coping with the various problems of identity, with trying to find some mechanism for uniting the identity with the human being to whom it is assigned. Now we must turn to the matter of substance, the content and ingredients that make up identity. At the outset, we should make the point that the existence of a real, live human being is not, in itself, a necessary ingredient.[19] An identity can be created, having an existence of its own, without any real attachment to a human being. But, conversely, a human being cannot exist without *some* identity; some have tried, but such efforts are doomed to failure ab initio. People have identities; identities do not have people. Despite this caveat, it is evident that the content of identity, its substance, proceeds from human experience; essentially, its ingredients are recognizably human, as relating to humanity, the way people think, feel, and view things.

Each of the following elements, therefore, has such an origin, but it is important to see them for what they are, namely *products* which, along with other essential ingredients, comprise in total that elusive, socially constructed and perhaps artificial thing we call identity. Yet an identity is, and always will remain, an intangible. It cannot be seen and inspected like the human being who claims it as his own. It can only be *evidenced*, manifested through the appropriate processes. When we say to someone, "I'd like to see some ID," we are inviting him to allow us to begin that process. How far we take it before we are satisfied, how well we undertake it so as not to deceive ourselves as to its results, depends on how well we understand what we are doing and what it is we are looking for. Wearisome though it may be, we must reiterate that when someone says, "I'm Mr. Jones, the tax man," it is not enough that he is able to produce an official document that says he is Mr. Jones, a tax man. We must turn to the intangibles themselves for the proper enlightenment.

For the purposes of the present work, the following ingredients of human identity are suggested for examination:

Names
Appearance
Race/ethnicity
Personal characteristics and peculiarities
Personal history
Experiences
Achievements
Relationships to other people
Relationships to things
Memories

This arrangement is quite arbitrary. It is recognized that particulars that could be placed under one descriptive heading might very well have been considered under another. What is set out does, however, have a useful symmetry for our purposes and any compression would tend to obscure the basic outline, which it is hoped might serve as a practical, operational framework. The data generated by submitting a particular human being to the rigors of this outline produces an identity for that individual, something serving in the aggregate to distinguish him from others, however similar in some respects they may be. From that comprehensive product can be extracted certain key items that serve as *identifiers* for incorporation into documentation that the individual can, at his discretion or as he may be required, produce to others to certify that he is who he claims to be (namely the human being who, above all others, alone could have generated the body of data in question). Somewhere within that body of data are key elements establishing it as pertaining to *one* human individual and no other. Clearly, what we have outlined above is worthy of extended examination. Here, the considerations of space and dictates of purpose militate against such an exercise, but some consideration of these categories must be essayed if the concept of identity and what is comprised in backgrounding are to be better understood.

Names have always had a singular importance in relation to identity. In some cultures, an almost mystical quality is attached to one's name; one's name is, literally, who one is.[20] Possession of it by another is tantamount to a surrender of an important part of oneself, so that names become a jealously guarded secret rather than an article designed to facilitate social relations. In our own society, names are important identifiers, and the ease with which they can be altered and assumed tells much of the changing character of the times and of the real value of names in relation to identity. In the simplest terms, "I am John Smith" or "Ivan Ivanovich" or even "Sabri Khalil al-Banna" really stands for very little as an identifier. Yet it is hard for us to conceive of a person who has no name; he would seem, somehow, excluded from the human race.[21] For a name, however false, is a kind of handle, a connection to something larger, a circle of reference. It tells something of the person who bears it, of his relationships, of his antecedents and, perhaps, how and why he acquired it. It may, on occasion, tell something approaching the truth as to his origins. It is an important part of a person's identity, but it must be studied in context. The most useful thing that can be said here is that no identification document can be considered complete without it.

Appearances can, as we have seen, be deceptive, but they have a high degree of importance in the matter of human identity. We most usually believe we "know" somebody because of their appearance. Obviously, appearance can be altered and such tinkering in the world of espionage ranges from changing clothing styles or shaving off a moustache to using padded cheeks, wearing dark glasses, and having cosmetic surgery. Appearances change with the years, and not only in the matter of fashion. While it is sometimes possible to see, with a fair degree of accuracy, the child in the adult, these metamorphoses offer considerable opportunity for creative impersonation or outright substitution. Appearances *are* important; why else have photo IDs? In the world of espionage, however, it is what can be done with people to create false appearances that has to be specially watched.[22] The old adage has it that you cannot tell a sausage by its skin. Appearances should never be evaluated in the abstract or without their proper supporting context.

Race/ethnicity is an important factor in situating identity. It goes without saying that peculiar racial/ethnic characteristics, especially physiognomy and language, are very difficult for a person of a completely different group to impersonate. Some races have ingrained characteristics quite as distinctive as any physical peculiarities, and unfamiliarity with them ruins any attempt at convincing impersonation.[23] A multiracial/ethnic society, such as that of the United States or Canada, opens up all sorts of possibilities; nationality is distinct from race. An Asian with a United States or a Canadian passport is, nowadays, commonplace. A Caucasian with, say, a North Vietnamese passport would attract official attention and inquiry almost anywhere. Race/ethnicity and culture are important indicators of *origins*, and hence a vital component of any identity even where distinguishing factors are visually unlikely to be apparent. Race/ethnicity and speech are therefore important characteristics for the keen observer.

Personal characteristics and peculiarities, along with appearance, are major factors in facilitating recognition. Some are hard to disguise or simulate. Age is a personal characteristic, although it may be hard to establish with precision in particular cases. Physical disabilities, such as the loss of a limb or debilitating infirmities (palsy or a withered arm, for example), often become part of a person's perceived identity ("one-eyed Joe," "peg-leg Pete," etc.). Other characteristics are more subtle but no less memorable.[24] They help to fix the individual in a certain framework and the mind's eye; they invest him with something peculiarly his own, helping to mark him out from the rest. Birthmarks, scars, tattoos, blemishes, and imperfections of all kinds are often pressed into service as identifiers. Three require special mention here: fingerprints, dental work, and blood types. Records of these will often serve to identify individuals when, for a variety of reasons, other identifiers are absent or suspect.[25]

Personal history is an intangible component of one's identity that stretches back to one's origins, however overlaid with rubble it may have become. Personal histories can, of course, be faked. They are more commonly so than many would admit, as a glance at the potted biographies in *Who's Who in America* of those whose history is known independently to us would reveal. But for the counterespionage specialist, personal histories are a mother lode waiting to be mined. If we know who you *were*, we are usually in a better position to tell who you *are*.[26] A history leaves an indelible impression upon the person to whom it belongs. It can only be escaped by judiciously covering the trail or inventing an alternative one, a history that will stand up to vigorous scrutiny. All serious tests of identity must begin here.[27]

Experiences are, of course, a part of one's personal history, but they are treated separately here because they are things that, most usually, are shared with others and, as such, are susceptible to independent recovery and appreciation from a different perspective. Having been a concentration camp guard is a part of one's personal history that is understandably hidden, but the experience, shared with others less fortunate in their day, might well surface as a result of *their* being able to recall and reconstruct it, situating you within its context. Experiences of all kinds *shape* identity, even where they are suppressed; the experience of having suppressed them makes its own contribution.

Achievements, from learning to ride a bicycle to attaining high office or other public renown, are a formative part of one's identity. They mark a progress through life that enriches the individual in some permanent way and helps to make him what he has become. Yet they are sometimes discarded or hidden as may be politic given the circumstances. Some can be recovered and reinstated, like old trophies taken down from the attic. Others lie buried, yet something of them protrudes, like a tombstone, as an identifier of what once was. The problem most usually lies in making the connection. How can we tell that this spindly, unattractive creature before us was once a strapping athlete, holder of some bizarre endurance record commemorated by an entry in *The Guinness Book of World Records*? A particular problem is posed for the counterespionage specialist by the faked achievement.[28] It is always a question of examining the evidence to see whether the claim can be sustained and the necessary connection established. It would have been difficult for one to have swum the English Channel in, say, 1934 if the evidence should show that the claimant was only four years of age on the date in question.

Relationships to other people are the links that connect an individual to the world in which he dwells. They define and limit his identity in a distinctive way, for they impinge upon his identity as he does upon the identity of others. Blood relationships are very important, and their acceptance or denial is sometimes crucial to the chain of evidence. Different cultures have different systems of kinship and recognition of paternity and its consequences. People are known by the company they keep.[29] Any time these connections cannot be found and adequately examined, it is evident that something is seriously amiss. John Donne, perhaps, said it best in *Devotions*, Chapter 17: "No man is an island, entire of itself; Every man is a part of the continent, a piece of the main."

Relationships to things are often eloquent testimony to who a person is or was. Attachments of all kinds are part of our identity, of our progress through life. The possessions of even the most wretched attest to their condition, who and what they are.[30] In our materialistic society, the "paper trail" is its own testimony. Without a specific relationship to certain things—in some societies a special pass or ration book—life itself might not be possible. Property and the human individual are closely linked in such a way that the individual may be located as surely as the item over which he exercises dominion.

Memories are perhaps the most poignant and persuasive evidence of identity. Whether they are our own or those of others, memory is more than a process for recalling the past; it is the very substance itself of that which is recalled. Minute scraps of evidence relative to identity are stored somewhere in memory, in someone's memory.[31] The spy-catcher must ever seek out the key to unlocking them. Memory often supplies the only link between some human being and the identity he claims or denies. This human being can remember what only he and the subject in question have shared or shared in a significant way. Such facts are, on occasion, preserved only in memory.

Having thus examined identity from these different perspectives, it remains for us to consider its place in our own scheme of things. An entire book might usefully be devoted exclusively to the use of false identity in the field of espionage. Who is not familiar with the temporary assumption of a false name for the purpose of purchasing travel documents, renting a hotel room, or meeting a casual contact? The purposes motivating such short-term expediencies, or those with a longer-range objective in mind, are essentially the same in all cases—namely, concealment of the person, his business, or his intentions.

Obviously, there is an infinity of permutations possible in all instances. The trick, operationally, is to be able to slip convincingly into the role, to "become" the person we claim to be at such times so as to deceive those we meet casually and fight off any more problematical challenge from those who claim to "know" us in some other capacity, inconvenient to reveal. If we are traveling in foreign places rarely frequented by those who are ordinarily acquainted with us, a change of name, accompanied by a slight change of personal appearance, will often suffice for our purposes. Such deceptions are part and parcel of the life of the secret agent, and their execution is a routine part of the spy's tradecraft. With the appropriate documentation, it is not too different for most to resist convenient inquiry over the short term.

For longer missions, much more is needed than a cover

name, corresponding documentation, appropriate alterations of appearances, and a certain flair for carrying off these undertakings. To actually "become" another person is a very demanding task, requiring greater discipline, iron nerve, and a certain amount of histrionic ability.[32] Some transformations, such as those involving a change of racial characteristics, size, and shape, are so dramatic as to be worthwhile only under heroic circumstances and with the exercise of considerable professional assistance. Nevertheless, cosmetic surgery is now by no means uncommon for effecting changes of appearance that would once have been firmly eschewed. The most difficult problems involve impersonation, the substitution of one person for some known other. Not only is a high degree of acting skill required to carry off the deception, it can very rarely be attempted without the active, wholehearted cooperation—even though it may be unwitting—of at least some of the key persons who have "known" quite intimately the individual whose existence has been taken over by another. These substitutions can generally only be attempted after some sort of separation or break with the past has occurred, some event which has taken the individual in question out of his ordinary course of life for such a period as to make his reemergence, in somewhat altered form, at least plausible and explainable to those who are supposed to accept the new for the old. While there are always some risks in such enterprises, they are sometimes of considerable value to those engaged in espionage and, again, would merit extended study in a work devoted exclusively to the topic. Here, we must confine ourselves, from the perspective of counterespionage, to a consideration of what may be necessary to carry off these deceptions and how they might be detected or prevented.

Many activities in the world of espionage, as well as in the world of crime, are premised upon the point that by the time inquiries are initiated and the deception exposed, the spy (or the criminal) will be long gone and the false particulars that have facilitated the deception will not lead to the perpetrator. The spy needs something that will stand up long enough to enable him to get the job done and get away safely. Ideally, therefore, identity verification procedures must be speedy and well performed if the impostor is to be detected and caught in the act. Effective spy trapping is predicated upon such dictates, and we shall return to a more detailed consideration of these matters in the following chapter.

We must take a brief glance at some factors that facilitate the ability to deceive. The spy-catcher needs to look closely at the conditions that make these deceptions, both major and minor, possible. Prominent among these, in various forms, is the *need to believe* on the part of the person or persons deceived. There is a predisposition toward belief that is adroitly recognized and exploited by the perpetrator of the deception. This need is often allied to other needs, personal, social, and economic, that set up a climate favoring the deceiver.

In the examples of the commercial transactions we earlier examined, if the need to sell is sufficiently great, the requirements of trust that might have safeguarded the transaction had they been heeded will be substantially overridden and the verification procedures waived or attenuated. In general, as the need to deal increases, the concern about whom one is dealing with diminishes. When the need to deal is great enough, the person experiencing it ceases to care who the person is with whom the deal is to be struck—as long as it can be struck.[33] These factors have more profound implications than are generally recognized. Systems for establishing and verifying identity are constructed and maintained on the basis of these principles.

When it is important to "know" who the person is in relation to some business or others, the system will be more elaborate, more rigorous than when it is not so important. It will not necessarily, however, be more efficient. Efficiency depends upon wisdom and skills that are not necessarily allied either to the need or the desire to know. Here, we would only observe that the efficiency of a system of identity checking is bound up not only with its design and construction, but most practically with its operation. It is in this that we see the roots of the failure of most ineffective security systems.

Few systems are, in the nature of things, conceived, designed, constructed, and operated by one and the same individual. There is, therefore, often a marked divergence between the aspirations and objectives of those whose interests the systems are intended to serve and those who operate them on their behalf. Thus, in the illustration we gave concerning the use of the charge card, it may be that if each step of the required procedure were diligently complied with, the chance of a card being used fraudulently would be extremely slight, but if the merchant's poorly paid assistant is perfunctory, disinterested, or simply overly hurried in checking as he should, the likelihood of fraud is substantially increased. The best systems are those that reduce operational discretion to a minimum and require the person claiming it to follow carefully prescribed procedures, deviation from which can be quickly spotted and, if necessary, penalized.

The operation of checking identities and, in particular, what we have called backgrounding, should be depersonalized; the operation design should be concerned primarily with process, not with personalities. The injection into the process of a coloring of humanity tends to distort the judgment of the operator. Ideally, at the lowest level, the work should be compartmentalized so that the verification of paticulars is separated not only from all personal reference to the human being under examination, but from other facets of the identity that have no immediate bearing on the matter in hand. Thus, it is not necessary for the person making a fingerprint comparison to know whether the subject of reference is a housepainter or the spy of the century; indeed, it may be highly undesirable to introduce such a diverting consideration. The check to be performed is essentially a technical one. The point is well illustrated by considering the conventional inspection of the photo ID so commonly carried out on entry into the workplace in so many commercial and industrial establishments around the United States. Where large numbers are processed and transit is heavy, the production and inspection of these documents is often reduced to a mere formality. Motivation to conduct a rigorous check is usually absent, and familiarity breeds its own kind of contempt for the process. The checker "knows" the regulars and substitutes that knowledge for the process itself. The ID card is redundant and receives only the most cursory inspection; were another, similar one substituted for it, the substitution would most likely pass unnoticed.[34] The implications are endless. Whenever "knowledge" is exchanged for process, there exists the possibility of that knowledge being mistaken or taken advantage of by unscrupulous persons seeking to defeat the system. We are not concerned here with the nuts and bolts of such systems or with the devices for making them less vulnerable. We *are* concerned to make a simple point that correspondence between the identity and the person claiming it can never be taken for granted. The more a society relies upon documentation to establish who a person is and what he is entitled to do, the more vulnerable it is to deception by those who have a fine understanding of the system and the way it works.[35] Only by a return to basics can the problems be identified and corrected.

The kind of scrutiny we have been considering here under the heading of backgrounding has two broad purposes in the field of counterespionage. The *first purpose* is of a *preventive character*. We seek to learn as much as we can about a prospective entrant to our universe so as to be able to exclude those we fear might harm our interests in some way. This kind of security check usually follows a prescribed form and is carried out by assigned personnel according to standardized procedures that allow them little discretion or independent initiative. It is very important, therefore, to get the design right before operations of this kind are commenced. Something of a checklist is developed; routine questions are formulated and posed. If the answers fall within the parameters of the preestablished pattern, the candidate is regarded as having passed scrutiny satisfactorily. Other necessary conditions being met, he is admitted to our world. His status changes. He becomes an insider.[36] The body of data collected may or may not be retained on file for any great length of time, but it is rarely reviewed or substantially added to unless some new event or development calling for such action takes place.

Having let in the postulant and worked with him for some time, we assume we have come to "know" him well enough to drop the formalities. We substitute our own knowledge-gathering techniques for the formal process designed to screen the stranger. There is nothing wrong in this provided we recognize the dangers. Clearly, what we learned through the original, somewhat mechanical process is very circumscribed. The "identity" that shines forth from the collected data has a certain stiffness and unreality that suggests to the trained observer that a more accurate rendering lies behind or beneath what has been discovered by this means. The question for us is whether what we have learned suffices for our purpose. We "know" the person examined to the extent we deem safe and necessary and no more. As we have seen, there are important cost/benefit considerations governing the scope and effectiveness of these exercises. The collection process is limited to items that seem to spell out the requisite margin of safety. Clamoring for inclusion are questions that demand an answer, for the information is seemingly crucial to our decision regarding the person to whom they are addressed. Neither the process nor the formula may, however, lend themselves to the exercise if what we are after is of a really sensitive character. Failure to recognize this can lead to unsatisfactory and misleading results. For example, the inclusion of items such as profound inquiries as to whether the subject has ever belonged to a subversive organization is unlikely to elicit the information we are seeking.[37] The well-prepared spy has little to fear from backgrounding such as this, for the objectives, parameters, and procedures are well known in advance, and it is not difficult to construct a "legend" that will stand up quite satisfactorily to an investigation of this kind. The real danger, for those relying on these processes, lies in according too high a value, from a security perspective, to the information produced, or of regarding that which is learned as being equivalent to knowing "all" about the subject in question. Interpretations are made that the data cannot really bear. Nasty surprises are consequently not uncommon in this area. Some of these could undoubtedly be avoided were counterespionage specialists encouraged to play a greater role in the development and employment of the instruments used and in the backgrounding operations that take place in those instances where substantial security matters are involved. Backgrounding has tended, even in sensitive industries, to become a personnel or human relations function rather than a security one, to the detriment of its true purposes.

The *second purpose* is fundamentally an *investigative* one, and it is here that we enter the true domain of the spy-catcher. We have used, when appropriate in this work, the term counterespionage specialist. While most certainly a specialist in the true sense of the word, such an individual still ordinarily enjoys a wide radius of permissible activities within the realm of his specialty. Here, we would opine, is a genuine field of further specialization, a narrowing down of the necessary skills of the spy-catcher to a very fine point indeed. There are routinely found in the world of espionage those whose exclusive function is the creation of identities for use by others. They spend their days patiently weaving legends and storing them for operational employment when the need and opportunity arise. Some specialize even within this extremely confined compartment, being experts in but one aspect of the design and confection—the haute couture, almost—of the garb of personality to be worn by the espionage agent for whom it is tailored. Building an identity or adapting the existing one to meet the exigencies of some operation is an extremely arduous task. It calls for the most painstaking of work, a proper sense of perspective and history, and an up-to-the-minute knowledge of the real world into which the artificial model is to be inserted. Detail is all important, for some slight incongruity can cause the entire construction to come tumbling down. These specialists are craftsmen of the highest order. It follows, in our view, that no lesser degree of skill, diligence, and specialization is called for among those whose job it is to disassemble identities and subject their component parts to the most minute of scrutinies.

Such an intensive, specialized process will be broadly required under two circumstances that call for differing exercises of the techniques involved. In the first, an active case is being pursued, but the suspect spy is at large and must be observed from a distance. The limitations imposed by this are evident. In the second, the spy has been apprehended, and now it is necessary to make the case against him, to learn all that is possible of him—his activities, purposes, and affiliations. There is an obvious advantage, in this second case, in that the spy is available for interrogation. Thus, if skillfully conducted, the interrogation can supply data of a different order from that available from third parties. Such interrogation is an art in itself. It is not something to be hurried. If the system obliges the interrogator to speed up his efforts, he is almost bound to fail, for it may be presumed that this is known to the person being interrogated and will have been taken into account by his control. A special kind of mind is required for these exercises, one combining infinite patience with ruthless persistence. Brutality is rarely effective, and may, in the worst case, result in the loss of the only person who might supply the missing pieces of the puzzle. The quantity and quality of the data, as well as the effectiveness of the analysis and interpretation are usually determinative of the outcome. While the need for results is understandable, haste is more than likely to lead the pursuers down blind alleys and into traps that have been cleverly laid for them.[38]

Good preparation and an appreciation at an early stage of the need for specialist assistance are important adjuncts in the process. In the spy-catcher's armory, these skills have many applications, and considerable "technology transfer" is possible. In particular, the value of these skills in the debriefing of defectors and determining whether or not they are genuine is evident. Such skills are only acquired by long training and constant practices. Careful analysis must be made of past cases involving impersonations, substitutions, and other chicanery lending by adaptation to the purposes of espionage. Some of the most interesting and informative cases are to be found outside the field of espionage per se, but the lessons to be learned from them are of the clearest relevance here.

Those who would become truly proficient in all the finer points of the matters we have been discussing must, then, undertake a detailed study of cases in which identity has been a substantial, if not the principal, issue. Fortunately, such materials abound, and they can be approached from many different angles. Many people, not only spies, have compelling interests in escaping from an inconvenient identity or hiding from an embarrassing past.[39] In our modern-day, mobile society, tens of thousands of people every year successfully engage in arranging their own exits from lives that have begun to pall or have become oppressive or dangerous in some way. Usually, these staged disappearances involve very little by way of arranging an elaborate new identity. The task of connecting up the old with the new and showing the necessary continuity is well within the competence of anyone with a reasonable knowledge of how identities are put together and evidenced. The time and financial resources to devote to the task are needed as well. Nowadays it is depressingly easy to drop out of sight for a time and reemerge elsewhere as someone else. There may be some wholesome curiosity in the new creature, but the world being what it is, most perpetrators are likely to get away with it, provided their ambitions remain modest and they are careful to keep within the bounds of the law—at least until they have grown a new, less-sensitive social skin. The problem for some, however, is more grave; they are being sought under their old identity by earnest and tenacious forces, and they need to go and stay deeply under cover.

There is no shortage of case materials for study, and our consideration of these should focus upon how the old identity was discarded, how the new identity was acquired, how the divorce between the two was managed and kept secret, and how the whole scheme began to come apart (if it did so). Broadly, the materials fall into two categories: those which involve a person with an acknowledged new identity and an unacknowledged old one, which he is desperately anxious to hide and deny; and the case of those who, in the identity by which they are currently recognized by the world, are just as desperate to receive acknowledgment of some old identity, which they claim, often against all the laws of probability, as their own. Both sides have their own peculiar fascination. Both are equally instructive from our own point of view here, offering important lessons on these matters from the espionage perspective.

In so many ways, identity is an imprisoning thing. Identity is an iron cage that tends to shape the human being trapped inside it as much as it is itself influenced developmentally by that inmate person.[40] Given enough time, people tend to grow into their identities, to "become" them. If enough time and distance are involved, it is possible to outgrow or outlast any who might have known the subject as anyone or anything else. When no one else cares, the stage is suitably set for plausible denial of the past. Yet identity is a cloying thing, sticking at times and in spots, inconveniently, to those who would completely slough it off. It is rarely easy to get rid of an old identity so completely that the new one can be convincingly assumed and defended against tenacious, well-informed inquiry. Yet there is a social effect worth noticing. An aura of respect attaches to a "good" current identity that tends to deflect intense scrutiny from its origins. Many great fortunes had inauspicious beginnings, but their very size and present state give them a respectability that defies uncharitable investigation. In our society,[41] the reaction is a resigned or bored, "So what?" It *is* possible for the successful to bury the past, and there are stories to prove it. Here we need only make the point that the keen student of these matters is primarily interested in knowing how it was done and what factors made the maneuver possible. What lessons do these cases hold for the subject of spies and spying?

Instances of those assuming new identities to escape the past are legion. In our times, some of the best and best documented involve the disappearance of Nazi war criminals and their assumption of new identities. Such identities have enabled them to live out their lives, albeit ever-fearfully, without paying the proper price that might have been exacted for their crimes. A recent flurry of interest in these cases has led to the apprehension of some aged Nazis in the United States and elsewhere, having, almost incredibly, lived out lives quite different from those that served the interests of the Third Reich, protected by identities into which they had comfortably and convincingly grown. Others, less spectacularly, have been taken care of by time. There are yet others, much sought, who, by taking on new identities, have eluded their pursuers throughout the long years since 1945 and may, in some cases, continue to do so until they die in obscure anonymity.

The cases of Josef Mengele, the infamous death camp doctor, and Martin Bormann, Secretary of the Third Reich, need not detain us here, but the copious literature to which they have given rise is commended to serious students of identity.[42] The classic case, from many points of view, is that of Adolf Eichmann, the zealous administrator of the Final Solution, apprehended in Argentina in 1960 by the Israeli intelligence services and finally brought to justice in Jerusalem. Eichmann had escaped Europe and taken the identity of Ricardo Clement in his new country, living in appropriate obscurity for some twelve years. The story of the work that went into finding him, while not perhaps as exciting as the account of his abduction, is much more interesting from our point of view, representing as it does the triumph of tenacity and the counterespionage specialist's art.[43] Given the lapse of time and the comfortable non-threatening surroundings, Eichmann must have been growing confident that he would live out the rest of his life undisturbed by the ghosts of his horrendous past. There were, however, just too many loose ends and too many interested parties looking for those loose ends. Once his whereabouts had been discovered with certainty, linking the past to the present was almost a formality and Clement/Eichmann made no attempt to deny who he had once been or insist that his captors were mistaken. The Mengele corpse, of course, is capable of neither affirmation nor denial. That is the beauty of it. Those interested can only ponder the available evidence, most of it highly technical, and draw their own conclusions. Mengele, it may be observed, was from a wealthy family, one that continues, somewhat curiously, to be respected in Germany and has never drawn to itself the fires of revenge; Eichmann had no such respectability on which to lean in his hour of need.

Alive or dead, these sought-after figures present the same enigma: Who are they? Are those we know now in other guises, those who once had the dreaded identities that make them the objects of our search? The ways in which that question has been variously answered form a fascinating counterpoint to the matters we have been examining in the present chapter. The acid tests are the same whether we are dealing with a fugitive war criminal, an artful con man, or a spy. This is an area where the adage *cherchez la femme* might be more usefully replaced by the injunction *cherchez les epreints digitales* (fingerprints). The really knowledgeable, like the professionals of the criminal fraternity, are careful to leave none behind.

Perhaps the most intriguing cases concern those who have lost a former identity and are seeking, often desperately, to reclaim it and secure recognition in the eyes of a changed world. As the former identity was most usually one of some renown or had substantial property interests attached to it, these claimants are often regarded as mere adventurers, opportunists, publicity seekers, or, at best, harmless cranks who would challenge what seems to be the incontestable verdict of history. Every mysterious death or disappearance of a prominent person seems, after awhile, to generate tales of miraculous survival and reemergence. Statistically, very few of these cases have resulted in reinstatement. Yet the mystery lingers on, with a kind of forlorn, romantic aura attached to it, even after the matter appears to have been conclusively disposed of by the courts. It is an interesting phenomenon that it seems impossible to convince all of the people (or even all of the important people) all of the time of the final resolution in these cases, even where the story told by such claimants truly beggars the imagination. Some of these stories, excellent and instructive enough, scarcely warrant serious consideration on our part here. Did the Lindbergh baby really survive? Did Hitler have male or female issue? Was Amelia Earhart a prisoner of the Japanese?

There are, however, stories of greater moment that not only challenge the authorized version of history, but leave a certain disquiet concerning process as well as substance. The story of Anastasia, daughter of Tsar Nicholas II who was supposedly murdered along with her family at Ekaterinburg in 1917, is well known, and its details are fascinating.[44] Enough people were convinced of Anna Anderson's claim to make the case worthy of careful study by those interested in the problems of identity we have discussed. No less remarkable, and with perhaps even more instructive features for our purposes, is the case of the man who in nineteenth-century England claimed to be Sir Roger Tichborne, heir to one of the greatest fortunes of the time, who had supposedly drowned many years previously off the coast of Australia.[45] The Claimant, as he became almost universally known, arrived in England from Australia with an extraordinary story of his survival and metamorphosis. Although he looked and sounded nothing like the remembered Sir Roger, the Claimant managed to convince many, including Sir Roger's mother, but in the end he failed to convince the courts, thereby proving, in a certain sense, that you are who the system says you are.

Becoming separated from one's original identity under circumstances that permit no proof being taken along by the human being who claims to have passed through the looking glass is a terrifying experience. Fiction writers thrive on all the many plots that can be wrung out of these very real tragedies. The resolution of many is bedeviled by the fact that the human being claiming the former identity simply does not look sufficiently like the person available witnesses remember as having borne it.

Once again, we see the importance of appearances. Modern technology, especially the analysis of photographic evidence, has helped enormously in some of these doubtful cases. While the more obvious imposters can now be detected and their claims disproved more readily (though positive proof remains as difficult as ever), there remain a few where even the most advanced techniques, given the sparsity of the evidence, prove inconclusive.[46] What these cases clearly demonstrate is the separateness of identity and the human being, and the nature of the connection between the two. The point also needs to be made once more that the attachment of a particular identity to some human being is largely a matter of belief, *other people's belief*. Whether that is manifested in the form of sotto voce folklore or loudly proclaimed through a decision of the highest court of the land is immaterial if the end result is the same.

One case is so extraordinarily instructive that it must command special treatment here. In the mid 1920s, there emerged a writer of fiction whose works, originally published in German, quickly came to be known around the world in many different languages. The supposed author, B. Traven, seemingly a resident of Mexico, whence the first manuscripts were seen, managed to elude all efforts positively to identify him during his lifetime. These efforts were ongoing and not inconsiderable. The literature, which was abundant, clearly had a human source, and curiosity about it never flagged. Scholars the world over analyzed the texts and studied every scrap of information they could lay their hands on in order to identify the writer. At times, the search for Traven took on the air of a parlor game, but many were deadly serious and well equipped in scholarship and other resources for the task they had set themselves. Eventually, the works of Traven, many of which were filmed, generated a considerable amount of money. Yet, extraordinarily, this was regularly paid out to agents on the flimsiest of evidence for supposed onward transmission to a human being that no one claimed to be able to positively identify, physically situate, or convincingly demonstrate was still alive and legally entitled to receive the proceeds of his labors. There were (and may still be) many candidates for the mysterious B. Traven, the author in the shadows. What is of especial interest to us here is the character of the writing and, particularly, in one book, its preoccupation with questions of identity. From the earliest times of his significantly productive years, the author was evidently obsessed with the questions we have discussed in this chapter. Clearly, his own experiences or introspection gave him extraordinarily lucid insight into them. It would be a travesty to try to give a synopsis of the work of Traven here, nor would it be particularly profitable for our purposes.

What is urged most strenuously is that those who have pretensions to specialize in this field of identity should study *most* closely all the available literature on this remarkable case. The excellent book, *The Secret of the Sierra Madre: The Man Who Was B. Traven* is recommended as a starting point, for not only is it in itself an exceptionally informative work on the central subject, but it is also most instructive as to method and reasoning. It is a model for investigations of this kind that has much to teach the counterespionage specialist confronted with similar problems of re-creating a deliberately obscured past. We would permit ourselves but one original observation on this case, and it may well serve as a concluding commentary on all we have set down about identity. Suppose, during the quest, a man calling himself Hal Groves, for example, had come forward and actually claimed to be Traven. How would he have sustained his claim? Would he have been believed? Might he not have been laughed out of court? Perhaps the author, who from personal experience evidently knew so much about these questions of identity, was wise to remain anonymous. Perhaps, knowing what he did, that is precisely *why* he never risked revealing himself?

POINTS TO REMEMBER

1. Identity is a constructed arrangement of individually and socially significant data related to some human being. The spy-catcher must always question the relationships between the human being and the presented and claimed identity. When presented to others, personal identity, as an assemblage of selected data, is often thought to represent the true self of the person. Yet, identities thus presented are always partial and are constructed to be situationally correct. The attachment of a particular identity to some human being is a matter of belief—*other people's belief*.

2. Identities develop and change over time and have an experiential base, roots in history, and nests of statuses and roles. In the presence of others, the construction of identity involves moving backward into past experiences (real or imagined) and other identities (whether totally or partially "real" or "bogus") as recollected. It also involves taking bits and pieces, fitting them together, and presenting the manufactured product. Because a human being's identity is situationally related, pieces of old identities (indeed entire old identities) can become dormant and/or decay and "die." For an identity to be socially relevant, it takes at least the person presenting it and one other to receive the presentation. Dormant identities can thus be called forward by either the presenter *or* any number of past receivers with remembrances of times past. All good spy-catchers understand this, and they understand the problem of verification.

3. Backgrounding, done properly, is the process of verification in which the relationship between the evident human being and the claimed identity is carefully and meticulously examined. Nothing can be taken for granted. *Continuity of record* is of the highest importance; gaps give rise to suspicion. Attention must be paid to the chain of evidence and to any weak links in the chain, for they signal moments, places, times, and situations at which the chain might have been refashioned and substitutions made.

4. Ten key areas of identity inquiry are names, appearance, race/ethnicity, personal characteristics, personal history, experiences, achievements, relationship to other people, relationship to things, and memories. Each presents probabilities or likelihoods of being true representations. Together, they represent *conditional probabilities*, an "n adimensional" web, or link between the claimed identity and the human being.

5. The ability to deceive is directly related to other people's *need to believe, the urgency with which they must make a decision, and the urgency and need to make transactions.* In general, as urgency rises and needs grow intense, careful checks on identity claims are forsaken. Thus, it becomes important for spy-catching that those who check identities have no needs attached to the claimant, and also that those for whom they work always try never to require intense needs to believe, decide, or conduct business.

NOTES

1. *The British Cross,* New York: Crown Publishers, 1983, page 35.

2. *Fric-Frac,* Boston: Houghton Mifflin, 1979, page 214. Spaggiari is a fascinating character and his disappearance lends particular poignancy to the reference cited here.

3. *Strangers on a Bridge,* New York: Atheneum, 1964, page 37. This observation by the redoubtable defender of "Colonel Abel" shows the importance he attached to appearances.

4. *Deadly Games,* New York: Berkley Books, 1985, page 85. This short quote speaks volumes for the meaning of documentation in a society such as that of the USSR.

5. *The Fourth Protocol,* Toronto: Corgi Books, 1985, page 194.

6. This line of thought, inspired by a chance reunion with Don Hepworth of Ontario, Canada, formerly of 2 SIB and the Metropolitan Police, London, England, is gratefully acknowledged here.

7. On this, see the very clever and perceptive novel, *Amanda/Miranda,* Richard Peek, New York: Viking Press, 1980.

8. A great deal of popular literature has now been generated about this, most of it of the "nuts and bolts" variety. On the topic, generally, see the thorough analysis undertaken in the Report of the Federal Advisory Committee on False Identification, *The Criminal Use of False Identification,* Washington, D.C., U.S. Government Printing Office, 1976.

9. Society is organized on the principle that any individual who possesses certain social characteristics has a moral right to expect that others will value and treat him in an appropriate way. Connected with this principle is a second, namely that an individual who implicitly or explicitly signifies that he has certain social characteristics ought in fact to be what he claims he is. Consequently, when an individual projects a definition of the situation and thereby makes an implicit or explicit claim to be a person of a particular kind, he automatically exerts a moral demand upon the others, obliging them to value and treat him in the manner that persons of his kind have a right to expect. See the acute observations of Erving Goffman, *The Presentation of Self in Everyday Life,* New

York: Anchor Books, 1959, page 13. For a very clever and entertaining fictional treatment of this, see *Deceptions*, Judith Michael, New York: Pocket Books, 1982.

10. "In their first encounter, unacquainted people face the problem of identification in its purest and most agonizing form. Who is the other person? Who am I in this situation? Who *could* I be? What do I *want* to be? Who does *he* want me to be? . . . Each party must read the person with extra care for any clues to identity that he may give or give off." *The Human Connection*, Ashley Montagu and Floyd Matson, New York: McGraw-Hill, 1979, citing George J. McCall and J. L. Simmons, *Identities and Interactions*, New York: Free Press, 1966, page 182.

11. " 'You ought to have some papers to show who you are,' the police officer advised me. 'I do not need any papers; I know who I am,' I said." *The Death Ship*, B. Traven, cited in *The Secret of the Sierra Madre: The Man Who Was B. Traven*, Will Wyatt, New York: Doubleday, 1980, page 149.

12. Ludwig Wittgenstein cautions, "One is often bewitched by a word. For example, by the word *know*." *On Certainty*, Eds. G. E. M. Anscombe and G. H. von Wright, New York: Harper Torchbooks, 1969, page 57e. He makes the pertinent point for us here that "My *life* consists in my being able to accept many things." Op. cit., page 44e.

13. The logical confusion that underlies what we are grappling with is explained by Wittgenstein in another context: "It is self-evident that identity is not a relation between objects." *Tractatus Logics-Philosophicus*, London: Routledge and Kegan Paul, 1969, page 105.

14. *Business Week*, 22 September 1986, page 95.

15. "Even babies have identity crises." *The Economist*, 18 October 1986, page 100.

16. For an interesting methodological instance of this, see Wyatt, op. cit., supra note 11, page 74.

17. "Face-to-face communication normally begins at extended visual distance, during the state of *approach*—the prologue to meeting—when the participants come into mutual view and the internal mechanisms of person perception, 'checking up,' and self-presentation are set in motion." Montagu and Matson, op. cit., supra note 10, page 2.

18. Those interested in the practical implications of this are

recommended to consult the *Paladin Press* catalog, where standard texts and new works are conveniently displayed.

19. A careful study of the Traven materials makes this quite evident. But there must always be some human being who is the initiator of the process by which the body of data representing identity comes into being.

20. "Is there truth in the belief that names carry magic? Later, Tik would come to feel that there was, and that when Philip was given the name 'Nanook,' his future was altered." *The White Shaman*, C.W. Nicol, Boston: Little, Brown, 1979, page 60. This remarkable novel contains many insights into the question of identity development.

21. Wittgenstein makes the important point that "I know my name, only because, like anyone else, I use it over and over again." Op. cit., supra note 12, page 75e. For an interesting twist on this in relation to lie-detector tests, see *The Sisters*, Robert Littell, New York: Bantam Books, 1986, page 206.

"I could alter my appearance or change my name, but I would never have another identity in my own mind." *Breaking with Moscow*, Arkady Shevchenko, New York: Alfred A. Knopf, 1985, page 14.

22. "A month earlier, while visiting my parents in Vienna, I learned that Hugo had been arrested for nonpayment of debts. I covered the relatively small sum for him and offered him a job with the firm. From all reports, Hugo was a shrewd businessman, and I needed him badly. On my departure, it was understood he would join me. I had already explained the firm's objectives, omitting Modiin's involvement until Hugo received security clearance. We had to do something about his Jewish appearance; so we passed him off as an Armenian by the name of Krugian." *Decline of Honor*, Avoi El-Ad, Chicago: Henry Regnery, 1976, page 170.

23. "The British once uncovered a double agent in Egypt because he forgot to urinate in the approved fashion of the native men, with the knees slightly bent. And as Americans operating on the continent one of the first things we had to teach our operatives was how to 'eat continental' without shifting the knife and fork from hand to hand with each mouthful of food." *No Bugles for Spies*, Robert Hayden Alcorn, New York: David McKay, 1965, page 2.

"I had noted that the Swiss officials who examined travelers' papers as they inspected trains, particularly those leaving Swiss frontier stations for the interior of the country, seemed to pay extraordinary attention to the feet of the individuals whose papers they were examining. After some quiet investigation I ascertained the reason for this. The ordinary Swiss citizen is extremely careful of his appearance. He rarely travels in dirty or muddy shoes unless there is a good reason for this." *Great True Spy Stories,* Ed. Allen Dulles, New York: Harper & Row, 1968, page 131.

24. The simple fact of circumcision has often presented spies with an identity problem. It was a big factor in unraveling the "Lonsdale" legend. Avio El-Ad recalls his own problems: "Aside from the general transparency of my cover identity, a particular shortcoming disturbed me. I was Jewish— and circumcised. Only a small portion (28%) of the German male population had had the operation. I broached the problem to Motke and Shlomo, and after a moment, Motke's face brightened. 'I have a suggestion. We will have a foreskin made of plastic. Something you can slide on or off.' " Op. cit., supra note 22, page 19.

25. It may be stated, in an espionage context, that wherever the history of a case has in it a body burned beyond all recognition or without arms or a head, most serious questions are raised as to identity. Suicides are not infrequently fixed outside the realms of espionage by persons having a need or desire to disappear from the scene. The former British M. P. John Stonehouse faced such a suicide after the failure of a bank in which he was involved, only to be found in the 1970s, alive and well in Australia.

26. " 'If you come in and tell us who you are,' Kaat said with a nervous laugh, 'I'll tell you who you were.' " Robert Littell, op. cit., supra note 21, page 306.

27. Wyatt's search for Traven was, essentially, a historical one, seeking to connect the progress of a historically verifiable person by following the tracks he had made. See, especially, op. cit., supra note 11, page 301.

28. On this and other related matters, see that indispensable book, *Catch Me If You Can,* Frank Abagnale with Stan Redding, New York: Grosset and Dunlap, 1980. The concluding comment of the author should be borne in mind in

evaluating the impress of experience. "Actually, I haven't changed. All the needs that made me a criminal are still there. I have simply found a legal and socially acceptable way to fulfill those needs." Page 253.

29. Raphael Patai makes some interesting observations on the formation of the desert Arab. "Here there is no anonymity. Everybody is personally known to everybody else and this in itself makes for very effective social control." *The Arab Mind*, New York: Charles Scribner's Sons, 1983, page 78. See also pages 283–284.

30. See the wonderful Sufi story "The Secret of the Locked Room" in *The Wisdom of the Idiots*, Idries Shah, New York: E. P. Hutton, 1971, pages 97–98.

31. For some revealing memories concerning Frederick Sidney Cotton, a very colorful figure in British espionage before World War II, see *The Spymasters*, Charles Whiting, New York: Saturday Review Press/E. P. Dutton, 1976, page 13.

32. For an excellent description of what is involved, see *The Shattered Silence*, Zwy Aldouby and Jerrold Ballinger, New York: Coward, McCann and Geoghegan, 1971, the story of the Israeli spy Eli Cohen.

33. See the extraordinary story of agent A54 as it is recounted by Frantisek Moravec in *Master of Spies*, New York: Doubleday, 1975, pages 58–69. Frantisek recalls: "Now suppose it was *not* a trick? The indisputable fact was that the Karl who wrote our letter had access to unique material. If he *could* deliver what he was promising . . . The odds against it were heavy but I felt we simply could not afford to pass up the chance." Page 61.

34. The authors have collected and documented a large number of instances of this occurring, and their own experience is confirmed in discussions with others who have taken the trouble to investigate the phenomenon.

35. For some fascinating, contemporary examples of this, see *The Crimes of Patriots*, Jonathan Kwitny, New York: W.W. Norton, 1987.

36. The following is worth pondering. "Yet there is one potential weakness in this vast and complex system—the cognizant agent. 'We define a cognizant agent,' said Earl David Clark, Jr., the N.S.A.'s deputy chief of communica-

tions security until he retired this year, 'as a cleared individual, with all clearances, who for some reason decides to work for a hostile intelligence organization.' " "Spy Ring," Howard Blum, *The New York Times Magazine*, 29 June 1986, page 17.

37. Lest there be any misunderstanding, we are not arguing that these matters should not be raised; they may, indeed, be most material. What is at issue here is the method, the way in which the matters are raised. It is like trying to approach a partially closed door from the wrong angle.

38. The long, and some would feel, inconclusive interrogation of Soviet defector Yuri Nosenko by the CIA offers much instructive material on these matters.

39. Every disease has the capability of giving rise to its own antibodies. The massive erosion of privacy that has been made possible by the processes of the electronic age has produced a manifestation of the human spirit designed to resist and defeat the intrusiveness of the machine. The role of the computer in this onslaught upon humanity has given rise to some very thoughtful literature, such as David Burnham's *The Rise of the Computer State*, New York: Random House, 1982, but we have yet to see an exploration or even awareness of the counter-revolution that is taking place. The latter is very important from an espionage perspective.

40. We referred earlier to identity as being in the nature of a tool. Burnham, op. cit., supra note 39, page 151, makes the useful point that "Tools, for example, shape man's imagination. Identity shapes the way we think about people as well as the way they think about themselves."

41. The time and place of this writing, obviously, contribute to the formation of this perspective. We would argue, by reference to the evidence of our times, that the United States has in many ways become very forgiving in these matters, more so, perhaps, than many contemporary societies.

42. Especially interesting in the present connection is *Aftermath: Martin Bormann and the Fourth Reich*, Ladislas Farago, New York: Simon and Schuster, 1974. John Demjanuk is the only person since Eichmann to be tried under the 1950 Israeli law for the punishment of Nazis and their collaborators. He is now 65 and was extradited to Israel, after lengthy delays, from the United States, where he had been living for

many years and where he had become a citizen. He was accused, on witness identification, of being the dreaded Ivan the Terrible, a brutal concentration camp guard at Treblinka during World War II. Unlike Eichmann, Demjanuk insists he is the victim of mistaken identity and claims to have been framed by the KGB (he is Ukranian). See *Facts on File*, 1986, 36282.

43. See *The House on Garibaldi Street*, Isser Harel, New York: Viking Press, 1975.

44. See *Anastasia: The Riddle of Anna Anderson*, Peter Kruth, Boston: Little, Brown, 1983.

45. See *The Tichborne Claimant*, Douglas Woodruff, New York: Farrar, Straus, and Cudahy, 1957.

46. We need only allude here to the many photographs published from time to time of the elusive, supposed Abu Nidal. Most of these, whatever their provenance, simply resemble the conventional Western idea of a rather disreputable Near Eastern individual of undetermined nationality. There is no reliable way of linking the photograph with the person it purports to represent. An act of faith is required here or, at best, a certain gullibility.

4

SPY TRAPS:
Building and
Maintaining Them

Even the most careful predator leaves a trail.
> Marilyn Moats Kennedy[1]

Some of Man's Best Friends are Spies.
> Ladislas Farago[2]

It is a very poor trap that looks so much like one.
> Frantisek Moravec[3]

The radio set is both the spy's most useful tool and his Achilles' heel.
> Anthony Read and David Fisher[4]

Spy traps can be as small as a microchip or as large as Africa. Sometimes they are of a strictly material character, while at other times they have a more elusive, intangible quality. On occasion, they are a way of doing things. In short, a spy trap is anything designed to facilitate the detection, identification, unmasking, and entrapment of spies.

However large or small, these traps must be capable of zeroing in with precision not merely on individuals as such but also on their indiscretions that might lead to their exposure and undoing. A spy trap should be capable of showing, for example, a person's unfamiliarity with something he might supposedly know if he were genuinely what he represents himself as being.

Spy traps, too, have both deterrent and protective purposes. They serve as a screen or a fence. These purposes may be served whether or not they actually catch any spies. There is a rugged practicality about all this, in which the improvised, the jury-rigged, may be quite as important as the most carefully prepared and sophisticated of devices. Spy traps are as old as spying itself, and most of them have been in more or less constant use since the earliest times. Although they are notorious among their intended prey, they are ever good for the odd incautious, overconfident, or naive victim.

Yet there is always the need to keep abreast of the game, to avoid being outwitted or outmaneuvered. There are few real novelties remaining to be introduced, but the currents of change flow strongly in this department as elsewhere in this murky netherworld. Consequently, spy traps are ever being updated through the adaptations of advancing technology while the ideas behind them and their employment have remained surprisingly constant over the years. This is truly an area of human endeavor where there is little, if anything, new under the sun. There is always a certain delicate balance between espionage and counterespionage. Sometimes the balance of advantages tilts one way; at others, it inclines in the opposite direction. Developments in spying techniques contribute to the elaboration and introduction of inspired countermeasures. The two processes rarely keep in perfect step, but, over the years, a rough kind of homeostasis is maintained.

The room for real innovation, nowadays, is comparatively limited, and the matter comes down to finding new and better ways of doing old and well-tried things and disguising the traps themselves. It is thus in the skillful employment and deployment of spy traps that the true expertise of the spy-catcher really shows itself. As in other departments of this great pastime, hunters and trappers can go about their business with identical equipment over much the same ground; while some will come back bearing handsome trophies, others will return empty-handed. There is no denying that the equipment itself is important. Obviously, the trap itself must be appropriate for the task in hand; a mousetrap, however excellent for ensnaring small rodents, will not suffice to catch an elephant. But even the selection of equipment is rarely as simple as suggested by this example. It is a matter in which the exercise of great technical skill and discrimination is required. Essentially, selecting the right tools for the job, placing them in the right place at the right time, and concealing them and their purposes from the intended prey all call for very special qualities related to knowing the attributes and habits of the prey. Those who hunt and trap spies must know their game as well as knowing "The Game" and how it is played.

Before turning to the minutiae of the practice, we must take a quick look at the theory. Fundamentally, all forms of entrapment rest upon an underlying theory of *assumed vulnerability* in the intended victim. A weakness is postulated, which can be detected and exploited so as to bring about the hoped-for ensnarement. For the particular species, experience has demonstrated the fatal appeal of the bait. Thus, it is theorized that the hungry tiger will not be able to resist the lure of the tethered goat. Both the hunger and the predilection for live goat are assumed, as is the presence in the area of one of the big cats that will investigate the succulent offering staked out to tempt it. Experience shows such weaknesses to be generally shared to the extent that they can be usefully incorporated into standardized hunting procedures for tigers. The assumptions are applied to all hungry tigers in the area and are found to be true enough in practice to make the design a useful one, one capable of being employed with profit on a sufficiently large number of occasions. A police stakeout of, say, a bank, proceeds from similar assumptions enhanced by specific knowledge concerning the particular interest of the criminal quarry in the lure in question.

Espionage itself is based upon the calculated exploitation of the weakness of others. The spy literally tries to trap others into betraying secrets or into helping him in some way to realize his objectives. Clearly, entrapment of any kind calls for an extensive detailed study of the prey in all its aspects; some will fall into traps that others will easily spot and avoid. Some have poor sight but acute hearing, while others rely on smell to warn them of danger. Some traps are by their nature more difficult to avoid than others.

The spy-catcher must always build the learning curve into his calculations. Spies will be taught what to look for, what to avoid.[5] This introduces a new dimension into the game. Yet the lessons of experience need to be drawn by the spy-catchers and reduced into the form of usable, future precepts. The spy-catcher needs to know what spies are likely to do in certain situations, how they are likely to react to certain kinds of stimuli. There are situational as well as psychological factors to be taken into consideration. The problem, for our purposes, lies in the dimensions of the subject matter. Whatever may be said in the abstract, it is manifest that all men are very far from being created equal. The weaknesses of one may well be the strengths of another. While there is some methodological utility in propounding general rules, these clearly serve only as a guide and way of organizing the work; operationally, more flexibility is needed.

Each human being is unique, and spies are among the most varied and variable of their species. Spying itself, what spies do, is far more standardized. There are certain things spies must do that are common to all. This, then, is a good starting point for any general approach to the subject of spy traps and how to use them profitably. We must examine, at the outset, the basic vulnerability of spying itself before proceeding to put the individual weaknesses of spies under our operational microscope.

At the start, there is one glaring, obvious weakness that invites the closest attention, namely the spy's imperative need to communicate the product of his endeavors. Here a comparison is worthy of note. Spies and kidnappers have the same fundamental, operational problem and what they do is sometimes fatally flawed by this problem. They can both arrange and conduct the *initial* portion of their labors in perfectly clandestine fashion. Thus the careful kidnapper can seize his victim without ever revealing anything whatsoever about himself or his purposes. If the operation could stop at that point, the kidnapper need never fear for his safety; but what use would what he had done so far be to him if he proceeded no further?[6] The spy, similarly, can engage in the clandestine acquisition of information with relative impunity, provided he follows, sedulously, a few basic rules for his own security. As in the case of the kidnapper, this is only half the job.

The problems for both begin when these operatives seek, as they must, to capitalize upon their respective enterprises. The kidnapper, in order to profit from his illicit undertaking, must communicate with those from whom he is seeking to extort the desired ransom; otherwise, what he does is not kidnapping at all. However cautious he may be, however cunning his design, and however much he tries to deal at arm's length, the very act of communicating critically exposes him in a way that his seizure of the victim did not. A spy who cannot communicate what he has learned is of no value to those whose interests he would serve, however important the information he has obtained; acquisition is only half the battle—sometimes the easier half. Setting up and protecting secure lines of communication and being appropriately cautious in their use are in the nature of a sine qua non for the active spy. The spy and the kidnapper are inevitably connected to their communications system at some point. That connection is the key to the operation. The spy's lines of communication are his vital links to all with whom he is associated as a spy; they carry traffic in both directions.[7] Finding, interdicting, and backtracking offer excellent opportunities for the well-prepared spy-catcher. They are useful tracks along which appropriate traps can be set and sprung. However efficiently the spy may otherwise have covered his tracks, these essential operational emanations will lead back to him and his associates if they can be properly studied in their entirety.[8] Thus for the spy-catcher, while the proper study of his craft begins with that of the spy, he is unlikely to make much operational headway without a most thorough and intensive study of spy communications.

Developments in communications technology have greatly favored the spy and made his job easier—and safer—than it was even a few decades ago. Miniaturization, solid-state circuitry, and artful concealment now enable the spy to carry around rather sophisticated communications equipment, capable of transmission and reception over great distances, in even hostile environments.[9] The spy's job with respect to his intelligence product is somewhat like that of the journalist: get it first; get it right; and get it there—fast. Some information is of a highly evanescent nature; it is of little use to those who would do something about it to learn of an event after it has occurred.

From an espionage perspective, speed in communication is almost as important as accuracy, certainty of transmission, and security of method. Problems of time and space are at the heart of all communications issue, and technology is directed at transcending both in the most convenient forms consistent with the preservation of the integrity and comprehensibility of what is to be communicated. The human voice *en clair* can now be transmitted directly over great distances at great speed, but such facility is of comparatively slight utility for espionage purposes due to the security problems involved.

Most usually, speeding up communication involves the transformation of the substance, changing ordinary human language into electric, electromagnetic, or electronic impulses. It involves a machine language that has to be translated or reconverted to a form understandable by human beings. This is a different function from encryption, which is designed to preserve the integrity of the message and to ensure that it cannot be captured, read, or understood by those not entitled to receive it. These requirements impose certain obligations on their own account. Signals have to be dispatched in a fashion compatible with the sender's technical and practical competence and must be received in such a form that their meaning accurately reflects the dispatcher's intentions. Errors and misunderstandings must be kept to a minimum; every clarification represents an added danger to the spy. The signals must be sent by such means whereby they can proceed to their destination unimpeded, or they must be conveyed in such form whereby they cannot be read and understood by those for whom they were not intended if they are intercepted en route.

These basic requirements remain unaltered by the advances of technology. When intelligence is reduced to writing and the actual communication is to be physically delivered in the form in which it was prepared and dispatched, some form of courier system has to be employed. The same is true when samples or other objects (such as photographs) have to be sent, for although their transmission is now technically possible by electronic means, it is not usually practicable in the context of clandestine operations. Human couriers have been used from the earliest times to carry both oral and written messages, and the speed with which they can carry out their functions is limited by physical considerations, the environment, and the means of transportation available to them.[10]

Security considerations sometimes dictate that couriers be unaware of the substance and nature of what they are carrying, but most often some form of concealment is resorted to which requires the courier's complicity and cooperation. To speed up the process and traverse areas practically impassible to mankind or in unfriendly hands, such adjunct devices as pigeons (until comparatively recent times) and hot-air balloons have been employed. Scheduled, regular mail service has been and continues to be an important avenue of commu-

nication where these means are established and have [...]
been interrupted by hostilities or other causes and speed
not of the essence. The reliability of the mails in our ov[...]
times is highly questionable. Primitive signaling by heli[...]
graph, semaphore, and smoke emissions all carried the risk [...]
almost certain detection and the interception of the commu[...]
nicated intelligence. The truly great advances, in every re[...]
spect, came with the development of the telephone and
wireless telegraphy.

Thus in our own age, where time is the crucial factor, the
spy's messages to his principals pass directly through some
system of cables or across the ether. Encryption, scrambling,
one-time pads, and the new speed of transmission have all
helped enormously with the problems of security, requiring
complicated equipment, however small and portable, for dispatch and receipt, the technical competence to operate it,
and, most importantly, from a security perspective, a human
being at each end to send and receive.

Human agency simply cannot be eliminated from the process entirely. The human element, especially in these times
of increasingly complex and formidable technology, must be
seen as the spy-catcher's point of focus, the weak link in the
communications chain. From the spy-catcher's perspective,
communications have to be evaluated in the light of the
intensity and openness of human participation. The vital question is, where in the process is to be found the most vulnerable human agent? As interception and interdiction of what is
communicated becomes more and more difficult for technical
reasons, it becomes more profitable to try to trace the lines
back to the human operators.[11] If these can be traced, the
payoff is often considerable. Moreover, such operators are
often in possession of a great deal more than is necessary to
enable them to perform the purely technical tasks of communication in which they are primarily engaged. Thus, a basic
job for those who set up espionage communications networks
is to try to shield or insulate the human beings responsible
for operating and maintaining the integrity of the systems.

As a general rule, as few human beings as possible will be
used; their knowledge will be strictly limited to what is
needed to undertake the task or mission with which they
have been entrusted; they and what they do will be kept as
separate as possible from all others in the system so that the

loss of one component does not necessarily compromise the functioning of the rest. Dead drops, post office boxes, and cover addresses, for example, will be used in substitution for knowledgeable human beings wherever feasible. Those who service them will know little beyond their assigned task that might jeopardize the system; key operatives will be insulated from each other by cutouts, and receivers and senders will operate from secure environments, protected by the appropriate displays of trade-craft. Yet, however carefully and craftily such espionage networks may be operated, their structure and functioning inevitably call for some form of human intervention at some point, some form of human interface with others, some activity that can be undertaken only by recognizable human beings however limited in scope their participation.[12] None of these activities stands entirely alone. Each is a link with the others in a complex and often long chain. It is the *connections* that the spy-catcher must seek out, and it is there that he must station himself to spot his quarry and set his traps.

Here we find ourselves obliged to interpose a short but earnest caution. We have advisedly sought, where possible, to propound general rules and principles in order to facilitate our explanations. Indeed, experience does lend itself to the distillation of such guidance provided the pitfalls are taken, appropriately, into the reckoning. An appropriate level of abstraction is essential if the lessons of experience are to be imparted satisfactorily. But there is a danger of viewing such instruction as operational truisms to be followed uncritically. It is especially dangerous in the present context, where there is an understandable tendency to argue from a basis of generalizations: under such and such conditions, spies are prone to do this and thus. The spy-catcher must be ever on guard against the operational seductiveness of generalizations, particularly when they proceed from their own experience. There is no sadder preface to the tale of the one who got away than "whoever would have thought that. . . ."

All trapping is postulated upon creatures of habit following their habits. That, indeed, is why we study their ways so avidly. Those accustomed to working with or around rattlesnakes know the perils of basing approaches solely upon general rules supposed to govern the behavior of these dangerous reptiles. Handlers must always expect the unexpected, for it is the exception rather than the rule that teaches the painful, sometimes fatal lesson. What we really get out of this is another kind of rule that bids us to look out for and heed the exceptions. Though less convenient than that which points specifically to what ought to follow, both rules are of necessity to be observed in good practice. General rules are the basis for a kind of betting on probabilities. The value of their guidance is no more than this: when things are seen to happen fairly regularly, they are likely, given the same circumstances, to go on happening in the same way. Just don't bet the farm on it! This has important implications for the design and employment of spy traps.

What we must look at are *ideas* for traps rather than actual trap models themselves. To the undiscriminating, these will seem rather like generalizations, but it is hoped that the distinctions will be perceived by those who would use what is suggested for operational purposes. Human behavior is full of surprises and paradoxes, and the human animal is more unpredictable, often calculatedly so, than the rattlesnake. The good spy cultivates his own unpredictability; he consciously strives for the unexpected as far as his adversaries are concerned. There is an artificiality about this process that should be noted. This is a very trying thing physiologically as well as psychologically, but many spies build up an extraordinary tolerance for stresses that would be unacceptable to those who relish a more placid existence. Nevertheless, there is a point in each individual where this tolerance level is exceeded.

Burnout is common among field operatives, but its warning signs are not always recognized or heeded by those in whom they manifest themselves or by those responsible for control and management.[13] Spies, especially those who have been in the business for a long time and have achieved a fair measure of success, tend to grow careless, often to the point of becoming contemptuous of the dangers by which they are beset. Many of them seem to have been remarkably lucky and to have survived and prospered rather after the fashion of Maxwell Smart than through any inherent skills and application of their own. There is a saying in aviation circles that there are old pilots and bold pilots, but there are no old bold pilots. The same adage does not seem to hold true for spies. While care and careful observance of tradecraft appear to enhance the spy's prospects of continued survival in a hostile environment, other random factors seem to be constantly at work to defeat the best prepared of spies and, incongruously and often quite inexplicably, to protect others whose blatant disregard for their own safety extends far beyond what odds would have suggested on their being caught.

Many spies push their luck. The spy-catcher's job is to find ways of making them push it too hard or for too long. Interesting traps, baits, or lures will suggest themselves in concrete cases to this end. Yet, it seems to be the case that while much of the spy-catcher's work is directed toward forcing his quarry into becoming careless, lulled into a false sense of security or rushing headlong into traps that have been set for him, it is rarely possible to take advantage of these circumstances in any really scientific fashion. It is simply a matter of using the fact to improve the hunting climate, a judicious use of counterespionage catnip.

What does seem to bring results for the spy-catcher is the intensity and thoroughness of the hunt itself.[14] Persistence, long after it would have seemed reasonable or prudent to have abandoned the chase, is often productive of success. Even the most experienced and securely entrenched spies seem to fall in the end if the hunt continues long and fiercely enough. Many a fox has come out of the covert after the pack has been called off.

Spy-catchers must carefully evaluate the ground over which the hunt is to take place. The climate and conditions of the terrain are often determinative of what trap can be employed. All democratic societies must cope with the problems of maintaining an acceptable balance between a respect for individual privacy and the need to ensure a reasonable standard of collective security.[15] It is axiomatic that as the exigencies of the latter impose their demands, private rights, and expectations must cede before them. Security for all calls for individual sacrifices, which, however abhorrent to the libertarian purist, are regrettably necessary in the interests of preserving a climate in which at least some respect for individual rights might continue to be preserved. It is not an easy balance to establish or maintain. It is all too easy for security considerations to be urged to the point where all privacy disappears. This latter nirvana is the goal toward which many counterespionage specialists will, not unnaturally, strive. It is, however, one with which our own intensely individualistic society would never be comfortable under even the most dire of conditions. Indeed, the climate of recent years, certainly that which had its genesis in the wake of the Watergate crisis and which has persisted with but slight modification into our own times, has favored the preservation of individual privacy over even the most urgent intromissions of the state.

The growth of what has been called the "computer state" and the establishment of vast public and private data banks (so jealously guarded yet so easy to enter) have certainly eaten away at the expectations of individual privacy that many had reasonably entertained.[16] Nevertheless, it would be a most imprudent spy-catcher who sought to extend these developments in this country beyond their socially defensible limits. A nice sense of what these are is a prerequisite, on the practical level, to the design, construction, and maintenance of spy traps. This is especially true with regard to any that are designed to be used in connection with lines of communication of any kind. It may be stated, as another of our general rules, that any spy trap designed for use in connection with lines of communication must violate someone's privacy. In a society such as that of the United States at the present time, it is imperative to retain the effectiveness of the trap for the purposes for which it is intended, while reducing its intrusiveness to the bare minimum to ensure that it works. This is an enormously difficult task. It is similar to what medicine undertakes in, say, chemotherapy; it is a matter of getting the dosage right in regard to the condition to be treated and the overall state of the body, taking into account the virulence of the disease. Sometimes the body politic is so riddled with spies that truly heroic measures are called for. These represent a severe and serious attack upon the fabric of the system itself. The greatest care must be taken to see that the disease is not eradicated at the expense of vital components of the body politic.[17]

In a democratic society, it is always dangerous for even the most sensitive and dedicated of public servants to assume that their own diagnosis of the seriousness of the disease will coincide with that of the patient. The most well-meaning of efforts have sometimes gone awry through failure to pay proper attention to this. Democratic societies tend to attribute a higher importance to the purity of the means than to the therapeutic value of the ends they are designed to attain.

Spy traps that do not conform to these dictates are doomed not only to failure, but also to embarrassing exposure for those who designed, made, and set them. If you live in a society that stipulates "thou shalt not listen in on thy neighbor's conversations"—and truly means it—you disobey at your peril, whatever your function and status in life. In real democratic societies, morality tends, sooner or later, to triumph over expediency. The spy-catcher who would serve such a society, as opposed to the sometimes inconsistent demands of his own calling, must take these strictures into the reckoning.

All this makes spy-trapping in a democratic society a very difficult business. It must be ruthlessly effective against those it is designed to catch without unacceptably hurting those on whose behalf the task of eradication is undertaken. It follows that anything that makes things more difficult for the spy-catcher favors the intended prey and improves his prospects of escaping. Clearly, this has a marked and quantifiable effect on the odds.[18] The spy-catcher must have a very exact appreciation of the parameters within which he must work and of the degree of elasticity he might enjoy within their confines. Much ingenuity is called for if he is to reduce the handicap under which he is placed.

At the outset, we must clearly lay down the following proposition: in the present context, the spy trap and the character of its employment are by their very nature intrusive. They are meant to violate the target's privacy, for that is what he relies upon to shield his own enterprise. Accordingly, they are meant for surreptitious and insidious employment against ruthless, unprincipled opponents for whom the very notion of a right to privacy for others is patently absurd. This is a war with no quarter offered or accepted. Neither can afford to concede any advantage to the other. As between the contestants, therefore, matters of chivalry, honor, or morality do not enter into the picture; taking account of the givens of the situation, the whole thing comes down to a question of percentages. Hence the peculiar relevance of our reference to betting on the probabilities. It is a well-known fact concerning commercial gambling enterprises that the percentages favor the house—and measurably so. This must be taken appropriately into account by any who would try to defeat the system. It is a built-in advantage against which complaints are of no avail and concerning which concepts of fairness are quite irrelevant. The logic, the mathematics of the matter, are essentially value-free; this is just the way things are. If you do not like the game, you can elect not to play. The contest between the spy and spy-catcher in the vital field of communications is informed by very much the same set of considerations. There is a numbers game here that can be stated in each case with a fair degree of certainty in the light of the existing state of technology. There remains a further component that cannot. The whole thing, on any sensible analysis, can be reduced to a matter of mathematics plus luck.

We shall devote some time to a consideration of this critical imponderable in its turn, but, for the moment, we would content ourselves with drawing a useful comparison with something we have earlier observed in another connection. Just as the comparison between the kidnapper and the spy in a certain context was suggested above, we would now offer by way of illustration a parallel between the assessment of the hostage-taking dynamic and an evaluation of the percentages that interest us in the use of communications in the espionage business. There is an interesting analogy to be drawn between those faced with the problem of rescuing hostages and that of the spy-catcher seeking to trap a spy by exploiting any inherent weaknesses in his lines of communication. Hostage rescue is another situation that can be reduced quite conveniently to a set of somewhat exact calculations—plus luck.[19] Thus if, by the appropriate means of measurement, it is seen that the hostage-holder can kill the hostage before the hostage rescuer can intervene or interpose a screen of safety between the assailant and his victim, any attempt at rescue is futile *unless* the hostage-holder's advantage can be nullified or reduced to manageable proportions in some way by the would-be rescuers. We need not enter into a discussion here of the niceties of these matters, for we are interested fundamentally in the parallels with our own subject.

We must begin with the proposition that the sender of the message enjoys a built-in advantage in time over the person who would intercept the communication and undertake any operation designed to trace it to its point of origin. An historical study of the technology of this area of communications shows that advances made in speed of detection and tracing have always been roughly countered by commensurate advances in the speed and security of transmission so as to preserve, however slight, the advantage in favor of the sender. The most the spy-catcher can realistically hope for is that the technology of countermeasures may advance to such a point that, *practically*, the advantages have become so reduced that the elusive element we call luck comes into play. Luck—real luck—is always up for grabs.

This brings us to a most important question. What is luck? Almost everyone has some commonplace experience with the phenomenon, for it is part of the fabric of our everyday lives. Each of us tends to have our own explanation for the mysterious things that rule our destinies. Some believe in it almost religiously, while others are prone to discount its existence as an independent determinant, attributing the course of events to other causes more amenable to human intervention.[20] It is not difficult to define what we mean by it in the present context. It is the aggregate of all those (more or less) randomly associated facts and circumstances that contribute in substantially unmanaged fashion to a particular outcome. Something happens, good or bad, seemingly without the exercise of any conscious human control over the matter. Luck is not something that might be expected if certain things eventuate (like a good quarterly dividend if the trade cycle is favorable) but, rather, something outside the compass of rational calculation (like the receipt of a wholly unanticipated legacy at a time when an element of desperation was oppressing the management of one's personal finances). The distinctions are often close indeed but they must be properly appreciated by those who would take advantage of what is often the decisive element in a finely drawn engagement. True luck cannot be usefully imagined or allowed for, nor rationally managed by way of incorporation into our plans, although we often say, somewhat wistfully, of a close-run thing, "This will work—if only we have luck on our side."

Much of what we call luck is not such at all, but is merely an advantage which one party to the proceedings has perceived at the expense of the other. Real luck is not altogether outside the realm of logic, but its presence and influence are discretionary and even capricious. But careful study suggests that luck smiles on those who are ready to receive it; such preparedness, rather than luck itself, is often enough the deciding factor. Some react more quickly to windfalls than others, while there are some who are consistently more adept at dodging the slings and arrows of outrageous fortune that would take most summarily out of the fight. This, too, is something worth extended study in the context of what we are exploring.

So we see that the advantage naturally enjoyed by the sender of a communication is not a matter of luck; it is preordained in the established scheme of things, and allowance can and must be made for it. We are working with the known rather than the unknowable. Luck enters the picture in the way in which the advantage is used or in the failure to perceive or employ it. This can be readily appreciated from the study of actual cases, a study that must be conscientiously undertaken by those seriously concerned with these matters. While not denigrating the hard work put in by those engaged in the chase, we see, not infrequently, that the trapping of some spy must be attributed to pure luck, some circumstance so serendipitous that it could not sensibly have been built into the plan or managed in such a way as to maximize the possibilities of success on the part of those it tended to favor.[21]

Luck, good or bad, is not something the efficient manager ought to build into his plan so that the result depends upon it. This is not management at all; this is leaving matters to the fates. What becomes very clear, as one examines these matters in detail, is that many outcomes conventionally defined in terms of the impact of luck ought not strictly to be so considered at all. The determinants are items that have been abandoned or surrendered by one actor or another in the drama as being too difficult to manage or influence or which on a cost/benefit basis are given up to the demands of some other expediency. We would observe here that in matters of security, one ought never to ride one's second-best horse into battle.[22]

It is here that we see the emergence of a school that would claim, somewhat over-ambitiously in our view, that there is truly no such thing as luck. Certainly, were human beings capable of the minute and timely analysis of *every* situation in which they act, so as to account for *every* influential item capable of having *some* impact on the outcome, luck could be reduced to infinitesimally small—even insignificant—proportions. This is what the good manager aims for, while recognizing that the chances of securing the absolute elimination of luck as a factor are as elusive as the search for the perfect vacuum. We need not pursue this interesting line of discussion here beyond observing that the greater the preparation and diligence of execution, the smaller the terrain within which luck per se can be determinative of the outcome. Ideally, the spy-catcher must leave as little as possible to chance. He must prepare for every possible eventuality and some of the less probable besides. What modern technology has done greatly to aid him in his task is to permit the more efficient use of time and enable the possibilities to be weighed in a fashion that simply could not have been contemplated before the invention of the digital computer and super computer.

Turning once more to the practical aspects of this, we see that the reduction of the spy's advantage or what is assumed to be the munificent goodwill of Lady Luck often involves a massive assault upon private liberties and, moreover, those of persons substantially innocent of any involvement in the matters with which the spy-catcher is directly concerned. The latter is hardly deliberate, for with time and resources at a premium, few spy-catchers would concern themselves with such innocents were they certain this indeed were the case. A trap capable of catching all, provided it can be efficiently handled, obviously ensures the guilty do not escape, although it must, at least temporarily, inconvenience the innocent.

Technological developments have encouraged the all-encompassing approach. Formerly, it would have been impractical to have interdicted, say, *all* the communications emanating from or proceeding to a particular area of the world. The resultant product would have been beyond the scope of human competence to handle within the time over which it might have had some utility for those undertaking the operation. When codes and ciphers are introduced into the equation, the time factor is further compressed in favor of the originators of the communications. Moreover, until comparatively recently, interception of communications in a clandestine fashion from a distance has not been possible. Now, the modern computer, allied with the evolving technology of interception, has brought the efficient acquisition and management of such huge amounts of information within the reach of many on quite an economical basis. There is thus the encouragement to procure such data, to store it against any eventuality, and to use at least an initial blanket approach to the entire communications question. From the spy-catcher's perspective, there is an undeniable attractiveness to such an approach provided it can be competently and not too expensively undertaken. Properly undertaken, with the right kind of net, such a fishing expedition allows the large fish to be hauled in and the smaller ones to be returned unharmed to the ocean. Experience has shown, even in the more modest endeavors of the past, the rich dividends that can be reaped from such wholesale operations.

The primary purpose of censorship of the mails may be to ensure that sensitive information does not get into the wrong hands, but its secondary employment as a spy trap has been attended by some remarkable successes.[23] Even in this day and age, spies do continue to send highly incriminating things through the mails. Modern methods facilitate their interception, examination, interpretation of content, correlation with other relevant information, and its onward transmission with such dispatch and in such a way that evidence of its untoward, intermediate inspection is scarcely suspected by those parties who would be the only ones privy to the contents of the communication. Trapping spies by these methods, even given the latitude of wartime conditions, has, however, always been very much of a hit-and-miss affair. What we have called "luck" has played an overly large part in the successes to which we earlier adverted. Yet other people's correspondence has an irresistible lure for the curious.[24] Clearly, knowing who writes to whom and who receives what in the mails is of the greatest interest to spy-catchers, even where they are legally denied a peek at the contents.

It is not to be expected that spies would write directly to known and obvious official addresses of their employers, but heavy correspondence with, say, a particular post box in a particular city may serve to alert the authorities and suggest a pattern worthy of further investigation.[25] The much criticized, but effective, CIA mail-cover operation was an attempt to utilize the benefits of a large-scale interception for the purpose of ascertaining whether foreign influences were at work in American society for the purpose of generating unrest and civil disorder. Its termination and the restricted scale of the operations themselves are a clear indication of the limited utility of such undertakings in the United States for the purpose of trapping spies under peacetime conditions.

A few words must be introduced here concerning the supposed sanctity of the diplomatic mails. Be it sent by general service or personal courier, a high degree of respect has always been extended (even by countries not generally known for such niceties of conduct) to the diplomatic bag or pouch. It has long been recognized among the family of nations that without such confidentiality, relations among countries would be extremely difficult, and denial would lead to clandestine communications being operated on an even greater scale than at present. There are, however, no absolutes in this matter. When the need *is* great enough, diplomatic communications will always be violated and many egregious instances can be cited from all ages.[26] In our times, there has been unquestionable worldwide abuse of diplomatic privileges, especially in connection with espionage and terrorism. The spy-catcher must be ever alert to these abuses, what they portend, and how knowledge of them can be turned to good account. Great caution has to be exercised in both the acquisition of knowledge in this area and the use to which it is put.

The greatest deterrent to overenthusiasm by the spy-catcher in this regard is not the law, but the fear of reprisals by the other side. There are conventions and niceties that dictate restraint in the interests of one's own espionage activities. Knowing what is going on, even though it is allowed to continue without let or hindrance, is an important and delicate part of the spy-catcher's work. This is very different from turning a blind eye and is entirely preferable to the perils of good-natured ignorance. Yet sooner or later reaction is inevitable. This kind of abuse of diplomatic privileges almost always leads to a countervailing abuse of the conventions safeguarding the confidentiality of diplomatic communications. Personal surveillance, for example, has become part of every diplomat's everyday life. The astute spy-catcher must be ready to catch every turn of the tide. Hindsight is valuable operationally only to those who specialize in the Parthian Shot.

Despite the constitutional constraints in regard to individual rights operating in the United States, we ought not to be too squeamish about discussing these issues in depth. They clearly have a peculiar importance for the spy-catcher and vitally affect his ability to do his job well. Our own age is certainly no time for a reversion to a Stimsonian, head-in-the-sand policy on these matters. We need to remind ourselves occasionally that there is no constitutional right to inspire or encompass the overthrow of the United States. Nor is there any constitutionally protected right to serve, in clandestine fashion, the interests of a foreign enemy—or even those of a foreign friend[27]—where these conflict with the interests of the United States. What is always the sensitive issue is how far those who are innocent are to be inconvenienced and disturbed in their privacy in order that the authorities might get on with protecting all from the few who would work their mischief in secret while claiming the very protection they would themselves take away from the rest. This cannot be tolerated by any society zealous for the protection of its responsible, law-abiding members. There are many useful parallels in modern life. Very few air travelers seek to endanger aircraft or the lives and property of those who travel in them. Yet all must submit to similar security procedures to ensure that those who would do so are denied the opportunity. All must be prepared to submit to a customs inspection in order that the authorities might detect and apprehend the comparative few who smuggle. Shoppers in many stores are required to permit inspection of packages and personal items as a precaution against shoplifting, which is now rampant and costs us all dearly. The patent intrusiveness of these procedures for the many can only be ameliorated by the manner in which these necessary incursions upon privacy are carried out and the way in which the authorities take pains to avoid making the innocent feel like wrongdoers.

Secretiveness is an ingrained quality in the human social animal. Privacy is most jealously guarded because nearly everyone has something to hide, some embarrassing little secret, not even a peccadillo perhaps, but nevertheless a matter that person has no wish to share with strangers. For most, this desire for privacy is a right that is perfectly comprehensible and acknowledged as a necessity in every free society. Yet it must have its sensible limits. It can never be an absolute, for in its extreme forms, it becomes a shield for those who would maximize respect for their own privacy solely to engage in activities ultimately designed to deny the right to others.[28]

Here we must, accordingly, take a long, hard look at privacy and the mails. As a means of trapping spies, covert examination of the mails has a well-established track record. It offers a way of obtaining concrete, often voluminous, information about espionage activities that cannot be readily acquired through the employment of any other devices or techniques. As electronic transmission of information increases and becomes the normal mode of communication, it is fair to assume that the value to the spy of the regular mails and written, sealed communications of all kinds will become even more common. Communication by this means enjoys the benefit of excellent cover, particularly in a free society; it seems on the face of it such an innocent—and indeed desirable—activity. This is especially true if it is engaged in by persons whose correspondence seems only to record and register the commonplace and who have no connection, so far as their addresses betray, with officialdom of any kind. If a comprehensive examination of everything sent through the mails is not legally or practically possible, it remains to be considered how selective targeting might best be arranged so as to ensnare those who use this avenue of communications for espionage purposes. It can be safely presumed that the diplomatic mails will always be used to this end in the belief that they will be broadly respected by the international community in the absence of positive indications that they are being unacceptably abused. But diplomats can also be expected to use the regular mails for espionage purposes where this better suits their book.[29]

We must interpose an observation here that is certain to offend the moralists, and quite rightly so. It is offered not by way of a recommendation, but rather as a sad commentary upon the reality of international relations as it is in our times. When the need to intrude is perceived as sufficiently urgent, it is open season everywhere for even the diplomatic mails. What is "urgent" varies from nation to nation, and some clearly have a very low threshold of tolerance in these matters. Consequently, all diplomatic communications, through whichever avenue they are transmitted, must be regarded as potentially targetable. They can only be protected by means of codes and ciphers, and the wise will take care not to mix their regular, diplomatic representation with impermissible espionage communications. The only real questions for the spy-catcher are when and how such communications should be targeted. These questions open up other relevant matters for consideration here.

Along with diplomatic communications, all mail sent to certain destinations, which in the context of their own time and place indicate correspondence with elements hostile to those the spy-catcher serves, must be considered fair game. While, for example, at the present time, much innocent correspondence obviously passes between the United States and those countries we have come to regard as being behind the Iron Curtain, it would be naive to assume that nothing useful to the spy-catcher is transmitted by these means. The very openness of the postal system and the volume of materials sent and received are a standing invitation to the espionage professional to use the mails. Prudence would dictate, at the very least, careful scrutiny of all mail sent and received as it pertains to Soviet Bloc countries and an attempt to establish patterns among correspondents that are suggestive of a need for further investigation. That same openness may well have induced a certain carelessness that can be turned to advantage by counterespionage specialists prepared to exercise some imagination and daring. Inspection of the mails, on a selective basis, should be a permanent, ongoing undertaking for the spy-catcher. The program can be expanded or contracted as conditions suggest. Automation of mail handling lends itself most usefully to the operation of these programs within the postal service. Spy traps should never be obvious or easily detectable.

So far as the United States is concerned, counterespionage specialists should reconcile themselves to the virtual impossibility of keeping anything secret.[30] What this means, in practice, is that the best that can be hoped for is that a program such as that suggested might be suitably disguised so that its true purposes do not become known to hostile elements or those who would evade the net or, alternatively, that the details of its operations can be protected by inducing an element of uncertainty concerning its scope and methods. At some point, however, there will always have to be direct intervention by some department of the counterespionage services, and it is this interface that must be most carefully disguised and protected.

The actual extraction of items from the regular mail flow and their material examination should be undertaken by specially trained counterintelligence specialists who are carefully insulated from other personnel engaged in the routine inspection program and the interceptions made under it. In short, the entire program should be heavily compartmentalized so that it is difficult, except at the very highest levels, to put together knowledge of its various components, even by inference, so as to envisage a coherent whole that would evidence the existence or operation of such a program. Operations of this kind should be undertaken in a form compatible with the ordinary workings of the postal system. In times of constant innovation and experimentation, with programs designed to be more economical and efficient, it ought not to be too difficult to introduce security measures without raising suspicions or concerns about their purposes. Ideally, specific counterespionage purposes should be annexed to something else that can be satisfactorily explained and justified on its own account (for example, routine examinations for contraband).

What is necessary in every case is the development of a system whereby mail requiring special inspection of this kind is channeled through a limited number of gateway offices so that the traffic can be routinely and comprehensively monitored by a relatively small number of handlers whose performance and allegiances can be similarly under constant review. Distinctive franking or bar codes can be used to facilitate the routing process.

Except for very special cases involving careful, personal surveillance of specifically targeted individuals, it will usually be impractical to intercept suspect items at the point of their introduction into the system. By the same token, it is difficult to establish a system of inspection too close to the point of reception of individual communications, for these are too numerous and scattered. The trap must be in the nature of a filter sitting astride the distribution mechanism where its operation and presence are difficult to detect. Modern developments have tended to favor the spy-catcher's purposes in this. Delays in the ordinary mails worldwide have become so commonplace and expected that rapid transmission rather than the reverse would be likely to arouse suspicion.

The prerequisites for an effective operation are, however, always the same: unobtrusiveness in the highest degree, and operational secrecy so far as this can be established and maintained. If innocent parties are inconvenienced as little as possible and the system is not abused for purposes foreign to its objectives, it is likely to remain effective and undiscovered.[31] Spy traps used for purposes alien to their creation quickly become useless and dangerous to those employing them.

It is to be anticipated that those who send incriminating correspondence through the mails will take precautions to test whether there has been any tampering with them in the course of transmission. Over the years, some fairly sophisticated methods for this purpose have been developed and these are well known both to those who have occasion to employ them and those against whom they are directed. Much ingenuity is expended on the creation of new devices and new ways of using them. A good system for keeping up with these developments comprising research, experimentation, and proper dissemination of what is learned is most necessary if these operations of interdiction are to be successful.

Given that mail can be comprehensively reviewed and sorted for more careful inspection, and those items that are to be opened are extracted, it remains to devise practical methods that are as speedy as possible and which are capable of resisting the most careful inspection by those eventually receiving the intercepted item and who, it may be presumed, will submit it to professional examination to discern evidence of tampering. Opening and resealing communications passing through the mails call for special technical skills that can be taught to relatively low-grade operatives to whom these tasks may be assigned on a regular basis.[32] The physical extraction of contents, their copying (where desirable), and their replacement are, similarly, technical tasks calling for a certain amount of delicacy and special skills, but little by way of out-of-the-ordinary judgment. This latter enters the picture when decisions have to be taken concerning the product of the exercise.[33] It is here that speed and soundness of decision are of the essence if the proper flow and concealment of purpose are to be maintained.

A procedure for evaluation has to be introduced into the operation at a point where it can be most effective. Someone with the requisite competence, knowledge, and authority has to pronounce upon what has been intercepted in order to be able to make what, in effect, is the critical decision: Is the intercepted item to be allowed to pass unimpeded to its ultimate destination or is it so sensitive or damaging that some immediate action is called for in order to prevent its reception by those for whom it was intended? Difficult decisions are involved here that sometimes have to be taken at the highest level. Such decisions call for considerable breadth of understanding, an appreciation of the whole picture rather than a special segment of it.

It may be more valuable, in the long run, to sacrifice some secret information than to risk exposing the means by which its loss has been detected. A calculated loss of this kind may even be taken or engineered so as to encourage belief in the inviolability of the mails. Similarly, if the transmitters or receivers themselves are to be acted against as a consequence of what is discovered by these operations, the cost to the operation as a whole has to be weighed against the value of effecting or foregoing the capture. In general, the trap—its character, operation, and location—should never be exposed simply in order to take the prey. The kind of system we have been considering here is not a one-time trap. At the same time, it may be cautiously observed that a trap so sensitive that it does not permit the extraction of what has been caught when it is useful to take this product is probably too delicate for anything but the most exceptional use. A mechanism that is intended to catch spies is of limited value if it is so constructed that it provides evidence of their activities but does not effectively allow for their capture. It is not necessary here to delve into the means by which these difficulties might be overcome, but, rather, to draw attention to the need for developing a way in which these problems can be spotted early enough in the proceedings to permit speedy decisions to be taken at the proper level of responsibility.

What has been set out above with respect to the mails can be applied with suitable modifications to any other kinds of communication except those taking place face-to-face. Some factors will be more prominent and influential in the case of certain types of communication than others. In a majority of instances involving electronic transmissions, the really vital factor affecting judgmental matters will be speed. The human mind cannot hope to emulate the speed of the technology now employed in the business of transmission. Rapidity of transmission is adequately matched by speed of interception, while deciding what to do about what has been intercepted is substantially limited by the capacity of the human beings

entrusted with the business. The world of espionage has yet
to produce and be serviced by anything in the nature of a
Zappa-like Central Scrutinizer. Those who employ codes and
ciphers know that even the most secure can be broken provided there is enough time for the job. In a practical sense,
success or failure in this area is dependent, often enough, on
winning the time to do the job. Computers have speeded up
the job exponentially. The time to capture the communication, plus the time to decipher and understand it, represent
the maximum period of grace permitted those who communicate under these conditions. This may usefully be regarded as
the spy's margin of safety so far as his communications system
is concerned. The spy-catcher's endeavors must be directed
toward reducing this margin to the point where it is thin
enough to permit useful interception. Reducing this margin
will also increase pressures upon the spy to the point where
he begins to make mistakes or the pressures simply become
intolerable to him.

Electronic surveillance of communications over a distance
has, over the last few years, become an increasingly auto-
mated process.[34] That process is very effective, provided the
human element necessary to make informed decisions concerning the product is satisfactorily integrated into it. The
detection of secret transmitters and their location through
goniometry has been greatly simplified in the last decade
notwithstanding remote operation, "squirt" transmission, and
miniaturization of transmitters allowing easy portability. All
transmissions carry or develop some sort of "signature" necessary for the identification of the sender. This is difficult to
make anonymous and wholly untraceable. The spy-catcher
needs a lot of patience once he has picked up a lead. Fear of
losing contact is a huge spur to precipitate action. When the
contacts are measured in microseconds, there is little time for
reflection on the merits of pursuit versus ambush.

Capturing communications is relatively easy today. Capturing those who send and receive them is probably as difficult as it ever was and remains, in principle, the same as it
has always been: a tracing job dependent on the length and
strength of the lead. If you are lucky and/or good enough to
spot and recognize the animal, you can follow it if you have
the requisite skills and can do the job without alerting it to
what you are doing. Hearing and identifying its call are just

the start. Otherwise, you are left to read the signs, interpreting what it has done, is doing, and is likely to do, so as to prepare to meet it somewhere along the way. Communications, however sophisticated, are just another pathway the quarry must tread. The end is the identification and apprehension of those who do the treading. Tracking is fundamental to both the hunting and trapping of spies. But a spy trap, properly speaking, is for catching spies—real people—not simply indications of their presence.

Spy traps, then, are intended to catch persons, people employed about a special kind of business. But this is very far from being the whole story. A trap designed and constructed for catching elephants must be large and sturdy enough for the job, and it must be employed in the right way and in an appropriate location if it is to serve its purpose. When an elephant has been caught in it, however, the trap's function is fulfilled; the beast it was intended to take has been captured. A smaller animal might conceivably fall into the trap, but it can be kept or discarded as an incidental matter; it is clear, to those who know, that it is not an elephant. The point being made here is that such a trap has no function as an identifier; it does not announce, as a matter of purpose, that it has taken an elephant rather than some other animal in fulfillment of its function. A spy trap, however, is very different in that it must not only capture quarry of a certain species, but it must as a secondary, no less important function, authenticate its capture. The spy trap must be capable of demonstrating that the person caught *is* a spy, and not something else.[35]

The spy trap must not only be capable of operational discernment, it must also translate its discrimination into a certain result. This is true whether the trap, functionally, is directed strictly at the spy himself or is used against what he does. This is important, for, most usually, it will be what the spy does that shows him up for what he is in reality, his modus operandi, his contacts with his masters, his disloyalty to those whose trust he has abused. Spies are identified as such by what they do and how they do it. The trap must strip away the mask, expose the deceit, and show the creature as it really is—all the while holding the spy in a vise-like grip from which he cannot wriggle free. And the trap must be capable of doing all this, if necessary, without the spy knowing that he is in the trap until he is ready to be extracted and his disposition or disposal arranged. The spy sometimes has nowhere to go and nowhere to escape. Yet his safety is assured simply because his true nature, while perhaps suspected, has not yet been revealed with certainty.[36] While there remains a serious doubt that the person under suspicion really is a spy, he is reasonably safe from anything too final in his case, except where he is a prisoner of a regime so barbarous or paranoid that the matter is moot.[37]

Nagging doubts are often the spy's best protection, even in societies where the Rule of Law is respected in but small measure. Those seeking finally to dispose of the matter cannot afford to leave unresolved doubts. Flight may settle the matter, but confessions procured under duress, whatever their formal or propaganda value, cannot always be trusted. Doubt is the real enemy of resolution, and the trap sometimes cannot be closed while doubts remain. The best spy traps have a kind of labyrinthine quality. The victim is never quite sure whether or not there is a way out, and his struggles with himself and with his predicament are revealing or suggestive of what he would keep hidden. There must, accordingly, be a built-in provision for ongoing, surreptitious inspection.

A spy trap, then, is both an engine for capture and a kind of field litmus test to determine the nature and quality of what has been taken. The trap itself should be benign rather than destructive; the prey, in best Buck Rogers fashion, needs to be taken alive for best effect.[38] If destruction should be necessary or decided upon, the act ought to be undertaken well away from the trap; otherwise, the benignity of the trap could be compromised. Finally, a good spy trap should be capable of showing for whom the spy is working. While, in the last resort, the spy's real loyalty is to himself, modern market conditions dictate that a spy must have a client or a master, if only for the time being. A trap that leaves this question undecided only does half the job.

The possibilities for building spy traps are limitless, for the basic ideas lend themselves to the most extensive range of design, adaptation, and implementation. Each case calls for careful study to see what is needed, what will work, and what materials are required to transform the idea into substance. The easiest way to proceed is to reduce the ideas to their simplest form and to consider them and their applications in regard to the case at hand. The trap is then built around the core idea, which is to shape it and direct its use. Each of the idea categories set out below is oriented toward the exploitation of a weakness in who or what the spy is, or in what he does or for whom he does it.[39] The weaknesses are thus personal, organizational, situational, or methodological. The kind of trap used, where it will be placed, and when and how it will be sprung will depend on the trapper's analysis of what is required for the case at hand. In most instances, the need for the process will be initiated by something happening, things going wrong, a loss of information or material items, or some other circumstance suggesting that a spy is at work.

Even the existence of a spy at the outset may be conjectural so that the exercise may have the most abstract of qualities. The appropriate idea is then selected and the spy-catcher sets about molding it to suit his purposes. For example, an idea for a trap based upon some assumed personal weakness will only serve where the spy has emerged so that a useful assessment of weaknesses can be essayed. The more that is known about the prey, the more exactly the trap can be designed to capture and accommodate it. Thus, while an idea can be expressed in general terms, the trap itself must have a particular character if it is to satisfy the objectives of the spy-catcher. Generic traps do catch spies on occasion, but their existence quickly becomes notorious and their employment self-defeating. The best traps are custom-made.

Spy traps are not simply protective barriers; although they have an incidental deterrent value, they ought not to be used indiscriminately to serve secondary or subsidiary purposes. All traps seeking to exploit a personal weakness will involve some sort of prior surveillance of the individual it is to capture. Photographic surveillance, especially video or moving image photography, is not just an indispensable preliminary; in its evidentiary aspects, it is an integral part of the trap. This type of surveillance may be needed in other cases, too, in order to show what was done, how, and with whom.

Where the core idea is closely related to exploitation of the qualities of a particular individual for whom the trap is intended, careful attention is indicated and the spy-catcher (or those working to his order) will, in effect, have to sit up over the trap.[40] Trapping becomes an active rather than a passive process. Once something (or, more correctly, someone) has been taken, it remains to be determined who and what he is. This is a very important moment for the success or failure of the operation, and the quarry has to be cautiously approached, weapon in hand. Here, interrogation is the weapon most commonly used, for ultimately it is the explanation given by the spy on which he will be judged in relation to the other evidence that has been collected.

The techniques of interrogation will provide many opportunities for the creation and insertion of traps into which the spy may fall. All these are built around the core idea of *information,* which is used in the sense of what the spy may or may not know. The *pit of ignorance* is among the deepest and most dangerous of traps into which the spy can fall. His struggles to extricate himself have a certain appeal for the sadistically inclined. When it is skillfully dug and carefully sited by the experienced spy-catcher, this trap is extremely effective and very difficult to avoid. What the spy does not know—but ought to—can easily prove to be his downfall.[41] A great deal of what we have called spy-trapping is premised, in one form or another, upon this core idea.

The spy who has to pretend to be what he is not is especially vulnerable to this type of trap. Those who would pass for something other than what they really are must know how to do so and know how to appear, behave, and relate to those among whom they must function without giving rise to suspicion of imposture.[42] The more complex the task undertaken—the more radical the impersonation attempted—the more necessary it will be to have a thorough familiarity with every detail and nuance of the environment into which the spy has been introduced. The example of language may be briefly considered in this context. The rich texture of modern languages gives those who speak them fluently not just the means of effective communication of thoughts and ideas, but also a special way of relating to their fellows.

Language is, in itself, an important identifier. Its employment (or nonemployment) tells much about a person and what he is like ethically, socially, and culturally; it also reveals much about his way of thinking. Content, style, vocabulary, tone, and articulation are as important as the choice of language itself. While English is now spoken as a native or second language by enormous numbers of people worldwide, marked variations in accent as well as meaning and style serve to distinguish the different users of the spoken word along racial, cultural, and geographic lines—often to an extraordinarily fine degree. A skilled student of this matter can often determine with remarkable accuracy where, when, and under what circumstances a person learned the language, as well as much about the circles in which he is accustomed to move. Archaisms are especially revealing and have been, on more than one occasion, the downfall of spies. There are "languages" within languages, an argot known fluently to only a very small class of speakers, an arcane means of communication, often a verbal shorthand, carrying a wealth of information in a special, protected form. Confidences are established among those displaying the ability to communicate in this way, even if they have no other references concerning each other. Similarly, the stranger or poseur is quickly exposed through his lack of fluency or his shallow understanding of the medium.[43]

In technical spheres, language not only allows certain tasks to be performed that would otherwise be impossible, but it produces the comradeship of the knowledgeable that transcends boundaries that would otherwise be set up along other lines. A spy of foreign extraction who is introduced from the outside into a community distinguished by linguistic considerations often has a difficult task in passing for a native-born speaker. A few well-directed questions soon establish the lines of inquiry. There is a natural (as opposed to a forced) use of language that can be quickly detected by the expert ear. Jarring anachronisms and out-of-date slang can be spotted by even the most casual of listeners. Clearly, this is but the slightest reference to a highly complex, many-faceted subject. It is introduced here as being central to the spy-catching theme and as a means to construct an endless variety of traps.

Codes and passwords are based upon specialized knowledge of language and its uses. The spy who does not know the correct password will be unable to enter the system or may draw unwelcome attention to himself through his endeavors to acquire it. Setting up such a password may be utilized, under certain conditions, as a useful spy trap. Any well-constructed system of defenses based upon special knowledge of language and its employment will alert those responsible for its monitoring and maintenance if there is undue interest being shown in it. Unauthorized attempts to learn about secure systems of communication have to be undertaken with great delicacy and subtlety if they are not to arouse suspicion. It might be presumed that anywhere passwords are used there will be attempts by unauthorized persons to acquire them for some reason or another and to break the security of the system. In practice, there is a shocking laxity about these matters that has been encouraged by the now-common use of access codes to all kinds of computerized systems on the part of persons who, but a short while ago, would never in the ordinary course of business have been entrusted with anything as exotic as a password.[44] This can be turned to good account by the spy-catcher who, by introducing an effective system of his own for learning unauthorized approaches, can entrap the incautious spy who is relying upon conventional gullibility to easily acquire the information he is seeking.

A fascinating use of these ideas for the purpose of spy-catching involves a very special kind of *disinformation* trap. Again, the core of the matter is the presumed ignorance of the spy concerning what he should or should not know and how information might be manipulated to his disadvantage. This trap is particularly valuable where information of a certain kind is closely held, in the sense that precise knowledge of it is restricted to a very small group of readily identifiable persons.[45] Once more, in practice, the possible variations on the major theme are legion, but the broad form is quite easily recognizable. The idea finds an interesting and instructive expression in the Koran, where we are told: "When the Prophet confided a secret to one of his wives, and when she disclosed it and Allah informed him of this, he made known to her one part of it and said nothing about the other."[46] Where a loss of secret information from a very restricted circle of persons privy to that information is suspected, carefully controlled items of information (and disinformation) of different kinds can be circulated to specific individuals. If the information escapes from the controlled environment, those who were not privy to it can be eliminated from suspicion and the hunt can be focused upon those who remain. If this exercise is skillfully and systematically conducted, it will eventually pinpoint the individual wrongfully disseminating the information.

This trap can be likened to the *barium meal* where tracers are introduced into the human digestive tract and their progress observed as they pass through the system. This "radio-active" disinformation is useful not only for revealing who is responsible for unauthorized disclosures, but for showing up the lines of communication to the intended recipients. There must, however, be the most careful and continuous monitoring of the tainted information as it passes through the various channels and on out of the system. Once a spy has been identified by these means, he can, with but a little ingenuity, be used as an ongoing conduit for feeding false or doctored information to his controllers. The spy is turned against his masters without either of them realizing that this is the case. The spy is not only trapped, but he also becomes a part of the trap in its extended employment. Moreover, the spy becomes the engine for his own identification and destruction; by his own actions he shows himself up for what he really is.

This trap can be used wherever there is strict and limited control over information and its flow. In practice, the main problem is that the spy-catcher will ordinarily (and quite properly) be excluded from the "magic circle," the loop privy to the information bank from which the losses are being incurred. There is a natural and understandable tendency in such closed communities to be highly suspicious of outsiders and to resent even the slightest suggestion of treachery within. Traps of this kind can rarely be laid without the highest degree of cooperation from those who control the information and its circulation. There is the greatest danger that the value of this trap can be nullified by too many knowing of it and its use. It goes without saying that in a situation where the spy must be privy to this spy-catching operation or, worse, is the person responsible for authorizing or overseeing it, the trap cannot work; those who set the trap and monitor its use expose themselves to embarrassment and loss. The appropriateness of such a trap has to be most carefully considered by reference to the preliminary investigations and what they have revealed. Despite the undeniable attractiveness of this kind of trap, it has some very sharp edges that can prove painful to those who handle it incautiously. Where treachery at the highest levels is suspected, it should never be employed alone, but in conjunction with other devices designed to make up for its inadequacies.

Another trap which uses information as its core idea has uncertainty as its dynamic. The spy is deliberately confused about what he is supposed to know, and his ignorance is critically exposed as he seeks to make an appropriate selection from among an equally plausible number of possibilities. No amount of training or advanced preparation can provide against every contingency or equip the spy with all the answers. In an uncertain environment, the spy is constantly at risk of exposure through some small error with respect to the unseen. Even knowing too much can be a danger.

The purposeful utilization of this climate of uncertainty is very important for the spy-catcher. It lends itself nicely to incorporation into a great many effective traps. The spy is cunningly conducted through the valley of doubt, with ever-increasing loads imposed upon his tolerance for stress until he finally comes to the *multiple choice* trap. In essence, he is required to choose from competing alternatives in the knowledge that the wrong choice may lead to his exposure. This type of trap has a maze-like quality about it so that once the spy has embarked upon his journey within its interior, there is no turning back; he must either find the correct way through to the exit or perish in its maw. These traps are premised upon the construct that while there are many suggestive possibilities, there is but one correct answer. The spy must be denied the opportunity for acquiring by regular means the information he needs to resolve his dilemma. Again, the control of key information and its dissemination are a prerequisite to the design, construction, and employment of this kind of trap. As a general rule, the larger the amount of information employed in these exercises, the greater the uncertainty engendered by its use. This kind of trap lends itself particularly well to employment in the course of interrogation, especially the sort of lengthy questioning to which the captured spy suspect must expect to be subjected.

The effectiveness of the multiple-choice trap is greatly enhanced when it is unexpected. Sudden, unanticipated choices are more difficult to cope with when the person called upon to handle them is tired, confused, or poorly prepared. This type of trap must also be designed and constructed with much care if it is to be really effective. The proper answer to the question must leave no room for doubt as to the required information. It must, too, be something which the spy is most certainly required to know, not just something which he might know. Multiple-choice traps can be used in series, each tending to validate the results of the preceding exercise. They can be concealed in such a way that their administration in the course of a lengthy interrogation is scarcely perceived and their true purport goes unnoticed. The multiple-choice trap is very useful against those for whom an elaborate legend has been prepared. Its judicious employment tends to erode the confidence of those required to answer the kinds of questions it raises for them. Its effectiveness is enhanced still further where the interrogator is not only reduced to a non-person, offering no hints, but is able to evaluate very quickly the answers given to the questions posed. The computer program using the multiple-choice trap is more than a match for all save the most thoroughly prepared (even those brought up on a steady diet of video games) or those who, as a matter of course, know the correct answers. Pre-employment screening using these methods provides an efficient barrier, as well as serving as a spy trap into which the unwary might be drawn.

The most potent of all traps directed against the person have at their core the idea of *temptation*. What one human being finds enticing, another may well find repulsive, but there are certain well-known basic drives that are shared by a great many individuals in one form or another. Somewhere, somehow, something can be found to tempt every human being under the sun. All that remains is to package it suitably and enclose it within the proper mechanism that will shut tightly upon the unfortunate who has been drawn in by it. This is a kind of "Venus spy trap," consisting of a lure and an engine of capture. Once again, it will be seen that actual examples are limited in design and employment only by the boundaries of human imagination, available resources, and exigencies of the case at hand. We would reiterate the stricture that the trap must not only firmly ensnare the prey, but it must serve to identify it as being of the genus "spy."

Sex and greed are powerful drives that lead to all kinds of dangerous temptations for the spy—even the most highly trained, dedicated, and highly placed of spies. The literature is replete with tales of strong men ensnared by their desires, seemingly in the most banal of ways. Giving in to temptation is often tantamount to placing the noose around one's neck.

The temptation to acquire a certain piece of information and thereby fulfill one's role as a spy may be one of the most powerful temptations of all. Sex as an article of temptation is alive with all sorts of effective possibilities for the imaginative spy-catcher.[47] Again, it is an element to be handled with the greatest of sensitivity and care, for it contains the most volatile of human components that are difficult to employ and maintain in stable condition.

The spy's sexual relationships are a source of strength as well as an area of great potential vulnerability. No form of sexual relationship is immune from exploitation by those who have this intent and are in a position to gather and evaluate the requisite information concerning it. Casual sex, as well as more enduring romantic entanglements, can be turned to good account by the spy-catcher. Any temptation that will increase the spy's risk quotient will serve as a lure. Sexual attraction can make some less cautious in their dealings than they would be were this factor absent.[48] People are naturally protective of their deeper, personal commitments and will often take risks to safeguard them that would be unthinkable under other conditions. Many a spy has been persuaded to give up everything for love of some other human being.

The so-called *honey trap* is a particular favorite among spy-catchers of all nations and is as effective today as it has been throughout the long years of its employment. The lure may be a highly trained agent in the regular employ of the spy-catcher or a person selected for the task on an opportunistic basis. The agent may know a great deal about the operation and its objectives or, alternatively, may be acting in comparative or even total ignorance of them. If the objective is to compromise the spy by placing him in an embarrassing or even illegal situation, the contact with the lure will be transitory and unlikely to set up problems of attachment. Other operations, however, focus upon longer-term relationships, and the use of a skilled and completely loyal agent is a prerequisite to entrapment of the intended target.

At the root of all traps using temptation lies another idea, namely that of *striking a bargain*. The spy is tempted with something he seems to desire in some degree. The spy-catcher holds out the illusion that he can provide what is wanted—at a price. It is dangerous for the spy to negotiate, for to do so is to put one foot firmly inside the trap. Those who are willing to listen are well along the road that has no return, for the fact of their having listened can be used against them to impeach their loyalty.[49] Here, too, we see suggestive parallels with kidnapping and hostage-taking. The comparison is especially apt in the case of a deal involving a love object that is being held or is detained in a quasi-hostage mode against the spy's good behavior. By means of this trap, the spy-catcher holds out the illusion of a better, fairer deal than he has been given by his own side. It is often enough an offer too tempting to refuse.

Yet other traps are built around the idea of *incrimination*. The spy is trapped through those with whom he is linked by association, by reason of something he does or omits to do, or by reason of something found in his possession. He is contaminated by contact with someone or something pointing to his guilt. This trap puts the spy on the defensive, for it connects him with something that he has to explain if he is to escape the damning implications of the connection.

Certain equipment is incriminating per se unless the possession of it in the particular circumstances, time, and place can be given an appropriately innocent explanation. The possession of sophisticated photographic equipment can be readily and, perhaps, acceptably explained as the appurtenances of an enthusiastic hobbyist. When such possession is, however, associated with the possession of photographs of, say, sensitive military installations, convincing explanations of innocence are more difficult to fabricate and sustain. Simultaneous possession of microdot processing equipment, useful if not essential to the active spy but few others, renders explanations more difficult. Where, for example, the clearest indications are given to all that photographic equipment is forbidden in a certain area, possession of it raises a presumption that it is intended for purposes contravening the order barring it, and explanations are in order. The same goes for other incriminating items, especially sophisticated gadgets for recording information, copying documents, or transmitting or receiving communications by other than overt, regular means. The standard components of these traps are *surveillance, search, seizure, and interrogation*. Their design, construction, and employment will be dictated by circumstances and any limitations imposed by law and practice upon the exercise of the various essential components.

Again, an important element of the entrapment process involves that the spy knows or does not know about it. If he does not know how, when, or where he might have been incriminated as a result of his actions, he is in a difficult position to cover his tracks. This is especially true where he is incriminated by reason of association with others already known to the spy-catcher, who may or may not have disclosed something of a damaging nature as far as he is concerned. The trap makes use of what is known to the spy-catcher concerning the association while concealing this from the spy. His actions are watched and any deviations from what may be regarded as normal are noted. Only the truly innocent or the most steel-nerved are able to act normally when those with whom they have been associated in some incriminating enterprise disappear suddenly from view.

The well-tried gambit of uncertainty can be brought into play to drive or lure the spy into the trap. Should he flee or stand his ground? Can he explain away his associations, activities, and paraphernalia found in his possession? Whatever the system under which he is brought to book, at this stage of the game the spy cannot realistically be given the benefit of the doubt. There is no presumption of innocence here but, rather, a prima facie accusation of the facts which the spy must answer satisfactorily if he is to absolve himself. *Confrontation* astutely managed is a most effective trap and lends itself to a variety of adaptations. Under some systems, *denunciation* is an element with which to conjure. It can, however, catch many innocents, especially in times of spy hysteria.[50]

The trap must be so constructed that the spy is unable to wriggle free if he is truly guilty. It must force him to account, in the minutest detail, for all that has brought him under suspicion. If the trap is well constructed and diligently employed, the spy will dig himself in deeper and deeper by his own efforts. Such traps catch the spy on the horns of an awkward dilemma. If he refuses to explain, he may be condemned forthwith, a fate that few save the most heroic and abnegating might contemplate with equanimity. Any spy worth his salt knows such a stance must bring his mission—and possibly his career—to an abrupt end. Yet every explanation, given the absence of knowledge about the context into which it is launched, is perilous and perhaps incriminating. Cover stories, however carefully prepared, cannot hold up against those who know or, with good reason, suspect the truth; they themselves become engines of entrapment. The spy finds himself blundering about in uncharted territory. He is trapped by a combination of his own ignorance and uncertainty. A caution must be offered here. The effectiveness of these traps is dependent upon the tolerances and gaps built into their construction. Many a spy has literally talked his way out of a tight corner because the trap was too loosely put together and poorly manned.

This leads us to another trap, based on an offer by the spy-catcher to provide a kind of solution to the harassed spy's dilemma in those cases just discussed. The spy-catcher takes the initiative and becomes the problem-solver for his quarry. He points the way into the trap, standing aside to allow his victim to enter it gratefully. We may call this trap the *illusion of safe haven*. It may be set up in many ways, dependent upon the circumstances and what might be available for the purpose. The trap makes use of another of the spy's basic problems: he cannot trust anyone. Yet to do his job, he may have to trust someone. He may not like, much less trust, those with whom he is assigned to work. He may take extensive, even excessive, precautions against betrayal by them and by his own side generally. But, in the end, if he is to do as he is told or ordered rather than setting himself at dangerous odds with his controllers, he is forced to establish some sort of relationship with them. The lonely, the incautious, and the inexperienced will, naturally, be more susceptible than most to this kind of trap. They are eager to grasp what appears to be the helping hand.

What is involved is a *deception* by means of which the spy is induced to believe that he is dealing with friends, people who serve the same interests as he does. He is fooled by substitutions who are working against him and who induce him to reveal himself and his purposes in the process. This trap is very effective in rolling up a network provided it is used intelligently, sparingly, and not overenthusiastically. The moment its use is detected or even suspected, it loses all effectiveness, for operations will be closed down and all territory and approaches will, pending further arrangements, be considered hostile. The trap can be operated from a distance—as in the case of the famous British Double Cross system of World War II, where unsuspecting Nazi spies were lured into the trap by others of their ilk who had been earlier captured or turned—or it can be set up in face-to-face, hands-on encounters.[51] The lure can be a specially trained agent introduced from outside in simulation of an expected friendly contact, or it can be a turned or double agent working unsuspected against his former employers. This is a trap that must be sprung very carefully if it is to be really effective.

All spies are, by nature, suspicious, and the good spy is more suspicious than most. He will limit his contacts, even where these are made under instruction, and he will be careful to reveal as little of himself and his purposes as possible. This is not a trap that works well when time is running against the spy-catcher, for great patience has to be exercised so as to make sure the spy is well into the trap before it is closed. There must be no room for him to feign innocence or to warn others of impending danger. He must be well deceived, letting down his guard in such a way that he can be exactly identified for what he is. The spy-catcher must have absolute control of his lure. Every spy worth taking by this means should be regarded as a barracuda capable of snatching the bait and leaving the hook.

There is probably no such thing as a reliable double agent; this is a contradiction in terms. The possibility of a further volte-face must be realistically allowed for in any operation. More complicated versions will deliberately play on the spy's vanity and his barracuda propensities. He will be persuaded to snatch for the bait by what he is induced through deception to see as the clumsiness of those fishing for him. He is caught by his own ego and an underestimation of his adversaries. This kind of trap may best be likened to a kind of espionage "sting" operation. To be convincing, there must always be a lot of "give" in the hope of eventually getting a larger "take." It is also, in a sense, like a game of chess, although admittedly, of a most deadly kind. There comes a point at which the good player realizes that he is beaten, that further moves are useless and offer no prospect of victory. The trick is to secure graceful acceptance and concession at this point rather than an angry upsetting of the board. The feeling of being trapped should never be startling to the point of engendering a violent response and should be ameliorated, where possible, by the prospect of some countervailing advantage.

The spy-catcher wants the spy to play the game, and to

play it by *his* rules. Most spies are only too well aware of the price of being found out as disloyal to their own side, or, at least, of being portrayed as such. The illusion of safe haven as an alternative can be appropriately extended in some cases at the moment of capture; it lulls the fears and holds out, however momentarily, the prospect of safety in a time of extreme danger. If the spy-catcher can play successfully upon the fears and suspicions that reside in the spy's psyche about his position vis-à-vis his own side, capture may not only be complete, but the spy may be ready to be "turned" so as to become yet another element in the ongoing process of trapping others. This is yet another side to the bargaining coin.

The professional spy lives with three major concerns in regard to his own safety. He can have no control over these matters that so vitally affect his personal security, and he must rely upon the system—and others—to protect him. History can hardly lead him to be sanguine about his prospects in this regard, and he must learn to live with the risks and accommodate himself to their operational implications for him. The truly great dangers to the spy come from the agent in place in the system that employs him, who is in a position to know of his work and whereabouts and to pass that information to those seeking him; a penetration of his own organization by those against whom he is working, his own mirror image as it were, who are able to learn of him and his doings and to get that information back to those who can find him and act against him on the basis of it; and, perhaps most deadly of all, the defector who brings with him the knowledge of the spy's identity and activities or perhaps even the tiniest fragment of information concerning them that will enable those in whose midst he is working to effect his capture. It is difficult to compartmentalize the handling of agents in such a way as to provide against the unpleasant consequences of defection of the knowledgeable.[52]

In each of these cases, the spy is caught because his back is not adequately protected. There is a failure of security in the system that employs him. No spy can afford to ignore or overlook the dangers posed to his position by these facts of professional life but, as a practical matter, there is very little he can do about them save to redouble his own caution—and worry. Turning that understandable concern to profitable use is something with which the diligent spy-catcher will want to acquaint himself. The subject of agents in place, especially the mole, is of such importance that a separate chapter is devoted to it in the present work. Here, we need note only this special, offensive use of this kind of agent for spy-catching. All these agents are an extension of the spy-catcher's hunting capabilities, capable of seeking out and providing him with valuable information concerning the spies he is trying to identify and apprehend.

Penetration of hostile services is another hunting technique involving the active, aggressive seeking-out of information concerning these matters at the source; an agent, a spy, is sent in to get it. Defection, on the other hand, comprehends a process whereby the information is brought out by the detachment of a knowledgeable component of the opposing system itself. From a counterespionage perspective, all penetrations are in the nature of a hunting technique and a highly dangerous and difficult one at that. They can rarely be mounted on short notice and are a long-term investment in the general rather than the particular. They are strictly spying operations, ventures or forays into unfriendly territory, even where this is comparatively local. They give rise organizationally to considerable problems relating to responsibilities and management of resources, as well as competition with other agencies having different purposes in view.

Mostly, the counterespionage aspects of all these penetration operations will be incidental to some other objectives sought by those primarily concerned with running them. While acknowledging a subsidiary role in these matters, the spy-catcher must be organized in such a way as to be able to take advantage of the opportunities they present, especially in the matter of debriefing and evaluation of obtained information.

As in all other departments of endeavor, the difference between success and failure often lies in the minute attention to detail. Spy-catching, whether seen in terms of trapping or hunting, is often mainly a matter of accurately putting two and two together and doing so before the quarry is alerted and has time to escape. Meticulous record keeping and indexing and a reliable system for speedy retrieval of data are essential to any spy-catching operation, but human memory is the secret ingredient that sometimes makes the difference. Stripped of all adornments, spy-catching always comes down to a painstaking search for clues to something hidden that is being sought. The basic information is produced by monitoring people or things and remembering the results.

Good, productive hunting and trapping are expressed in the effective use of information about people and other activities and the establishment and maintenance of sound, systematic procedures for making use of that information. There is no off-season for spies. All mechanisms for hunting or trapping spies are part of the overall defensive system that we loosely call security. Any system that practices a strict form of population control has the materials at hand for the most effective means of spy-trapping.[53] From the very earliest times, the Soviet Union has institutionalized population control and adapted it to these ends. Indeed, the possession of the right kind of documentation, especially that connected with identity, is no less than the state's acknowledgment of one's right to an existence. Most modern states, however moderate, regulate life and well-being through some system of controls, bestowing the right to work or to live within certain areas, etc.[54] On a more limited scale, all organizations that employ any sort of a pass system by means of which they restrict access to their property practice a form of population control. These are all-season spy traps.

Special spy traps, built around some of the ideas we have discussed, have their particular utility, but there is no substitute in this field for regular, sound security procedures rigorously—religiously, almost—applied in defense of what the spy might target. The careful, conscientious background check is a veritable mine field through which the spy must pass, whether or not we are aware that he is making the attempt. It serves not only to test his nerve, but to reveal his flaws. Access control is another procedure by means of which unauthorized intrusions are detected and those who undertake them might be trapped. Just like barbed wire, every security procedure, well enforced, is a trap for the unwary.

Shevchenko's account of the security procedures relating to cable traffic at the Soviet Mission to the United Nations is very instructive. He writes: "The *referentura* was a fortress . . . I was certain that hidden peepholes let security men watch us in the cubicles as we read."[55] Clearly the very sensible (and necessary), if stultifying, procedures designed to protect the secrets it housed constituted, as a by-product, a most effective spy trap against all except for the spy prepared to carry out the secrets in his own head. No system of physical security is proof against the eidetic memory, and thought control can only go so far. But efforts to defeat a system such as that described by Shevchenko are bound to defeat or trap the most courageous or imaginative of spies sooner or later. This type of system has the added advantage of not looking too much like a trap.

Search and surveillance are regular, admissible security procedures in even the most permissive of societies.[56] The only real question with respect to them is how far they can be extended before they become objectionable to those subjected to them. Where the line is actually drawn is what, in practice, distinguishes the traditional liberal democracy from the police state. Protection from unreasonable search and seizure is enshrined in the United States Constitution. But opinions differ, as indeed they must, on what is both a legal and a philosophical question, as to what is unreasonable. Searches for contraband coming into the country have a long and respectable history, and even where the term *contraband* has been extended beyond that conventional usage, the practice of search is widely upheld. The regulation of commerce has always seemed at least respectably compatible with the notions of Western democracy that have been economically sustained by it. Similarly, the protection of property, even intellectual property, has long appeared a laudable purpose, giving license to what might be called "security" measures in defense of such objectives. While few commercial undertakings in the United States would wish to go to the lengths described by Shevchenko in order to protect their information and its employment about their business, there is little doubt that their right to do so could be brought both within the spirit as well as the letter of the law. Certainly, specific categories of government information can be—and are—so protected. We may, in certain circumstances, insist upon a lot of concessions from those with whom we do business or, perhaps more exactly, from those who hope to do business with us. It is precisely here that a competition of ideas and rights enters the picture. Neither commercial considerations nor personal references are, understandably, allowed to dictate the outcome of these conflictual encounters; politics is brought to bear in order to produce a resolution consonant with the balance of power at any given time in society. The swing of the pendulum depends upon a number of finely tuned social, political, and economic factors.

In the present context, the swing in the United States toward the recognition and protection of individual rights to privacy has had a marked chilling effect upon the adoption of sensible security measures designed to protect intellectual property in the private sector. This state of affairs is a spy's delight. In some instances, background checking has been reduced to a charade that has undoubtedly favored the entry of predators and unreliable persons through this noticeably weakened perimeter fence. The utility of the background check as a passive trap for spies has been noticeably reduced accordingly. In the United States, we have over the years become infected with a strange sensitivity about inquiring into matters that, while understandably and admittedly of a private nature, might be highly damaging to us were we not to take them into account in assessing the trustworthiness and suitability of those we admit to our secrets. The really good security check on individuals is in itself a most effective spy trap. Moreover, it is unlikely to harm those who intend no harm to us. Its integrity must be preserved at all costs, and attempts to erode its character and content in the name of privacy must be seen for what they are.

While this initial hurdle is an important one in defending the perimeters of the system against intrusions, ongoing reviews are essential if the effectiveness of the security machinery is to be maintained. Again, we see how a certain reticence in our own society contributes to a kind of professional myopia that prevents us from detecting and doing anything about obvious security risks already lodged within the system.[57] People change over time. Life and all its exposures alter objectives, efficiency, and loyalties. We must now allow an over-tender attitude toward privacy to blind us to the dangers or to impede us in the search for useful mechanisms by means of which we can monitor and evaluate these dangers. The hardest part for the spy (and his masters) is often no more than getting through the gates. Once within, this presence tends to be taken for granted and he can set to work on the not-too-difficult task of building his credibility. Once this reaches a certain point, he is almost impregnable. Those who are inside—the special flavor of the term "insider" is no linguistic accident—are viewed differently. Relationships and outlooks change, subtly in most cases, but there is a drawing together of insiders in a distinctive way. Insiders are regarded and trusted in a manner that strangers are not. They (and their foibles and eccentricities) are tolerated and even excused on the footing that "they are our own."

It calls for a certain, rare strength and clear-sightedness to admit that one of the insiders may indeed be bad. To confess the fact is to suggest something unfavorable about ourselves, our procedures, and our judgment. It is always chastening to have to confess how little we truly know about our nearest and dearest and those we have trusted. We are also prone to mistake "knowing" people for simply liking to do business with them ("Great guy, I've known him for years!"). In some societies, these tendencies are more pronounced than in others, but in general the more closed the community, the more forgiving of frailties it is to those admitted within its ranks. It is this, more than anything else, that explains the curious tolerance extended from time to time to members of the espionage and security services accused of having acted against the interests of those by whom they are trusted.

There is a collective resistance to a belief in betrayal. It is as though belief in the accusation, even to the point of giving it consideration, might threaten the very existence of the system itself. The possibility of a traitor within the gates must be evaluated with these attitudes in mind, not simply by reference to the adequacy or otherwise of the admission procedures. Positive vetting or "expert" appraisal (what a comforting expression!) is no more than a controlled access point through which the postulant must pass to be admitted within. It is no absolute guarantee of inherent purity or, more to the point, of continued, unswerving loyalty to those who have granted admission. Getting to know someone requires much more than an act of positive vetting. Positive vetting itself usually means no more than someone we trust vouching for someone we wish to trust or at least consider trusting. And we trust those who do the vouching because we "know" them or assume that others have already vouched for them. Realistically, we must recognize the fragility of all this and allow for it in our calculations. The bad *can* get in, however formidable the traps set for them but, more to the point, the good can go bad or be corrupted during the time they spend within. Presence—even likeable presence—within the inner circle is far from being a warranty of continuing loyalties or an unreserved sharing of values. An insider may well be accepted without himself accepting. In this day and age, loyalty oaths are for the superstitious, the simpleminded, or the primitive.

A somewhat Leninesque aphorism may usefully be interjected here: the job of the spy-catcher is to catch spies. All spies are dangerous, but some are more dangerous than others. The most dangerous are those closest to our most important secrets, who can purloin and communicate them to those who would learn them, or who can, by their place and position, influence people and, through them, events. The spy within—so close and yet so far—is the spy-catcher's greatest challenge, the one for whom the most cunning of traps must be devised. His trap must be particularly strong in the department of justification, for even if he is caught, those who really count will need much convincing that their friend, colleague, perhaps even family member, is a spy. Here, too, the greatest delicacy and discrimination are required, for laying traps in your own living and working space opens up the real prospect of catching, quite uncomfortably and almost certainly to the common embarrassment, some of *your* own innocent "associates." The spy-catcher is rarely a true insider; he is inside on sufferance. Getting inside so as to be able to lay his traps where they may be used to their best effect is often the most difficult task of all for the spy-catcher, but it must be undertaken, for in the final analysis, inside is where the action is. This is where the good security officer must be; if necessary, he must act like a real bastard, but in such a way that none dare question his paternity.

The sensible spy-catcher prepares his ground. He is not a poacher but a gamekeeper,[58] though he may, on occasion, find himself obliged to act after the fashion of his adversaries. Those who would hunt or trap over land they do not own or control must make the proper arrangements with those who can concede the right. These are often touchy matters, but ignoring them invariably leads to problems, recriminations, bitterness, and wounded feelings that can frustrate the exercise and much else besides. Anyone who has ever worked in a government agency will readily appreciate the practical implications of these admonitions and what they portend in terms of actual cases.

The spy-catcher may well have to be a bastard from time to time, but he would be most unwise to act so as to appear an arrogant bastard.[59] The Western counterespionage specialist may, at times, wistfully envy his KGB counterpart, but he would do well not to be even thought of as emulating him. The spy-catcher, wherever he works and however efficient and good at his job, needs cooperation. When he encounters obstruction, he ought not to be too hasty in attributing it to sinister motives. Only where these can be objectively established to his satisfaction should he consider the alternatives open to him. The desire to keep him and his traps out may be no more than an extreme manifestation of the insider syndrome. The spy-catcher may need to make a very persuasive case to be allowed to hunt and trap outside his accustomed or assigned preserves. He will certainly have to show evidence of the presence of the game he hopes to take. He can only do this by careful observation and equally careful documentation of what he has observed. The hunter may well be placed in the awkward position of having to prove both the presence and nature of his quarry before he is given the requisite license to pursue.

Those interested in protecting the spy from his pursuers will obviously seek to use natural advantage, especially the sentiments we have outlined, to confuse the trail and hamper the chase. It is self-evident that these efforts are greatly aided in a climate where lax security measures are the norm. Very few of those inconvenienced by stringent security would really pretend to enjoy the experience; this is like affecting to relish a very unpleasant-tasting but efficacious cough medicine. The conscientious and honest-minded will see the need for such measures if proper explanations and indoctrinations are given. In our society, there is, however, always a sufficient cadre of "libertarians" to whom all such measures are anathema and whose motivation, though of the very best, can be perverted to serve the enemy interest. Such abstract idealism is often touchingly out of tune with objective reality. The spy-catcher is a distasteful reminder of that reality. The real world, even that of the cloister, is not peopled with saints. It is inhabited by men and women who often enough maintain a bold, scrupulous public facade, concealing private spaces into which they dread others prying, and with good reason.

Those in high public places have the most to fear from such

private exposures; even in the most permissive of times, the public does not like to see the feet of clay of its idols. A facade of total competence, brilliance—genius even—can hide a core of self-doubt, shame, secret lusts, and worse. The secret tippler or user of hard drugs, the pious church-goer who in former president Jimmy Carter's famous phrase "lusts after other women in his heart," the staid-fronted clandestine gambler is all of us—or none of us.

It is always the other fellow, and we delight in his exposure in our stead—provided it does not touch us too closely. The danger in such secret weaknesses and their indulgence is precisely that they are secret, and the price of their indulgence can be exacted by any spy master able to discover and exploit them. In dealing with these matters, the spy-catcher must still the censorious side of his own nature. It is not for him to judge, condone, or condemn, but to understand and to use that understanding to further his work. He knows others are tempted (he may often be tempted himself), for he, too, uses temptation as a trap. What he must do is be ever vigilant for the telltale signs of temptation in his own camp. For the skilled tracker, these are not hard to spot. The experienced hunter looks for *indicators of change* that alert him to the presence of the wolf among the lambs.[60] The indicators looked for are those that might signal the emergence of hitherto unsuspected weaknesses (even a cry for help) that can be manifestations of a predisposition to altered loyalties or susceptibility to manipulation and exploitation by others. The spy-catcher must develop the means of reading and interpreting these signs and putting their meaning to his own uses. Ideally, the spy-catcher should arrange observation of every target-worthy individual within his area of responsibility, bearing in mind that rank and position are not the sole determinants of target-worthiness; the secretary may be more profitable as a direct target than his or her superior.

The spy-catcher should look for changes in personality (depression, melancholy, carelessness, excessive cheerfulness, violent outbursts); physiological changes (especially where these may be stress related); cosmetic or appearance changes (the dowdy, middle-aged, female secretary who sports a new wardrobe and fashionable hairstyle or the neat, soberly dressed manager who is suddenly unkempt and slovenly); lifestyle changes (the workaholic who develops the surprising habit of taking short, unexplained spells of leave; the straitlaced book-keeper who shows up under the influence of drink or drugs); economic changes[61] (the poorly paid employee who drives a new Porsche and wears a gold Rolex or the affluent business-man suddenly smitten with an urgent need for a relatively small sum of money)[62]; and emergence of irregular sexual practices (unusual liaisons, "coming out of the closet"). The list can obviously be expanded and fleshed out in detail. When a sensational spy case has broken, how many times do we hear, "Didn't anyone notice?" The question, more prop-erly put, would be, having noticed, what did they do about it? The answer in most cases, sadly, is: Nothing.

If he is wise, the spy-catcher realizes that he wants to put an end to the spying; he does not necessarily want to put an end to the spy. Many become involved in spying only to regret it quite quickly, continuing because they can see no way out. They are coerced and fearful (fearful mostly of what punishment might be inflicted on them by those they have harmed through their betrayal). Some have become spies as a result of succumbing to a weakness; others have done so under pressures they could not resist. These are agents of others, more committed and professional, who have used them and what they have to offer for the job at hand. They are reluctant spies—yet spies nevertheless—and they con-tinue to spy because they feel they have no other choice. Many of them are to be found by the methods just discussed. Yet, for the most part, they are but the tip of the iceberg. What the spy-catcher needs is a means of unobtrusively neu-tralizing them while using the knowledge gained in the process to go after the more dangerous elements comprising the part below the waterline. A variation upon the safe-haven trap is useful for this purpose. The spy-catcher discreetly offers an alternative for the spy who wishes to come in from the cold but does not know how to do it or where to turn for help. The spy-catcher becomes a kind of father/confessor who, while holding out no guarantees of absolution, is sup-portive and understanding in a way that suggests compassion and hope of rehabilitation. The experienced spy-catcher will be ever on the alert for false converts and false contrition[63], and those who are only too quick to seize upon the chance of forgiveness to avoid punishment for their misdeeds. Spy-trapping in most cases involves a tradeoff. Scalps and pelts are useful trophies and look great on the wall, but their value has to be set against what might have been gained had these spies been put to other uses. Such reflections are not the product of 20/20 hindsight.

There is an understandable belief that Donald Maclean was a regenerate, dyed-in-the-wool ideologue, whose flight to Moscow and his reception by the Soviets was merely evidence of the strength of his commitment and the small likelihood of useful steps toward reclamation succeeding in his case. A more careful, detached view of his behavior at critical times suggests otherwise. On any assessment, the way he behaved, especially during the Cairo years, can only be regarded as bizarre.[64] It drew attention to him in a way that neither he nor his Soviet masters can have considered desirable; it certainly did nothing for his cover, nor did it facilitate any espionage activities in which he might have proposed to engage. It seems to have been—and should have been recognized as such—a cry for help. There are many indications indeed that it did not go unrecognized. But what was done about it? It is there that the unencumbered spy-catcher might have thought it worth his while to have extended a helping hand. Suppose it were objected that no one knew at that point that Maclean *was* a spy. So much greater the need for probing what was evidently an extraordinary exhibition of weakness by one who had been (and still was) in a most sensitive position. Maclean was, on what we have set out above, eminently targetable, manifesting clear indicators of change. The hunting instincts should have been set in motion.

It is tempting, but unprofitable, to speculate what might have been the result had the clues been followed and the snares set. The case is offered here as an object lesson in missed opportunities. The system ought to afford spies who are important enough the chance to atone by offering more appealing terms than the prospect of a life in hiding, among strangers. Realistically, the absence of such a prospect is a major defect in the Soviet system. It is difficult to strike the right balance between smart enticement and soft-headedness, but the astute spy-catcher must learn what is required to do so and how he can accommodate it within the parameters of his instructions. Ideally, the knowledge that such an escape hatch is there should be built into early training for high responsibility. The right kind of earned forgiveness can be a very cost-effective trap, for it can put an end to the spying and lead back to those who have greater culpability in the matter.

Even the most careful of spies leaves a trail of some kind, a footprint here, a track mark there. In these days, it is hard for the spy not to leave a paper trail of sorts, even if this is falsified and deliberately confusing to the hounds. Spy-catching is, at bottom, a work of patient investigation.[65] In this respect, it is much like police work of the more conventional kind. It is the final pounce, the moment of the catch, rather than the techniques of pursuit, that mark it out as something special and distinctive. Catching the spy, as distinct from merely spotting him whether by hunting or trapping, depends, in the final analysis, upon power and authority. There were those who had long marked Philby for what he eventually showed himself to be, but were unable to do anything about it. The spy hunter may well identify his quarry and be able to describe him and his doings in the minutest detail. But if he is held back or lacks the power to take his prey, his work is largely academic. The most cunning of traps is rendered nugatory when the trapper is forbidden to use it.

The spy-catcher in the United States must learn to live with the fact that he operates under a very limited license, one that does not allow him to use effectively, if at all, some of his best weapons and techniques. In other cases, the restrictions may be of a more temporary character. There may well be good reason to stay action on occasion in the interests of some wider, less immediate objectives. It may be, at times, impolitic, unhelpful, or even dangerous to pounce, though the catch is sure and the work of the hunter impeccably performed.[66] The hunter must learn to cope with these disappointments and not allow them to influence future performance. He needs to constantly look down his sights and keep his finger on the trigger. The trapper, too, needs to keep his traps well oiled and ever ready for employment. The blacksmith's arm is strong because he uses it. In the same way, spy-catching requires much practice for proficiency. It is wise to stalk many lions before trying to shoot one. Even those exercises that are not consummated with a kill have their utility. It is possible that just being able to identify the spy and appropriately communicate the knowledge of that identification will put a stop to the spying. These admonitions have a respectable antiquity.

The only real novelty in this business lies in the ability to find new wrinkles in what essentially is very old cloth. Modern man with his Winchester 30.06 does exactly what his counterpart did in the Stone Age. He stalks his prey until he is within range of it, using all the artifices at his command to avoid frightening it off while he settles it into his sights. He may have to range far and wide to bring his weaponry into play, or he may use his knowledge of his quarry's habits to choose a convenient spot for an ambush.[67] Even Paleolithic man needed reliable information and the ability to interpret it if his hunt were to be successful. Basically, he needed to know what his prey looked like; how big it was; what it did; what it liked and disliked; where it was; and what he needed to do to lay it low. With but a little adaptation, these fundamental requirements still serve the modern spy-catcher very well.

POINTS TO REMEMBER

1. Spy traps can be anything designed to facilitate the detection, identification, unmasking, and entrapment of spies. In designing and choosing traps, the spy-catcher must understand the attributes of what is to be caught.

2. The theory of *assumed vulnerability* postulates that for every prey there is at least a single weakness that can be exploited. Weaknesses can be habitual and/or situational. Situational weaknesses stem from the structural features of the situation—the physical layout, critical times of the day, possible technologies, etc. Habitual weaknesses stem from preferred patterns of behavior which have biological and psychological bases. Both situation and habit limit the range of options. Elements of situations which remain relatively constant are *structural*. One structural weakness of the spy is that he must communicate with his handlers about the product(s) of his endeavors; traffic and the tracks it makes are key areas of vulnerability. Yet, one must keep in mind that the best spies cultivate unpredictability.

3. It is often the exception rather than the rule that teaches the lesson. Rules work when the situations remain similar and the people for whom they are relevant also remain similar. For this reason alone, spy traps must sometimes be designed de novo, while at the same time the traps must fit

within the accepted cultural framework of the group or society within which they are to be employed. In general, spy traps—their character, location, and operation—should never be exposed simply in order to take the prey unless they are to be used only once.

4. In terms of communications, the maximum period of safety is the sum of the time it takes to send the message, capture it, decipher and understand it, and decide what is to be done about it. The spy-catcher attempts to reduce the amount of time as close to zero as is possible without, of course, compromising the operation. Two variables which condition communication and the people to which it leads are the length and strength of signs and signals. The worst possible case is one in which the signs are weak and short; the best, in which they are long and strong.

5. Spy traps must perform two key functions: they must catch the quarry and authenticate that the quarry *is* a spy. A third function performed by the best traps is revealing for whom the spy is working. Traps should not be destructive; the prey should be taken alive and as unobtrusively as possible so as not to compromise the trap.

6. Spy traps are built around a central or *core idea*. Traps are set out to exploit weaknesses in persons (say, for example, in habits), organizations (repetitive rules and collective behaviors), situations (specific organized sequences of collective exchange), or method (step-by-step procedures utilized by actors). Traps built around the core idea of *information* are temporary interventions of the mail (mail traps), language ability traps (argot and/or dialect traps), information ignorance traps, access code traps, disinformation traps, and multiple-choice or uncertainty traps. Traps built around the core idea of *temptation* include sexual (including honey) traps, greed (including money) traps, and bargain or exchange traps. Traps built around the core idea of *incrimination* include those of association, possession, and entrapment, while there are a number of trap variations centering on *confrontation*. Other traps, such as double agent and betrayal traps, play upon the central notion of *trust* and the fact that spies cannot trust anyone.

NOTES

1. *Office Warfare*, New York: Macmillan, 1986, page 168.

2. *The Game of the Foxes*, New York: David McKay, 1971, page 397.

3. *Master of Spies*, New York: Doubleday, 1975, page 61.

4. *Operation Lucy*, New York: Coward, McCann & Geoghegan, 1981, page 157.

5. For an interesting example, see the roller-skating story in *The New KGB*, William R. Corson and Robert T. Crowley, New York: William Morrow, 1985, page 194.

6. On this very complex subject, see *Special Problems in Negotiating with Terrorists*, H. H. A. Cooper, Gaithersburg, MD: International Association of Chiefs of Police (CTT Series), 1982.

7. A work deserving of special study in this connection is *Handbook for Spies*, Alexander Foote, New York: Doubleday, 1969. It should be read in conjunction with Read and Fisher, op. cit., supra note 4.

8. That master of espionage literature, Eric Ambler, wrote an engaging novel around the problems discussed here. See, *Send No More Roses*, London: Weidenfeld & Nicolson, 1977.

9. This was a principal element in the case so entertainingly described in *The Falcon and the Snowman*, Robert Lindsey, New York: Simon & Schuster Inc., 1979. What had been put at risk, incidentally, by the espionage activities of the protagonists was the very advanced system the United States was developing to communicate with its own agents in hostile territory. See, too, on the U.S. Joan-Eleanor system developed by the OSS during World War II: *Piercing the Reich*, Joseph E. Persico, New York: Viking Press, 1979, pages 157–183.

10. One of the most extensively documented cases is that of Harry Gold, the self-confessed Soviet agent, who was a government witness in the Rosenberg case. See, *The Rosenberg File*, Ronald Radosh and Joyce Milton, New York: Holt, Rinehart, and Winston, 1983. Gold authored an unpublished account of his work while in prison.

11. On a strictly related topic, a computer security expert writes: ". . . the primary reason for poor computer security today still lies with the inadequate sensitivity to security needs of people in data processing operations. Perpetrators of

computer abuse have told me time and time again, 'Why go to all the trouble of technically compromising a computer center when all I have to do is con one of the trusted people into doing anything I want him to do?' " *Crime by Computer*, Donn B. Parker, New York: Charles Scribner's Sons, 1976, page 282.

12. "All communication is person to person." *Hostage: London*, Geoffrey Household, Boston: Little, Brown, 1977, page 21.

13. Worth detailed study in this regard is the well-known case of Eli Cohen. See *The Shattered Silence*, Zwy Aldouby and Jerrold Ballinger, New York: Coward, McCann & Geoghegan, 1971. Accustomed to working so close to the fire, Cohen simply did not appreciate how hot he had become.

14. It has been well said that "In the field of observation, chance only favors those who are prepared." *The Prevalence of Nonsense*, Ashley Montagu and Edward Darling, New York: Harper & Row, 1967, page 202.

15. See "Comparative Law Aspects of Wiretapping and Electronic Surveillance," H. H. A. Cooper, in *Commission Studies of the National Commission for the Review of Federal and State Laws Relating to Wiretapping and Electronic Surveillance*, Washington, D.C.: U.S. Government Printing Office, 1976.

16. On this, generally, see *The Rise of the Computer State*, David Burnham, New York: Random House, 1983.

17. A cautionary note is sounded by Thomas Plate and Andrea Davis. "America's patience has not often been severely tested. In a crisis atmosphere, America might impatiently reach for seemingly easy solutions." *Secret Police*, New York: Doubleday, 1981, page 301.

18. See "The Erosion of Law Enforcement Intelligence and Its Impact on the Public Security," Report of the Subcommittee on Criminal Laws and Procedures to the Committee on the Judiciary of the U.S. Senate, Washington, D.C.: U.S. Government Printing Office, 1978.

19. See *Hostage Negotiations: Options and Alternatives*, H. H. A. Cooper, Gaithersburg, MD: International Association of Chiefs of Police, CTT Series, 1977, page 12, note 31.

20. See, for example, *How to Make Your Own Luck*, Bernard Gittelson, New York: Warner, 1981.

21. The defection of Reino Hayhanen, which led to the

arrest of "Colonel Abel," must be regarded as such a lucky circumstance. Abel had left no traces of his work or presence up to that time.

22. "Ponsonby, the Brigade Commander, was among those killed, and lost his life because of a false economy. He had left his best charger, worth far more than the government compensation fund would pay if it were killed, behind the lines and chosen to ride instead an inferior hack. The French Lancers caught him struggling to safety over heavy ground, easily rode him down, and speared him to death." *The Face of Battle,* John Keegan, London: Penguin Books, 1978, page 151.

23. On this, generally, see *Secret Intelligence Agent*, Montgomery Hyde, New York: St. Martin's Press, 1983, pages 68–70.

24. "Every counterintelligence man's dream is to be able to secretly read the enemy's communications," for then, " . . . we would achieve the ultimate counterintelligence goal, complete control of the enemy's moves against us." *The FBI-KGB War*, Robert J. Lamphere and Tom Schachtman, New York: Random House, 1986, page 79. This is a very useful book and one which should be read with care and attention.

25. "We had the post office send us photostats of the outsides of all envelopes and postcards mailed to Elitcher's residence (this was called a 'mail cover')." *Ibid*, page 92.

26. The matter has been exacerbated in our times by the undeniable use of diplomatic facilities by some countries in the assistance of terrorist groups which they sponsor. Electronic invasion of diplomatic communications is now the norm. See, on this generally, "Diplomatic Immunities and State Sponsored Terrorism," Frank Brenchley, in *Contemporary Terrorism*, Ed., William Gutteridge, New York: Facts on File, 1986, pages 85–108.

27. The Pollard case, to which frequent references will be made in this text, is an outstanding example of the latter.

28. *The Age of Surveillance*, Frank Donner, New York: Alfred A. Knopf, 1980, a useful work due to its extensive documentation alone, should be approached with this caution in mind.

29. See the interesting account of the trapping of the Portuguese diplomat Peixoto de Menezes by H. A. R. Philby, in *The Third Man*, E. H. Cookridge, New York: G. P. Putnam's Sons, 1968, pages 103–104.

30. The price of freedom is the diligent, investigative journalist, who makes his living informing his readership of matters that many, including the authorities, would prefer to keep under wraps. The line between espionage and journalism is thin indeed, and the issue will not be argued here beyond pointing out the obvious parallels between the work of the spy and the investigative journalist bent on learning (and publishing) the secrets of some matter.

31. Big Brother, a la Orwell's *1984, is* watching you, to a greater extent than many would credit. As long, however, as he is content merely to watch, most people remain unconcerned and accepting.

32. See Montgomery Hyde, op. cit., supra note 23, page 87.

33. While this work is of a sedentary nature, it ought not (as it has been in some cases) to be regarded as an occupation for the super-annuated. A certain zest and agility of mind are called for if these reponsibilities are to be diligently discharged.

34. On this generally, see *The Puzzle Palace,* James Banford, Boston: Houghton Mifflin, 1982.

35. This point is very well illustrated by Lamphere's account of the Coplon case. Op. cit., supra note 24, especially page 112.

36. The copious and instructive literature on H. A. R. Philby offers widely divergent views on the man and what he is said to have done, but it is in broad agreement in reflecting the doubts as to whether he was truly a Soviet agent that remained unresolved from 1951 until his own defection to the Soviet Union in 1963, which appeared to resolve those doubts once and for all.

37. See the observations attributed to the Soviet prosecutor, Krylenko, cited in Corson and Crowley, op. cit., supra note 5, page 74. While such exemplary handling may have a political purpose, it does nothing to resolve the doubts and is as discriminating a method of waste disposal as throwing the baby out with the bathwater.

38. The trap set for the United States in the matter of the true nature of Gary Powers' U2 mission depended upon the fact that the Soviet Union had taken Powers alive and concealed the fact over the crucial hours from the Eisenhower administration. From a spy-trapping management perspective, this is a case worth close study. A good starting point is

Ike's Spies, Stephen E. Ambrose, New York: Doubleday, 1981.

39. The task of the spy-catcher in the procurement of information on the point for evaluation is really very little different from that of the spy recruiter. With respect to the United Nations, we are told, "Since it had its own people in the personnel office of the Department of Administrative Affairs, the KGB could review the files of those seeking a UN job or a promotion. They were looking for exploitable weakness." *Breaking with Moscow,* Arkady N. Shevchenko, New York: Alfred A. Knopf, 1985, page 247. Shevchenko speaks with firsthand knowledge on these matters.

40. For an instructive, journalistic account by one well versed in matters of espionage, see "The Spy Who Got Away," David Wise, *The New York Times Magazine,* 2 November 1986, passim.

41. Farago recounts an interesting example involving the British double agent Johnny/Snow, who operated under the control of the XX system. His German handler had some doubts as to whether or not his agent understood German, something he claimed not to be able to do. In Snow's presence, he told his secretary in German, "Watch out! I'm going to turn over this lamp here so that it'll fall right smack on the little fellow." He was apparently convinced that his agent did not understand the German language by what followed. Farago, op. cit., supra note 2, page 154.

42. An amusing, apocryphal story circulating in Washington had it that the United States, disturbed at the quality of its HUMINT with respect to the Soviet Union, spent many years and a great deal of money training a specially selected agent for a penetration. Trained to meet every imaginable contingency, he was infiltrated across the Finnish border. Feeling in need of a drink and eager to try his cover, he entered a bar and asked for a vodka. The barman looked at him quizzically and enquired, "40 proof or 80 proof?" His training had not encompassed this small item, and he was cast on his own resources. Not wishing to become inebriated so early in his mission, he requested the lower-proof vodka and while he was drinking it, the barman observed casually, "You aren't Russian, are you?" Thoroughly alarmed and wondering how his cover may have been penetrated, he mumbled a reply, drank up, and sped out into the night. His

trained mind led him to conclude that his initial response to the barman had been incorrect and, anxious to prove his theory, he confidently entered another bar and requested a vodka. Once more he was asked, "40 proof or 80 proof?" This time, without hesitation, he opted for the latter. As he was drinking, he observed the barman looking at him strangely. Finally, the barman said, "You're not Russian, are you?" The blow was so traumatic that the agent, who saw his years of effort going for naught, replied, "All right, I'm not Russian, but how did you know?" "Because we don't get too many blacks in here," answered the bartender.

43. The same observations apply to those who profess a familiarity with computer languages, although these, of course, are not spoken languages.

44. For Maclean's abuse of a top-security classification pass and the ways in which it was procured as well as employed, see *The Philby Conspiracy*, Bruce Page, David Leitch, and Phillip Knightley, New York: Doubleday, 1968, pages 190–191.

45. This was one of the traps used in the Coplon case. See Lamphere, op. cit., supra note 24, page 105.

46. Sura 66:1.

47. "Now, there is an old adage in the FBI to the effect that there has never been an espionage case in which sex did not play a part." Lamphere, op. cit., supra note 24, page 103.

"Sex has been used as a lure, persuader, and bargaining point by espionage agents for hundreds of years and things haven't changed." *The Bureau*, William C. Sullivan with Bill Brown, New York: W. W. Norton, 1979, page 173.

48. "During the week, however, Sissy's mama used the vaginal wrench to slowly, gently turn her husband's objections down to a mere trickle. Mabel's plumber, with his full set of tools, could not have done better." *Even Cowgirls Get the Blues*, Tom Robbins, New York: Bantam, 1980, page 26.

49. The recruitment of Shevchenko, as he recounts it, is an interesting parallel. There came a point when, in his own words, "I realized I was trapped." Op. cit., supra note 39, page 22.

50. Provocation is a commonly used adjunct, especially in totalitarian countries or those in which the Rule of Law is observed largely in the breach. The spy is tricked into revealing himself or his purposes. Something of this seems to have been present in the Sam Hall case in Nicaragua in 1986. This is certainly what was alleged in the Daniloff case.

51. See *The Double Cross System in the War of 1939–1945*, J. C. Masterman, New Haven, CT: Yale University Press, 1972. See, also, *The Cat with Two Faces*, Gordon Young, New York: Coward and McCann, 1957.

52. Modern espionage systems have effective damage control mechanisms designed to limit the harm done by leakage of information at all levels, but the problem always lies in the time it takes to operate them effectively.

53. On the Soviet system and its beginnings, see Corson and Crowley, op. cit., supra note 5, pages 42–44.

54. The United States has many such controls, but their implementation is weak and, for the most part, ineffective for counterespionage purposes.

55. Op. cit., supra note 39, pages 30–31.

56. In the United Kingdom, the Prime case revealed a shocking laxity in this regard. "At both establishments all entrances were manned by a security officer at all times. But searches, regular or random, were not made of GCHQ personnel, their bags, briefcases, or automobiles." Corson and Crowley, op. cit., supra note 5, page 365. Prime removed considerable quantities of highly secret material from GCHQ during his service there, which he passed to the Soviet Union.

57. Perhaps the most useful and percipient part of Corson and Crowley's considerable work is their observations on this point at pages 364–365, op. cit., supra note 5.

58. The late Earl of Stockton's urbane rejoinder is recalled here: "I don't expect the gamekeeper to come and tell me every time he kills a fox." Page, Leitch, and Knightley, op. cit., supra note 44, page 273. Such cavalier delegation is fine, but it does open the door and more to the Mellors.

59. "Major 'Sammy' Sansom, the incumbent of this post (British Embassy security officer, Cairo), remarked in the course of the investigations for this book, 'I was the most hated man in the Embassy.' Sansom, a blunt, bull-like man who rose from the ranks, said this with evident satisfaction. He believed that a security chief doing the job properly must inevitably be an unpopular figure, a questionable thesis, and accordingly he was exceedingly tough with any secretaries who were having affairs with local gigolos. He had succeeded in having several sent home for comparatively minor misbehavior, which nonetheless prejudiced Embassy security and he now wasted no time in reporting Maclean." Page, Leitch,

and Knightley, op. cit., supra note 44, pages 209–210. Security professionals will read the above with a peculiarly sensitive ear.

60. In Corson and Crowley's picturesque phrase, "If there are wounded in the herd, the Soviet predators will find them." Op. cit., supra note 5, page 365.

61. See Cookridge's interesting "means test" on Philby, op. cit., supra note 29, page 154. For those who might like some practical assistance with these matters, see *The Seventh Basic Investigative Technique*, Richard A. Nossen, Washington, D.C.: U.S. Government Printing Office, 1975.

62. "We were looking for people in special positions who were debt-ridden." Moravec, op. cit., supra note 3, page 36.

63. Such, it is suggested, as was exhibited by Klaus Fuchs. For a contemporary who was clearly not deceived, see *The New Meaning of Treason*, Rebecca West, New York: Viking Press, 1964, pages 273–274.

64. See Cookridge, op. cit., supra note 39, pages 167–175.

65. "You must work systematically at information gathering." *Salary Strategies*, Marilyn Moats Kennedy, New York: Rawson, Weir, 1982, page 131.

66. "International political repercussions were feared if we arrested and tried a Soviet national during wartime when Russia was our ally—though I've never understood to this day what we had to fear from exposing a spy." Lamphere, op. cit., supra note 24, page 23.

67. ". . . it is not necessary for me to disturb an animal by following it around. After a period of patient observation I know what it is likely to be doing and where it is to be found at any given time." *Watcher in the Shadows*, Geoffrey Household, Boston: Little, Brown, 1960, page 14.

5

MOLES AND OTHER SUBTERRANEAN CREATURES

One last confession: the title may be misleading. However descriptive of a penetration agent it may be, the word mole *was not in the intelligence lexicon in my day. John le Carré found it—Marx had used it, but in a political sense—and popularized it. Mole is, however, so apt an expression that, for all I know, it may now be a part of the professional vocabulary.*

William Hood[1]

An agent of penetration and subversion; orig. espionage, since late 1940s.

Eric Partridge[2]

Mole: An agent who has penetrated the enemy intelligence or military service. The term probably originated with spy-novel writers and was picked up by the real-life spooks.

Don Ethan Miller[3]

For KGB officials, a possible solution to this problem might be found in examining the feasibility of training and equipping an agent who, if successful, could not only gain important access but also have the background to do something about improving it. It's a very old idea, probably predating John Thurloe's first use of the term mole *in the mid-17th century.*

William R. Corson and Robert T. Crowley[4]

A mole is . . . a genuine KGB term for somebody who

*burrows into the fabric of a bourgeois society and
undermines it from within.*

John Le Carré[5]

Spying, like politics, is the art of the possible. The professional spy spends a great part of his working hours contemplating, in honor of the well-known commercial, the art of
mastering the possibilities. The really successful spy has a
greatly extended notion of the possible. While it would be
going too far to aver that, for some, all things are possible,
history furnishes us with sufficient examples testifying to the
truly amazing ambitions of some of the more audacious. But
these ambitions are always strongly tempered with a sense of
the practical.

The spy and the spy master know well the harsh realities of
their profession. They understand their place in the overall
scheme of things. They are suffered because they produce,
and their product—this treasure, almost—is often enough not
susceptible to being acquired by any other means.[6] Hence
their peculiar usefulness.

Despite the commonplace and mundane character of much
espionage, spying is at its best when it is undertaken sparingly and with the greatest discrimination. Why go to the
trouble of mounting a costly, clandestine, and possibly illegal
operation when the information you are seeking can be obtained in the ordinary course of business from a public library
or from some government agency authorized to supply it?
Spies are very necessary, but are undeniably used many
times quite unnecessarily—if not counter-productively. Spying
is certainly debased by some who, by this means, seek control to assure themselves that they "know what is going on"
and that they are keeping a steady finger on the pulse of the
body politic. Spying then becomes an indulgence in neurosis.
The line between regular inquiry and espionage (as some
journalists have found to their cost) is a very fine one and may
indeed be difficult to draw without careful investigation of the
facts in a particular case. Many times, much mystery is made
out of perfectly straightforward inquiry.

It is probably true, too, that there is much immature
"playing at spies" that tends to confuse the picture and con-
fute the inquirer. There are certainly enthusiastic amateurs,

often of a Walter Mitty bent, who muddy these waters, but there are also, unfortunately, professionals who, with perhaps more money than a real sense of the game and how it should be played, are inclined to throw spies at every problem situation where it seems that knowledge is being withheld from them or their masters. Spying becomes promiscuous.

Running spies can be very addictive; it is not always very productive in terms of real intelligence. In some ways, it is a little like trying for the grand prize in a lottery. You may spend a fortune and a lifetime only to be left in the end with useless ticket stubs and a vague, dissatisfied feeling that while the playing was good and in some way gratifying, there really ought to be more to the matter than the end result would allow. Yet, there are winners, and winning seems to justify the game, however slight the logic or the moment at which the grand prize might fall. The prize is the spur, and even the most hardheaded of spies and spy masters must ever dream that it might one day be theirs, the one great, awe-inspiring coup that will make it all worthwhile. For such a coup *can* be pulled off, and the exploits of a single spy have, on even the most sober of assessments, changed the course of history. This then is the spy's dream—the rationale for the banal, the risks, even sometimes, the absurdity. For this is no quest for the pot of gold at the rainbow's end. The prizes *are* there, well guarded in most cases, but attainable for those who dare and know their business. You cannot win the lottery if you do not play.

The great prizes are tightly held. None could pretend that they are given away cheaply. The secrets the spy would pry loose are often shrouded in multiple layers of security. They will mostly be confided to very few. In the most crucial of cases, they will not be committed to permanent form but will be carried in the heads of those who have conjured them into being and hold them ready for use. Physical security measures are invariably stringent. There may be complicated procedures for gaining access to secret materials which are reduced to writing or some other permanent form which involves identification, authorizations, and measures constituting an assurance against their being copied and carried away. Casual theft and amateur marketing are possible, but there is no career in this. Spying—spiriting away these secrets and conveying them to others whose need for them is so urgent within their own scheme of things—calls for more than mere opportunity and opportunism. It calls for that rare artistry that can carve out the opportunity and turn it to proper use.

A handy truism may be appropriately interjected here: it is never an easy matter to acquire intelligence worthy of acquisition by resorting to spying, as it extends the imagination and resources that must be devoted to its collection. The essence of the problem may, however, be simply stated: it involves getting close enough to what is desired to be able to make a successful grab for it, whether it be an intangible (such as influence or information) or something of a strictly material nature.

Close, in this context, is a relative matter. Some things can now be "grabbed" from extraordinary distances; information transmitted by satellite can be effectively intercepted in outer space from properly equipped stations operating on earth.[7] Telespionage carried out by accessing computers at a distance has become frighteningly commonplace and a popular pastime for curious and curiously talented adolescents. Surveillance of the earth's surface from the limits of outer space can produce high-resolution photographs that in some circumstances could hardly be bettered were they taken directly at short range by a human agent; indeed, few humans could attain the perspectives necessary for such acquisitions.[8] There remain those few crucial items that can be secured only by a human agent in close enough proximity to what is to be taken so as to be able to acquire it when the "right" opportunity arises. In the physical sense, proximity is the key to the matter in these cases—getting close enough to be able to do whatever may be required. There are operations where nothing else will suffice to get the job done. The artistry lies in the positioning.

There is no substitute in these hard cases for being there; the next best thing is being able to be there when the need arises. For in operations of the kind envisaged here, there must be no disharmony that might give the game away. The spy must be a part of the scene. He must already be there on stage waiting to perform. Or he must be introduced from the wings in such a fashion that his entrance causes no surprise and certainly no alarm. In these cases, spying comes down to having an agent in place who can do the job or having the ability to place one. The artistry is often to be seen at its very best in the intricate maneuvering involved in the latter. This is rarely something that can be done in haste. These things take time to organize and accomplish if they are to be done successfully. Some of the great espionage coups are years in the making.[9] They are not conceived and executed on a hurried, improvised basis, but are part of a comprehensive, long-term strategy. These are the examples that are of particular concern to us in the present chapter.

Someone will have invested substantial time, effort, and money on spies of this order. It is unlikely that they will be caught without a commensurate expenditure on the part of the counterespionage specialist. That effort must begin with a thorough study of the species and its employment. A great diversity of types and subtypes is to be found within the categories we are considering here, but whatever their particular description and variations upon the major theme, they have this in common: to fulfill their purpose, they must reside deep within the organism whose secrets they would acquire and whose fabric they would undermine or unravel. It is that depth which gives them their special character, peculiar power, and dangerousness. This is the quality that makes them so very difficult to recognize for what they are and to eradicate. Their strength and protection lie not in their invisibility, but in the unwillingness or inability of those around them, who have accepted them, to see them for what they really are. These cunning creatures have not only to be located and trapped. They also have to be unmasked and revealed demonstrably as spies, betrayers of the trust reposed in them, before an audience predisposed to give them (often against all reason) the benefit of any remaining doubt.

While it may have a ring of triteness about it, it is necessary to emphasize that the kind of spy with whom we are concerned here cannot do his work until he is situated in the right place, namely where the job is to be done. However highly trained or motivated, his exceptional qualities go for nought if he cannot approach his target. The spy on the wrong side of the looking glass accomplishes nothing. We are not concerned here with a review of the manifold ways in which this placement of the spy might be accomplished; that subject is large enough for a book of its own. Nevertheless, it is necessary to consider the matter here in broad outline for it is most material to an adequate understanding of the present topic.

Basically, there are three distinct ways in which the task can be accomplished. The *first task* involves what amounts to a kind of conversion. One who is already at the heart of things, legitimately in place, volunteers or is persuaded to do the job.[10] In effect, one of the insiders goes over to the enemy. It is useful to regard such agents as defectors in place. In their hearts and minds they have abandoned their former allegiances and are serving the interests of others essentially antagonistic to them. There are most obvious advantages in this. No maneuvering into position is needed; such individuals are already in place to do whatever may be required of them. Moreover, the changes they have undergone are internal; if they have been appropriately cautious, nothing will have changed or be seen to have changed. They are at the center of things (and will remain so) by right of what they are assumed to be. Whatever their subsequent transformation, they attained their place and position licitly, and the only pretense required of them is that they be seen to retain unreservedly their former loyalties. Recruiting and servicing such agents may be far from easy. Generally speaking, though, they will need comparatively little instruction concerning what is required of them to get the job done, for that job approximates a perversion of that with which they are already familiar. As spies, they already know the job's potential and how they might exploit it.[11] Provided their consciences can bear the new burden they have assumed, they have mainly to go on doing what they have always done. If they are volunteers, they will have a very good idea of how to go about serving the interests of their new masters. Thus, the play goes on with no apparent change in the cast. Provided the actor can square what he is doing with his conscience and exercise the appropriate degree of caution called for by his changed status, nothing will be obviously amiss. Such agents in place are common enough at all levels. They are the meat and potatoes of every clandestine intelligence organization, a staple and much appreciated diet. They only approach the gourmet level when they are very high in the hierarchy or have special responsibilities allowing them exceptional opportunities to do what is required.[12]

No special name seems to have been coined for these

agents in place. If a characterization were needed, the good, old-fashioned "traitor" would suffice for most. The point is of some importance, however, in relation to what will be later discussed. There is more than a matter of nomenclature in all this. It goes, in many ways, to the heart of the disinclination of those affected by this kind of spy's activities to admit of them. We have come to accept burglary—the intrusion into our world of the felonious stranger—as one of the nastier incidents of social life. Larceny by a loved one, friend, or trusted servant is harder to take. There is a reluctance to call a spade a spade due to the deep-seated unwillingness to admit to treachery in our own ranks, even when the evidence points irrefutably to it. We do not like to believe that one of our own can go bad in this way. We prefer, therefore, to look for external causes for the mischief and to attribute, if we can, what has occurred to those causes. Nor do we like to boast of our own capacity to induce treachery in the organization of others, for we recognize, quite rightly, that if this lies within our powers, then we, too, can be victimized in similar fashion. This kind of calculated denial is a great hindrance to the spy-catcher and appropriate allowance must be made for it.

By way of contrast, the *second manner* of accomplishing the task is an alien undertaking from start to finish. It is harder in most cases to organize and execute, but at least we all know where we stand and what is involved. For it is a foreign organism that is insinuated into the enemy's heartland to do the dirty work. Someone has to be maneuvered into position from the outside—outside the magic circle, that is— and situated where he can do what is required of him. He may come from afar or close at hand. Foreign, in the present context, does not necessarily refer to race or nationality but, rather, to an estrangement of a nonpathological order from one's fellows that sets one apart in the matter of interests and allegiances. Clearly, the spy is not going to be allowed into the inner sanctum under his true colors, in the guise of a foreigner, one working for the opposition at that.

As in the first instance, there is a deception involved here but, obviously, one of greater artificiality. Something is manufactured to resemble that which it is not, namely a genuine, loyal person whose position, trust, and responsibilities have been earned in virtue of, as it turns out, wholly erroneous assumptions. All spies pretend to be what they are not, but the pretense in the two classes we have distinguished here proceeds from different standpoints, and the matter is extremely important from an operational and attitudinal aspect. The spy who has turned and continues to work from within has a genuine exterior and a false heart and mind. Those we are now considering are false through and through, but they are supplied with a carefully fabricated exterior that can pass muster for the real thing. Having manufactured a suitable article, the next phase of the operation requires that it be maneuvered into position. Whatever this may involve, the essence of the operation is *penetration;* this kind of spy penetrates the organism within which it is intended he shall function.[13] He must get to where he is going, to where he can be effective and do the job required of him, by boring his way through the flesh of the body into which he has been introduced. Whether this takes a very long while or is accomplished quite quickly, it is an operational step that cannot be eliminated.

Obviously, the selection of such a penetration agent calls for some accurate matching of qualities and potential. If the penetration agent is to be successful in accomplishing his mission, he must be able to fit, in a rather special way, into the organism into which he has been introduced. He must be accepted. He must pass for the genuine article. He must not deteriorate along the route so that he is passed over or shunted into some backwater. His suitability for his eventual destination must be there from the start and manifested at appropriate moments. The task is made less difficult by starting with the right material. It is easier to lay siege to some citadels than to others. Those that are stoutly guarded hardly admit of a conventional frontal assault. If they are to yield up their secrets, considerable sapping and mining will be required. The route of the penetration agent will mostly be long and arduous. He may have to travel a very long road before he reaches the point where he might become effective as a spy. This calls for stamina and fortitude. He can rarely pause to smell the roses along the way. Aside from sheer distance, he will clearly have many obstacles to overcome. As a counterfeit trying to pass for the real thing, he must earn acceptance. He will have to play himself into his part. When he is finally accepted, his treachery—if he is discovered—is therefore felt as keenly as that of any true insider who has changed sides.[14]

It would be wrong, however, to regard such agents as traitors, for although they undoubtedly misled us as to where their true allegiances lay, they were in truth never ours. They were foisted on us from without, and we mistakenly nursed them to our bosoms. If the right selection of material has been made, our anger may well be of no lesser order, for such individuals seem to be of our own, our class, our team, our tribe. But while there has certainly been a massive deceit which resulted in dangerously misplaced confidence, there is no real betrayal. We have been tricked in classic fashion, but we might console ourselves with the thought that they set out to trick us from the start. They were never on our side, and our assumptions about the matter were plain wrong. They were the enemy and, like the Trojan horse, we let them within the gates. We can hardly criticize their success in effecting the penetration by complaining that it was achieved by less than honorable means.

There are many interesting philosophical excursions on which we might embark here, but we must resist them. The point that we now need to make in anticipation of the discussion to come, is that while *all moles are penetration agents, not all penetration agents are moles*. Clearly, then, the term mole can only be properly applied to a select group in this second category of spies we have been considering here. It is clearly inapplicable where nothing in the nature of a penetration of the sort we have just been considering is involved, and it is straining the spirit as well as the more literal meaning of the term to apply it outside these limits.

We shall return to the topic of the mole shortly, but we must first deal with the *third way* of accomplishing the goal of approximating the spy to his objective. Although quite distinct in form, technique, and management, both of the categories already dealt with involve something in the nature of a transformation. Appearance substitutes for reality. The first two categories both rely on an illusion based upon deceit. They have in common, too, the fact that those who control the spy and his work as an agent have no control over the environment into which he is inserted and in which he must work for them. This environment, often hostile, is a tangible barrier between the spy and those for whom he works. The

difficulties presented by this fact have to be faced and overcome by making operational use of the distinctive advantages
described. For both categories, the effort is substantially
impacted by this factor. No less of a transformation is observable in the third example, which is strikingly similar in many
ways (in its purpose and operational aspects) to the penetration mode.

This third mode may, in all its many variations, be usefully
seen as a kind of *passive penetration*. In one variant, some
sort of positive insertion is certainly necessary, but this characteristically lacks the aggressiveness we associate with a
more typical penetration operation. The introduction or, in
some cases, the leaving behind of the spy, is altogether more
subtle and unthreatening and is designed to achieve the
highest degree of naturalness; the agent is slowly submerged
and even the telltale bubbles soon disappear from the surface. In other cases, although the spy may be gently pro-
pelled toward his target, the launch is less like that of a
rocket than the release of a balloon on a favorable current,
and by night at that. Perhaps the extreme variant shows this
method at its best and best defined, for the agent is readied
for his task by planting him deeply in soil that is to be
abandoned or given up to the enemy. In this case, the
operation resembles nothing so much as the laying of a mine
field where these deadly agents are later activated from a
distance by those who have sown them. These, then, are the
true sleeper agents surreptitiously placed in position in innocent form, only to be later transformed at the behest of their
masters to do their assigned tasks as spies.[15]

Here, too, we see the conversion of one thing to another,
the deception, and the artifice. The sleeper is a very long-
term investment, which must remain largely unattended and
even ignored. He is an alien embryo, almost, at the time of
his insertion into the element in which he will subsequently
develop and work. He will mature and grow into his part, all
the while taking on the character and familiarity of his surroundings. He will be naturally absorbed into the host organism rather than having to burrow his way through it. The
living, breathing human being is, of course, wide awake as he
goes about his business of making his way in the society of
which he has become a part. It is the idea of the spy buried
within that person that lies dormant, awaiting the call to

action. The human aspects that are recognized are subordinate to the artificial that constitute yet another device for hiding the spy and his true purposes.

Another analogy suggests itself: that of the thief who enters a department store as a regular customer during business hours and then secretes himself on the premises until the hours of darkness enable him to consummate his felonious mission. The night may indeed be long for the sleeper, but there comes a moment when the work for which he was prepared has to be done. He must then awake and seize his opportunity. It remains for the spy-catcher to ensure that the sleeper does not undergo a second transformation by morning's light that will enable him to slip out the front door as an innocent customer with his loot. The sleeper is a deadly device planted unobtrusively in the enemy's midst which can be activated when the time is considered auspicious.

Inherent in the concept is the idea of delay and metamorphosis, the awakening after long slumber to become something else. The creature is no mere programmed automaton, but a live, sentient human being who has had to suppress much in the interests of satisfactory integration and equip himself for the tasks ahead. It takes very special qualities to be able to maintain the posture necessary to complete the job. Somnolence can be dangerously corrosive of purpose. However well prepared he may be, the sleeper, once awakened to an altered world of which he never dreamed in the course of his slumbers, suffers a rude shock to the system. For things *are* changed by the passage of time.[16] For some, it may be hard to resist the impulse to go on sleeping, to ignore the call to action, and to stay as a chrysalis rather than hatch as a butterfly. The metamorphosis to spy is not inevitable; the conditions for incubation must be right. The sleeper needs a strong sense of identity and a burning zeal, however low for safety's sake the flame may be set, that will sustain his purpose through the long night of hibernation. From an espionage point of view, he lives in a cocoon of inactivity that is his present and future security.

Unlike the mole, properly speaking, whose days even at their dullest must be spent in purposeful activity in aid of reaching an assigned goal, the sleeper must endure long periods of inaction of the most enervating kind that are preparation for his eventual task. In effect he becomes by doing nothing. When he is finally activated as a spy, his cover should be as perfect as that of the home-grown article, the agent in place discussed in our first category. Yet, like the mole, he too was counterfeit from the start. His long sojourn in our midst has made him "one of us," and our anger at his betrayal, however misplaced, is no less real than if he had been the genuine thing. It is well to remind ourselves that the sleeper, like the mole, was against us from the start. We can only expect to recognize his danger when we are able to see him begin to work against us.

It is easy to see how the various strong points of similarity among the three types of agents can serve to confuse the incautious or the untutored eye. To the undiscriminating, these three categories certainly appear sufficiently alike to be lumped together under one umbrella heading and, consequently, to be given a single, easily remembered name. Indeed, making distinctions in this regard seems to be the exception rather than the rule. For the writer of fiction, the exercise is burdensome and the antithesis of entertaining. Even where one might expect to encounter the employment of some discrimination, it is strikingly absent.[17] Most of these omnibus usages seem to be of comparatively recent vintage, perhaps reflecting a growing contemporary interest in spies and spying. Thus, we are informed that a mole is: "A secret intelligence agent who builds a legitimate cover over a period of years by not engaging in spying activities until he is tapped for an important mission."[18] A careful analysis of this passage indicates that all three categories outlined above could be subsumed within it without the need for procrustean exercises of any kind. Were the writing not of a definitional character, this attempt at harmony might not be altogether objectionable but, as it is, the endeavor must be protested. For it does indeed purport to define but one of our three categories and, moreover, a certain variant of that to which a very specific name (mole) has come to be assigned. It is therefore frankly misleading, for not only does it lump together certain things so as to offer an unfortunately skewed presentation, but it loses in the process the essential "moleness" of what it is supposed to be defining.

A comparison of this definition with what we have outlined above concerning the mole makes clear what essential, definitive elements are absent if what is written is to apply to but one class of agents and not to another. What is somewhat curious is that the principal source cited for this composition is a slightly extended version of the Le Carré statement cited in our headnote to the present chapter. Whatever objections may be taken to a part of that statement, it clearly features *the burrowing aspect* of the undertaking that is the most prominent characteristic of the mole's endeavors. The unfortunate result of this lack of precision in usage is that the term mole has now come to be applied by many writers as a catch-all description for all agents in place and especially those who by good fortune or otherwise have lain undiscovered over a lengthy period of time..

Under such conditions, "mole" is in danger of losing its most useful singularity; almost any spy in the enemy's midst might, then, not improperly be called a mole. Indeed, to carry matters to their extremes, mole might then become no more nor less than a colloquialism for spy. That this represents a real and present danger can be seen from the acute, socially significant observations of one of our British correspondents: ". . . at that time, the early 1980s, we could hardly open a newspaper or magazine over here without stumbling over the term. It was applied ad nauseam to almost any informant giving news from inside any organization or establishment. The word is of course still around, but the fashion is fading slightly."[19] Perhaps the all-time record for its use (and with not too much discrimination at that) should go to Christopher Andrew for a review entitled "Molehunt," published in the *London Review of Books*, 22 January 1987.[20] It is, of course, a very evocative word and one which rolls nicely off the tongue—or pen—in this connection. But this excessive application carries with it the danger that the term will lose any very useful and exact meaning. Its very popularity with writers, especially fiction writers, has tended to strain it in unacceptable ways, causing a blurring and inexactitude that have in turn affected professional usage. This would perhaps be unimportant—after all, the same thing happens so often in all departments of language—were it not such a useful term in its more exact sense. We voice, then, more than mere academic concern at what we have observed of late in this regard.

It was not our original intention to write an extended essay on the meaning and origins of the term mole. As our research deepened and focused more narrowly, however, the need for this became strikingly apparent. In the first place, the growing popularity and uncritical acceptance of the term alarmed us, for this overuse and abuse suggested that the mole, in its espionage sense, might be on its way to becoming an endangered species.[21] We are not prompted by sentimentality in this matter, but it did seem to us that the preservation of this useful term required some careful investigation of its original and contemporary meanings and an effort at reconciling, purifying, or reclaiming them. As a necessary first step, it seemed desirable to establish, if possible, how it gained admission to our professional lexicon and whether it passed from there into common parlance or vice versa.[22]

Our initial inquiries established a number of fundamental points with a fair degree of certainty in the sense that no contrary opinions appear to be reliably entertained on the matter. It seems that the term mole, as applied in the espionage context, is truly a native English one and does not derive by way of adoption, translation, or corruption from some other language.[23] Even the idea itself has a strangely foreign ring about it for many whose native language is not English.[24] Furthermore, the term is not of American coinage and certainly did not originate within the United States intelligence community. Indeed, it did not acquire a place in the professional vocabulary of that community until comparatively recently, most probably, it would seem, as a consequence of its having become so popular with writers of all kinds.

Whether life imitated art or the reverse is a much-debated question in this connection. It may be shortly disposed of here. The term did not become common currency among writers of spy fiction before the 1970s, and it was mainly during the latter half of that decade that it achieved anything like the popularity and recognition it now enjoys. Much of the fiction was clearly inspired by the Burgess, Maclean, and Philby spying revelations of the 1950s and 1960s, revelations which had generated an enormous amount of literature in their day on both sides of the Atlantic. The factual treatments of these cases, mainly from the late 1960s, do not, however, seem to have spawned the use of the word mole. It is significant that novelist John Le Carré (David Cornwell), whose name is so often associated with the term mole and its popularization, did not use it in his introduction to *The Philby*

Conspiracy published in 1968. Nor is it used by that well-versed writer on spies and spying, E. H. Cookridge (Edward Spiro), whose book, *The Third Man,* was published in the same year.

It is as well to make the point here that there were some very literary and scholarly figures writing about these absorbing matters, many of whom had been active intelligence officers in some capacity or another during the 1940s.[25] The conflict with the Axis powers gave rise to a lot of picturesque terminology,[26] some of which remains actively in use among us to this day, even more of which has now passed into that limbo where such linguistic inventions end up after they have served their purpose. It is safe to say that the word mole, in the sense we are exploring, did not arise from the life-and-death struggle with Nazi Germany and its cohorts in which the Allied intelligence services were engaged until 1945. The nature of that struggle really precluded the parturition of such a notion; it simply was not that kind of a war.[27]

Mole is a term that had its birth or, more properly speaking, its discovery, in the more frigid years of the Cold War. It takes on its meaning, coloration, and significance from that struggle although it can have the widest range of applications. Dictionary entries begin quite late, dating in England and Australia,[28] for example, from the early 1980s. The cited sources for these entries help little in the quest for origins or precision of meaning. The editors of *The Oxford English Dictionary* were kind enough to share with us the earliest reference to the term they had encountered in print (a nonfiction work published in 1960).[29] The reference,[30] which is to an attempted Russian emigre's penetration of the Soviet services in the mid-1930s is, however, misleading as an authority for the origins of the espionage usage of the word; it does not support the general use of the term as a penetration agent but, rather, refers to a specific operation in which the agent in question was recruited under the alias *"The Mole."* Clearly, he could as easily have been recruited as "The Weasel," "The Snake," or any other name evoking the mood of the operation or catching the fancy. What does emerge from a reading of the work in question is that the term under inquiry here was not part of the espionage parlance of the day.

We were thus left with the problem of discovering how and by whom this recent fashion was started. This has proven to be a fascinating, if somewhat inconclusive, quest. We came across a number of hints, distressingly vague, that the term in the sense we seek to establish might have been much older than we had originally suspected and that its recent popularity represented somewhat of a rebirth or rediscovery under some circumstances that, while unclear, suggested a scholarly recognition of its appropriateness to modern conditions. This was, after all, the age when scholars had begun to flood the intelligence services of the West. While a number of lines of inquiry suggested themselves consequent upon this notion, it seemed somewhat strange, if this were indeed the case, that the term in this usage was so singularly absent from the standard works of reference or even those arcane repositories where such things are often prone to find lodgment.

Even if the term had been in use in precisely the sense we are discussing since the late Middle Ages,[31] it is obvious that it had passed unnoticed into a very long period of disuse before reentering our world with a flourish in recent times. It is certainly curious that this had not been remarked upon by any of the remarkably scholarly minds addressing themselves to the matter in the wake of Burgess, Maclean, et al. It is especially interesting that a number of very definite pronouncements have been made concerning origin without citing any authority at all or citing one so vague that the diligent researcher would have to scour the arid deserts of the literary scene in the hope of finding the one odd footprint which might lead him in the right direction.

There is something most unfortunate about this. If such pronouncements are made with sufficient confidence by those upon whom a certain authority has been conferred in these matters, there is a real danger that they might be uncritically followed and accepted unchallenged by later generations whose resources for investigating the puzzle might be somewhat slighter than those of contemporary investigators. As has been well said, "The fact that an error had been accepted by Aristotle did not make it any less an error."[32]

Does all this matter, save in the interests of a rather prissy scholarship and a somewhat persnickety desire to set the world to rights in some small and obscure detail? We believe it does, for the keen observer of these things will immediately realize that there is something incongruous and inappropriate about the choice of the term mole to describe this kind of penetration agent that invites the attention and suggests something about the way it crept and crept back into the language. We shall have to deal with this at some length in its turn. There is another reason that impels us to look closely and exactly at the matter. What is coming to be called "Spookspeak,"[33] the jargon of the intelligence community, is starting to be recognized as an interesting, vibrant, and developing branch of contemporary neology. Some small collections and selections have already been published; others, attended by more rigorous scholarship, will almost certainly follow. Mole has already found its niche and is destined to make something of a permanent home for itself in any intelligence lexicon of our age and language.[34] These are the works to which those interested in these matters will refer to for guidance in the next decade or so.

We feel an obligation, therefore, not to mislead them or to put our own imprimatur along with others on unsettled business. What gives rise to the greatest concern is the extent to which quite serious errors are already being perpetuated through a kind of careless cross-pollination of half-understood and poorly formulated ideas. It is clearly time for a fresh start regarding the assembled materials, and we have accordingly felt it incumbent upon us to make sure that use began from a firm and certain base. To this end, it has been necessary to go back to take another look at certain original sources used to support some of the interpretations with which we disagreed. We would insist that we do not regard this as a diversion from our main purpose in this chapter but, rather, as a necessary shoring up of the foundations. We are sure the mole, that assiduous burrower, would appreciate the allusion.

From the earliest times, humans have invested animals with anthromorphic qualities.[35] The lion is far from being the largest, fiercest, or most dangerous of animals, but he is regarded in lore and literature as the king of the beasts. Attempts by other animals to supplant him are the object of human ridicule. There is something regal in the bearing and comportment of *panthera Leo* that might be thought to justify such a characterization, although in a literal sense, the lion rules over but a tiny corner of the animal kingdom if he rules at all. The owl is thought by many to be endowed with special wisdom and was consequently adopted by the ancient Greeks as a symbol of Pallas Athene. There is something in the owl's solemn appearance and bearing to suggest these qualities,[36] although none but the fanciful or the superstitious would really ascribe them to a mere bird. On a more scientific level, the field observations of naturalists and others do suggest that certain animals evince special qualities in their struggle for survival which make them especially worthy in the eyes of humans and whose characteristics might stimulate emulation by man. Not only is the comparison with human thought and behavior suggested, but in admiration and perhaps by way of sympathetic magic, the name of the animal itself is sometimes appropriated descriptively to that of the human being (for example, Running Bull, Hafez el Assad, or Richard the Lionhearted).

There is an innate, almost universal recognition of the appropriateness of these ascriptions, for there is something that enables people (especially primitive peoples who live close to nature) to recognize how man is related to the animal kingdom and of which he is inescapably a part. Few who are close to the land would regard the fox as a stupid animal, yet there are many legends showing how this cunning predator might be tricked. What is clear is the anthropomorphic image of the fox that shines forth from the folklore. These practices, so deeply ingrained in our social being, are very important in the formation of thought and action. Comb the literature from whence you will; it is impossible to find an image of the mole as an astute, cunning gatherer of intelligence.[37] Indeed, the very reverse of the case is true. The mole is near-blind, inoffensive, and never seen as a sensible, cooperative creature in the political undertakings of others. There are no folktales or legends in which this is remotely suggested.[38]

On the contrary, the mole traditionally tends to be regarded as solitary and inclined to mind its own business. While we talk of people as being "blind as a bat," with increasing scientific knowledge, we have come to recognize the miracle of the bat's "radar," which enables it to perform extraordinary feats of evasion in low light and at high speed. By comparison, the mole's weak sight is not thought to be compensated for by other extraordinarily developed faculties in such a way as to evoke human admiration, though doubtless, on a biological basis, it is perfectly adapted to its environment and has the appropriate qualities in good (even generous) measure to make up for its visual deficiencies.

Moles are innocuous creatures with few natural enemies, largely intent on minding their own business and living at peace in those areas of the world favorable to them. While not as manifestly industrious as ants, they do create minor earthworks—molehills—that have found a reference of their own in literature.[39] Their capacity for burrowing and the seemingly ceaseless toil beneath the surface this entails suggest, unfairly perhaps save to those like greenskeepers directly affected by it, a capacity for mischief, albeit unconscious, that might interfere with human plans and activities.[40] This is about the sum total that can be sensibly deduced about the mole, either from a perusal of the way it has been regarded in the literature, a reflection of human attitudes down the ages, or by way of direct, scientific observation of the creature and its habits. Moreover, there is little mystery about the mole; it has never been held in awe or dread. The point we are making here is that the mole can never have stood for *the spy* in the imagination of anyone familiar with the animal or its habits. With this as our starting point firmly in mind, we must therefore look to see how such an extraordinary transformation can have taken place.

We began our research in the literature of Elizabethan England for a number of reasons. First, we were prompted to try to verify recent suggestions that it was there that the true origins for the word mole in its espionage usage were to be found.[41] Second, the earliest dictionaries of the English language to which we might have had recourse date in their compilation, if not publication, from this age.[42] Third, this was the age of the printing press and, consequently, of a burgeoning diffusion of knowledge of all kinds. And fourth, it was an age in which, it is generally conceded, the modern English secret service had its birth. We must begin here by pointing out two salient facts which ought not to be overlooked. The English of the period (even the gentry) were an earthy lot. They were close to the soil; even the most miserable of town dwellers had a closer link to the land, its ways, and its denizens than their counterparts in later times. The literature is redolent with the flavor of the rural, the pastoral, and all pertaining to it. The England of the day did not harbor exotic, wild animals. Those in a feral state were generally small and well known, and references to them in the literature, even the fanciful, are exact and appropriate. The idea of an Elizabethan writer taking the mole as a representative figure for a spy of any kind is, frankly, ludicrous to anyone familiar with the English countryside, its society, and the notions of the period. The idea of the mole as a burrower, nuisance, and meddler, capable of undermining the neat agricultural undertakings of man is, however, one that could be well understood and appreciated in both a literary and a political context.

The English writers of the Elizabethan and Stuart ages were a sophisticated lot, familiar with the learning of the ancients and many tongues, especially Latin, Greek, and Hebrew. They were also most elegant and stylish in their own writings as well as being colorful and exact in their choice of metaphors. Hence, we were surprised by William Safire's citation (which we must set out here in full) in its context of "spookspeak." Safire writes: "Take 'mole' which professional spies and readers of spy thrillers know means an agent clandestinely placed within another power's intelligence agency. That word, insists former Director of Central Intelligence Richard Helms, was never used by professionals—their term for that dread activity was 'penetration.' But today, as life follows art, CIA men have adopted mole, and intelligence historian Walter Pforzheimer even found a 1622 citation in Francis Bacon's history of King Henry VII: Hee was careful and liberalle to obtaine good intelligence from all parts abroade. . . . He had such Moles perpetually working and casting to undermine him."[43] So struck were we by the syntactic curiosity of this last illusion in relation to the meaning it was put forward to sustain, that we consulted the source from which it is abstracted. Only thus does the meaning of the word mole become properly intelligible, and it is immediately evident that this mutilated citation is no authority whatsoever for the modern usage of mole in the espionage context; Mr. Helms' insistence takes on a newer and more solid light.

Lord Verulam, as he was when he penned this history in the last full year of his life, was a most elegant writer[44] and would have taken great pains to have used technical words in their exact, contemporary sense. A distinguished lawyer, his writings have a breadth and style of marked contrast to those of his arch rival, Sir Edward Coke. His later editors have been at pains to reproduce his text as he intended; where a word was used in a meaning no longer extant, it has been so signified by placing it in square brackets. *Mole* has not been so treated and a reading of the full text makes it quite clear why resorting to such a device was considered unnecessary. We must, accordingly, reproduce that text below:

> "*He was careful and liberal to obtain good intelligence from all parts abroad, wherein he did not only use his interest in the liegers (residents) he, and his pensioners* —which he had both in the Court of Rome, and the other Courts of Christendom—but the industry and vigilance of his own ambassadors in foreign parts. For this purpose, his instructions were ever extreme, curious and articulate, and in them more articles touching inquisition than touching negotiation, requiring likewise from his ambassadors an answer in particular distinct articles, respectively to his questions. As for his secret spials, which he did employ both at home and abroad, by them to discover what practices and conspiracies were against him, surely his case required it; he had such moles perpetually working and casting to undermine him. Neither can it be reprehended; for if spials be lawful against enemies, much more against conspirators and traitors. But indeed to give them credence by oaths and curses**—that cannot be well maintained, for those are too holy vestments for a disguise. Yet surely there was this further good in his employing of these flies and familiars; that as the use of them was cause that many conspiracies were revealed, so the fame and suspicion of them kept, no doubt, many conspiracies from being attempted.*"[45]

**Spies and others, who received pensions from the king in return for supplying information.*

***i.e., to have his spies publicly cursed, in order to reinforce the general opinion that they were his enemies, and so make them more acceptable to those who were plotting against him.*

It is quite plain what is meant by moles in this context, namely those conspirators who would undermine the careful superstructure erected by Henry Tudor and upon which his none-too-secure claim to the English throne rested. That he was enormously preoccupied with matters of security in this regard is evident to any who take the time and trouble to study the matter.[46] His own methods of obtaining intelligence, both overt and covert, are well set out in the passage cited. It is significant that the word *pensioners* as meaning "spies," hidden, secret agents in the jargon of the day, is used. Note, too, the employment of "flies and familiars," a picturesque and perfectly comprehensible figure of speech in this context. Some one hundred and odd years later, Dr. Samuel Johnson was to write in his dictionary that a pension is "an allowance made to anyone without an equivalent; in England it is generally understood to mean pay given to a state hireling for treason to his country." There is no way in which what Lord Verulam wrote can be sensibly construed as describing the mole as an espionage agent, and it would be a disservice to one of the greatest scientific minds of the age to suggest that he had any such figure in mind when constructing this careful and apposite passage of English history. It is equally clear that the term mole was unknown in such usage at that time; even if it were thought necessary to explain "pensioner," it would have been considered doubly so in the case of "mole."

The 1755 dictionary of Samuel Johnson,[47] a standard by which so many later works are judged, contains but four entries for mole, none of which is in any way related to espionage usage. In regard to Dr. Johnson's penchant for adding acerbic comment quite freely, his failure to point up such usage is the strongest evidence that such a meaning of mole as spy or penetration agent (into whatever medium the penetration was to be effected) had never come to his attention. He is content to characterize the *talpa*, in delightfully Harry Whartonish[48] fashion, as "a little beast that works underground." Kersey,[49] whose own dictionary preceded that of Dr. Johnson by some forty-odd years, gives "a little creature that *lives* underground," and Dr. Johnson's acute observation and enthusiasm for exactitude may have led him, not accidentally, to stress the mole's industry as a defining feature.[50]

We would not have proceeded to such lengths were it not for the reinforcement that seemed to be given to this theory of origins by the Corson and Crowley citation given in our headnote above. It was this that we found most disturbing, for such a use by an authority of the order of Thurloe would have unquestionably clinched the matter. By any standards, Secretary Thurloe was a remarkable state servant, and his reputation as a spy master seems to have been well deserved.[51] He was not a prolific writer for publication and was more written about by others in the matter of his espionage work than is evidenced by his own pen. As far as we have been able to discover, unlike his predecessor (and short-time successor),[52] he wrote nothing of his own work by way of explanation or defense in which he might have made use of the word mole in either the sense it was employed by Bacon or in the origins of which we are seeking here. The absence of any reference to the source made our task more difficult,[53] and none of the sources on Thurloe we consulted supported the statement made concerning his use of the word. Accordingly, we had no alternative but to seek it, if it were to be found, in the seven-volume collection of Thurloe papers, which themselves have a curious history.[54] No such reference was found, although these and associated materials in other collections provide a good deal of evidence of the extent and character of Thurloe's work as spy master. Moreover, there is no one among the galaxy of agents he employed to whom the term, in the sense we attribute to it in our age, could have been appropriately applied: Thurloe simply did not use moles. What he did use, most effectively, were agents in place, whom he persuaded or coerced, or who for venal motives or otherwise placed their positions and knowledge at his disposal. Some very scholarly work on Thurloe as spy master has been done, and some of this is most interesting and on the point for our purposes. It is, however, completely devoid of any indication that "mole" was a part of the espionage lexicon of Thurloe's day.[55] If he did use or understand that term, it would undoubtedly have been in the Baconian sense, for Thurloe, like Henry VII, was primarily concerned with the security of the realm and the attempts being made from abroad to undermine it.

There are many contraindications. Of particular interest is the life of John Wildman,[56] one of Thurloe's spies, whose remarkable, colorful career ranged across the entire gamut of the espionage spectrum. The discourse attributed to him on the management of intelligence is replete with operational detail and is written in the professional idiom of the day, identifying the author as one thoroughly familiar with his subject in all its facets.[57] It contains no reference whatsoever to moles although the different kinds of penetration agents are dealt with, perspicaciously, *in extenso*. Colonel Sexby's correspondence with Wildman does, however, contain an interesting animal allusion:[58] ". . . he outlined details of his plans to Wildman and assured him that once money 'which will not only gain the bodies of men but their souls also' were distributed he could be revealed as possessing. 'Jackals in the forest amongst the lions and some cubs who hath seasoned claws and teeth . . . which I warrant will help us beat their own kind out of the den.' "

We are then led to the conclusion that the term mole, meaning a penetration agent,[59] has no Elizabethan or Stuart origins and that any interpretation to the contrary placed upon its employment by Lord Verulam is mistaken. It is clear that an age that readily used such terms as "decoy ducks" for agents provocateurs would have made more than a casual reference to the mole had it entered the espionage lexicon of the day and all the evidence speaks against it having done so.[60] We returned, accordingly, to our original area of investigation, namely, the early days of the Cold War.

While we do not have the benefit of the writings or recollections of those who undertook the crucial Comintern recruitments during the inter-war years, especially those in the British universities, there is no evidence to suggest that they used the word mole in connection with their own work.[61] The use of the word is clearly a posterior literary device of those who have researched, analyzed, and described it in our own times. It is not clear what John Le Carré had in mind when he described mole as a genuine KGB term,[62] but our own inquiries show that this is not the case, at least so far as origins or employment are concerned.[63] It remains to be considered how the term actually came into being, and under what circumstances, for there can be no doubt that its popularity and place in our present-day lexicon are the result of easily traceable literary efforts from about 1974 onward. There is, accordingly, a gap between the late 1940s, say 1945 on, until the early 1970s in which mole, if the term was used at all, was confined to speech rather than writing of the published kind. As this speech cannot very well be that of those who earn their living by the pen, it must have been professional spookspeak. The most careful research has not turned up any professional American intelligence officer serving between the years 1945 and 1960 who claims any familiarity with the term in connection with operations in which he was personally concerned. Such operations against the Soviets were so few and, on the whole, unsuccessful, that the generation of a new word such as mole is highly unlikely. While many successes were registered in a wide variety of efforts elsewhere, their emphasis was generally secondary to the effort against the Soviet Union and, most often, complementary to it in terms of the struggle between the great powers. There is an abiding sentiment, however, among those who have any recall on the matter at all, that mole somehow is derived from a consideration of operations undertaken *against* the Western intelligence services rather than by them; that it is a counterespionage (from our perspective) term rather than an espionage one in this context, hence the illusion that the *term*, as opposed to the operations themselves, emanated from the Soviet Union's own services. A sense of these operations and their dimensions of how long and intensively they had been pursued only began to emerge as their damage became apparent. It was the defection of Burgess and Maclean in 1951 that triggered this latter assessment. On the basis of our own research, we would conjecture that the term mole was not used among members of the British intelligence community before 1951. Certainly we have found no written record of its employment before that date. This still left us with the aggravating problem of discovering, within these reduced parameters, when, how, and by whom the term was introduced into the professional lexicon.

If our assumption that the term came into being and acquired its present meaning(s) in the wake of the revelations concerning the sorry state of affairs affecting the British intelligence and security services at the time indicated, a number of possibilities were in view. On the basis of our experience, we made the perhaps not uncharitable assumption that the working vocabulary of writers in these arcane areas is rarely original but, rather, derived from their own experience, observations, and synthesis of their subject matter. This is especially true of journalists, who do not invent words but, more usually, report them after having learned them from others and been struck by their aptness and utility. Had we found a very early reference to mole in the journalistic accounts of the Burgess/Maclean scandal, we would have suspected their derivation and pursued our suspicions accordingly. The word did not, however, appear in those earliest writings, and it is only much later, after taking up residence in the Soviet Union, that it comes into the accounts.

By then another complicating factor comes into the picture. For the commentators, who so enriched the literature in this matter, were a different breed altogether.[64] Many had firsthand knowledge of the clandestine world in which the traitors had operated. They knew the language, the way of thinking and speaking about these things, what had been done about them, and the direction matters were likely, in consequence, to take. Moreover, many of these persons were scholars who might have been expected to have had recollections of any earlier usage of the word mole and might, themselves, have reintroduced it, prompted by the extraordinary circumstances of their times. There were some obvious candidates in this regard.[65] It seemed reasonable to suppose that these intensive contacts among intellectuals bent on understanding what had happened and their own role in these events might have produced the sort of picturesque language of which mole might be an example. But it seemed to us equally possible that in the closed, confidential damage-assessment sessions that proceeded at different levels of the political and intelligence communities, there could have been one who, blessed with a neat turn of phrase, might have hit upon the term mole to describe not only those who penetrated the British intelligence and security services but were bent on undermining them from within. It seemed quite credible that such a notion, fostered and refined in discussion, could have been taken up by others, entered the vocabulary of the day, and eventually escaped from its confined, hothouse atmosphere to achieve consecration in print.

On the evidence we have examined, if this were the case, the word had quite a lengthy gestation period. Such a conceit is unlikely to have had multiple authorship, although its eventual refinement suggests something of the committee. Our own researches have not so far revealed any claims to authorship, but we entertain a sincere hope that our inquiries and a reading of what we have written here might prompt the retiring (or retired) author to come forward and tell all. We are still left with the vexing problem of precisely what the term was intended by its author(s) to mean at the time it was introduced into our modern spookspeak. As we have indicated, this is no more idle, academic curiosity.

In a vulgar sense, mole has long stood for a penetration agent of sorts, and mole catcher, by extension, has an equally vulgar, if entirely appropriate, meaning if the first significance is accepted.[66] But, clearly, anyone familiar with the innocuous creature who ruins lawns in pursuit of his daily diet would know that it is quite incapable of acquiring intelligence on its own account, much less of passing it on to others. No one would sensibly see a parallel in such penetrations and those of the human agent whose endeavors we have described. Even more to the point, in a representational context, is the patent advertisement of its activities in which the mole engages. It is almost a surface creature; it does not burrow deeply or unobtrusively, but calls attention to itself and its doings in the most obvious way.[67] Can the author of the espionage usage have known so little of the family *Talpidae* as to choose so inappropriate an allusion? Yet it is precisely the inappropriateness that has come to constitute the main ingredients of "mole" as it has now come to be understood in contemporary spookspeak. And here, we are tempted to suggest, is to be seen the product of later minds less immediately concerned with the practical aspects of espionage and counterespionage and more with literary flourish. These latter accretions have all the seeming incongruities of the camel, that horse designed by committee.

But we may very well be struck with the product, for despite its inelegance, it has undeniable utility, so we had better become accustomed to its peculiarities. In particular, we must reconcile ourselves to accepting the strange fact that it is the "mole's" job to gather intelligence for his masters and only incidentally to undermine a task for which real moles are by nature more properly equipped. We can, however, do our best, at this stage, to stem any further debasement and arrest the disturbing promiscuity in the use of the term mole. We must avoid some of the extravagances that have crept in, as well as the limitations that would alter the character of the concept.

We need a practical, working definition that will enable us

to see what has to be done to cope with the problem of the mole from a counterespionage perspective. Accordingly, we propose the following definition:

A mole is a penetration agent introduced into the service of another with the hidden intention of his attaining a position enabling him to be useful to those to whose interests he is really devoted.

Armed with this definition, we may now proceed to consider the problems posed by these "little beasts that work underground."

Moles are not easy to catch. Clumsiness must be avoided at all costs. As a general rule, moles are trapped rather than hunted. Riding to hounds after the mole is a spectacular exercise in imbecility that is likely to ruin the landscape. A mole hunt is no place for showiness or fancy tricks. If a hunt is decided upon, it must take an appropriate form, for it is well to recall Grivas' famous aphorism: "You do not send tanks to catch field mice. A cat will do the job much better."[68] Any hunt for the mole must be discreet, carried out by experienced, sensitive personnel who do not advertise their presence or intentions and who, above all, tread carefully and do not, by their own clumsiness, obliterate the tell-tale signs. Mole hunting is not an amateur field sport; it is a job for professionals. A mole hunt clumsily conducted can be very disruptive. It can be highly destructive of the interests of those who engage in it and harmful to innocents. It can tear apart organizations and sow the seeds of distrust that will grow untended into an enduring, impenetrable forest.[69]

Unskillful performances of this kind bring joy to the enemy camp. They are a bonus to the opposition, whatever their final result. It takes, then, a very special kind of hunter indeed to track and actually catch a mole. Usually, it calls for a very particular and unusual hunting technique. If the mole is to be hunted, it is necessary to pick up his trail, patiently stalk him, and then effect his discreet disposal in a way calculated to cause as little damage as possible to the environment and structures in which he has operated. There is a surgical quality to the successful mole hunt.

The mole, like his namesake in the animal kingdom, is usually not a violent creature; he is unlikely to put up a fight when cornered. A mole is not generally selected for his James Bond qualities. His defenses reside in his ability to remain undetected and to maneuver himself into a position from which he can fend off any challenge. This is the principal danger for those who seek him and are trying to realize his eradication. If his burrowing has gone on long enough and has been attended with the right amount of success, his position might be practically unassailable.[70] As in all matters of a cognate kind, in the end it comes down to who believes what about whom. Mole hunting is often enough a solitary business, calling for great patience, tenacity, personal integrity, and the ability to build and present a convincing case. For what one might see incontrovertibly as a mole may well appear to others, however well informed, to be quite a different creature. Catching the mole may well prove an easier task than establishing to the satisfaction of those who matter that what has been caught really is a mole.

The mole moves in a twilit world where nothing is ever quite black or quite white—unless those with the power to make it so choose that it shall be done.[71] This is very frustrating for the hunter, but it is a predictable part of the hunt. Neutralizing the mole, removing him from a position where he can do any more harm, may be all that is possible and even preferable to the difficult task of dealing with him in his true guise.

There is a fundamental problem with this whole business of mole hunting that is worthy of note here. The mole will not usually give much evidence of his presence *as a spy* while he is working his way toward his target area. His progress, while it will obviously leave traces of where he has been and what he has done, will not ordinarily give rise to suspicion of improper activities until he begins to carry out those tasks directly associated with his espionage work. It is usually only after things start to go wrong that the presence of an agent in place or a mole begins to be suspected, and the necessary measures are set in motion to discover what—or who—may be causing the problem. By that time, if the penetration has been organized with skill and patience, the trail will have grown cold or been swept clean so as to confuse or divert the tracker. The hunter may well have to start with an old, cold, or false trail. In cases of this kind, he will most likely commence with a suspect, whose most recent trail he will have to take up in the hope of working it back to its beginnings and, perhaps, the point of penetration.

The mole hunter must be a connoisseur of detail; he cannot work in broad strokes. He will be aided in this process by the small field of candidates he will have to consider; only a limited number, with certain responsibilities when he begins his hunt, will have been in a position to have done the damage that has brought him upon the scene. This, on the other hand, may be but a doubtful advantage. The hunter will often be challenging figures in high positions and of considerable reputation whose origins and obscure beginnings have long been left behind.[72] In the course of a mole hunt, much may turn upon matters of perspective: how individuals and their actions are to be seen and measured and against what background. So much turns upon questions of interpretation. The mole may be in a position to throw sand (or worse) in the eyes of the trackers.

Moreover, a doubtful beginning is *not necessarily* conclusive of, or even good evidence for, some later treachery. The mole hunter also has the problem of deciding whether what has engaged his attention is truly the work of a mole or of some other creature among those we have discussed; their spoor may be very different, but the evidence of the damage they have occasioned may be so similar so as to be indistinguishable. Clearly, all this adds up to a very bleak picture, suggesting a much higher degree of security for the mole than is probably the case in reality. For moles *are* caught, or at least stopped in their tracks. Our point here is that those who equate the mole hunter's task with that of catching the little beasts who ruin our lawns and who thus expect to use similar methods are likely to be greatly disappointed. The similarity lies in the name and little more.

For a mole hunt to even begin, there must be credible evidence of the presence of a mole rather than some other creature; this must be something rather more than a simple mess after the style of a molehill. Something resembling a mole, at least in its outlines, must have become apparent in the course of addressing the problem or what has occurred so as to touch off a real mole hunt. Much mole hunting is a kind of verification procedure. There are sufficient indications of the mole's presence, and some likely candidate or candidates have emerged. Such a hunt narrows itself down to finding the means to prove that one or more of those indicated is/are of the species that would warrant action being taken against them on that account. Obviously, mole hunting cannot usefully proceed on the basis of some sort of "beating the bushes." It tends to be at best a reactive exercise, touched off by events which in themselves may be quite damaging. Mole hunting has thus often to be undertaken in a psychologically unfavorable climate in which the security services, in many cases without any great justification, are regarded as derelict in their duty or even incompetent.[73] By an elliptical and unfair process of reasoning they are thought unfit to engage in such a hunt because they were unable to prevent the circumstances that have given rise to the need for the hunt. This puts them at a distinct disadvantage in dealing with those persons of a closed elite from whom they must necessarily secure a high degree of cooperation if their efforts are to be crowned with success. When the mole is well ensconced, as is often the case when his machinations come to light, it will usually be extremely difficult for the mole hunter to get to him unobtrusively.

All closed elites strongly favor some form of self-policing or another. Trial by one's peers is very far from being the kind of "democratic" process we pretend it to be. The problem is grossly accentuated when a relatively junior mole hunter, however competent, is in pursuit of, say, his own director or other senior officer. Not only will all his efforts be under the closest scrutiny, but there may well be attempts to sabotage or derail them by using the regular power available through the normal channels of command. Highly placed moles have extensive, officially sanctioned powers for organizing and carrying out cover-ups. If they are popular to boot, they will attract much sympathy, which will surround them like an invisible wall of protection behind which they can wait and observe. The mole hunter is therefore under the additional serious handicap of having to pursue a hidden adversary while operating in plain view himself. There is something of the Alice in Wonderland about all this that has certainly not been lost on those brought up on a diet of Lewis Carroll. Nor, we would observe, is mole hunting proper work for a committee. It may well be that such collective endeavors have their place in proceedings to establish the facts of the matter, but they are not equipped to gather them or to follow the trail that must be pursued if the mole is to be tracked with certainty. Commissions of inquiry rarely discover anything new or startling, but they are adequate enough spreaders of whitewash or pitch. The mole hunter needs tracks, but, above all, he needs authority. The mole's tracks may well wind across many different areas, crossing and crisscrossing all manner of jurisdictional lines in the process. While remaining sensitive to susceptibilities in these matters, the mole hunter should never have to be placed in a position where he might be warned off for trespass. But, for the reasons we have outlined, he may well be tempted to take shortcuts, and obstacles placed in his way may lead him to explore extralegal or at least extraofficial avenues to go around them.[74] He must tread very warily lest he become unseated. Happiness for the mole hunter is never having to apologize.

In all this, it is important to keep in mind that a mole is a mole by virtue of the techniques he uses to put himself in a position to do his work. There is nothing distinctive, *qua* mole, about the way he will undertake his work as a spy once he is in position. Once he has begun that work, he is just like any other spy—insofar as these wonderfully varied creatures can be heaped together as a species. There are certain things he must do, as we have earlier recounted, that leave him exposed to countermeasures. The mole enjoys no immunity if he is seen to do things that would give rise to suspicion of espionage in his case. A mole is no different in this respect from his fellows. His relative safety subsists only while he is on the way to work, and then only if he does nothing to reveal his real nature and intentions.

All that we have said heretofore about the hunting and trapping of spies applies without qualification to moles—once they presume to act the part of the spy. Once this is grasped, its corollary makes itself apparent. The mole on the way to work is really but an incomplete creature, an inchoate spy. He is perfected, consummated if you will, only when he becomes like all the other spies and does a spy's work. A mole is a mole only until he arrives. This is the reason for the primary ineffectiveness of most hunting techniques so far as moles are concerned; they are simply premature. We would reiterate, too, that it is rarely apparent when the damage evidences itself whether this is truly the work of a mole, as we have described this office, or of some other creature capable for other reasons of doing the same work. A Pollard, for example, is quite capable of leaving the same signs as a mole when his destructive activities are first uncovered.[75] Short of some monumental foolishness, a rather masochistic change of heart by the mole, or an extraordinary stroke of luck on the part of the pursuer, there is only one way the hunter is going to waylay the mole on his way to work and that is by being informed by someone of his identity, location, and purposes in sufficient detail so as to be able to track him. Obviously, such information can *only* come from someone on the other side who knows these things and is prepared to impart them. Even comparatively scanty information is valuable to the well-prepared mole hunter, and the possibility of its being transmitted through some sort of treachery is ever the mole's greatest nightmare. The mole can do little to guard against such dangers. Time is often of the essence in these cases. If the mole and his controller learn quickly enough of this breach in their own security, they may be able to move so as to cover the tracks or take steps to avoid discovery. Again, the same will be true of any agent in place likely to be revealed by a defector who has sufficient knowledge of his operations. These fortuitous advantages must not be allowed to go to waste. It is indispensable in these matters that there should exist the greatest cooperation between the intelligence services and their security service counterparts. While compartmentalization may be desirable, even essential in many cases, it can work to great disadvantage here, and this is but one instance in which a well-run, comprehensive, integrated service, which has all its functions under a single command structure,[76] has much to commend it. Failure to transmit vital information or a delay in doing so which results either in the mole's escape or losing his track may not always have the most sinister implications. It may simply be a bureaucratic problem that must obviously be addressed due to the effects it might have on other aspects of the system's operation.

Given the definition of mole we have offered and of his purposes, the most important questions the spy-catcher must answer are where, when, and how the mole entered the system or that part of it with which the penetration is concerned.[77] This will most usually involve a detailed backtracking of the mole's movements. If the mole has been in the system for a long time and has had the opportunity to cover his tracks, this may be a tedious and frustrating business. It must be thoroughly and painstakingly undertaken. Much will depend upon the circumstances of the investigation. If it is to proceed without the knowledge of the mole (who will in such a case presumably be left in place under close supervision while the investigation is undertaken), it will have to rely upon information in the records or from third parties. In some systems, the record keeping deficiencies will hamper the investigation substantially.[78] If the mole has been confronted or has been apprehended and charged, his cooperation can be sought and the extent to which it is sincerely given will determine how many of the blanks can be reliably filled in. Confrontation is an irrevocable step and not one to be taken lightly. The extent to which useful cooperation is likely to be given will depend upon the gravity of the peril in which the uncovered mole perceives himself to be; his steadfastness in adversity; the degree to which those who have employed him are prepared to "own" him and assist in extricating him from his predicament; and the effects of his own exposure upon other persons and operations being undertaken by his own service. For an espionage service, little is more precious than its operational methods.

It is to be expected that in the event a mole is apprehended, every effort will be made to protect the knowledge of how he was introduced into the system and how he was supported while doing his job. Only with the mole's fullest and most wholehearted cooperation is anything useful about such matters likely to be learned. The mole who is caught has therefore a great deal with which to bargain. This idea of striking a bargain should be given careful thought by the spy-catcher. He must have a realistic appreciation of relative values.

There is no room for sentimentality or high-toned morality in these matters. It is useless to appeal to past loyalties, for there were none. Only a practical appeal to self-interest is likely to succeed, and it must be strong and urgent enough to overcome the mole's perceived obligations to his real masters. The mole must be persuaded to see his own salvation in being appropriately cooperative. There is often a visceral distaste for bargaining with those who have wronged us in this way. It is understandable that we should be angered by presumed treachery, but such emotions ought not to be allowed to dictate action in these matters. It is better to coax what may be usefully learned from the mole, even at a price, than to exact vengeance and inter useful knowledge along with the mole's carcass.[79] The debriefing of a captured mole should be expertly conducted with a view to learning as much as possible about the opposition's operational methods. If the mole has to be treated gently in the process, that is but a small price to pay for the knowledge that is to be gained in this way. In the last resort, the mole may serve as a useful item of exchange in some future spy swap. The important thing is to squeeze him dry before the exchange is made, for even the presumption that this has happened may serve as an inhibitor to the opposition as to the mole's future usefulness.

Some fish are caught with rod and line, while others are taken in a net. The preferred method of taking the mole is the trap. We have already said a great deal about spy traps in general, and most of what we have outlined is fully applicable in the case of the mole. It should be noted that trapping techniques are especially useful against the unrevealed, the dangerous pest who enters our domains with secret, harmful purposes. This is all part of the strategy to keep such creatures out or to apprehend them on the way in. The questions that face the trappers are always: What kind of trap? And where shall it be set? The mole in the animal kingdom has weak sight but a greatly enhanced sense of smell and acute hearing to compensate for its visual weakness.[80] It also has a highly developed sense of the dangers that might threaten it and, given its nature, it prefers avoidance to confrontation. Our metaphorical mole cannot afford confrontation either, and his senses are accordingly highly developed to enable him to appreciate and evade snares, generally avoiding detection. He will be on the lookout for traps and will have little difficulty in avoiding the crude and unconcealed ones in his path. The careful trapper must take these qualities properly into account in choosing and setting his instruments.

The uncritical temptation to counteract these qualities would be to design and employ clever, complex traps intended to defy detection and make avoidance difficult. While such traps might have their special utility, they are usually just too expensive, on a cost/benefit basis, for everyday employment. The mole has so many potential points of entry. To cover them all this way would be prohibitively costly and of doubtful efficiency. What is needed is a combination of simplicity and defense in depth. We cannot rely upon a single line of traps covering only the possible area where the mole might infiltrate the system.[81] We must lay traps for him all along the route, especially at those sensitive places where his progress is marked by advancement in status and responsibilities. Applying and adapting our standard traps for these purposes ought not to be too difficult. All this is posited upon the assumption that our system is not totally mole ridden (or infested with other creatures working for the opposition) to start with.

Nothing could be worse than to entrust the guarding of the henhouse to the fox.[82] This has been done in the past on a sufficient number of occasions to make this renewed admonition worthwhile. If the administration, supervision, and oversight of the mole-trapping program are in the hands of agents in place or the moles themselves, or can be strongly influenced by them, it is obvious that the trapping process will not have the desired results. The well-advertised failure of the British security services during the late 1940s, Fifties, and early Sixties to ensure that this was not the case was the principal reason behind the unsatisfactory results of the various "housecleaning" operations then undertaken. The mole trapper should always assume that the mole can count on some sort of help to evade the snares set for him, and they should be designed, constructed, and set with that in mind.

Perhaps the only thing special about mole trapping as opposed to the trapping of other types of spies is the care and cunning that must be applied. The trapper must try to put himself in the mole's position, in effect thinking like a mole in order to practice his own craft to the best advantage. The mole is a long-term investment for any espionage service. Enormous resources are expended on the mole-planting operations, and the potential payoff is commensurate with the effort expended. Mole catching is a highly specialized business, and those who would be successful at it must be prepared to commit the appropriate time and resources to the task. Otherwise, catching moles simply comes down to a question of luck. We are not concerned, in the present work, with the catching of spies by accident.

All that we have said with regard to countermeasures in

the case of the mole can be applied with equal force to that of the sleeper. While the mole, according to our estimate of him, is hardly considered man's best friend, the sleeper is, in some ways, even more dangerous. For one thing, his period of inactivity may be longer, thus giving him more time to take on protective coloring, disguising himself and his true purposes. For another, the technique of his insertion will probably be different from that of the mole, making him difficult to trap; he may simply be left behind. This essentially was the problem posed for those concerned with the denazification of Germany after World War II.[83]

While the picture is obviously distorted by the rapid onset of the Cold War and the changes in emphasis it brought, there are nevertheless many lessons pertinent to the present theme to be learned from this exercise. Chaotic conditions, where records were destroyed and regular administration disrupted; hordes of displaced persons, often in appalling physical and mental condition, for whom no records existed at all; a focus on the hunt for war criminals; inexperienced security personnel with uncertain direction—these all gave a definite edge to those whose purpose was to get lost in the crowd. Provided his past had not made him too notorious, the unregenerate Nazi's concealment on his own ground was not too difficult. The native soil was still fundamentally favorable, and those truly interested in denazification and all it implied were, in the main, the alien victors. In this case, the sleeper had a ready-made, well-concealed bed. Unlike the mole, introduced into a hostile terrain through which he has to burrow unobtrusively to reach his objective, these Nazi sleepers could simply lie concealed and unnoticed, awaiting a change in the climate that might allow them to emerge once more to re-establish the Party hegemony. Most had nothing but a fanatical faith to sustain them, for real plans for a Fourth Reich were the stuff of novels rather than serious business in the conquered territories in the bleak, confused days after the Allied victory in Europe.[84] The central directive force of the NDSAP and the bureaucracy and armed might that had sustained it, making it for a time the undisputed master of all Germany and the greater part of Europe, had disappeared in the fires of defeat.

The sleepers awoke to a changed world in which the dark forces that had sent them on their way had become quite different in form and substance. Some had gone to their places in the belief that the Allied victory was an ephemeral thing and that Nazi Germany would rise phoenix-like from the ashes, and that they would play a part in the ultimate triumph of those to whom their allegiance never wavered. Others, more realistic in the event, had long seen the writing on the wall but had gone forth in the belief that World War II was but a tragic interlude or prelude to the inevitable War against Communism that would see a risen, though chastened, Germany take its rightful place alongside its Western conquerors in the new struggle against the barbaric hordes sweeping into Europe from the East. These hoped that there might be a conditional welcome for those with a not too objectionable Nazi past and a place for them in the direction of the great, new struggle that would restore Germany to her proper position as leader of an anti-Communist Europe. As history shows, this was a not unrealistic hope, and the groundwork for this was being cautiously laid before the War's end.

Yet others saw the need to go underground in order to save not the Nazi ideals they cherished, but Germany itself, wartorn, divided, and sorely in need of those who would save it from permanent dismemberment and perhaps even total destruction. Some of these sleepers were undoubtedly wellprepared and professionally briefed on their tasks, while others seem to have conceived them spontaneously or by a process of personal reflection. But the history of the Federal Republic of Germany, from its creation through the early 1960s, is perhaps the most instructive for any who would study the problems of the sleeper on the grand scale. Indeed, the period 1945 through 1949 may usefully be regarded as the "Years of the Sleeper." These creatures *did* survive, and they eventually emerged in numbers from the woodwork to carry out their tasks, shaping the destiny and direction of the new state, albeit in ways modified by the exigencies of the times. The sleeper has to endure with his faith intact until the time comes when he can show his mettle. He may awaken spontaneously or be awakened by a prearranged signal from those whose interests he serves.

The sleeper is stimulated to action by the approaching scent of victory for his cause, and the emanations of the Cold War undoubtedly encouraged many Nazi sleepers as it assuredly assisted in their transformation over the course of time.

By 1948, hunting them down had already become an overwhelming task for the erstwhile victors preoccupied with newer, more urgent concerns. Even the hunt for war criminals was becoming attended by something approaching ennui. Trapping them had turned into an embarrassing exercise few were anxious to conduct or extend.

All that remains is to learn the lessons and to see how they might usefully inform the spy-catcher's work elsewhere. The sleeper (in the guise in which we have treated him here) is the conqueror's problem everywhere, be it the Allies in post-World War II Europe or victorious Vietnam after 1975. These lessons are more than suitable for synthesis and application to other situations on a micro- or macrocosmic scale.[85] Moles are to be found burrowing their way through great commercial and industrial enterprises as well as through the organs of the body politic. Our own definition is generous enough to embrace the activities of such creatures, and we regard them as fair game for the spy-catcher, especially in our own times where treachery has taken on a new, more ample meaning. Sleepers, too, are to be found in such organizations, and security officers should be especially alert for such creatures where there have been mergers and takeovers, the equivalents of conquest in the world of capitalism.[86]

It is not necessary here to give special treatment to the case of those we simply called agents in place. As far as we are concerned, our task in this chapter was mainly to distinguish them from moles and sleepers in the interests of providing a better focus for the problems of catching them and controlling their activities. All the techniques we have thus far discussed have their place in the struggle against such spies and must be organized and applied accordingly in proper measure. That such separate attention has not been bestowed upon them should not be construed as suggesting that they are considered of lesser importance or necessarily easier to detect or apprehend. On the contrary, in practice, these agents in place can be very dangerous and difficult targets. They should never be underestimated, and in a work devoted to recruitment, management, and support services they might well warrant primacy and extended treatment. The spy-catcher will want to pay special attention to these features for his own purposes, but it is not necessary to explore them further here. There are distinctions and commonalities. We are concerned with both only in so far as a knowledge of them aids in furthering the aims and objectives of the spy-catcher.

There is a clear lesson in this as far as all these hidden subversive elements are concerned: the most effective measures are prophylactic. The very soil itself must be made unwholesome for these creatures, whatever their nature, categorization, or purposes. This is a comprehensive, long-term project, but it is one in which the spy-catcher has an important, technical part to play. Something like a *cordon sanitaire* must be constructed around sensitive enterprises. Only the harmless may be allowed to pass; there must be a proper filtering process and constant sampling to monitor who is passing through the system. Naturally, this means a degree of regulation and interference that may well be unwelcome to those for whom such ideas are philosophically objectionable. But a slight scrutiny of the facts of our modern world show such ideas to be naive, unrealistic, and outmoded. The laissez faire doctrine in human relations is incompatible with a world in which high-stakes competition makes impossible demands on those who engage in it. There are simply too many prepared to stoop to treason, murder, or theft to secure a timely advantage. No business can be successfully conducted without some sort of inventory control. Knowing where things are, their condition, how they are moving through the system, and who is doing what in relation to them is essential to the ordinary working of the enterprise. Any businessman who shirks such responsibilities is not merely inefficient; he is heading for bankruptcy. The national security, if nothing else, imposes no less stringent obligations with respect to human assets.[87]

The freedom of movement everywhere, by everyone, at all times is chimerical. We all accept the need for some restrictions however libertarian our philosophy. The more closed the system, the greater the controls and restrictions—and the need for them. The moment the point is conceded, the only issue, realistically, for civil libertarians in our society becomes one of degree; how much population control is acceptable and compatible with our security interests? What is wanted is a system that is suitably tolerant yet watchful. No steel mesh and barbed-wire fences, but a serene landscape which nevertheless carries indelible footprints identifying those who pass across it, showing where they are going and where they have been. Modern technology makes such landscaping possible. What has to be guarded against, with ever-increasing vigilance, is the counter-technology that can confuse and create false trails of its own. What is advocated here is a kind of crime control through environmental design. There is a real need for high-intensity lighting to illuminate some of the darker corners of our system where penetrations and other dirty dealings are presumably too easy for the wrong-doer. While its implementation is hardly likely to spell death to the ubiquitous mole or agent in place, some Oscar Newman[88] of the counterespionage world may one day give a material aspect to the chosen epitaph of a modern "C": ". . . it would be a waste of time. Nothing worth nicking there, guv'nor."[89]

POINTS TO REMEMBER

1. **Moles** are *penetration agents* introduced into the service of another with the hidden intent of attaining a position which will make them useful to those whose interests they really serve. Moles are a heavy investment for an intelligence service and are generally part of a long-range strategic plan. All moles are *penetration agents*, but not all penetration agents are moles. Moles should never be confused with *converts*, or *defectors in place*, or *sleepers*. A key distinction between moles and sleepers is the degree of attention handlers must pay: as a rule, true sleepers receive very little, if any, attention.

While different, all three must reside deep within the organization whose secrets they wish to acquire in order to fulfill their purpose. They generally do not leave footprints or tracks until they begin sending information, although with defectors in place, there may be a number of indications through changes in behavior. For the spy-catcher, the most important questions are where, when, and how (long ago) the penetration was achieved.

2. The term mole appears to be of recent use and was generated by literary as opposed to intelligence sources (even though intelligence sources *may* now use the term to denote penetration agents). The correct use of the term as depicting the spy-catcher's quarry is important because *language in-*

forms thought and structures thought in important ways. It follows that inaccuracies in language will lead to sloppy thinking and insofar as the thought leads to planning and planning to action, poor outcomes and often misfortune. The spy-catcher must always examine the possibilities and details and not be fooled by slovenly thought.

3. One of the major defenses of moles and other long-term penetration agents is to maneuver themselves into positions from which they can fend off challenges and inquiries. Once ensconced, the mole as an agent in place can begin work, and it is then that things begin to go wrong. Spy-catchers, brought in on such a scene, must sometimes challenge those in high positions who possess considerable power and reputation.

4. For an effective security policy, the minimum information requirements necessary are to know where things and people are, what their condition is, how they are moving through the various systems, and who is doing what to them.

NOTES

1. *Mole*, New York: W. W. Norton, 1982, page 16.

2. *A Dictionary of Slang and Unconventional English*, London: Routledge and Kegan Paul, 8th edition, 1984, ed. Paule Beale, page 746.

3. *The Book of Jargon*, New York: Macmillan, 1981.

4. *The New KGB*, William R. Corson and Robert T. Crowley, New York: William Morrow, 1985, page 355.

5. *Listener*, 22 January 1976, page 90.

6. A good example of what is stated here is provided by one who carried out indispensable economic espionage for the Allies during World War II. See *The Counterfeit Traitor*, Alexander Klein, New York: Henry Holt, 1958.

7. "They have placed a huge antenna in northwest Cuba to intercept telephone calls relayed by satellite across the United States." "Why Americans Become Kremlin Agents," Stansfield Turner, *U.S. News and World Report*, 12 August 1985, page 32.

8. See *Secret Sentries in Space*, Philip J. Klass, New York: Random House, 1971.

9. See, for example, the instructive *Agent in Place: The*

Wennerstrom Affair, Thomas Whiteside, New York: Viking Press, 1966.

10. An instructive and tragic minor example is the case of William Marshall, exquisitely outlined by Dame Rebecca West. *The New Meaning of Treason,* New York: Viking Press, 1964, pages 255–263.

11. This has a very special, contemporary relevance. See, for example, *Techno-Bandits,* Linda Melvern, Nick Anning, and David Hebditch, Boston: Houghton Mifflin, 1984. This book should be required reading for all having security responsibilities in the private sector.

12. Or when the scarcity factor plays a dominant role in the market. This is well illustrated in the case of Petr Popov, the subject of William Hood's excellent account, op. cit., supra note 1, who was not really a mole, but an agent in place.

13. The oft-cited story of the Israeli Eli Cohen provides one of the best-told accounts of such an operation. See *The Shattered Silence,* Zwy Aldouby and Jerrold Ballinger, New York: Coward, McCann and Geoghegan, 1971.

14. We ought, really, to reserve the full measure of our righteous anger for those truly of our own who inevitably are to be found, for reasons of their own, helping these agents of deceit to establish themselves and do their work. These are often the true traitors, and those Syrians tried with Cohen provide a good example.

15. *A Supplement to the Oxford English Dictionary,* Vol. IV, 1986, page 249, has the entry, *Sleeper:* "A spy, saboteur, or the like, who remains inactive for a long period before engaging in spying or sabotage or otherwise acting to achieve his ends; loosely, any undercover agent." A 1955 source is given for this. The final part of the entry points up the problem of the undiscriminating application of these terms.

16. Man's search for purpose, for his real meaning in the scheme of things, is very strong; it is shaped and directed by external forces as well as those within. "Is a man nothing more than this—an obscene shape drifting through Time, reproducing itself and dying with no more reason than Friday's trout." *A Spy for God,* Pierre Joffroy, New York: Harcourt Brace Jovanovich, 1969, page 27.

17. "Of the bright young men recruited at Cambridge, Kim Philby and Donald Maclean became Soviet spies in 1933. Guy Burgess was certainly approached at the same time but

may not have been formally recruited until 1934, when he visited Moscow. In describing these men as 'Soviet spies,' it should be stressed that they were 'sleepers' or 'moles' in intelligence parlance; they were not expected to provide information for a number of years, until they had worked their way into high confidential positions." *The Shadow Network*, Edward Van Der Rhoer, New York: Charles Scribner's Sons, 1983, page 77.

18. *Second Barnhart Dictionary of New English*, 1980, page 310.

19. Paul Beale, who very kindly wrote to us at length on January 29, 1987, in response to our query regarding the entry in *Partridge's*, op. cit., supra note 2. Mr. Beale made a number of helpful suggestions that assisted in focusing our research. That his last observation might be prematurely optimistic, at least on this side of the Atlantic, is to be seen from a report in *U.S. News and World Report*, 6 April 1987, page 10, entitled, "The French Nab an Iranian 'Sleeper Cell.'" "We used to watch for bomb-carrying terrorists flying in from Damascus, Beirut, Tehran, or Tripoli," says a Paris-based source. "But the real threats are the moles they've put in place all across Europe—either people they've sent in to settle or militants they have recruited on the spot."

20. "Molehunt," *London Review of Books*, 27 January 1987, page 6. See also *Her Majesty's Secret Service*, Christopher Andrew, New York: Viking Penguin, 1986, passim. Mr. Andrew, unfortunately, provides no clues as to the origin of the term.

21. One particularly egregious example caught our attention. "Mole—a foreign spy placed in one's own national intelligence agency. Safire says that the term was either coined or reported by John Le Carré in his novel, *The Spy Who Came in from the Cold*." *Kind Words*, Judith S. Neaman and Carole E. Silver, New York: Facts on File, 1983, page 304. This does not, as we shall see, do any more justice to William Safire than it does to the poor mole.

See also *Family Treason*, Jack M. Kneece, New York: Stein and Day, 1986, page 219: "For years a faction in the Navy had believed there was a mole somewhere with access to top-secret and cryptographic information as well as other technical data." Perhaps such underwater creatures should be called "dolphins"?

22. A very useful entry is to be found in *Newspeak: A Dictionary of Jargon*, Jonathon Green, London: Routledge and Kegan Paul, 1984. "*Mole/Espionage*. A deep cover agent, put in place many years before he/she can be of use, but on the assumption that such an agent will gradually gain access to the centres of power, increasingly useful as time passes. Mole is a perfect example of the blurring of fact and fiction. While Francis Bacon uses the word in his *History of the Reign of King Henry VII* (1622), it was otherwise to be found in the works of John Le Carré, notably *Tinker, Tailor, Soldier, Spy* (1974). In a BBC television interview in 1976 Le Carré claimed that mole was a genuine KGB term, but it was the televising of *Tinker, Tailor . . .* plus the revelations of the *Fourth Man* (Anthony Blunt) in October 1979 that took mole out of fiction and into the headlines for good."

Forbes, 25 April 1983, page 94, carries a review by Donald Moffitt of *The Circus* by Nigel West, which contains the statement, "John Le Carré (himself, as David John Moore Cornwell, of MI5)." Of such gossamer threads are the web of authority spun.

23. At least, we should say, we have never seen this suggested anywhere in the literature. It seems to have had no place in the German spy lexicon, where the word is closest to its English cousin. Talpa, or Topo, would have a strange ring in any espionage context.

24. And even for some whose English has been transplanted to other climes. See, for example, *A Dictionary of Canadianisms*, Toronto: W.J. Gage, 1967, page 482: "Mole 1964 *Calgary Herald* 25 May 23/1. While the pests colloquially are called 'moles' they are really pocket gophers and our gophers are ground squirrels." Gopher has not yet crept into the espionage lexicon on its native side of the Atlantic.

25. One point we find very telling is that Sefton Delmer, an accomplished wordsmith whose professional talents were put to use in the secret intelligence services of his country during World War II, makes an incidental reference to Philby in *The Counterfeit Spy*, published in 1971. Although this makes effective use of an interesting item of insider's jargon (bigotting) on page 174, it does not characterize Philby as a mole.

26. *Fifth Column*, a very popular term during World War II and of some interest in the present context, originated

during the Spanish Civil War and is attributed to General Emilio Mola Vidal. See *Crossroads on the Left*, Robert A. Rosenstone, New York: Pegasus, 1967, page 22. Although *mola* has a special meaning of "mole" in the sense of a false pregnancy, the connection here would seem to be purely coincidental.

A fifth columnist could, however, be appropriately brought within the bounds of what we have been discussing here, as the many references in *The Spanish Civil War*, Hugh Thomas, New York: Harper & Row, 1977, will indicate.

For the way in which "mole" was understood by intelligence professionals during and shortly after the close of World War II, there are two outstanding pieces of evidence. Walter Schellenberg, writing in his memoirs (published in 1956) of a group of infiltrators and detailing the measures taken to catch these elusive spies, tells of one of them: "He kept himself shut up like a mole." *The Labyrinth*, New York: Harper and Brothers, 1956, page 127. His meaning here is quite plain. Professor H. R. Trevor Roper, in a work written in 1945 but published in 1947, writes: ". . . The persistent Bormann. This mole-like creature, who seemed to avoid the glare of daylight and publicity and to despise the rewards and trimmings, was nevertheless insatiable in his appetite for the reality of power." *The Last Days of Hitler*, New York: Macmillan, 1947, pages 13–14. Interestingly, this is cited without comment on the usage as late as 1969 by Perrault in *The Red Orchestra*, page 455. Professor Trevor Roper (now Lord Dacre) was a member of the British Intelligence community at this important time for our proposed purposes, and his preface recalls that his study was undertaken at the instance of "My friend Dick White . . . Brigadier commanding the intelligence bureau at the time when Hitler's death was still a mystery." We wrote to Lord Dacre on this and other matters but, unfortunately, have not received a definitive reply at the time of going to press.

27. The reasons for this are apparent from a reading of *Piercing the Reich*, Joseph E. Persico, New York: Viking Press, 1979. The British in particular attached very little importance to penetration operations, especially those of a long-term character, presumably on the basis of their evaluation of the German security services. We would, however, regard Kurt Gerstein as having been a mole, by our defini-

tion, within the SS, although, at best, he was a mole on his own account. It is significant that his careful biographer does not refer to him in these terms in 1969, and this, too, is an interesting piece of evidence. Op. cit., supra note 16.

28. See, for example, the excellent *Macquarie Dictionary* (1981).

29. Letter to the authors from the Assistant Editor (*New Words*), *The Oxford English Dictionary*, 23 January 1987.

30. *The Conspirators*, Geoffrey Bailey, New York: Harper and Brothers, 1960, page 124. The interesting *Commissar* [by Thaddeus Wittlin, New York: Macmillan, 1972], spanning Beria's entire career, makes no use of the word mole, though it uses many Soviet colloquialisms (and some interesting vulgarities). It does use Fifth Column.

31. No such reference is to be found in the authoritative *A Middle English Dictionary*, Francis Henry Stratman, Oxford: Clarendon Press, 1891, which contains words used by English writers from the twelfth to the fifteenth centuries.

32. Roger Lockyer, Editor, *The History of the Reign of King Henry the Seventh*, London: The Folio Society, 1971, page 13.

33. It is interesting that *Jargon*, Joel Homer, New York: Times Books, 1979, contains no reference to mole under "Spook Talk." This would seem to be historically significant when considering the time necessary in preparing this work for publication.

34. See, for example, *The Dictionary of Espionage: Spookspeak into English,* Henry S. A. Becket, New York: Stein and Day, 1986. This work seems to have become a CIA favorite and was referred to these authors by that agency when assistance was sought on this subject. A recent publication has recognized the term "mole" in the context of the United States intelligence community. While this belated recognition is an acknowledgment of a linguistic fact, it casts no light upon the origins of the term nor the date of its impartation into U.S. Intelligence parlance.

See *The Central Intelligence Agency: A Photographic History*, John Patrick Quirk, et. al., Guilford, CT: Foreign Intelligence Press, 1986, pages 144, 156, and 253.

35. *Aesop's Fables* are a striking example, as are the many Sufi stories which resemble them. A pertinent illustration is found in *The Red Orchestra*, Gilles Perrault, New York:

Simon & Schuster, 1969, page 176: "Was it a wolf the enemy was trying to introduce into the fold?"

36. But see on this Aesop's "The Owl and the Wren."

37. Aesop records two fables featuring the mole, from which ancient thinking regarding this creature's principal qualities can be readily deduced. The mole does not appear in the guise of a spy. It is too busy minding its own business.

38. *The Oxford Dictionary of English Proverbs*, Third Edition, F. P. Wilson, Oxford: Clarendon Press, 1970, contains one especially interesting entry: "Doe you not knowe, that (as the Proverbe is) we see better a farre of, than hard by us, that at home we see no more than Moles, but abroade as much as Argus," (1581) Guazzo. The sentry, Argus, unlike the mole, had a hundred eyes, which after his death were said to have been transferred to the peacock's tail. Well might he have been the Patron of all security services.

It did not surprise us to find in *A History of the British Secret Service*, Richard Deacon (Donald McCormick), London: Frederick Mullen, 1969, page 55: "Thurloe was succeeded as head of intelligence, or Number One Argus, as that office was named by Thomas Scott." Unfortunately, the reference cited does not support this statement, but there is no reason to believe that the title was not used. The importance of this in relation to Thurloe will become apparent in our own text. It is interesting that no reference to the contrasting term "mole," apparently not unknown in those times, is to be found in an espionage context.

What is interesting is the chapter entitled "The Eyes of Argus," in *Code Number 72*, Cecil B. Currey, Englewood Cliffs, NJ: Prentice Hall, 1972. The book deals with Benjamin Franklin and the British Secret Service at a time when it was particularly strong and active. There are many instances of penetrations mentioned, but no moles are referred to therein.

39. It is said that Foxe's *Book of Martyrs* (1563) first recorded "makeying mountains of molehills," and is cited in *Animal Crackers, A Bestial Lexicon*, Robert Hendrickson, New York: Viking Press/Penguin, 1983, page 149. Bailey, op. cit., supra note 30, records, "Then, too, by now he [Tukhachevsky] probably agreed with Napoleon: Europe was a rabbit warren—Napoleon had actually used the word 'molehill' " (page 181).

40. We have found an interesting modern reversion to this, more sensible idea. See "Mole's Lib," *The Economist*, 16 February 1985, page 12: "The Pointing case is a mole's charter." It has never been suggested that Mr. Clive Ponting was a mole in the espionage sense, but his industry certainly disturbed the British government's neat greensward.

41. "Although mole has it origins in Elizabethan usage . . ." William Hood in *The International Journal of Intelligence and Counterintelligence*, Vol. 1 No. 2, 1986, page 177. Mr. Hood kindly wrote to us and explained that he should have said "I *think* mole had its origins in the Elizabethan usage." A suggestion by Mr. Hood led us to a play by Thomas Singleton, written between 1625 and 1642, entitled *Talpae Sive Conjuratio Papistica* ("The Moles or the Popish Plot"). This survives only in manuscript in the Bodleian Library Ms Rawlison D. 288, and it is evident that mole here is used in the sense we have indicated in the text and is in conformity with Lord Verulam's usage. We are indebted to Ms. Judith Farley of the Library of Congress for the reference. We referred our inquiry to the Bodleian and were advised by Dr. B.C. Barker-Benfield that the general theme of the piece is conspiracy rather than spying, referring as it does to the Gunpowder Plot. He kindly offered a translation of the Prologue: "We examine and reveal the tricks of the moles (for so they are called) and the blind paths of purblind and underground evil, the crime of darkness." He adds: "So my tentative conclusion is that while 'mole' is a peculiarly apt term for Guy Fawkes and his fellow-conspirators, it does not seem to be being used in the modern sense."

42. See *A Table Alphabeticall of Hard Usual English Words, The First English Dictionary by Robert Cawdrey*, Robert A. Peters, Gainesville, FL: Scholar's Facsimiles and Reprints, 1966. This is a facsimile reproduction of the only known surviving copy of Cawdrey's approximately 2,500 entries, which is in the Bodleian Library. This list does not contain an entry for "mole," a sufficiently common denizen of the English countryside which, like "cat" or "dog," is not thought of sufficient curiosity to merit inclusion; crocodile is found therein. So, of interest to us, is "conspire"—agree together to do evil. Peters (XIV) writes: "Thus the first English dictionary was given birth in 1604 in Cawdrey's Table Alphabeticall." Cawdrey

records: "Now such are thought apt words, that properly agree unto that thing, which they signifie to plainly expresse the nature of the same." Had an espionage usage for mole been common at that time, it is probable that it would have found a place in Cawdrey's compilation.

43. *On Language*, William Safire, New York: Times Books, 1980, page 256. This entry is accompanied by a delightful cartoon. It had occurred to us that a search of illustrations might also be of value in pinning down the entry of the term into the literature.

44. As his latest editor observes, the work "is written in superbly elegant English." Lockyer, op. cit., supra note 32, page 20.

45. We have used the Folio Society edition because of the quality of the editing, the care with which the text has been studied with respect to unusual terms requiring explanation, and the fact that its year of publication (1971) brings it into a significant time frame from our own particular perspective here.

46. See, for example, *Henry VII*, S. B. Chrimes, London: Eyre Methuen, 1972, pages 68–94, "The Problem of Security."

47. The authors wish to thank Mr. Marvin Stone of the Dallas Public Library, Rare Books Section, for facilitating reference to this work. For some interesting observations, see *Dictionaries and THAT Dictionary*, James Sledd and Wilma R. Ebbitt, Chicago: Scott, Foresman, 1962. With respect to Dr. Johnson, see the article, "On Dictionaries," Ernest Weekley, *The Atlantic Monthly*, June 1924, pages 762–791: "One would give a good deal to have Dr. Johnson's definition of a bolshevist" (page 16).

48. Generations of English schoolboys were brought up between the wars on a diet of japes and such in delightful period language in the pages of *The Gem* and *The Magnet*, wherein Harry Wharton, Captain of Greyfriars, featured prominently. So did the word "beast" in a context quite familiar to the Cambridge bounders and those who wrote about them. The transatlantic Fisher T. Fish springs to mind, but no mole.

49. This work, entitled *A New English Dictionary or A Compleat Collection of the Most Proper and Significant Words*

and Terms of Art Commonly Used in the LANGUAGE, London: Robert Knaplock, 1713, is most important as a source because it treats terms used in relation to "Affairs of Sea and War."

50. *An Universal Etymological English Dictionary*, N. Bailey, London: R. Ware, 1796, also gives four entries for mole, giving as that which concerns us the following: "a little creature that lives underground." It is shown to have quite ancient English origins, remarked on by other lexicographers as deriving from "Mold" = Earth, and the Saxon word for "to throw up." A further interesting and unique entry gives mole as "a river in Surrey, so called because like a mole, it forceth its Passage under ground and thereby mixes its water with the *Thames*." But no mole in the espionage sense.

51. See XIX DNB, page 821. Marjory Hollings writes: "The efficiency of the intelligence system established during the protectorate by John Thurloe was the admiration of his contemporaries and has been fully recognized by historians, though little has been said of his debt to his assistant, Samuel Morland, in the technical part of the work of censorship, through which so much of his intelligence was acquired." Thomas Barrett: "A Study in the Secret History of the Interregnum," 43 *The English Historical Review* (1928), pages 33–65, on page 33.

Miss Hollings further concludes, "Thurloe's organization of intelligence, so justly yet so mistakenly admired by his contemporaries, needed no such 'masterpiece' of corruption as they believed" (page 65). This scholarly work was an exploration of Thurloe's relationship with Sir Richard Willys, a secret counselor of Charles II, who belonged to a small, superclandestine organization known as the "Sealed Knot," then working in England for the Restoration. To have had an agent in place in this organization would have represented a remarkable coup by Thurloe, and the uncritical might today have referred to Willys as a mole.

He was certainly not so described in his own times. Professor Underdown, in more modern times, writes: "It is impossible to establish whether Willys was a regular spy for Thurloe, or one who only occasionally supplied information." Cited in "Sir Richard Willys and Secretary Thurloe," *The English Historical Review*, 1954, pages 373–387, on page 384.

See, too, *Royalist Conspiracy in England 1649–1660*, David Underdown, New Haven, CT: Yale University Press (1969). "The objection that slow, painstaking caution had always been characteristic of the Sealed Knot is answered by documentary proof that there was a traitor in its midst. He has justly been called Thurloe's 'masterpiece of corruption,' and his name was Sir Richard Willys" (page 194). And again, on page 332: "The Royalists were used to plots. They had organized or sympathized with them themselves. Is it surprising that they regarded the use of spies and agents provocateurs as part of the standard procedure of government, and accepted their depositions at face value or at least as convenient political ammunition?" No mention, in this scholarly work, of moles in the seventeenth century.

52. Thomas Scot (or Scott) was executed (unlike Thurloe) shortly after the Restoration. See "Thomas Scot's account of his actions as Intelligencer during the Commonwealth," C. H. Firth, 12, *The English Historical Review*, 1897, page 116. Sir Charles Firth writes, on page 117:"It is evident from the tenor of Scot's paper that he had been led to hope a full confession would save his life, but his revelations were not considered sufficiently valuable." In any event, they contain nothing about moles.

53. On a number of occasions, we wrote to Messrs. Corson and Crowley but were not favored with a reply. Having gone through the publisher, we cannot be sure our requests for information ever reached the authors.

Our research on the point led us, however, into another byway. Knowing of Mr. Crowley's former association with the CIA, we wrote to that Agency in the hope of ascertaining whether anything in its library had provided the reference sought. Again, we had difficulty in obtaining a reply. Thanks to the intervention of the Honorable Phil Gramm, U.S. Senator for Texas, this difficulty was overcome, and an unsatisfactory and somewhat patronizing correspondence ensued. We decided to conclude this on receiving a letter from David D. Gries, Director of Congressional Affairs, in which he stated: "I have no way of knowing the source of the statement in the book *The New KGB*." That statement can be allowed to speak for itself. We are left in the uncomfortable position of having to admit that if Secretary Thurloe ever used the term, we cannot find it without further assistance.

54. *A Collection of State Papers of John Thurloe, Esq.*, Ed. Thomas Birch, London, 1742, seven volumes. The DNB entry concerning them, written by Sir Charles Firth, tells of their history and observes: "Thurloe's vast correspondence is the chief authority for that history of the Protectorate." XIX DNB, page 824.

55. See, for example, "Thurloe and the Post Office," C. H. Firth, 13, *The English Historical Review*, 1898, pages 527–533, which contains a very technical description of Thurloe's methods of operating. There is one very interesting allusion, from our point of view, on page 530 ". . . to plow with their owne heifers and soe to frustrate all their designs against him." But no reference to moles is found.

56. See *John Wildman: Plotter to Postmaster*, Maurice Ashley, London: Jonathan Cape, 1947. This should be required reading for all interested in spies and spying.

57. Firth, op. cit., supra note 55, page 529.

58. Ashley, op. cit., supra note 56, page 108.

59. Wildman can certainly have been properly described, at a certain period of his life, as a penetration agent. Ashley, page 112, writes of him: "Was Wildman the traitor? Naturally, in view of his peculiar relations with Thurloe, suspicion must rest upon him." But he is not spoken of, even in these comparatively modern times, as a mole.

60. Professor Underdown reports that the picturesque language of the day had it of "Scot's informers, swarming over all England as Lice and Frogs did in Egypt." Op. cit., supra note 51, page 20. But not, again, as moles.

61. We have the work of Alexander Orlov, *Handbook of Intelligence and Guerrilla Warfare*, Ann Arbor, Michigan: University of Michigan Press, 1963, but this is really too slight for firm guidance in these matters.

I Was An NKVD Agent, Anatoli Granovski, New York: Devin-Adair, 1962, is very informative but contains no mention of moles. Granovski does refer to Fifth Columnists (page 139). Indeed, none of the Russians defecting before or shortly after World War II seems to have used the word mole or anything like it.

62. We wrote to Le Carré (Mr. David Cornwell) on a number of occasions but were not favored with a reply. He is, of course, too young to have had personal knowledge of this

usage, and the statement must be presumed to be based on derived knowledge. When that knowledge was gained, as opposed to when it was employed, is of interest.

Another possibility suggests itself from a reading of *Smiley's Circus*, David Monaghan, New York: St. Martin's Press, 1986. Monaghan writes on page 11: "The final important element in the creation of Le Carré's world is the invention of a language of spying. Authenticity is rooted in thoroughness because, rather than introduce a few terms designed to give a flavor of espionage 'jargon,' Le Carré offers nearly two hundred words and phrases." This does raise the real possibility that the word mole is a "genuine KGB term" only within the artificial confines of Le Carré's world. The impression is heightened by another reference of Professor Monaghan on pages 162–163: "By the end of the decade Smiley appears to be a spent force and he earns himself the nickname mole." Shades of Bormann and Bailey, if not Barnum and Bailey!

63. We are advised by Soviet sources that the statement by Le Carré is not correct and that the term became known to the Soviet Union from Western sources in the early 1970s. We have sought a more ample verification from the Philology Institute, Moscow State University (MGU), but this had not been received at the time we went to press.

64. Dame Rebecca West, a most elegant, well-informed writer with exceptional gifts of expression, does not use the word mole in her seminal work, *The New Meaning of Treason*, published in 1964.

65. Among the most notable is Lord Dacre (Professor Hugh Trever Roper). Of course, H. A. R. Philby, himself no mean philologist, might have been able to shed some light on this.

66. On these meanings, see Partridge, op. cit., supra note 2, page 746.

67. The flyleaf of the novel, *The Mole*, Dan Sherman, New York: Arbor House, 1977, records the following: "*Mole*—A deep penetration agent, so-called because he burrows deep into the fabric of the enemy's intelligence structure."

68. "The Cat Can Do What the Tiger Can Not," *The Dermis Probe*, Idries Shah, New York: E. P. Dutton, 1971, page 138.

69. For a novel that illustrates this well, see *Wilderness of Mirrors*, Donald Seaman, New York: Harper & Row, 1984.

70. For a perhaps unequaled fictional treatment of this, see *The Private Sector*, Joseph Hone, New York: E. P. Dutton, 1972.

71. A society such as our own does not call upon the mole, in the ordinary course of events, to make any extraordinary profession of loyalty. Different is the case where we try to penetrate, say, a terrorist organization with a mole of our own. "Some of the groups are so fanatic," warns former CIA Director Stansfield Turner, "they will put your agent to a test that he can't possibly accept." "Spying on Terrorists—It's a Tall Order," *U.S. News and World Report*, 8 July 1985, page 30. Obviously, a latter-day Azev is called for, but such an agent is a danger on his own account.

72. This was the problem of Mr. Peter Wright, formerly of MI5, in his crusade to prove his Director to have been a Soviet mole. For more on this, see Chapter 6.

73. Dame Rebecca West makes the interesting observation that "The government would have been well advised to specify the reasons which had made the security organization so long nourish this viper in their bosoms, and to announce the resignation of some of the bosoms. But this was not done, and the Philby affair is an unhealed sore in the public mind. Doubtless there were sound reasons for this failure to solve the mystery, but all the same the sore did not heal." Op. cit., supra note 10, page 365.

74. The last resort of the frustrated mole-hunter is the Fourth Estate. How effective—yet perilous—this can be is to be seen from the works of Chapman Pincher, especially *Their Trade Is Treachery*, London: Sedgwick and Jackson, 1981, and *Too Secret Too Long*, New York: St. Martin's Press, 1984, and the Parliamentary responses they evoked.

75. See "The Spy Who Came Between Friends," *U.S. News and World Report*, 30 March 1987, page 32. We have still seen but the tip of the iceberg in this matter.

76. Since the early 1960s, there have been a number of proposals to combine the British Secret Intelligence Service (MI6) and the Security Service (MI5) by placing them under a single directorate or the oversight of a single coordinator with responsibility solely to the prime minister. None of these proposals has prospered.

77. If the proposal made to Christopher Boyce had been accepted, he might well have become a genuine Soviet mole. See *The Falcon and the Snowman*, Robert Lindsey, New York: Simon & Schuster, 1979, pages 202–203. An interesting intellectual exercise may be indulged in by assuming acceptance and consummation of the arrangement and what would have been necessary to provide the answers called for in this text.

78. This was certainly the case with the initial investigations of Philby. Record keeping in the *Dritte Reich*, by comparison, was so meticulous and detailed that it survived the war in such a state as to allow whole histories to be reconstructed. What this means, in practice, is that different methods have to be used to obtain the evidence.

79. On the by no means proven assumption that Donald Maclean was a Soviet mole, how much better it might have been had an early determination been made to strike a useful deal with him rather than trying to nail his carcass to the wall. For an interesting side note on this idea, see "Lots of Smoke—Little Fire," Fredric Mitchell, *International Journal of Intelligence and Counterintelligence*, Volume 1, No. 4, 1986, pages 111–118.

80. "My eyes are small, it is true, but that has made my ears sharp, and they serve me well now. I hear a sound which seems to come from where you stand, and it tells of a foe." The lynx and the mole, *Aesop's Fables*.

81. We are especially of the view, in common with that taken by the late Sir Maurice Oldfield, that there ought not to be an overly great reliance placed upon polygraph tests and that these should always be used in conjunction with other control measures. Recent disclosures concerning Sir Maurice must now call into question his aversion to the polygraph.

82. There are, of course, subtle ways of handling even this problem. See "The Fox Who Was Made a Sufi," Idries Shah, op. cit., supra note 68, page 168.

83. "The initial reaction was 'We have missed them!' For it was virtually impossible in those early days after the war to even consider the possibility that there were no secret Nazi groups in action, engaged in clandestine political activity to keep alive the myth of the 'thousand-year Reich.' " *The Fourth*

and Richest Reich, Edwin Hartrich, New York: Macmillan, 1980, page 29.

See also *Denazification*, Constantine Fitzgibbon, London: Michael Joseph, 1969.

84. See, for example, *The Trial of Adolf Hitler*, Phillipe van Rjndt, New York: Summit Books, 1978.

85. Modern demographic movements fueled by war, persecution, and economic considerations provide endless opportunities for the painless insertion of sleepers. In the dissident movement, the Soviet Union has an excellent vehicle for the task, and it cannot be doubted that it has been effectively used, especially with respect to Israel and the United States. Hispanic immigration, which has defied all attempts at even the imposition of minimum security procedures, is an excellent means of introducing sleepers into the United States.

An excellent example is furnished by Leopold Trepper, the great Soviet spy master. "Hechalutz was a Zionist body financed by wealthy American Jews. Its aim was to promote immigration to the Promised Land. . . . Hechalutz was responsible for picking the small, privileged band of immigrants officially allowed into the country each year. With typically American regard for future returns, the organization's backers sought to fight Communism even as they furthered the Zionist cause. Preference was therefore given to candidates who appeared to be easy prey for the Party's recruiting agents." Gilles Perrault, op. cit., supra note 35, pages 16–17. There is no reason to believe matters have drastically changed.

86. Such creatures are most usually to be found huddled at the lowest end of the scale, where suspicion is minimal yet the opportunities for effective espionage abound. Even in these days of extensive, executive networking, the secretary remains the key figure (though rarely appreciated as such) in most organizations. Beware of the secretary left behind after the boss is fired or has moved on!

87. The year 1984 now lies behind us, without too much damage to our psyches or our social systems. These have not noticeably become intolerably restrictive, and totalitarian systems in general have tended to become more relaxed. Yet there is a real need at times for Big Brother to watch more vigilantly that these tendencies do not find themselves in need of a drastic reversal.

88. *Architectural Design for Crime Prevention*, Washington, D.C.: U.S. Government Printing Office, 1973.

89. *"C": A Biography of Sir Maurice Oldfield, Head of MI6*, Richard Deacon, London: Futura Publications, 1985, page 1. This work now has to be approached with extreme caution in view of the latest disclosures concerning Sir Maurice. It nevertheless contains much of real value for the discriminating professional reader.

6

FOOTPRINTS:
Tracking the Spy
Through the System

Maybe I ought to look like a Wall Street laywer.
                                   Rudolph Abel[1]

*But today there are millions of people as common-
place as Houghton who, by their employment in certain factories or offices, have access to documents
which can deliver us over to death, with help from an
arsenal concealed behind the most innocent piece of
half-timbering in suburbia.*

                                   Rebecca West[2]

*How had the Gestapo found out all this information?
Had they spent time, and money tracking down this
irrelevant data about Erickson's early business career
just to be able to scare him with a demonstration of
their thoroughness? Only years later, when the war
ended, did the OSS learn how simple it had all been.
Months before Pearl Harbor a German agent in America had contacted the Cornell University Alumni Association and obtained a record of all of Erickson's
changes of address and his jobs since he was gradua-
ted. It was as easy as that.*

                                   Alexander Klein[3]

*Like every other art, spying has its unknown men of
talent; they are needless to say its greatest prac-
titioners.*

                                   Gilles Perrault[4]

I took the massive document and as I couldn't read Chinese then, the scribe did it for me, sitting next to me and reading aloud. It took several hours, and it was a frightening revelation. On those hundreds of pages were handwritten denunciation forms from colleagues, friends and various people I had encountered only once or twice. When I returned to my cell I was relieved to have reached this important moment in my prison career, but my head was spinning—how many persons whom I had trusted without a second thought had betrayed me!

Bao Ruo-Wang[5]

Some spies are never caught. In some instances, this is a tribute to the skill and prudence with which they exercise their calling. In other cases, they have simply been extraordinarily lucky in the truest sense of that controversial term. There remain others who have eluded all efforts to identify and apprehend them. The counterespionage service has just not proven to be adequate to the task. While there is something galling about the result, for no one likes to suffer a professional defeat at the hands of the opposition, its ever-present likelihood should be sensibly recognized. The spy *can* do his work and get away, and many will do so more often than we would care to admit.

There is no such thing as a spy-proof system. Someone will always come forward to tackle the most daunting of tasks, even those where the prospects of success seem slim and the penalties of failure dreadful. Those who do succeed under such circumstances are truly remarkable—sometimes so remarkable that their tales have to be told, even though in heavily fictionalized form. It is hard to remain silent forever about some great exploit; it runs against human nature. But there are those whose story we shall never learn. They have successfully passed through the mine field without leaving any trace of their passage or mission. And having accomplished this, they have vanished as silently as they came. There are no witnesses to such accomplishments; it is as though they never occurred.

Such cases are undoubtedly uncommon, but we must assume that they can—and do—occur. They are as difficult to prove as murder in the absence of a corpse. Difficult, but not impossible. We are not concerned here with such exotic curiosities. But they do serve in the present context to make our point. Spies and spying can be evidenced by the apprehension of the human being engaged in espionage, a process of habeas corpus, if you will, or by evidencing the activities and their author by reference to their impressions upon the system within which they have occurred. If the system is so constructed that it retains no prints or they can be wiped clean, no trace of the activities will be found—unless we can produce a live body and that individual can be persuaded to disclose his activities to us. These initial premises must be kept firmly in mind as we proceed to consider what is involved in tracking the spy through the system.

Again, we must invite a short excursion to consider a point we have made in other forms in an earlier context. We may well observe and be able to fully authenticate a spy's progress through the system without knowing, in timely fashion, that he is a spy. That ugly fact becomes apparent only at some later time when we have discovered the damage and are looking for its author, or when we are backtracking to verify some posterior suspicion. Spies—the really good spies, that is—live among us, leading lives scarcely different from those of their neighbors. They do the same kinds of things, have (apparently) the same sorts of mundane problems to which they find very much the same types of solutions. If they are rich, they live among the rich and do as such folk are wont to do. If they are poor, we can expect to see much the same ravages of poverty in terms of nourishment, possessions, attitudes, and the like. There is no large (or even small) sign upon these people that marks them out as spies. These people are integrated. They blend in and have an essentially appropriate "fit" with the communities of which they are a part. And why indeed should they not? Spying, like any other calling requiring extreme discretion in its exercise, *can* be sufficiently divorced from other aspects of life as to call no particular attention to itself. After all, do we not have many neighbors of whom we would truthfully say, "I really have no idea what he does." This is particularly true of those who are self-employed, especially if that employment is reasonably conventional and of itself excites little curiosity.

How many of those who had dealings in the ordinary course with the quiet, mild-mannered Emil Goldfuss would have suspected that he was in reality a high-ranking Soviet intelligence officer working as the head of an illegal network in the United States?[6] Such people leave evidence of their presence among us through their daily contacts with ordinary people, going about their ordinary business. They pay their rent, buy their provisions, and talk with their neighbors about the consequential and the inconsequential. They leave footprints everywhere of varying kinds and degrees of permanence as they pass through the system. Their transactions may be recorded and documented, and they may be remembered, at least for a while, by those with whom they have dealt. If the interval between the event and the inquiry concerning it is not too great, they can be situated in a certain kind of social context, a sort of tableau or pastiche. To a greater or lesser degree, the same is true of everyone; life goes on, and willy-nilly, we are a part of it.

At the time they are occurring, many things seem to be of but slight importance, scarcely worthy of note. The doctor who had circumcised the real Gordon Lonsdale had probably performed a similar operation on others on many occasions. He would ordinarily have had little reason to single out one particular operation for recall; and it could hardly have figured in his wildest dreams that his evidence concerning the matter would, years in the future, be crucial in securing the conviction for espionage of the Soviet agent who had assumed the identity of the tiny infant who had been his patient. "I worked on Jonathan Pollard's[7] automobile" is unlikely to figure as a headline in the *National Enquirer*, unless the mechanic can, in some way, be tied to an extraordinary discovery germane to Pollard's life *as a spy*. A friend, an experienced police officer, had a chance encounter with Ronald Pelton[8] shortly before that NASA employee was exposed as a long-term Soviet agent. The chance meeting was inconsequential and was not less so after Pelton's arrest and trial. But that fact was not apparent at the time. Pelton had left a footprint, a remembered footprint, but it was not recognizably that of Pelton the spy. The point is of no little importance in the matters we are now considering.

Life is made up of inconsequential encounters—with spies, perhaps, and others—with a few events of real significance thrown in for good measure. From the perspective of the spy-catcher who comes upon the scene later, often much later, it is a matter of sorting the wheat from the chaff. It is easy to be overwhelmed with the sheer magnitude of the task; there seems to be so much chaff and so little wheat. Spies do not *necessarily* leave distinctive "spylike" footprints as they pass through our world. Those they do leave may very quickly fade from sight; even those that are clearly noticeable and can be attributed with certainty may not lead anywhere particularly interesting. To be meaningful to the spy-catcher, the footprints he has picked up must not only be those of the spy, but they must be made to relate to him *as a spy* in some way. It may be important to follow the spy in his transactions at the local supermarket if that is where he exchanges cash for information with a professional contact. It may simply be a waste of time if all he is going to do is buy groceries.

Any footprint, anything showing the presence of the spy somewhere in the system at a particular time, *might* be useful and even significant. But among the myriad crisscrossing trails, with their confusing patterns and triviality of meaning, there will be gaps. The spy, like millions of others among whom he moves, simply disappears off the screen. No traces of him or his doings are to be found. There simply are no footprints that can be seen with which he can be reliably connected. He may have been careful where he has trodden, or the ravages of time may have obliterated the impressions of his passage. But there is also the possibility that the medium over which he passed was unsuitable for registering any durable signs of his passing. The progress through life of many, if not most, of us is punctuated by such blanks; the trail disappears for a while, only to emerge elsewhere with no seeming connection to what has gone before. Yet it is all one life, and it tells a coherent story—if it can be stitched together by one who understands his business.

When we speak of footprints in the present context, we do not mean to be taken too literally. By footprints, we mean *all those indications, of whatever kind, which mark an individual's progress through life and serve as pointers to the direction he has taken*. They are the signs, tangible and intangible, of the trail he has followed. As a tracker can look at an impression in damp earth, at a bent twig, or a crushed plant and infer from these signs much about the creature who has made them (including, often, its intentions) so too can the expert who reads the spoor of spies inform himself concerning his prey. Some can read tracks across barren rock and know, after scores of miles, where a visible trail will begin once more. As in all such arts, skill and experience go hand in hand. The hunter may well have acquired much knowledge in these matters in a lifetime in pursuit of game, but if he is wise, he will always seek the aid of those who are truly expert in this arcane field and who are peculiarly familiar with the terrain. The hunter should ideally know enough so that he knows just what he does not know about these matters and be ever ready to avail himself of the assistance of specialists in these tasks. Most spy-catchers will be good generalists. They will know what is required to get on the trail, and they should know what is needed to be able to follow it. Those who are soundest in judgment will know when they are getting out of their depth and will know where to turn for the right kind of help. In this electronic age, this admonition is very necessary. The world of the computer and supercomputer is a veritable jungle. None should venture therein unless he is thoroughly trained to find his way in, out, and through the thickets. Tracking those who operate in this medium is a job for experts, and the spy-catcher should learn what advice he needs and how to obtain it. He should know, too, when he is not really getting it. Only the arrogant and the foolhardy plunge in unguarded, and the results are predictable.

There are periods in the lives of the most commonplace of people (as well as the most remarkable) that will appear as a complete black to even the most diligent of researchers. It is not that they have been inactive, or even that they have greatly changed their lifestyles or habitat. Rather, what they have been doing does not seem to have registered or made a particular impression. For most people, this is quite unimportant. Their lives are not subjected to especially rigorous scrutiny, and there is rarely much need to fill in the blanks later. For a few souls, the blanks are the rule rather than the exception, interrupted by only a few, brief interludes where something of significance can be evidenced in these matters. The professional spy is carefully educated in these matters. It is an important part of his training, whether or not it is consciously conducted in these terms. Those who must live the greater part of their professional lives in the shadows have to learn how to walk when they have to cross the occasional patch of bright sunlight. The professional spy learns how to leave the right kind of footprints—those he can explain to his own advantage. He will also know how to leave the right kind of blanks, where the trail comes or appears to come to a dead end. The professional spy will be adept at assuming many different identities and will have no difficulty in procuring all the necessary appurtenances and opportunities to evidence them. Multiple identities produce multiple footprints, often significantly different from one another and in widely different locations. By this means, the skillful professional spy can overcome the physical difficulties of being (or appearing to be) in more than one place at the same time.

We would like to recall here what we had written earlier about identity. In the present connection, we would reiterate the separateness of human being and identity. For it is the *identity*, as we defined it, rather than the human being as such that leaves what we have called footprints in our system and that these footprints are as artificial as that which was responsible for making them. The identity is a socially constructed extension of the human being. All manifestations of its being and presence are ultimately traceable to the activities of *some* human being, not necessarily the one regularly associated with the identity. Our point is that this artificial creation is capable of a life of its own to a large extent independent of those who have generated it. What we have called footprints tell a story concerning themselves; they do not necessarily tell the truth concerning the person who is supposed to have made them. What they mean and, especially, what they mean in relation to that person requires careful study and evaluation.[9] It is a failure to appreciate this that often leads the hunters off on the wrong track.

It seems important to bear the following in mind. First, the footprints can be allowed to speak for themselves, to tell their story without embellishment or corroboration. Second, the supposed maker of the footprints can tell of their making, and/or, independently, others can tell of their being made. Sometimes evidence from only one of these sources will be available. At other times, it will be supported by evidence from the others in some degree. Ideally, all three should coincide to a high degree if the proper authentication is to be obtained. Let us look at a simple example. An individual claims a degree from a well-known university. He produces a diploma showing him to have been awarded the degree in question. The paper speaks for itself and, if properly authenticated, will show a person of the name it bears to have had conferred upon him such a degree. *Res ipsa loquitur. Loquitur vere. Sed quod in inferno vult dicere?* The graduate can offer evidence to show that he is indeed the person entitled to display the certificate as his own by demonstrating knowledge of what was required to earn it, of his experiences in the course of his studies, of the award itself. Lastly, those who observed the performance (teachers, fellow students, administrators, family, and friends) can testify to the earning of the degree and of its being awarded. The various combinations necessary for conviction can be considered and conjured with, as well as a host of situations suggested by the imagination where one or more of the requisite elements is absent or defective. In a similar way, every footprint is susceptible to examination by the same methods. Only the evidence tendered and the standards of proof considered acceptable in each case will vary. The footprint paradigm, adapted as circumstances require, is an indispensable tool for tracking the individual as he passes through the system. All this assumes, however, that there *is* a footprint that may be considered in this fashion and subjected to the appropriate tests.

We, of our age and place, are beset with all the perils facing a pampered generation in these matters. A sudden loss of the advantages we take for granted can be paralyzing. For all our technological superiority, we are in some ways as handicapped in an emergency as the civilized man, suddenly bereft of all his accustomed appliances, who is set down in a remote jungle. The senses so highly developed in our early ancestors and still vibrant in those who do not enjoy our customary advantages have long since atrophied. Going back to basics under such conditions is a life-or-death matter of most uncertain outcome. The analogy here is not farfetched. In the so-called developed countries, we live in a society that has become extraordinarily reliant upon documentation and mechanization for the most basic and ordinary of human transactions. The digital computer in particular has revolutionized our lives to a remarkable degree even within the last decade. Investigation of records of all kinds is now dominated

by the computer. In public libraries, card catalogs are fast
disappearing and being replaced by ubiquitous monitors at
which quite young, solemn-faced children can be seen working with touching intensity.

By means of these electronic marvels, we are able to accomplish feats of tracking that would have been prohibitively
time-consuming but a short while ago. But these facilities
have been purchased at a high price in other departments.
Computers have not only changed our way of life, they have
radically altered our way of thinking about things and the way
in which certain tasks are performed. They have created their
own state of dependency, of indispensability. Record keeping, on a large scale, is now almost entirely entrusted to the
computer and those who operate it. It is not fanciful to state
that nowadays we owe our very existence (or, at the very
least, its recognition) to the operations of this vast, complex,
and all-encompassing machinery. Our vital data is fed into its
insatiable maw. Theoretically, it should be possible to rapidly
construct for those entitled to review it, a comprehensive
picture of our being and our doings once the appropriate
steps have been taken by the machine operator. Little wonder that the contemporary rage is a curious electronic figment
called Max Headroom, conjured into entertaining existence
as a reflection of the growing power and versatility of the
computer.

As we all know, often through bitter, personal experience,
things do not always work out as they are supposed to. It has
been well said that to err is human, but to really foul up you
need a computer. With such marvellously developed devices,
everything is on the grand scale, which means, in practice,
that errors, where they occur, are of considerable magnitude
and often surprisingly difficult to correct. These machines
have what appears to us to be an obstinacy, an arrogance
almost, which prevents them from recognizing that they can,
and do, make mistakes. It is all too easy to take an anthropomorphic view of these monsters and ascribe to them emotions
and sentiments that, rationally, even the most intelligent of
them cannot really have. They, software and hardware alike,
are still the creatures of their human masters, those who
design, build, and operate them. They are simply the magnifiers of human mistakes where these occur. We cannot sensibly do without computers. They are now a permanent fact of

our lives and we must learn to coexist with their quirks. But they do give a new and much more technical dimension to the business of tracking spies through the system.

The current emphasis (indeed, reliance) on computers does tend to give a distorted picture of what is involved in the detection and tracking of the spy's footprints. As a healthy corrective, we ought to perhaps reflect upon an earlier, less-regulated age where we can see more clearly what is involved in this process. What we would stress is that what we are seeking fundamentally to do has not altered very much as a result of the changes in record keeping that have been facilitated by these advanced forms of handling and preserving large quantities of data. We must keep firmly in mind, in the simplest of terms, our basic tasks—namely to find and keep track of a particular individual within our system—and to demonstrate by means of what we can establish concerning that person and his activities that he is a spy. What all this massive recording effort is designed to effect is a situation where it becomes increasingly difficult for any individual to pass *unnoticed* within the system. The individual is theoretically under scrutiny at all times so that what he does and where he is can be *evidenced*. Moreover, it can be evidenced so rapidly that it will be possible, once the data is available to those with this purpose in mind, to secure his physical presence in order that he can be examined in person or through his representatives.

One of the problems immediately becomes apparent. We have not yet reached the position where, at the touch of a button, the human individual (rather than the data concerning him) appears before us. Such feats of materialization belong only to the realms of *Star Trek* and *Dr. Who*. We must reconcile ourselves to the fact that our data retrieval systems, however comprehensive and efficient, can only produce footprints. The individual responsible for their creation is still somewhere on the trail ahead of us. All we can do, by means of our advancing technology and the way in which we employ it, is to constantly seek to reduce the gap so as to bring the prey within sight and seizure range. In the last decade or so, we have made extraordinary strides in that direction, but the fact remains that tracking is one thing, while capture is another. The key to integrating the two lies in the processing of the data so as to give it meaning and make it rapidly accessible in such form that it is useful to those who have the tasks of apprehension and categorization assigned to them.

Not only must the relevant data assist in the spy's capture, but it must also evidence that he is a spy within the parameters of whatever definition is used for that purpose.[10] As we have seen, most of the data relevant for the purpose of placing the individual to whom it corresponds somewhere, at some time, within the system, has very little utility as evidence for assigning him to the category of spy. This latter task is substantially one of interpretation. It is concerned with the meaning of data rather than its acquisition or retrieval. The data, however, is essential to the task, whatever way it is obtained. And the more data that is available and the more reliable it is, the greater the chance of arriving at its correct interpretation.

Most of what we have been discussing thus far turns upon what we might call *the sensitivity of the system*. Some sociopolitical systems are more susceptible than others to registering, in recoverable and recognizable form, the traces of those who have passed through or sojourned within them. Their texture is such that they retain impressions like light-sensitive paper used in some photographic processes. Some such impressions are general and transitory in character, while others are highly specific and intended to have an enduring nature. In some way or another, all are evidentiary. Thus, a bus ticket, for example, is within the first category. All fare-paying passengers are issued the same type of impersonal document, which has a primary life extending over the duration of the journey for which it is issued. It does not of itself identify the purchaser or holder. After its primary purpose has been served, it might be discarded or retained. If it is kept or acquired for some later purpose, all it will sensibly evidence is its issue to some person and possibly its use for the purpose for which it was issued. It requires something else to link it with a particular purchaser or passenger. Its utility as a footprint depends first upon its material content; it may have a date and time of issue and particulars of a route imprinted upon it. It may bear marks of inspection en route. Such facts have a peculiar value for the tracker because they enable him to situate the footprint in a context from which he may derive additional meaning and corroborative evidence. When this type of transaction is contrasted with the issuance and use of, say, an airline ticket, some of the distinctions we have made in abstract terms take on a special meaning.

A person taking a bus ride, where the ticket is issued for a relatively short journey and for a comparatively small sum of money, leaves a very different footprint than one who travels by air. The bus traveller desirous of remaining anonymous ordinarily has not the slightest difficulty in so doing. In the ordinary course of affairs, the person issuing his ticket and accepting his fare has no professional interest in his passenger's identity. He may be concerned with seeing that the passenger is not inebriated or disorderly in dress or conduct, but the issuance of the ticket will usually be conducted without formality or inquiry to anyone tendering the proper price of passage. A person wishing to travel anonymously on a scheduled commercial flight is, however, forced to adopt certain stratagems to that end, all of which involve a degree of inconvenience and may require actual deception. For well-founded reasons, air travel produces a more highly sensitized environment, in which those who tread leave a different and somewhat less transitory footprint. A careful examination of the procedures and their practical implementation will suggest not only ways to avoid their intent, but the degree of reliance that can be placed upon their product for the purposes of tracking any particular individual through the system.

At any one time, most of us are in possession of or have about our persons an extraordinary amount of inconsequential debris, all of which is capable of telling some sort of story about us and our doings, who we are, and where we have been.[11] Currency, ticket stubs, clothing labels, laundry marks, medications, pocket books, toilet articles, an odd candy, and a host of things too numerous to name may indict us or exonerate us if they can be made to speak. But, as we earlier observed, what do they have to say? And, can they say it alone or do they have tongue only in conjunction with other things, material or otherwise?

Such trivial items are far from being unimportant to the business of spying. Think of the London theater ticket stubs so carefully, yet with studied casualness, secreted in the uniform pocket of "Major Martin," Royal Marines, "The Man Who Never Was."[12] They were designed to give the impression to the finder of the corpse that the purported officer had attended a particular theatrical performance. A footprint was deliberately left for those who would find it. The footprint was neither true nor false. It was the interpretation of it that had to be so categorized. The tickets were genuine; the impression they were to give was not. A birth certificate is no more conclusive for the existence of the human being named therein than is a tombstone for the termination of the existence of the person whose grave it is supposed to mark. It is all data, however trivial, fragmentary, and unfathomable on its own. A mere bus ticket, then, may lead to the gallows or a prison cell as surely as the presence or absence of a foreskin.

In our search for simplicity, it is well to recall that spying is a clandestine activity, perhaps the clandestine activity par excellence. This trite and rather obvious fact of life tends to be taken for granted in the present context so that some of its less-striking consequences are overlooked. For the spy, it is difficult, if not impossible, to avoid leaving any footprints at all. The most he can hope for is that he will not leave any that will serve to identify him as a spy or, if even this is not possible, that he will be far enough along the trail when they are discovered that he will outdistance his would-be captors.[13] Practically speaking, clandestinity comes down to a constant search for the ideal modus operandi, one that will get the job done, but in such a way that nothing untoward seems to have been done at all to those whose interests are affected by the act. If there are no tracks going into or out of the house and nothing seems to be missing, no one is likely to cry thief! The spy's task is to avoid a suspicious presence and to devise a method of getting the goods without the abstraction being noticed. All spying comes down to some sort of variation upon these twin themes. Some objects of the spy's attentions lend themselves to being filched without any obvious evidence that a larceny has taken place.

Provided no one is watching, directly or by proxy, a secret document can be removed from a file cabinet, photocopied, and replaced without showing any obvious signs that would lead its custodians to suppose that its contents had been taken and carried away by this means. Spies have been doing this since the dawn of the age of photography and, in more primitive fashion, for centuries before that. An ordinary document is of low sensitivity. Its appearance will not normally be altered as a result of being photocopied. No evidence of it having been mishandled will be presented by the document itself. It is the system, the environment within which it is stored, and the procedures for gaining access to it and handling it that must be appropriately sensitized so as to provide security against what it contains falling into the wrong hands. The system must be so constructed that footprints *are* left by those who approach and leave; in short, a record is required of those who handle the document. Given these simple precepts, the imagination can juggle with the many possible permutations.[14] These principles are universal. The matter is only complicated in degree by the introduction of new technologies into the equation. Where data is stored electronically rather than in a file cabinet, a different kind of key and a different procedure are necessary to carry out the same sort of operation.

From a security perspective, the question we must always ask is whether it is possible to illicitly remove something of value from the system without leaving evidence of entry, handling, abstraction, and exit. Any system that allows such an operation to be carried out without leaving footprints is clearly insecure. But advanced technology has indeed created problems that did not exist in bygone ages. The electronic data bank is very different in many important respects from those repositories where secret information and other valuables were formerly guarded. Accessing these electronic storage facilities over great distances is now both feasible and commonplace. What enters and exits the system under human tutelage is a mere anonymous, coded representation, a phantom almost, that identifies itself and proceeds in the most perfect of disguises to its destination. Provided it wears the correct garb (password) and goes about its work in the proper, routine fashion, the intruder cannot merely enter and exit, taking with it whatever it has come for; its shape and connections may well remain a mystery for, to be successful, it must of necessity be exactly like all the other electronic messengers that come and go by the millisecond in this brave, new world. It is apparent that we are dealing with something analogous to what we previously discussed in connection with our airline ticket illustration. What is practiced is a deception favored by the environment. The intruder makes use of a false electronic identity or, more properly, a genuine identity falsely acquired and employed. The environment is sensitive, but it is not sufficiently discriminating.

For our present purposes, we may divide spies in general into two main classes, *scouts* and *infiltrators*. The scout is really a very special kind of military or quasi-military observer. Scouts go ahead of the main body to gather information and bring it back so that those whom they serve may be able to make intelligent decisions with respect to their purposes. This is a time-honored, unexceptionable activity.[15] The work of the scout may be offensive or defensive in nature but, in general, he will try to avoid entanglements. The secrecy of his undertaking is necessary to that end, as is the largely *external* character of his operations. His reconnaissances may carry him to the very foot of the enemy's defenses. He will perhaps seek the heights where he can overlook the walls. But his penetrations, if they are made at all, will be slight, temporary, and with the most limited of objectives in mind. They are likely to be opportunistic, dictated by events of the moment rather than conscious tactical decision. Every military commander expects the enemy to try to secure intelligence of his movements, strength, dispositions, and intentions by these means. Smoke screens of all kinds, real and metaphorical, will be thrown up to obscure and confuse, and technology has ever been pressed into service on behalf of the scout to try to overcome these defensive maneuvers. The technical problem has always been one of extending long-range vision and overcoming the difficulties posed by camouflage and concealment.[16]

The telescope, observation balloon, high-flying reconnaissance airplane, and earth-orbiting satellite are all developments of the same basic theme. These observation agents pose serious problems for those concerned with the protection of their own side's secrets. Historically, countermeasures comprehend everything from foraging patrols to killer satellites. While the occasional scout is indeed captured by these means—as was Gary Powers[17]—operations against them are not ordinarily within the province of those we have called spy-catchers in the present work. This is no reflection upon the relative importance of the scout as spy; it is an acknowledgment, rather, of his function. Fundamentally, the distinction lies in this: the scout operates in his own territory or, at the very least, that which is in dispute or of doubtful domain. Listening posts in Turkey or Cuba, AWACS that patrol Soviet borders, Soviet submarines and "trawlers" that lurk off the coasts of New England and Florida are all protected to a certain extent by the tacit recognition of their *military* mission. That Gary Powers was not a member of the United States armed forces at the time of his ill-fated flight and did not therefore have the protection of military uniform is of some significance in this analysis.[18] The act of belligerency was scarcely less, but the provocation was softened to espionage for which Powers, rather than his country, might suffer.

Most nations make a distinction between scouts and infiltrators based on what has been stated here, although there may be little difference in the quantity or quality of the intelligence that each, respectively, produces. A scout is normally less concerned with the footprints that his activities leave behind than an infiltrator; he is simply anxious to avoid being caught in the act. His seeming unconcern with his footprints does not stem from any lack of operational caution. It is simply recognition of their relative irrelevance in the wider scheme of things of which the scout and his activities are a part. There is, in this, a tacit tolerance that is not extended correspondingly to infiltrators and their doings. The scout's observations, at a reasonable distance, are an acceptable part of the other side's curiosity, and defensive screening rather than operational aggressiveness is the order of the day. Only when such external observation shades over into penetration, as in the case of the U-2 overflights, do countermeasures assume a more intolerant form. Powers paid the penalty of unacceptable intrusiveness as a result of arrogant miscalculation.

The spy-catcher is concerned, then, primarily with the footprints of the infiltrator, the spy who has made a calculated incursion within the domains of another to do that which cannot sensibly be accomplished from outside. It is evident then, as far as those having security responsibilities are concerned, that it is imperative to sensitize the environment to the point where it will register and recognize the footprints of strangers without serious inconvenience to the domain's regular inhabitants.

For his part, the infiltrator will do anything in his power to avoid leaving footprints that will give evidence of his entry, his presence, or indications of the direction he has taken. In the simplest of terms, this comes down to avoidance and disguise. It is difficult to avoid what you are not certain may be present. The spy rarely has a detailed, accurate, and up-to-date map of the hazards to guide him in these matters. If possible, he must make certain prudent assumptions about the difficulties he is likely to have to face and plan his route so as to avoid them. Thus, he will try to avoid inspections or scrutiny that may be carried out with unusual rigor.[19] If he is unable to do so, he must make sure that his story and its accompanying evidence are of a quality that will withstand such examination. If he is without documentation he knows he requires, he had better have a good explanation.[20]

It may be taken for granted that the exigencies of the spying profession in this modern age will allow the spy few safe opportunities for avoidance; there is little bare ground over which he might safely tread without leaving some sort of footprint. He must look for other options to enable himself and his purposes to remain concealed. That which offers the greatest possibilities in this regard is for the spy to try to lose himself in the crowd. He will try to avoid drawing attention to himself by doing the commonplace along with everyone else and after the same fashion; he will tread well-worn paths in the hope that the footprints he leaves will be indistinguishable from those of his companions. He will make use of fungibles, especially cash, in all his transactions, except where doing so would of itself suggest that the person concerned has something to hide.[21] He will try to avoid leaving a paper trail, for every document, every signature, might come back to haunt him at a later date. If he is forced to leave footprints, he will seek to confuse by multiplying them to the point where they contradict and bewilder.

The careful spy may avoid leaving any inconvenient impressions of a permanent or semipermanent character upon the structure of the system to which he has gained entry, but, in the nature of things, his mere presence will *always* leave a mark of some kind. That mark will be registered in the *remembrance* of those with whom he had, perforce, to come in contact in the course of his journeyings. The spy does not, cannot, work in an uninhabited desert. His labors as a spy force him to have dealings with other human beings on all levels. It is in their individual and collective memories that his footprints are to be found in some state of preservation.

Human memory, like human observation, is an unreliable,

imperfect thing.[22] It can sometimes perform prodigious feats of retention and recall, but it cannot be relied upon to do so. In this matter of footprints, evidencing some matter will often come down to a subtle duel between the spy and the spy-catcher for the sensitive areas of the human memory. This is an exceedingly profound and highly specialized subject area that must be thoroughly studied by those who would seek to avail themselves of the advantages that a sound knowledge of this terrain will afford them. There are no shortcuts to the knowledge required.

Our purpose here is not to educate in these delicate, highly technical matters, but to point up the need for education in them. There are important strategies involving this battleground that require consideration. The spy will develop techniques designed to enable him to exploit the frailties of human memory so as to leave upon it a confusing and contradictory picture of himself and his activities. At best, he wants to not be remembered at all. If he is recalled (shades of E. Howard Hunt interviewing Dita Beard),[23] he wants the outlines of what is remembered to be blurred and indistinct, worthless to those who are seeking him or trying to develop an image of him and what he does.

There are endless possibilities for muddying the still waters of memory. Physical conditions, light and darkness, human emotions, perceptions of danger, limitations of time, and distractions of all kinds play the strangest tricks with human memories. Sickness and health are also factors in what is remembered. Ideally, the spy seeks that all with whom he comes in contact might remember him differently, indistinctly, or not at all.

On the other hand, the human memory can be the most sensitive terrain of all, capable of recording, retaining, and recovering impressions of such infinite variety and exactitude as to represent a veritable cornucopia of useful indications for the discerning spy-catcher. People have items in storage that are of incalculable value to those with patience and the appropriate techniques for searching out the information they require. The expression "to jog the memory" is a useful and apt one. The appropriate stimulus has sometimes to be applied to cause an unclogging and a flow of memories that seem to have vanished forever into the pit of history.

There are, too, important problems of evaluation involved

here. Human beings register what impinges on them with little initial discrimination. A later process of sorting out and filing away takes place which tends to alter the original impression as it is received unguarded and with a vision unencumbered with any preconceptions of ultimate value. What is filed away may be relatively pristine, or it may be distorted, having been tainted with accretions that proceed from sources other than those from which the original impression emanated. What is remembered is very different from what actually occurred or was experienced; the retained memory is artificial by reason of other, unconscious processes that have altered the episode or impression before it was consigned to storage. People sometimes block out quite vivid memories; at other times, they highlight or touch up that which was originally dim and of somewhat formless character.

It seems that human beings tend to orchestrate certain major themes. In the course of filing away materials in our memory banks, we usually attach our own labels to them, mainly for the purposes of assisting in the process of retrieval. We all build our own filing or index systems with their own peculiarities, and chronology, as such, may play a minor role in selection or construction; we may file, by subject, for example, rather than other criteria. We tend to carry out this operation by reference to what all these items mean *to us;* we attach a significance to them which not only determines their place and associations in our storage system, but which is, in itself, a kind of value which we assign, often arbitrarily, to them. What is insignificant for us is sometimes of the greatest importance for others.[24]

We may well have priceless treasures buried away in the discarded lumber clogging the attics of our minds. Conversely, we may assign values to memories which are not commensurate with the worth they might more properly bear for others. All this goes to point up the constructed nature of *the content* of human memory. It is not a pure, unalloyed record, but a doctored collection that can be amended and rearranged under pressure to conform to a variety of dictates. It is, too, exceedingly frangible, for it is inevitably linked to the fortunes and caprices of the human vehicle that is its repository. The human being who is uncooperative, the one who is overly anxious to please, the one who is conscience-stricken or just plain nervous—all can alter or impact in some way the quality of what is remembered. Memory becomes a tool of convenience; people remember or forget on a defensive basis.

The human being who dies carrying with him to the grave what he has remembered represents a total and perhaps irreparable loss of valuable information. The human mind is, then, a very fragile and mercurial data bank. It must be approached with care if its contents are to be examined in a way that will permit them to be used to the best advantage. Yet for all its fragility and failings, the human memory is perhaps the most sensitive instrument for recording and retaining impressions, and it is uniquely valuable for capturing the fleeting footprints of the spy. It is probably true to say that most people who have had casual and unknowing contact with those engaged in espionage are unaware both of what they know and how valuable their knowledge might be to those who are seeking the spy. It is the task of the spy-catcher to probe these fertile fields in such a way that they yield a bountiful harvest of unreconstructed impressions. Having obtained all the information available to him by this means, he must then sift and arrange it himself before submitting it to any sort of analysis.

Let us pause here to consider the practical options open to the spy who is anxious to avoid leaving a trail that might be followed by his pursuers or who is desirous of creating a false trail or scent to mislead them in their endeavors. Broadly, these fall into two categories: concealment of person or concealment of purpose. In the main, the first is an emergency measure unless the spy is able to transform himself so that he is taken for someone other than who he really is. This is the *false identity* option. The trail is left, in all its different manifestations, in the guise of the other self. The security of the technique lies in the ability to discard the identity and "destroy" the person with whom it is associated once it has become inconvenient. There is nothing of substance left for the pursuer to follow because the tracks have been made by one who has simply dematerialized. This is effective only up to the point where it can be ensured that the human porter of the inconvenient identity baggage cannot be recognized in his new guise. Such identities must be discarded cleanly and completely. If any part of them clings to those who have borne them, a link is established that can be fatal to the succeeding masquerade. In this, we see quite clearly that the footprints are manifestations of an identity rather than of a human being who, for the time being, pretends it for his own.

The spy who makes use of multiple identities, unless these involve radical alterations of appearance, must be something in the nature of a quick-change artist. Yet, in a reasonably open society such as that of the United States, it is remarkably easy to have serial identities; provided the same trails are not walked—or walked too frequently—in different guises, it is quite possible to avoid challenge in the new identity. All that is necessary, for the most part, is a minimum of documentation to authenticate and sustain the illusion. This is never very difficult to acquire, and its availability to one engaged in the business of espionage may be taken for granted.

Anyone who doubts the ease with which the illusion can be created and maintained should try the simple experiment of renting apartments in two different sections of any large city and establishing a life in each by dividing one's time equitably between them. Two quite separate sets of footprints can be established that differ as widely as the subject cares. The human being is subdued and thrust into the background. It is the *persona*, the mask, that is emphasized and given prominence. If this is done with sufficient skill and care, it is only the identity which is really recognized and acknowledged; thus, the identity takes on a life of its own. These separate identities can develop a distinct, contemporary existence for different audiences. This is more than the adoption of hollow, social identities; it is the creation of the illusion of the simultaneous existence of all these different creatures and their baggage. With careful management of time and resources, the illusion can be maintained over a long period in even the most intimate of settings; bigamists have done this long before jet travel facilitated such undertakings.[25] Success requires the mobility of the performance and static audiences, or relatively static and separated ones.

Clearly, these principles have a great many applications in the realms of espionage. The human being is carefully hidden behind the false facade of an identity. It is the identity that is "known" to those involved in the different dealings that are transacted. Such persons involved in these dealings can only say, "I knew him as such and such. He did thus and so." The spy-catcher is left with the task of linking up the different identities and the footprints they have left and showing them to be professional equipment of a single, human individual. In the main, he will only be able to do this by mining the recesses of memory of those willing subjects who have had dealings with the spy in his different manifestations. By clever alterations of appearance and speech and by projecting a different personality in each role—in short, by the skillful exercise of certain thespian qualities—the spy can make it very difficult for his pursuers to connect him with all those with whom he is or has been in contact. The spy thus conceals himself by having many "social selves." The only sensible reason for such complication is to avoid responsibility for something that is done or which has occurred. In essence, it is the basis of the alibi: it was not I, for I am someone else. Those who have nothing to hide or who have taken care to hide their secrets effectively have no need for such contrivances. They can safely sail under their own colors.

This brings us to concealment of purpose. Here, the spy lives openly, known to all in the most extrovert of fashion. His life is seemingly an open book, and the footprints he leaves are without exception a matter of public record or easy verification.[26] He has no fear of any inquiry concerning his person for he is exactly what he appears to be. This, too, of course, is merely an illusion, but one which, if it is conducted and projected with sufficient care, is capable of standing up to all but the most rigorous and well-informed scrutiny. This life is like a screen, an extra skin worn for show, the proverbial wolf in sheep's clothing. For the job of the spy is to spy. And unless he engages in the activities which will bring him within the parameters of our definition, he cannot properly be said to be a spy. Once he engages in those activities, he does indeed have something to hide. The illusion of openness, of social purity as it were, may serve to deflect investigation, to act as a blanket behind which the quick changes are carried out. But once such activities are revealed, the mask is torn away and the spy is shown for what he really is. It is, to take a preposterous comparison, as though a person in holy orders were secretly and principally engaged in the business of prostitution. Once the fact is unquestionably established, all pretense at virtue must cease, for the actions themselves label the person unmistakably. The notion expressed here would indeed tend toward the absurd were it not for the undoubted fact that many of the most successful spies have managed to compartmentalize their lives so as to preserve the requisite illusion of virtue and integrity. Clearly, it is possible to live a life of the blackest sin while maintaining an outward show of purity that deceives and fends off inconvenient inquiry.

Most cases are hardly so extreme. The edges are less sharp, and it is not easy to determine where one facet—or role—ends and another begins. The spy will not ordinarily aim for saintliness when a more middle of the road position will be less conspicuous and serve better as cover. This is but an example of actions speaking more loudly than words. People are not necessarily what they say they are but must be more properly judged by what they do. But, what *do* they do? The spy *appears* to be one thing, whereas in reality he is doing what would lead him to be classified in a very different way, *were it known*.

What must be appreciated is that he is aided in this by a phenomenon that is oftentimes overlooked. Spying is a full-time occupation only in the sense that there is a whole-hearted commitment to a cause or profession. Even the most active, wholehearted, dedicated workaholic of spies is not putting out a one hundred percent effort *at being a spy* all hours of the day and night. Indeed, such fulsome devotion would be counterproductive and certain to lead to the most early discovery. Many of the most effective and useful of spies devote very little of their time, percentage-wise, to the business of espionage. This leaves a lot of time for other, quite innocent activities, all of which serve to build cover and to screen the true business of spying.

From the perspective of the spy-catcher, a spy is a spy even when he is not actively spying or engaged in ancillary activities in furtherance of the practice of his clandestine profession. But it is only when he is so engaged that it is apparent that he is a spy; anything else is inference. All the other connections may well be circumstantial and involve speculation with regard to the past and instances that might be characterized as espionage. There is plenty of room for victimization here, particularly in countries where xenophobia reigns and counterespionage services are inefficient or corrupt. For the spy, the problem of concealment, then, comes down to this: At all costs, he must avoid being caught in the actual business of spying, and being linked, even by implication, with spying that has gone on in the past. For the spy-catcher, cutting through the concealment means making the right connections. Suspicion, however well founded, is not enough to do more than point the spy-catcher in a certain direction. What is needed are methods or techniques for making the right connections.

When the matter is viewed in this way, it is easy to see in the abstract what is required to produce the evidence necessary to make a case that a particular person is indeed a spy. If it were possible to monitor what every person was doing, everywhere, every instant of every day, the disparity between appearance and reality, between word and deed, between saint and spy, would immediately and inevitably disappear. There would be no place to hide, no room for concealment. Such a spy-catcher's utopia is an impossible dream—or a nightmare the spy shares with most ordinary folk. Even the closest approximation falls far short of what is required for even minimal success along these lines.

Every good spy-catcher seeks to improve the odds, by whatever means are available. When these are rationally examined, it is evident that the spy enjoys considerable advantages. There is only so much of everything to go around. There has to be a sensible allocation of resources on both sides. The spy must divide his resources between what is required of him to get the job done and what is necessary to ensure that he does not get caught. It is not difficult to analyze the accounts in any particular case to see how and on what basis the actual distributions have been made. Those concerned with security, on the other hand, must eke out their own resources, dividing them between what is necessary to safeguard against depredation and what is required to catch the predator. The spy-catcher has to be content with this latter, usually smaller share for his own purposes. It is a useful operating truism that a spy must sooner or later act as a spy. The spy-catcher wants to be around when that happens, personally or by proxy. If that is to be within the realm of possibility, given what we have indicated concerning the scarcity of resources, a very discriminating employment of them is required.

The spy has to be caught doing something that unquestionably marks him as a spy; what is done with the evidence so obtained is outside the scope of our present consideration. Short of some utterly fortuitous or accidental circumstance revealing such activities, there is only one way in which the requisite evidence can be acquired and that is by organizing an operation to spy on the spy. Surveillance, whether by man or machine, is nothing more or less than this.

Such operations proceed by stages. In the first phase, a suspected spy is tentatively identified for targeting. This determination may have the widest range of motivations from mere suspicion or gut feeling through well-founded indications to that end. The amount of effort dedicated to what are really verification efforts will depend to some extent upon the credence placed on the suppositions forming the basis of those indications. Assuming the target to be worth the effort (an identified intelligence officer serving under cover at a foreign embassy, for example), the subject may be placed under surveillance in the hope that his actions can be observed in such comprehensive and conclusive fashion that the suspicions can be confirmed or caused to evaporate. Clearly, the intensity, thoroughness, and persistence of the surveillance are the keys to success in this regard. Any gap in time or place is fatal to the attainment of the objective; who knows what went on while the subject was not being watched? If it is impossible to get close enough to the subject, if he is elusive in his movements, or if surveillance is only possible at some times and not at others, the results must be regarded as being more or less inconclusive—unless a positive development occurs.

For some highly suspect targets, a twenty-four-hour regimen of surveillance is essential, but the difficulties of maintaining this over a restricted area and with limited objectives are to be appreciated by considering what is involved in undertaking such an operation against the regular personnel of but a single country's embassy (something which has become standard practice in most security conscious countries). It is small wonder that such human surveillance endeavors have to be supplemented by high-resolution, automatic photography over fixed areas and electronic eavesdropping, especially tracking and homing devices. Although these can greatly extend the range and intensity of the coverage, they are still very demanding in terms of labor, and it is not easy to conceal their employment from those who have the technology to detect them, neutralize their effectiveness and, when the occasion presents itself, turn this double-edged weapon, for propaganda purposes, on those who have employed it. These surveillance tactics have some undeniable utility in the case of diplomatic trade and cultural missions, and render some useful dividends, though they are anathema to honest diplomats. But they do produce a great deal of time- and energy-consuming dross for every nugget of precious metal. It is uncharitable to say, but sadly true, that every embassy is a nest of spies. Finding the truly rapacious among the songbirds is no easy task, and it takes more than a keen ear, patient observation, and length experience to pick out the distinctive plumage and the occasional discordant notes. And an embassy is a relatively soft target for the bird watcher, for the nest is in sight—the comings and goings of the birds and their visitors can be kept under discreet surveillance and their plumage (and some of what it hides) can shortly be known. Would that all nests were so easily spotted!

Clearly, even with this brief statement, some of the complexities of what is involved are readily apparent, as is the expenditure of effort for even minimal coverage of the obvious. And if one concentrates upon the obvious, the efforts of the opposition in unsuspected areas and directions will be safer and more effective. Once more, some discriminating calculations have to be made. The spy-catcher has to try to gain the inside track. He must try to effect a penetration of his own or secure an agent in place. The much publicized security problems at the United States embassy in Moscow ought to be appreciated in this light.[27] There are inconvenient limits to what can be learned from external observation of any embassy and its personnel, whatever the restrictions placed on their movements. The kind of surveillance permitted does not develop a sufficiently comprehensive picture without supplementation. On the not unreasonable assumption, on the part of the security services of the Soviet Union, that at least some clandestine operations against Soviet targets were being run directly or indirectly out of the embassy, it would have been necessary to mount countermeasures to discover what these were, how they were being conducted and controlled, and what measure of success attended them.

These investigations could not logically have been conducted from the perimeter; this was a job for infiltrators not scouts. Just as the infiltrator has scant respect for the opponent's sovereign domain, it should come as little surprise that the national or fictitious sovereignty extended by international law to the premises of foreign embassies and other missions should be so lightly regarded.

It is only by the infiltration of men or machinery that the job of finding out what the other side is up to can be done at all; those who do not stoop to such behavior when they are able to do so are simply electing to remain in the dark for whatever reason. An agent in place or a penetration agent can be selective in his labors. He does not have to work all hours of the day and night to get the goods on those on whom he is spying. The insider *can* find some very interesting footprints, but only so long as *he* remains undiscovered. Surveillance of this kind has to be undertaken most discreetly. Surveillance is really only a fancy name for observation; it is spying when it is done secretly. Those who are doing things they do not wish others to see are constantly on the lookout for unwelcome observers. This is so whether the observer is human or some device engineered and installed for the purpose. The observer's job is to provide evidence, to see what the spy on whom he is spying is up to, and to report accordingly.

He must presume that if a hint of his own activity is detected, it will be unwelcome to those he is observing. He can presume, too, that if his surveillance is known or suspected, what he is hoping to observe will not take place and measures will be taken to frustrate his observation or distort its results.[28] Therefore, he must observe secretly, for if he does not take precautions to that end, his activities can be challenged and defeated and perhaps even turned against his masters. There is a very special purpose in all this in the present context. The observer is really trying to see the footprints being made and to have a very clear idea of who is making them; then it can perhaps be seen where and to whom they lead. Position is a large part of the game here. The observer may be the watcher from the shadows or he may be an unsuspected, overt companion; all the while, what is concealed is his true purpose in being there. Effective surveillance requires a combination of the trained observer, being in the right place at the right time, while something worth watching is going on. In the nature of things, the spy-catcher has little or no control over the latter. In desperation, he may be forced to supply a staged substitute, a provocation.[29] While such contrived situations may serve the purpose of sending a warning or getting rid of one whose conduct cannot otherwise be challenged, they are unsatisfactory and virtually an admission of defeat.

Finding footprints that are useful to the spy-catcher is often no more than a matter of finding the right connections. The spy cannot function in isolation. He will have to make contacts of some kind that are designed to facilitate his work as a spy. These will usually be kept to a minimum to enhance his personal and professional security. The rules of tradecraft will prescribe how these connections are to be made so as to best compartmentalize the operation and limit the possibilities that these essential links form a chain to lead to and expose or incriminate others.

Assume a suspected spy has been kept under intensive and extensive surveillance over a lengthy period. He will be observed to have many contacts with other human beings during that time. Unless the observer is close enough in every sense to capture all that is transacted, even the most apparently innocent of these contacts must be suspected of having some professional significance. A seeming accidental encounter in a supermarket, the purchase of a newspaper from a street vendor, a visit to a theater or a sports function, having a haircut, or buying a new suit—all can be the most innocent, straightforward of activities having nothing but their ostensible purposes in view—or they can be pregnant with meaning in terms of the espionage activity suspected. Spy novelists revel in such wide-open possibilities. If such contacts take place between skilled professionals, they will be very difficult to detect for what they are. It is as fatal to move precipitously in these matters as it is to be caught watching. Here the skill of the hunter is truly tested. Over a period of time, a kind of tapestry emerges in which patterns among the contacts are seen to occur. These have to be studied and interpreted and, where possible, recorded in permanent form. In this time-consuming business of observation and evaluation of contacts, certain operational distinctions have to be made. The spy-catcher is interested in any person engaged in the actual business of espionage in even the smallest way. Some participants are more important than others, but those who would see the whole picture cannot afford to ignore any of them.

If the spy-catcher can effectively establish the existence of anything in the nature of espionage through the observation of but a single contact, he can use the knowledge so gained to expand his understanding of those parts of the tapestry that have yet to come into view. He may, for the moment, do nothing more than strengthen the surveillance of the person who has "tested positive." He may confront that person with the evidence he has already obtained and try to secure cooperation or even "turn" the person in question so as to secure a penetration and enhance the surveillance. If there is no disposition to cooperate, the spy-catcher may take such other measures as are deemed appropriate to extract whatever information is to be had from this contact, so as to use it in the furtherance of the main business. Clearly, under these latter circumstances, the person concerned cannot be put back in circulation. What may be learned from surveillance of a spy suspect is determined in large measure by the espionage-related functions of the person under observation. Those who work out of embassies and other official or quasi-official establishments will rarely be direct procurers of information. They will be facilitators, receivers and transmitters, organizers and inspirers of the efforts of others who are in direct touch with whatever it is that has to be done. What can be observed concerning their activities therefore is strictly governed by the exercise of these functions. This is not to say that they cannot be caught with "the goods" on them or in the act of some compromising business involving the passing of secret intelligence. Ordinarily, they will try to put distance between themselves and those activities they manage, direct, or control. There will be other intermediaries who obscure the character of what is going on and who, beyond their own limited role, may know very little of the business being transacted. The florist asked to deliver a potted plant to "Cynthia" may have no more idea that the accompanying greeting is a code transmitting a stolen secret formula than the innocent postal clerk who receives and transmits, in the ordinary course of business, a packet of confidential instructions to a Soviet agent in Mexico City.

There are many intermediaries in the espionage business, some of whom know at least a little of what they are really doing and others who are simply used. These "couriers" may or may not be innocent, and they may be used or abused by those more knowledgeable than they. But what can be learned by observing them is determined by the roles they play. The man "at the sharp end" is another matter altogether and is by far the most challenging target for any surveillance, for he is the one who actually does the jobs that set the whole thing in motion. Assuming the problem of getting a lead on him can be solved, he has to be observed at his place of business (where he actually is engaged in the espionage) or in the course of having contact with those from whom he must receive instructions or unburden himself of his product. We are not considering degrees of culpability here or even relative importance. It is simply that without him, there is no product, no business to be transacted. His are the most interesting and definitive of footprints, for he is what most people think of when the word spy is used, but there are no special ways of lifting the footprints. Only an appropriate adaptation of the standard methods we have discussed will yield useful results.

Surveillance returns its highest dividends when the subject under observation is caught in the act of spying, is found in possession of the product of his activities or the tools of his trade, or is taken in association with others whose company permits of no innocent explanation. The footprints leading up to such delicious moments have to be patiently collected and assembled before these triumphs can be fully savored. Direct surveillance is of comparatively little moment in the detection and collection of footprints; it is, rather, these that lead to the tool of surveillance being used against a particular target. The main purpose of surveillance is to watch those who have left footprints or are capable of leaving them. Every observer hopes to see the "smoking gun" and to be able to identify the hand holding it. This is not an uncommon denouement in espionage cases, thanks to surveillance. The drama tends to overshadow the patient tracking that has led up to the moment.

Next to leaving a trail that might lead to him and his operations, thereby allowing them to be observed, the spy's greatest concern is getting caught with the goods, either the product of his espionage activities or the means used to acquire it. As we have indicated, this may be the result of a surveillance. More usually, it will result from a search.

What we must say here may be horrifying to civil libertarians and even more shocking to those who assiduously worship at the shrine of the Rule of Law. We would emphasize that we are in no way advocating a position on these matters, much less suggesting a violation of any legal norms. What we are, however, under an obligation to do is to report on the reality of these practices and to indicate what is commonly done by those who would catch spies (by whomsoever they might be employed). This is the reality with which the professional spy must live. He cannot afford to rely upon some theoretical notion of "paper" rights to protect him and his business from those anxious to apprehend him and put a stop to his activities. The spy who is not trained to expect and prepare for the surreptitious search of his belongings is a spy already on the way out of the business. Whatever the law may have to say about such searches, they are conducted everywhere by counterespionage services with varying degrees of skill and thoroughness, and often produce important indications that assist the spy-catcher in his work. Sometimes all that is needed is that he find something that will point him in the right direction. Sensible spies keep incriminating elements to an absolute minimum and seek to conceal well that with which they cannot dispense altogether. The spy cannot afford to take risks in these matters. Every good spy course includes training in how to hide things and how to improvise.

The spy is at greatest risk when he is traveling and he must take the strictest precautions to conceal necessary appurtenances and recorded information relating to his business from random or snap searches. He should not carry drugs, weapons, anything of an illicit nature, or prohibited items likely to intensify the search if they are found, or any items which might lead to his arrest and detention on their account. All this is especially relevant when he is obliged to cross international boundaries, where he can expect to be subject to regular customs or security inspections of his person and property.

Every counterespionage course should include training in conducting the type of intensive search necessary to discover items that might be hidden by a skilled professional. Special techniques and equipment may be needed. Such searches must be highly methodical and thorough. They usually require a considerable amount of time, during which the searcher(s) can work undisturbed if such searches are conducted surreptitiously. Their work should ideally be so carefully carried out that they leave no sign of their efforts; a clumsy, obvious search may be used to cover the traces of another, more professional one. Particular care must be taken to avoid loss or damage to delicate items designed to resist tampering, such as photo-sensitive materials on which information may be stored. Concealment devices have now become highly sophisticated and are specially manufactured for the purpose, although almost anything may be refashioned and suitably adapted. The searcher(s) will be looking for anything that might enable the spy to acquire, store, or communicate information. Nowadays, many of these items (such as miniature cameras and tape recorders) will be common enough among even the most innocent of travelers. Searchers will be looking to connect suspicious items with the business of espionage and will be especially on the alert for anything related to methods of operation, marked maps, instructions, codes and ciphers. However good a memory a spy may have, he will rarely rely upon it exclusively. He may have his own peculiar forms of notation as *aides-memoires*, which the trained searcher will recognize. The more valuable the information in his possession, the more likely it is that the spy will seek to preserve it in permanent or semipermanent form.[30] This is especially so if it is a unique or original document.

Given their training and the occupational risks they are forced to run, spies are often surprisingly careless with important information entrusted to their care. This is particularly the case with names, addresses, and telephone numbers of contacts. Spies often evince the same curious, professional nonchalance of bomb makers and bomb-disposal experts who smoke around highly volatile explosives and diamond merchants who carry priceless wares in old cigarette packets. Even a search that does not turn up anything immediately incriminating of the person in whose possession it is found may yet render some small item of information that will usefully lead elsewhere. Everything examined in the course of a search should be logged, for its true importance may only become apparent at a later date. There can rarely be such a creature as a completely sanitized spy, at least not while he is going about his business. Somewhere among his possessions there is likely to be evidence of his occupation, his associations, his intentions. The trick, in the present context, lies in discovering such evidence without revealing that it has been found. The surreptitious, physical search we have been considering has much in common with clandestine surveillance. It is yet another way of spying upon the spy, of finding what he would rather remain concealed.

Even the spy who is, to all intents and purposes, completely "clean" must be carrying a vast quantity of highly incriminating baggage. How else could he function as a spy? To search for it requires the employment of very different techniques from those we have been considering, for such impedimenta are carried in the human mind. A very special type of inquiry is needed to track the footprints of the spy through such forbidding and forbidden territory. Some of these areas will be as closed and well guarded as a seraglio. We may begin with the somewhat trite but useful proposition that the only thing that is *entirely* locked in the human mind is personal fantasy; even this may be released on occasion. Such exotica are of no real concern for the spy-catcher; they may have some entertainment value or even stimulate his own thought processes in some degree, but they lead him nowhere in the practical sense. We are concerned with the portals, the necessary links to reality which pass through them. That which makes its home in the human mind has gateways and avenues to the external world. What passes through and along them is two-way traffic. It is what links the healthy human being with what we are pleased to call objective reality. This is yet another way of echoing John Donne's famous lines, "No man is an island, entire of itself. Every man is part of the continent, a piece of the main." The secret recesses of even the most closed of minds, save those of the hopelessly psychotic, have their useful, indeed, essential connections with the outside world.

Those who would resist intrusion by the "Thought Police" build extremely efficient defenses in their efforts to ensure their personal privacy. They carefully regulate the traffic flow, watching what goes in and out. In these matters, the professional spy is in a very high-risk category. His mind contains much that is essential to the performance of his work, and for his own safety, as well as that of his operations and those for and with whom he works. He must be as good at keeping his own secrets as he is at stealing those of others. His mind may be likened to a locked filing cabinet or, in more modern terms, a data bank secured, as far as possible, against unauthorized probing. It is difficult, if not practically impossible, to surreptitiously extract vital data from the human mind. Man has been searching for such awesome, divine power for thousands of years, and despite the Soviet efforts in the field of parapsychology,[31] there is little to suggest that real success is just around the corner.

Mind-altering substances, hypnosis, and other techniques are facilitative of inquiry rather than useful tools in the aid of surreptitious entry and extraction. Those who would enter the mind of another, must do so under fairly open conditions, at least in relation to their ostensible purposes, and be prepared to come up against the defenses designed to resist intrusion and prevent anything of value from being taken and carried away. This logically leaves a limited number of options if the operation is to be successful. If the mind of another cannot be entered unbeknownst to that other, there remains the possibility of concealing the purpose for which entry is intended. Techniques to this end are many and varied and, in some way or another, widely practiced by persons who would have a great deal of difficulty in articulating exactly what it is that they do. The professional must give them some serious consideration so as to be able to employ them to their best advantage. They are all designed to the same end, namely with a view to raiding the mind of another and despoiling it of those contents that would otherwise remain secure against outside interference. They must neither break the structure nor damage the material to be carried off if the exercise is to be accomplished to its proper ends. As the dentist learns to draw teeth from the cooperative and the uncooperative alike without breaking their jaws, so too must the spy-catcher learn to extract the information he needs to proceed about his business.

In short, the spy-catcher must learn and employ the art of interrogation. Somewhere in the minds of those with whom he deals are the answers to the questions that he must ask to satisfy his professional curiosity. These answers will not be easily surrendered. Those who seek to defend the information, with their lives if necessary, have many strategies at their disposal to turn aside the interrogator's probe. There may be nothing to be rendered up; the key to it may be lost or mislaid for a variety of physical or psychological reasons; the information may have been deliberately altered so as to make it unrecognizable or useless to strangers who come seeking after it, or it may self-destruct.

The mind is the last refuge of the hunted spy. The spy-catcher who would truly excel at his job must familiarize himself with its structure, mechanism, and contents. He must learn how to get at them without doing damage to the delicate vessel that holds them and without being deceived or deceiving himself in the process—truly a task worthy of a book in itself, and we would not demean it by treating it in an abbreviated fashion. For the moment, it is merely our obligation to show the role of interrogation in tracking the footprints of the spy through the system.

Interrogation is intended to open to inspection the minds of others. Those others may be suspects or simply persons having useful information that will assist the spy-catcher in his inquiries. The distinction between the two classes radically affects the willingness to make free and truthful disclosure of what is known and, consequently, the techniques to be employed in acquiring the information. Those who are not suspected of being spies or of having any degree of complicity in their activities may be divided into two broad categories: those who are willing to make available what they know, and those who are not. A wide spectrum of possibilities is encompassed within the first category, ranging from the diffident and retiring to the overenthusiastic collaborator. Their willingness to tell what they know, to the best of their ability, is not necessarily commensurate with the value of that which they have to relate. The interrogator cannot afford to be complacent merely on account of cooperation.

Laying out everything for inspection is a laborious, time-consuming business. Yet the interrogator cannot afford to overlook some minuscule scrap of information that, together with others from diverse sources, may be the key to the mystery he is seeking to unlock. The content of his questions and the way he poses them are all important. Very few people ever learn how to question others effectively. In matters of moment, interrogation is not something that can be accomplished at a single session.

There is a subtle chemistry between the questioner and the subject questioned that affects the quantity and quality of the information imparted.[32] Some interrogators have an unfortunate faculty for turning even the most cooperative of subjects against them. Interrogation of non-suspects ought not to be turned into an adversary proceeding. It is all too easy to make such persons resentful, uncooperative, and even hostile by underestimating the disagreeable character, for them, of the proceeding. For many, any sort of interrogation is an ordeal. It is equally easy for the interrogator to misunderstand and misinterpret the basis from which these feelings stem. Some people simply do not like being questioned at all, especially by the authorities. Others are fearful and guilt-ridden by nature; they live out their lives under a pall of dread of being blamed for something.[33] It ought not too readily be assumed that they are being deliberately obstructive or that they have something material to hide.

When latent antagonisms and general unhelpfulness occur, the problem may well reside in the questioner—his manners, techniques, and attitudes. Interrogation, if it is to be fruitful, must not be allowed to degenerate into a clash of wills; valuable information, as well as precious time, may be lost in the process. The questioning of suspected spies or those believed to be in some way involved in their activities proceeds from a different standpoint altogether. Here there is necessarily from the outset the presumption of a contest, with one side seeking to pry loose information that it believes the other to have, while those who are subjected to interrogation muster all their defenses against the assault. Interrogation takes place in an atmosphere of mutual distrust that the interrogator can do little to dispel save by acting with scrupulous fairness that may in itself place him under somewhat of a handicap. It is never helpful to the interrogator's purposes to allow such contests to deteriorate into a clash of egos. Too much energy is spent on irrelevancies, on scoring personal points. The interrogator is seeking accurate, complete information as quickly as possible. The more exactly he satisfies his needs in this regard, the greater will be the measure of his personal and professional victory. Anything else is unhealthy and counterproductive as far as the main purpose of the interrogation is concerned. The interrogator may have to use a carrot-and-stick approach, but he ought not to reward or punish according to how difficult or easy his job has been made by the subject under questioning.

The interrogator should always remember that it is he who sets the tone of the proceedings. He should avoid acting in any way likely to lose him the respect of his adversary. The interrogator is following a trail that he hopes will eventually bring him within sight of his prey. He must use all methods at his disposal to obtain the information necessary to that end. Given such an injunction, it is easy to see how an interrogator might well become unscrupulous in his methods. He may have to strike bargains to get what he requires, and the fundamental fairness of his methods will always be open to question, for coercion is an ever-present, underlying theme however muted its tones. What we are concerned with here is the effectiveness of the interrogator's methods: do they get the job done expeditiously and in a way that aids in the attainment of the ultimate objective?

The final link in the interrogation chain, no matter how it is arrived at, is the questioning of the suspected spy. For it is with this subject that the chain of footprints, of particular footprints, ends. Only that person can explain them fully if he should choose to do so, filling in the missing pieces of the story, ending up cleared of suspicion or accused. Clearly, this circumstance alone calls for a very different kind of interrogation, one which taxes those engaged in it on both sides to the limit of their abilities. For the spy, this is often enough the end of the line, the last-ditch stand. He must make certain critical choices that leave little room for error. What he says or does not say, as well as how he does or does not say it, will determine his fate. It is also for the spy-catcher a potential moment of truth: does he or does he not have a spy in his trap? His interrogation may be the only instrument capable of producing a clear, unequivocal answer.

We may start here from the not unreasonable supposition that everything the suspected spy is likely to say in response to inquiries concerning him and his activities will be self-serving, or, at the very least, serving of the interests of his masters. If he is indeed a spy, he will do everything in his power to conceal the fact—unless some manifest advantage is to be gained by admitting to it.[34] If he is a professional, he will be ready for a carefully concocted story, a "legend," to explain himself and his doings in the most innocent light, and he will be adept at countering any information suggestive of contrary conclusions regarding his person, history, and activities. To believe that matters might be otherwise is to be hopelessly naive or absurdly optimistic. The spy will lie through his teeth—until he comes to see that the lies he has told are serving no useful purpose. Then he will offer additional, but different, lies until the time comes when, in desperation, he might experiment with some version of the truth to see how it might serve his cause. By this time—which comes a lot sooner for some than for others—it is difficult even for the spy himself to know what is the truth and what is not. Indeed, if he has only a minor role and his training has been less than adequate, he may not even know what is fact and what is fiction in the various accounts he is prepared to offer. Then there are those brave souls who, when finally tracked down, retreat into silence in the hope that by saying nothing they can at least preserve some sort of consistency.

So any variations upon these different themes are possible according to the circumstances and the personalities of the actors in these dramas. We need to remind ourselves that we are not dealing with some vague abstraction here when at last we come to this point in the game. We are not confronted with a generic "spy," but a flesh-and-blood human being who is the repository of highly important information that we require for our purposes.

Each human being will respond differently to the approaches made to gain possession of that information. Each will assess his chances of hanging on to it, concealing it, altering it, destroying it, or bargaining with it for his life or some lesser advantage. At an early stage, he will have to make certain determinations so as not to foreclose future possibilities. The suspect, too, is in urgent need of information and, in his straightened circumstances, this may be difficult to procure and evaluate. He needs to know, if possible, the strength of the case against him and of what it consists; is he merely suspected and, if so, what is the strength of those suspicions? Has suspicion already hardened into certainty? Are his captors playing games with him? This may hardly be the moment for calm, objective reflection. His performance will have as much to do with his personality and training as anything his interrogator might do at this juncture.

For our present purposes, we may divide spies in captivity into two classes: those who will not bargain under any circumstances, and those who will. The first class is comprised of a very small part of the whole. Once such individuals are recognized for what they are (and such recognition is not always obvious or immediate), it is futile and even dangerous to waste time with methods presupposing cooperation of any kind, for there are masters of deceit in this category who know how to generate false impressions and take advantage of the smallest concession. There is a door which is firmly barred and bolted which denies entry to what is required by the interrogator. It is stoutly defended from within. Polite knocking will not elicit any useful response. Those who want what lies behind the door badly enough must be prepared to force it in the appropriate fashion. We will return to this shortly.

All other spies will, sooner or later, come to some arrangement to surrender what they know. The only issue is the price. Having determined at some point to sell out, the spy wants the highest price for his wares. What he will ask and what he will get depend on how well he has gauged the market, on the strength of his pitch, and whether he might be forced into a "fire sale." Nor is the spy above trickery. He will try to hold back the best goods until he judges the market is most in his favor. He will try to not part with the best at all; whatever the presence or absence of finer feelings, there is a strong notion of personal insurance underlying this. He will throw in as much rubbish as he feels he can get away with. The spy is, of course, no honest trader nor, in strictness, is he owed honesty in return. For the spy, this may be practically of little consequence, for he may well have reached the end of the road, but the spy-catcher stands in a different relationship to this question. He has to measure his own practices by more enduring standards.

What the spy-catcher does and how he does it *will* become known, however much he tries to keep these things a secret. Unfair dealing, sharp practices, and trickery as opposed to professional "smarts" will come back to haunt him and make his work, and that of his service, all the more difficult in the future.[35] This is a consideration which cannot be left out of account. The interrogator's reputation can be a help or a hindrance; it is only truly neutral in the ineffectual. In borderline cases, the reputation of the interrogator and how it is assessed by the person being questioned can be the deciding factor that will clinch the deal. All these things combine to impose heavy responsibilities on the interrogator. He must have very strong control over his own emotions and a very clear idea of what he is after by way of results. If he *really* wants information rather than some sort of sadistic pleasure out of the exercise of his calling, he must conquer or at least hold in check any latent distaste for bargaining with those from whom it can be acquired. Anything else leads to confusion.

It is axiomatic that the person with the best knowledge of how the market works and of the true value of what is being bought and sold is in a position to strike the most advantageous bargain. All the rest is technique and application. The spy certainly has something the interrogator wishes to know; indeed, he may have a lot of useful information that can be traded for something of value to himself. The interrogator is at a disadvantage because he does not know what or how much the spy may know that is of value to him. It is far too early to talk price, for it is not clear what is on the market. The parties are dancing around each other in the dark. The principal advantage that the spy-catcher has from the beginning is his power over the spy. He has to dramatize this if necessary. Theoretically, the spy-catcher can trade anything he wants, from freedom for the spy at one end of the scale to a glass of water or a quick smoke on the other. It is this power and what is implied by it that is his strongest bargaining chip. It is best employed when it is allowed to speak for itself.

The spy, on the other hand, is in the quandary of not knowing how ruthlessly and unscrupulously that power might be used. He cannot afford to make favorable assumptions under even the most benign of circumstances. His real defense against abuse is not the formal mechanism of the system but the knowledge he is assumed to have. He must trade very cautiously if he is to retain anything in the nature of a shield for himself and those in whose safety he is interested. For his part, the spy-catcher must not barter away his own advantages in this respect in too cavalier a fashion. In particular, he must avoid having his bluff called. If he decides to show the strength of his hand, he must be prepared to play it.

Time is always a very important element in any interrogation. The law or administrative dictates may impose very confining limits within which the interrogator may work. However efficient he may be, these are certain to cramp his style, especially if the person under interrogation is aware of them. Certain techniques simply do not work satisfactorily under conditions of haste.

Information is a perishable commodity. What the spy knows today that is of prime use to his interrogators may be quite worthless in even a few hours. Imagine a member of a spy network who is apprehended who has knowledge of the whereabouts of others who are associated with him. Once his arrest has become known (even his temporary disappearance from his usual haunts may suffice to give the alarm), his associates can take steps to make themselves scarce. The longer he can hold out, avoiding giving information he has concerning them, the more likely it is that they will be able to use the time thus won to avoid apprehension. Such considerations are extremely influential in deciding the choice of methods of interrogation. The important thing is to get the information, to get it accurately and in useful form, and to get it while it retains its full worth. Methods that require a leisurely process of persuasion, of softening up, to secure satisfactory cooperation are clearly of little value in these cases. They simply do not get the job done. The interrogator may have to settle for half a loaf, or even less, rather than going without bread altogether. He must make a careful assessment of the prospects. He must reflect most carefully upon the extent to which the methods he is contemplating are likely to prove successful *with the subject in question* and the extent to which the information he is trying to obtain is likely to be adversely affected, distorted, or lost as a result of his choice of methods. However bereft of humanity he may be, he will also have to give some regard to the effect of those methods on the human repository of the information, the spy himself. He does not want to destroy the toothpaste tube before he has squeezed out the toothpaste. Some hard market calculations are required here. What it comes down to in the end in every case is: Is it worth it?

Here we must broach another subject that many will no doubt find distasteful, if not downright offensive—torture. To ignore the subject would be to shut one's eyes to an unpleasant but demonstrably prevalent fact of life.[36] People the world over, in our own as in former times, *are* tortured to extract information. We would be foolish as well as remiss to pretend that these practices do not exist. They are unlikely to go away by ignoring them or writing about them in misleading or euphemistic fashion. Torture is an option the spy-catcher must consider even if he opts to reject the notion out of hand or is required to do so by the system under which he operates.

We would define torture as *the direct or indirect imposition of physical or psychological stress upon the body or mind of a human being with the intention of inducing unacceptable pain and suffering in that person so as to bring about a state of submission*. Leaving aside the moral and legal issues, we are left to inquire: Does it work? Does torture facilitate the acquisition of information that other, gentler methods would fail to produce? We raise the question very directly here for it is one that tends to be evaded; when it is answered, the response often springs from erroneous considerations that do not really address the issues.

The simple fact of the matter is that there are few who would wish to go on record as admitting that anything so patently horrible can, at the same time, be efficacious. The same considerations have muddied the water of the death penalty debate for years.[37] We understand these considerations all too well, but we must dispassionately put them aside if what we write is to serve the cause of inquiry into these matters.

We must not confuse the issue of whether torture is good (it is not) with that of its efficacy, with whether it works, producing looked-for results. Nor must we confuse torture as an act of spite, revenge, or punishment with its employment as an instrument of inquiry. There are many unsavory reasons why men deliberately inflict pain upon others. We are concerned here with only one of them: the use of torture to make spies talk, to tell what they know of the matters under investigation. This is a very narrow question indeed, and we restrict our observations to it accordingly. It does a disservice to the spirit of inquiry to confuse the issues or to state general propositions ,founded on a misguided credo rather than an objective examination of the evidence.

In our society, there are few passionate advocates for torture, but there are many whose objectivity is eroded by something approaching a passionate opposition to it. There is nothing wrong in this provided the credo is correctly stated. Thus we read the confident *assertion* of an experienced former United States counterintelligence officer: "In my experience as an interrogator during World War II, Gestapo torturers (many of whom really existed) never got more than a pfennig's worth of information from their prisoners. The same is true of every other country you can name."[38] From our own experience, we would categorically disagree. Moreover, what is expressed runs contrary to the overwhelming weight of the best evidence in these unpleasant matters. Used in the right way, at the right time, and against the right subjects, torture is tremendously effective; it produces the desired results. Over and over again, it can be shown to have elicited exactly the right information, promptly and without reserve. Even the threat or apprehension of torture will sometimes suffice.[39] Anyone who believes otherwise has not studied the evidence, is hopelessly naive or biased, or has no personal experience of what is comprehended within that pitilessly elastic term, *torture*.

Appeals to history are often equally confused. The Common Law distaste for the rack (so beloved of the inquisitors under other systems) had a prosaic, utilitarian basis: was a confession extracted under torture to be believed *in a legal proceeding?* The same issue, as most interrogators realize, is implicit in any coerced statement, hence the Miranda Rule and the like. Hardy souls *do* lie under torture, misleading their interrogators, but we are talking about information and not inculpation. In contrast to what is cited above, we would pose as representative of the experience of thousands of his countrymen, the words of the French Resistance hero, Colonel Remy, who, writing of the German practice of obtaining information by torture, averred: "It was very different with the Gestapo—whose inhuman methods, I am bound to admit, were more effective."[40]

Those who can resist true, carefully chosen torture, mercilessly applied, are few and far between and range from the

admirably heroic to the romantically stupid. There are those
who can naturally or through training resist extreme physical
pain; for them, effective torture takes other, no less vicious
forms. Many a strong man would be broken on the rack
before revealing his secrets, yet would tell all rather than see
his loved ones abused or put to death before his eyes. Everyone has some small weakness that can be exploited: claustro-
phobia, or a fear of reptiles or insects, or drowning, perhaps.
Many subtle forms of torture betray no visible marks of their
application, yet leave those exposed to them feeling violated
and ashamed. Professionals who train spies know these facts
of life, and their students are told the circumstances under
which they might resist and when they should submit. No
spy trainer would be so presumptuous as to assert that his
students are torture-proof, and this in itself speaks volumes for
the effectiveness of torture. The only useful resistance to
torture is to choose death, if that is possible, before it begins.
Once torture has begun, it assumes a relentless momentum
of its own and ends up in useless sacrifice. Those who have
the luxury of time may have no need of torture.[41] For the
rest, it is usually only a matter of choosing the right torture,
the one calculated to work in the particular case. The required information follows as inevitably as the spring thaw.

The basis of all torture for the purpose of securing information is fear: fear of pain; fear of exposure; fear of shame and
embarrassment; fear of the consequences. In even the mild-
est of interrogations there is the ever-present substratum of
fear. The interrogator must learn how to sense and evaluate
what is feared in each case and put it to good use. It has been
well said: "A man needs to have something to lose to become
frightened. Even only one thing that is his and that he values
will make it possible for threat to scare a man."[42] The interrogator must seek out this item of value to strike a bargain. If it
is worth more to the spy than the information the interrogator is seeking, he will be able to get what he wants by
preserving or offering to preserve that item of value for its
possessor. It may be anything from his life to his self-respect.
The right climate for trading has to be established.

The interrogator must be able to show he can deliver as
well as destroy. Torture is sometimes confused with a demonstration of power. Those who for the moment hold absolute

power over others are sometimes impelled by some inner necessity or a conscious policy choice to demonstrate the fact. This was common enough with the routine Gestapo interrogation, which almost invariably commenced with a vicious display of physical violence calculated to bring about submission and a sense of despair. Such indiscriminate brutality rarely served a useful purpose, as such;[43] it did not cow the truly heroic, the stoics, or those who had long since resigned themselves to their fate. As for the others—the vast majority— there was no need for such a demonstration to pry loose from them all they knew. This is a lesson in the economics of violence that the many spiritual successors of the Gestapo have sadly yet to learn. The power of the interrogator is for most all too obvious, as is the desperate nature of their own plight. Even where the need for the information is truly urgent, most can be prodded along the path more gently so as to tell what they know, provided an adroit use is made of their fears.

The greatest fear of all is produced by uncertainty. This was at the heart of the *Nacht und Nebel*[44] policy. The spy, however well trained and however fortified by precedent, can never be quite sure of what is going to happen to him if he falls into the hands of the opposition. He does not want to step into those realms from which there may be no retreat. He does not know what his interrogators are capable of— maybe they do not follow the norm—and, most importantly, how much they know. If he should try to trick them, will he be calling down deserved punishment upon himself? Have his associates already disclosed what they know about him? What can he still keep secret? How did they find his tracks?

The skillful interrogator will use the momentum generated by this uncertainty to keep the spy off balance and to increase his doubts and indecision. The most effective exploitation of this state of affairs is possible only if the interrogator is not placed under time constraints. Given the luxury of proceeding at his own pace, the interrogator can adopt what is perhaps the most effective technique of all. He will simply set the spy on the task of telling *all* he knows by, in effect, writing his own life story.[45] Such biographies are enormously useful and should be the basis of all interrogations in depth.[46] At best, they take months to construct. In the course of time, they will be reviewed and revised, over and over again, being added to and amended as fresh questions are prepared by the interrogator. They cover the entire terrain over which the spy may have passed, and no stone upon it should be left unturned. If the process is thorough, it will be difficult for the spy to avoid inconsistencies, contradictions, and plain misstatements. He should be deprived of the possibility of retaining any copy of what he originally provided and he should be examined in depth on all those items of special interest to the interrogator. Those interrogating the spy should constantly surprise him with small but significant revelations of what they knew concerning him and his activities from other sources. But they should be careful so as to arrange matters so that he is never able to retain in his own mind a comprehensive picture of the case against him or the identities of those who have furnished information. Interrogation is a constant battle of wits and in this, as in so many others, God is on the side of the big battalions.

Tracking the spy's movements through the system is, as we have seen, substantially a matter of acquisition and management of the largest quantity of *the right kind* of data. The spy-catcher must work with whatever the system has to offer. A system where human beings are the enthusiastic eyes and ears of the authorities can be as photosensitive as the most heavily reliant upon documentation as far as the recording of footprints is concerned. All European countries require hotel guests who are foreigners to temporarily surrender their passports and to complete alien registration forms which go to the police. By far the best sources of information, however, are the police spies on the hotel staff who supply details no form makes provision for. Only the techniques for lifting the footprints differ from state to state.

In a police state, everyone is a potential spy, but in some societies, those who inform for the state are more enthusiastic and committed than others.[47] The record human beings are capable of producing is often more exact and more full of useful nuances than any documentary indication. When properly constructed or reconstructed, it represents the materialization of human experience. The organization of data is a matter of the diligent application of the techniques we have discussed. Its management, the uses to which it is put, calls for different skills and equipment. The more data a spy-catcher has at his disposal, the better his chances of making those vital connections that will point him in the right direction and lead him eventually to his goal. The vacuum cleaner principle is useful; everything is swept up and then carefully picked through for what may be useful. If the spy-catcher has special knowledge, a more discriminating procedure may be adopted, like going after a pin with a magnet. But all great accumulations of data have their own pitfalls. They can be just overwhelming and offer too many hiding places of their own. Even with the modern miracles of the digital computer and the sophisticated techniques of cross-matching, there are dangers of vital interpretations not being made or not being made in timely fashion, of the spy falling through the cracks due to human operational inadequacies, man simply being unable to keep up with the machines. These dangers can only be expected to increase as information management becomes more and more centralized and networking the order of the day.

Yet even more worrisome for the spy-catcher is the problem of data security. The spy-catcher must expect that his own registries will be prime targets for enemy action. *Really* sensitive information does not belong in any kind of data bank at all[48]—at least not until it has been definitively acted upon. Information has a disturbing tendency to disappear, especially secret information concerning people and their activities.[49] Human memory is still the best policeman, but the tasks we have been discussing are truly herculean. Any unexplained gaps on conventional footpaths, records missing or purged without obvious reason, and unauthorized alteration should be discreetly and fully investigated. Electronic storage and retrieval of records have made the job of sweeping the trail easier for those concerned with the preservation of their spy's secrets. Everyone knows how fallible these systems are, even the most up-to-date and rigorously maintained. No one is surprised at the errors—but they should be.[50]

Every error should be satisfactorily explained. In this, as in all his other tasks, the spy-catcher must bring the proper degree of humility to his work. As in so many departments of his demanding job, he will need to make the proper use of the right kind of experts. A tracker who is an expert on the sandy, windblown wastes may himself be utterly lost in the verdant rain forest. An IBM systems analyst may be of little use to the spy-catcher on the waterfront at Marseilles, especially if he does not speak the local argot. The spy-catcher needs a lively interest in all things concerning his work, and in none more than choosing and listening to the experts. His quarry may cross many different kinds of terrain, but the signs will be there for those who know how to look, provided the scent is still fresh to the practiced nose.

The spy will try to look like what he is not, leaving footprints to match. Sometimes the deception will be good enough to fool even the experts. The only trail will be the damage he has done and the red faces he has left behind. There are super-spies, and every fisherman has his tale of the one that got away. Some are destined to escape the best laid (and made) of traps and elude the most careful of searches. Why do we take one path instead of another? The religious will see in this the hand of God; others will marvel at the quirks of chance. Against these forces, the spy-catcher struggles in vain. These are mysteries outside his province. He cannot, should not, reproach himself for failures that are beyond his control. His obligation is to do his best in those departments over which he is granted some dominion. There are enough of these to engage all his attention throughout his working life. We would reiterate that in looking for footprints, the spy-catcher is under a professional obligation to leave no stone unturned, however small or apparently insignificant. He has an obligation to exercise a very special kind of diligence, for what he seeks may not make its true meaning apparent for some time. The motto of the British Special Air Service, the famed SAS, is "Who Dares Wins." The spy-catcher's motto might well be, "Who Cares Succeeds Where Others Fail."

POINTS TO REMEMBER

1. Spies, really good ones, live in a society leading lives scarcely different from those of their neighbors and their social class, facing similar problems, solutions, and life chances. Class, neighborhood, work and organizational life provide both context and a basis for examination of "footprints." The

task of the spy-catcher is to find and keep track of particular individuals within the system and to demonstrate by means of established data about those individuals that they are spies. Central problems are availability of data, reliability of data, timeliness of data, *and* the interpretation of the data.

2. By *footprints* we mean all those indications of whatever kind which mark an individual's progress through life and serve as marks and pointers to the direction taken. *Both human beings and their socially constructed identities leave footprints.* While sociopolitical systems and subsystems within them vary in the degree to which they are concerned about the tracks, traces, and footprints of those who pass through, the good spy-catcher knows that a birth certificate is no more conclusive proof for the existence of the human being named on it than is a tombstone for the termination of existence of the person whose grave it is supposed to mark.

3. There are three basic elements for the spy-catcher: first, footprints "speak" for themselves in the sense that the tracks leave trails and tell stories without any embellishment; second, the supposed maker of the tracks can tell of their making in greater or less detail; and, finally, others can bear witness to the making. The degree of agreement among the three is an indication of the degree of authenticity.

4. Regardless of the technology involved, the axiom is that it is the environment surrounding the information or items to be protected that must be sensitized to record all who pass by.

5. Spies may be seen as scouts or infiltrators. Scouts operate in their own territory or territory that is in dispute or of doubtful domain. Any penetrations made by the scout will be slight and temporary with limited objectives in mind. Infiltrators, in contrast, make calculated incursions into the domains of others and attempt to do so without leaving any footprints or signs of their coming, their presence, or their going. The spy-catcher is most concerned with infiltrators.

6. For the spy interested in leaving as little as possible a trail, two options are generically available: concealment of person and/or concealment of purpose. The first involves fostering a false identity or identities; the second involves hidden agendas. The spy must avoid being caught spying or being linked to spying that has already occurred. The spy-catcher, on the other hand, must provide evidence of link-

ages and actions. One means to do so is through "spying on the spy," while another is through interrogation; both involve a great deal of planning, patience, and precise execution.

7. Interrogation is intended to open the minds of others for inspection and involves a variety of techniques and approaches. Technique and approach must be varied on the basis of who the spy-catcher is interrogating. There is, for example, a difference between those who might have information that is desired and those who are suspected of being spies. Those with information may or may not know they have information valuable to the spy-catcher and may be variably willing to disclose it. Except in a small number of cases, the interrogation of spies involves establishing the market value of the information involved and the present and future market value of the spy. For the interrogator with few time constraints, the life history approach is highly recommended.

NOTES

1. *Strangers on a Bridge*, James B. Donovan, New York: Atheneum, 1964, page 30.

2. *The New Meaning of Treason*, Dame Rebecca West, New York: Viking Press, 1964, page 293.

3. *The Counterfeit Traitor*, New York: Henry Holt, 1958, page 101.

4. *The Red Orchestra*, New York: Simon & Schuster, 1969, page 66. This is an excellent source for all aspects touching upon the subjects discussed in the present chapter, especially the German methods of tracking.

5. *Prisoner of Mao*, New York: Coward, McCann and Geoghegan, 1973, page 72. This is a most insightful book, especially concerning those matters involving the extraction of information.

6. One of the aliases of "Colonel Abel." See Donovan, op. cit., supra note 1.

7. Jonathan Jay Pollard was found guilty on June 5, 1986, of spying for Israel. The case attracted a good deal of attention on many counts, and those matters are raised elsewhere in the text. Although a lot of human interest items have appeared in the popular media regarding this case, there is

clearly a great deal more that the serious investigator would like to know.

8. Ronald William Pelton left many footprints crossing and recrossing many paths before he was finally unmasked as a spy. What is of particular interest is the vulnerability of this and other individuals employed by the NSA on financial grounds. See *The New York Times*, 6 June 1986, page 11.

9. For example, a credit card transaction by telephone, now not uncommon, merely shows a card bearing a particular name and number, issued by a certain company or institution, has been used to order goods or services. It is certainly not in itself evidence that the transaction was conducted or authorized by the person to whom the card was issued.

10. See *Making Spies*, H. H. A. Cooper and Lawrence J. Redlinger, Boulder, CO: Paladin Press, 1986, page 11.

11. An excellent exercise for a counterespionage course involves requesting one student, without prior warning, to empty pockets or purse and to ask the others to interpret and give meaning to each of the items disclosed.

12. See *The Man Who Never Was*, Ewen Montagu, Philadelphia: J. B. Lippincott, 1954.

13. Confronted by federal investigators in May 1986 at the height of the concerns raised by Pelton, Walker, Whitworth, Wu Tai Chin, Miller, et al., Glenn Souther, a Navy intelligence analyst, simply stole a march on his pursuers and disappeared. See *The New York Times*, 11 November 1986, page 11. There is no need to walk backward or employ sweepers, provided you can run quickly enough to get a good start.

14. This is at the heart of many of the problems that bedeviled the work of those investigating the Iran-Contra affair. It simply was not possible to establish, with respect to many important documents, who had handled them. The system was inadequate for the purpose.

15. See *Numbers, 13*, for example.

16. See, for example, *The War Magician*, David Fisher, New York: Coward-McCann, 1983.

17. See *Operation Overflight*, Francis Gary Powers with Curt Gentry, New York: Holt, Rinehart and Winston, 1970.

18. See *Ike's Spies*, Stephen E. Ambrose, New York: Doubleday, 1981.

19. For a very good idea of the practicalities of what is

involved, see Klein, op. cit., supra note 2, passim. Erikson set out to make an inspection of the German oil industry at a crucial period during World War II, relying upon the strength of his documentation and his own glibness to carry him through this very dangerous mission.

20. For a striking example, see *I Was An NKVD Agent*, Anatoli Granowsky, New York: Devin-Adair, 1962. This is a very instructive book, but it requires expert, discriminating reading.

21. Drug dealers have similar problems, and some have given themselves and the source of their wealth away in the course of paying cash on the grand scale.

22. "Here, I must repeat myself. I have an almost stereoscopic memory for events in their tiniest details, for facial expressions, gestures, and the spoken word. Yet that memory refuses to conform to any strict chronology." *Intimate Memoirs*, George Simenon, New York: Harcourt Brace Jovanovich, 1984, page 359.

23. For this fascinating episode, a Rococo vignette of modern times, see *Undercover*, E. Howard Hunt, New York: Berkeley Publisher, 1974, pages 198–204.

24. *The Islamic Bomb*, Steve Weissman and Herbet Krosney, New York: Times Books, 1981, an extraordinarily good work of investigative reporting, is full of instructive illustrations for the counterespionage specialist. Speaking of a key figure in Pakistan's nuclear program, "The Kindly Dr. Khan," the authors observe: "The neighbors noticed the cars, but hardly gave them a second thought. They simply assumed that Khan, like any foreign professional, had close friends in his country's various embassies. At least that is how they saw it until some five years later, when all the pieces began to come together." Pages 178–179.

25. For a modern instance, see *Boeing! Boeing!*, Marc Camoletti, New York: Samuel French, 1967.

26 For a good example see *The Champagne Spy* Wolfgang Lotz, New York: St. Martin's Press, 1972. His very openness was disarming.

27. These matters, which are referred to extensively elsewhere, should not in any way be regarded as exceptional, save in scope and ingenuity. Indignation is therefore misplaced. Focus, nowadays, is on how to do it rather than on whether it ought or ought not to be done.

28. "A counter-espionage agent has a paramount duty to the government: He must not allow himself to be uncovered. Whatever happens, an agent must always be anonymous to the people with whom he has to consort, otherwise he is a failure. I will put it bluntly: an uncovered agent is a failure. His usefulness to the State is at an end."

29. The Nicholas Daniloff case, to which reference has been made elsewhere, may usefully be seen in that light.

30. Most readers of spy fiction are familiar with arrested spies eating incriminating documents or seeking some pretext to have an opportunity to flush them down the toilet. Art and life tend to coincide quite remarkably in these last-moment disposal efforts.

31. These not very well publicized efforts have been proceeding for many years. See *KGB*, Brian Freemantle, New York: Holt, Rinehart and Winston, 1982. Israeli interest in these matters has been noted.

32. See the very interesting and informative *Eichmann Interrogated*, Ed. Jochem von Lang, New York: Farrar, Straus & Giroux, 1983.

33. For a very tragic and poignant example of this attitude, so familiar to psychiatrists, see Marie-Jo's book forming a part of the Simenon work, op. cit., supra note 22.

34. Spying and espionage activities of all kinds are sometimes admitted as part of a general pattern of disinformation. Some spies are occasionally sacrificed to take the heat off others.

35. The same problem arises in hostage negotiation. See *Hostage Negotiations: Options and Alternatives*, H. H. A. Cooper, Gaithersburg, MD: International Association of Chiefs of Police, CTT Series, 1977, pages 51–59.

36. For a discussion of the widespread character of torture in our times, see *Secret Police*, Thomas Plate and Andrea Darvi, New York: Doubleday, 1981, passim.

37. See, for example, "La Pena de Muerte: Reflexiones sobre la experiencia inglesa," H. H. A. Cooper, *Revista Peruana de Criminología y Ciencia Penitenciaria*, No. 4, 1968, pages 39–53.

38. "Tricks of the Trade: Counterintelligence Interrogation," William R. Johnson, *The Journal of Intelligence and Counterintelligence*, No. 2, 1986, pages 103-113, on page 103.

39. See, for example, the total cave-in of J. Matilde Carře, "The Cat," in *The Cat with Two Faces,* Gordon Young, New York: Coward-McCann, 1957. Madame Carře betrayed her entire network, including her lover, without a finger being laid upon her. Being shown to her cell was sufficient to convey the idea.

40. *Memories d'un agent secret de la France Libre,* G.L.E.T. Renault-Rouler (Colonel Remy), Paris: France-Empire, 1959, Vol. 1, page 317.

41. After showing Bao-Ruo Wang the disused torture chamber of the former Nationalist Chinese authorities, with which he was suitably impressed, his interrogator said to him, "We do not use such crude and inhumane methods. People who resort to torture do so only because they are weaker than their victims. We are certain of our superiority. And the methods we use are a hundred times more efficient than this." Op. cit., supra note 5, page 62.

42. *The Manchurian Candidate,* Richard Condon, London: Michael Joseph, Second Impression, 1973, page 210.

43. The "as such" is added, advisedly here. The Abwehr found it very useful to contrast the known brutality of the Gestapo with their own more moderate approach to these matters. They would then say, with something of regret, "If you are not disposed to cooperate with us, we shall have no alternative but to turn you over to the Gestapo."

44. "Deportations and secret arrests are labeled, with a Nazi writ which seems a little ghoulish, *Nacht und Nebel* (Night and Fog)." *Nazi Conspiracy and Aggression,* Volume 1, Washington, D.C.: U.S. Government Printing Office, page 146.

45. For an excellent example of the technique, see Bao Ruo-Wang, op. cit., supra note 5, pages 42–43. The process took some fifteen months, and it is interesting to note that even these assiduous interrogators did not get all they wanted. For the exception, which is very interesting, see page 146.

46. "It was also necessary to obtain at the earliest possible opportunity an accurate and detailed account of the agent's life from his earliest years, since this account almost certainly combined traces of other personalities with whom we were acquainted, and because any deviations from the truth would almost certainly be detected sooner or later. The greater the detail into which an agent goes, the more certainly will he

trip himself up if he strays into falsehood." *The Double-Cross System*, J. D. Masterman, New Haven, CT: Yale University Press, 1972, page 26.

47. The Chinese are, as amply evidenced by Bao Ruo-Wang (op. cit., supra note 5), almost excessively enthusiastic in this respect.

48. "The first rule in keeping secrets is nothing on paper— paper can be lost or stolen or simply inherited by the wrong people; if you really want to keep something secret, don't write it down." *The Man Who Kept the Secrets: Richard Helms and the CIA*, Thomas Powers, New York: Alfred A. Knopf, 1979, page 130.

49. See, on this: *Wanted: The Search for Nazis in America*, Howard Blum, New York: Quadrangle, 1977.

50. Security of electronically stored data is a highly technical matter, but the spy-catcher should familiarize himself with at least some of its complexities. See, for example, *Cryptography*, Carl H. Meyer and Stephen H. Matyas, New York: John Wiley, 1982.

7

NAILING
THE TROPHY
TO THE WALL

The work of the examining magistrate begins with the arrest of the criminal; the work of the spy catcher is to all intents and purposes finished when he slips the handcuffs on his prisoner—at least, it should be. For the examining magistrate is concerned with the arrest and confession of one man. The counter-espionage officer is after a complete network. The arrest of a single spy amounts to no more than the snapping of a link, whereas the real objective is to shatter the whole chain simultaneously. To achieve this it is necessary to shadow the identified agent, keep a close watch on whom he meets and where, put him in touch with a double-agent, and make every effort to persuade him to change sides. Of course, there may come a time when he must be arrested, but only when all else has failed."

Gilles Perrault[1]

A man who invests money at bottom prices in a gold mine with a shaky past history and a very dubious future may well be tempted to take a small and quick profit by selling out if the shares rise—but he will only make a fortune if he risks total loss by hanging on to his shares. With double agents we have, as it were, held shares in a great many mines, and some of them, on which we have in the early days expended labour and money lavishly, have indeed turned out to be El Dorados. Others of course have yielded nothing and cost much, but you cannot expect in any case to draw a fortune unless you pay in, and pay freely, first.

J. C. Masterman[2]

I would seem to have strangled my dreams on the altar of unbridled hubris.

Jonathan Pollard[3]

There is something essentially primeval about hunting. It is deeply etched in the human animal. There is nothing playful about it. It had originally nothing of the sport or pastime it has come to resemble for those in our times who no longer have to rely upon their ancient skills for survival. Hunting, in the primitive sense, is a practical activity. The thrill of the chase is all very well, and, no doubt, highly gratifying in its own way, but no real hunter can remain satisfied with such cosmetic contentment. It is what goes, metaphorically, into the pot that counts, and too many unproductive forays must sooner or later call into question the competence of the hunter.

The point stands even where, in Oscar Wilde's vivid phrase, we are talking of the unspeakable in pursuit of the inedible. Yet even the most practical of hunters is allowed his indulgences, be it only a feather in his cap. The tangible proof of his prowess requires a more demonstrative display than can be conveyed purely in terms of bodily nourishment or even the most extravagant of culinary delights. It was probably inevitable that this would degenerate into a pursuit of its own.

In our times, trophy hunting has been debased, becoming something of an exercise in dilettantism for the rich and famous. Yet behind even these vainglorious exploits, there are always those with real hunting skills who make possible the skins and horns that hang on the walls of others. Hunting requires the exercise of true ability. The disposition of the product of the hunt and even the reward of the hunter are a matter of power. He who has this in the proper measure calls the shots and is in a position to claim the trophy if he chooses. This is equally true whether we are treating individuals or institutions. The hunting of spies is no different from any other hunting activity in this respect.

The spy-catcher is the real hunter, the person endowed with the skills which, if properly applied over the right terrain at a propitious moment, will result in the trophy being taken. Whatever pride he might rightfully take in his own profession and the skills that have earned his success, renown, even, it is important for him to retain a sense of perspective, a suitable degree of humility. *He does not hunt on his own account.* That he is allowed to hunt at all is in the gift of others. The trophy belongs truly not to him who has taken it, but to those whom he serves and who, in a certain sense, have extended to him his license to hunt. The spy-catcher, it is true, will take the blame for the fruitless searches, missed shots, and empty bag. The prize is not a compensation for these responsibilities. It is destined to another end, of a more political kind, for ultimately the hunter's reputation rests as much on his political savvy and skill in the art of human relations as it does upon his abilities as a hunter per se.

All this may seem at first blush monstrously unfair, but it is perfectly consonant with what happens in other departments of life, and whoever said life was fair? These simple admonitions are very necessary here, for they are frequently overlooked through ignorance or design. Ignoring them can have very unpleasant consequences. The questions, whose trophy and what shall be done with it, are ones that must be seriously addressed.

There is always at least some utility in the simple elimination of the spy provided that, along with him, the spying is also eliminated. All too often, this is not the case. Something more is required, for the spy is usually but part of a larger whole, and the gap left by his extraction, varying in size and significance according to the spy's relative importance, is capable of being filled by others. Elimination, liquidation, termination with extreme prejudice—call it what you will—certainly has its place in the scheme of things. It plays an important part in any pattern of disposition, and its advertisement may well be significant in establishing the ground rules by which the game is, and is seen to be, played. *Smert Shpionem*[4] is a statement of policy as well as an operational arm of counterespionage. Whatever the rhetoric, in times of acute crisis, spies are not cockroaches.

What we are cautioning against here is overenthusiasm for

the quick disposal method. It is rarely as cheap or as efficient as it superficially appears to be. Apprehended spies do not just have to be properly evaluated to see what part they play and have played in the larger scheme of things. A concerted effort has to be made to squeeze them as dry as possible before consigning them to the conveyor belt that will carry them to their ultimate fate. Desiccated spies may be reconstituted and even recycled. Nothing should ever be discarded while containing anything resembling a useful measure of juice.[5] Moreover, the captured spy may have a useful value over and above these immediate considerations. He may, under certain circumstances, have a helpful role to play for a new master. This goes well beyond cooperating to save his own skin. He may decide to work actively for those into whose hands he has fallen. He may allow himself to be "turned" or even facilitate the process himself. The usefulness of this possibility is largely dependent upon the preparations that have been made to meet such a contingency. For his own reasons, the captured spy may be most willing to cut such a deal, but the proposition has little appeal if those who have him in their power lack the means to usefully handle him to their own advantage.

Making proper use of the "turned" spy is often a much more difficult and complex process than the act of turning him. A considerable investment of specialized resources of all kinds is needed, and the entire operation must be directed with vision and a keen sense of the strategic fitness of things. Since the remarkable and now well-publicized successes of the British Double Cross system during World War II, it may be assumed that every major counterespionage service will have some arrangements for handling turned spies, and it is prudent for those concerned with these matters to learn as much about these arrangements as possible. Employing the "turned" spy in any capacity, but especially where he is put on a long leash or allowed to roam at will,[6] is always a risky business, but it can pay the most handsome dividends when handled properly.

Clearly, the "turned" spy is not a trophy that can be sensibly exhibited by those who have made the capture and effected the conversion, at least not until the entire affair has passed into what amounts to ancient history[7] in espionage terms. This points up, incidentally, a useful fact: the successful spy-catcher may have to wait a very long time before being in a position to exhibit his trophies and to receive recognition of his professional achievements, if indeed he is ever able to do so. He must usually rest content with the personal knowledge that he has been successful without any of the satisfactions that might come from being able to publicize the fact to the world at large. Those spy-catchers who have large and voracious egos must find other, less overt ways of providing the necessary nourishment for them. The savoring of triumphs must be done modestly and with circumspection if methods are to retain their effectiveness for future operations.

The captured spy has yet another value, to which we have already occasionally adverted. Potentially, each spy so taken constitutes a more or less useful item of exchange. Moreover, seen as a trophy, this is certainly one capable of the most blatant and immediate of exhibition. Sometimes indeed the spy is "lifted" for no other purpose than to serve as an article of barter, and the capture and exhibition are well advertised so that the whole point of the affair will not be lost upon those with whom it is hoped to do business.

The bartering of professional spies occupies a significant place upon the international commodities market.[8] Each has a carefully assigned value, although it may take several expert appraisals to determine exactly what this is. Market conditions generally have a great deal to do with the setting of values; there may be a policy against trading at one time, for example, that is relaxed at others. Relations between potential trading partners may be so poor that, however great the desire to trade, on the merits, it is simply not possible to strike a bargain or even to be seen contemplating doing so. Factors of intrinsic worth are probably the most important in setting a price or impelling a trade.

What any particular spy may be worth is dependent upon a variety of matters, many of which may not be readily apparent to one of the bargaining parties at the material time. Clearly, Israel would have paid dearly to have secured the return of its captured spy, Eli Cohen.[9] Under but slightly different circumstances, it might well have been possible to have struck a bargain with Syria that would have saved Cohen from his ignominious public execution. The climate for trading was most unsuitable, and there would have been powerful and considerable internal opposition within Syria that would have made serious consideration of any Israeli offer very difficult at the time. It was simply more important (and healthier) for Syria to nail the trophy to the wall as quickly and publicly as possible rather than look for a different kind of and, perhaps, more worthwhile profit in other directions. Anyone who took part in the trading process on Syria's behalf was bound to be suspect as a consequence of Cohen's own widespread espionage activities, which had spread to the highest levels of Syria's ruling circles. Israel had no human quid pro quo to put up in whom Syria might have shown a corresponding interest, nor was anything in the nature of a three-way swap possible in that historic time frame. Even the most tempting offer the Israelis could muster would have been seen as tainted in Damascus (as well as in other Arab capitals), and it is likely that this consideration, far more than the undeniably deteriorated quality of the merchandise, was the most influential in preventing any deal from going through.

The ranking importance of the spy in the hierarchy of those he serves, while highly influential in stimulating efforts to get him back, is not by any means determinative of the matter. His having been taken at all may, under some circumstances, be considered a fatal black mark against him.[10]

There are many to whom the expression "Spy of the Century" has been applied, but few can be more deserving of it on all counts than Richard Sorge,[11] the incomparable Soviet agent who served the interests of the USSR so long, so faithfully, and so well. If ever a spy might have expected his master to move heaven and earth to secure his safe return from captivity, Sorge would assuredly have been that one. Sorge's expectations in this regard were not unreasonable, for Japan, by which nation he was taken, was not the principal target of his espionage activities and the Soviet Union was not at war with that country at the time. Moreover, Japan had no particular desire to claim Sorge as a trophy and may well have not appreciated his huge importance as a Soviet agent at that time. Yet, it seems clear (despite the rumors which, like those surrounding Mata Hari, persist to this day) that no serious attempt was made by the Soviet Union to procure his release, and the matter was hardly important enough to Japan for that country to take the initiative. Sorge himself was in a very difficult position, for besides the ferocious discipline by which he was bound, any promotion of such expectations on his part, however gently they might have been suggested, would have led the Japanese to investigate more closely his true contemporary value. There was little that he could do save rely on standing tradition, far from regularly observed, and a solid belief in his continued unique usefulness. That his expectations remained unfulfilled is a matter of received history, but the reasons for this are in need of some clarification. No decision of the kind involved in this case could at that time have been taken other than by the express approval of Stalin, and that he refused to intervene on Sorge's behalf seems to require some new consideration. It has long been held that Sorge's fate was tied up with Stalin's apparent failure to act on certain warnings from Sorge and that his return to the Soviet Union would somehow have embarrassed the Soviet leader. This can hardly have been the case, for a leader so firmly in control, so powerful and ruthless, who had no hesitation in clapping Rado and Trepper into prison upon their return and who summarily disposed of so many whose loyalty he had come to suspect,[12] would have had little trouble and no embarrassment whatsoever in doing the same with Sorge. Stalin was extremely shrewd and farsighted in matters of this kind. He would have seen that any sort of bargaining at that time would set an inconvenient precedent that could have no countervailing value. He thus established a policy that was to be severely tested not too far down the road. By way of contrast, it can be seen that President Reagan's "deal" in the Daniloff case had a more than incidental impact on the subsequent "arms for hostages" dealings of his administration. Stalin was determined to allow no such market to develop, even by implication, and Sorge's fate was sealed as a result.

Sorge's case must be regarded as somewhat of a historical aberration rather than a matter seriously affecting the workings of the market in these affairs. There are excellent reasons why nations should trade provided the climate is right and a good bargain can be struck. Nations want to get their own spies back if for no better reason than to debrief them on their experiences in captivity and find out what they may have revealed, punishing them as an example to others, if this seems appropriate. But the main reason for entering into these often Byzantine dealings is simply to keep the faith.

There is at the very least an unspoken commitment to those who unstintingly give their all in the service of espionage, that those who direct them will extend toward them whatever protection might be feasible in the event of their capture even though open or even tacit acknowledgment is impossible and contrary to protocol. Such notions have hardened into an almost unwritten law; certainly the matter goes well beyond mere one-sided expectations. Since the death of Stalin, the Soviet Union has indeed, by implication, made this almost into an ethic of the profession, one that is extremely reassuring to those who daily place themselves at substantial risk through their labors for Mother Russia. That is why for many, Sorge's case, despite its historical context, is so anomalous and seemingly out of character. Clearly, this is a rather carefully circumscribed obligation. It is owed to a comparatively small, select group of all those who serve as spies. Its exact parameters have never been, perhaps never can be, sketched.

The whole thing rests upon a curious kind of honor, an unstated understanding of what is met in the case. There is a sense of when these obligations should be met, and a certain kind of disappointment when they are not. Much of what all this rests upon is unarticulated, but it is important in the present setting that some sort of understanding emerges of the foundations upon which these practices rest. We can safely argue, on the basis of what is done, that more than considerations of utility rule in these cases; spies are not traded simply because some usefulness, of a positive or negative character, is seen to remain in them. *Trading is undertaken primarily to benefit the reputation and interests of the institution rather than those of the individual.* The service, apart from any practical benefits, aspires to being seen as reliable and trustworthy, a good employer. Those to whom these special obligations are tacitly extended are not defined exclusively by their conditions of employment, the character of their service, or such considerations as race or nationality. More exact criteria can perhaps be derived from a consideration not of those cases where a country has moved to get back its own captured spies by striking a bargain with those who have apprehended them, but by reference to cases of flight, where one who has spied for a particular country moves in advance of his presumptive captors to return to his employer's domains or seeks refuge in them to escape the clutches of those against whom he has spied. Thus, Philby, Burgess, and Maclean, all British civil servants, were welcomed to the Soviet Union upon the discovery of facts or concretization of positions with respect to those facts that would have led to uncongenial proceedings against them in their own land. Blake, convicted in Great Britain as a Soviet spy, was apparently welcomed into the Soviet Union following his escape from prison.[13] In his own way, each had rendered signal service to the USSR that ought to have entitled him to some sort of protection, recognition even, from those on whose behalf those services had been undertaken, notwithstanding his nationality, ethnic origins, or compensation he may have received for his services.

In the great Portland spy case, "Lonsdale" (Conon Molody) and the "Krogers" were the subjects of a spy trade, whereas Houghton and Gee, the two British subjects directly responsible for purloining the secret information in the case, were left to their own devices. It is not difficult to see why this should have been so, and few knowledgeable professionals would cavil at the results. But, it is pertinent to hypothesize on the case of Maclean. What if he had been arrested, charged, and convicted of having been a Soviet spy? Would the Soviet Union have acknowledged him to the extent of trying to do some sort of deal that would have allowed him to live out his life in Moscow? It might be thought most unlikely. Under interrogation, he could not have revealed much to harm the interest of the Soviet Union, and even were those modest disclosures considered intolerable, there were ways of disposing of him. But what of Philby, a ranking officer in the Soviet intelligence services? Might not a deal have been worked out in his case? Perhaps he could have been exchanged for Commander Crabb? And was the escape of Blake necessitated by the fact that no deal would have been possible in his case?

Such matters are not moot in our times, despite the now well developed practices to which the capture of spies and the exposure of their doings have given rise. A most interesting situation is posed by the case of Jonathan Pollard. Pollard,[14] a United States citizen by birth born into the Jewish faith, was a civilian employee of the United States Department of the Navy. He held high security clearances, and in the ordinary course of his employment had access to a great deal of sensitive secret material that would have been highly damaging to the interests of the United States had it been abstracted and conveyed to a foreign power by a disloyal servant. That Pollard owed allegiance to the country of his birth is indisputable and, moreover, that country had reposed a singular confidence in him and his abilities by appointing him to the sensitive post he had lately come to hold. Yet Pollard found himself in the uncomfortable bind in which so many Jews must have found themselves since the earliest days of the Diaspora, which has led to a veritable crisis of identity for some since the founding of the State of Israel in 1948. Who is a Jew when it comes to the crunch? When he sees his ancient people threatened by hatred and the possibility of extinction that recent memories of the Holocaust have fanned to fever pitch? Where, in moments of crisis, do his true loyalties lie? For many Jews, who regard their faith truly as a religion rather than an index of race or ethnic sympathies, Pollard's disservice has been extreme, for it has raised in the minds of those among whom they live and work, understandably, if not justifiably, a nagging doubt as to their trustworthiness and basic loyalties. What are these people, really, when fundamental loyalties are on the line: Jews or Americans?

The same question might quite properly be asked of the loyalties of so many of the minorities that make up the great pluralistic society of the United States (or, indeed, many others of our contemporary world), but it is not. It is asked here of the Jews, and they must, of necessity, answer. Pollard espoused an extraordinarily fervent adherence to Israel that led him to betray his own country and the duties owed to it, in favor of aiding, through espionage, the Israeli cause in matters of the most profound consequence to relations between the United States and Israel. That he was persuaded, encouraged, even enticed to do so by professional Israeli intelligence officers acting in the service of their country may have been reprehensible, but it can hardly have been surprising. Pollard was a valuable source of information and, moreover, enthusiastic in carrying out his task. He believed himself to be helping a cause to which he was wholeheartedly committed. He had little difficulty in rationalizing his thefts of United States secrets and their transfer for considerable personal reward to Israel. Was not the United States dedicated to the preservation of the State of Israel? Was not Israel a friendly power, a bastion of United States policy in the Middle East? Were not those secrets vital to the defense of Israel against the most dreaded and determined of her foes? And ought they not, in honor of the true relationship assumed to exist between the United States and Israel, have been freely and honestly shared in the ordinary course of things? And were they not, to the contrary, being unfairly and improperly withheld to Israel's detriment? At least, the Israelis thought so, for they made the most strenuous efforts through Pollard and others to lay hands upon them.

From the point of view of the United States, none of this can possibly justify Pollard's treachery, though it does help to make it more comprehensible. When this somewhat easily taken trophy was finally pinned upon the wall for the rest of his natural life, amid a great deal of rather hypocritical indignation, it seemed destined to gather dust among others of its ilk taken during what will go down as an extraordinarily trophy-conscious season for America's spy-catchers. Premature historians of the matter had, however, to reckon with "60 Minutes,"[15] that extraordinary contemporary blend of the banal and the significant, and an outpouring of Israeli feeling at the treatment of Pollard that seemed both insensitive to American susceptibilities and indifferent to an American backlash.

That Pollard was ill-used by the Israelis, especially once he had exhausted his worth as a source, seems a not uncharitable conclusion. That he was substantially responsible for his own misfortunes and ought properly bear the consequences, regardless of what might be meet to visit upon the heads of others, is a harsh but not unfair judgment. But two disturbing questions remain for us: Were the best interests of the United States served simply by tacking the trophy to the wall? And what ought the attitude of the State of Israel be vis-à-vis the current predicament of its naive, sacrificial lamb? The strangulation argued by Pollard in his own defense is hardly kosher. The hard question is really this: Does Israel owe him a better deal? If the answer is in the affirmative, how does that nation go about getting it?

We can usefully explore these matters here. On the merits, by reference to the character and importance of Pollard in the overall context of Israeli intelligence policy and relations with

Washington, it could well be argued that this miserable spy is now owed nothing save perhaps the opportunity of doing a graceful Wu Tai Chin,[16] having been amply paid for his treachery at the time. This is clearly not the view of the Israeli man in the street. Pollard was no Sorge in any sense, and taking Soviet standards as a yardstick (for the Russians now seem both rational and usually punctilious in these matters), he might be compared to a Boyce[17] or a Houghton,[18] a well-paid, perhaps overly so, spy who knew enough about what he was in for when he entered the game. It would be difficult to fault the Israelis for taking such a position, and only an appeal to the "Jewish" issue, to which we shall shortly return, might be raised to soften this stance. It could thus be argued that Pollard was paid, and he paid in turn; the account is settled as it stands, especially when Israel's own embarrassment is thrown into the scales. But, as we have seen, it is not the individual's position that really swings the pendulum in these cases. Israel, like other employers of spies, has a certain reputation to uphold—perhaps even more so. It cannot be said to be satisfactory in this regard to be seen simply to have left Pollard's hide tacked to a Washington wall. Others in the Israeli service, or those who might fancy entering it, would be apt to draw unfavorable conclusions. It does not pay a service like that of the Israelis, or indeed any other, to acquire a bad reputation in these matters.

But there remains the more pregnant question of whether Pollard was owed anything out of the ordinary by reason of the fact that he was an idealistic Jew doing, as he conceived it, something rather special for his own people and his own spiritual homeland. Certainly, the very suggestion puts the State of Israel, and Jews elsewhere who are not inclined in the slightest to follow the Pollard line, in a considerable bind. It casts the Israeli secret service in the role of the serpent and throws a pall of suspicion over many whose sympathies for Israel in no way extend to committing treason against their own countries on her behalf. Yet this is undeniably the central issue in the Pollard story, and its implications for Israel and Jews everywhere cannot be avoided by deepening Pollard's own sacrifice. He did not do what he did simply out of avarice; he was certainly not motivated by a hatred, however muted, of the United States. He did what he did because he was a Jew and felt an overriding loyalty to Israel on that account. Many Israelis certainly feel that his abandonment, however politic, is not merely an act of cowardice, but a retreat from a fundamental principle on which the State of Israel was founded. This is not a case that is likely to fade away of its own accord, for there is honor to be satisfied in the midst of dishonor. As some of the anger on both sides abates, there will be those with cooler heads and more detached perspectives seeking ways of satisfying that curious element of honor that so often resides amid these discreditable matters.

Here we must ask if it is really more difficult in these cases to strike a bargain between friends than it would have been in slightly altered circumstances between those whose situation places them in antagonistic relations.[19] For many, it is unforgivable for friends to spy upon each other,[20] but this is surely, in the present context, to carry naivete to its extremes. While we would not go so far as to aver that it is done all the time, it is certainly sufficiently common that the discovery hardly calls for more than raised eyebrows in professional circles—and that on account of indiscretion rather than a flagrant breach of the unwritten codes that govern these matters.

There are strong and sufficient reasons for visiting condign punishment upon those of one's own citizens who give aid and encouragement to the enemy through espionage. While its deterrent value is questionable, it does serve some important atavistic purposes, and it is as important in its own way to make proper exhibition of the trophy as it was to impale heads upon piles at the town gates in the early Middle Ages. Whether such spies have served friends or foes, they still have their worth in a pinch. A hungry hunter has little use for trophies; he renders every scrap of the beast into something of immediate or lasting utility. Only the voluptuaries and the affluent can afford to be prodigal with what they have taken. Most fall somewhere in between; having registered their catch for the proper credit, they are not averse to parting with it—provided the price is right.

It is suggested, by reference to what is set out here, that there is nothing eminently non-tradeable about Pollard or any of those who have fallen into Uncle Sam's nets in recent times. The only problem is finding a willing trading partner; even the Walkers might be worth something to the United

States. If it is objected that these persons are still United States nationals, notwithstanding their heinous behavior and manifest disregard for the obligations of citizenship, a useful parallel can be seen in the treatment by the USSR of Soviet Jews. The Soviet Union showed itself not averse to striking a deal over Anatoly Scharansky,[21] a convicted spy serving a long term of imprisonment, notwithstanding his nationality at the time of his office. He, too, evinced a love of Israel, to which he wished to emigrate, exceeding that borne toward his native land. The Soviet Union made a fitting example of Scharansky in much the same way that the United States did with Pollard, but wisely preserved him intact against some future eventuality which at last materialized. It was clearly worth it to the Soviet Union to do a deal for Scharansky, and such a possibility was obviously envisaged from the outset; it was simply a question of waiting until the right market was felt to have developed. We would suggest that there is nothing fundamentally wrong with a Pollard deal from the perspective of the United States—when the time is right. And if a deal can be struck, it may well be much more profitable than hanging on to the skin of a self-proclaimed ass. Whether Israel really wants Pollard is a moot question but, for the reasons we have indicated, it might be politic to appear to be prepared to strike a useful bargain if common ground can be established.

It is difficult to see, at first blush, anything that the United States might require of the State of Israel in exchange for Pollard that could not be obtained by other, less embarrassing means. Ruling out a purely fictitious deal of convenience, there is one area of interest that might usefully be explored. On numerous occasions, United States citizens have been kidnapped or taken hostage and their lives put in jeopardy for the ostensible purpose of forcing the United States to pressure Israel in some way, usually to agree to the release of Arab nationals held in Israeli prisons. Whatever the merits or demerits of such deals when viewed from the perspective of counterterrorism strategy, they have been considered in the past and will undoubtedly be considered, if not entered into, in the future. A state prepared to release a Kozo Okamato[22] and an Hilarion Capucci,[23] despite the popular, hard-line image, is not averse to doing deals of this kind when it sees some small benefit to itself. Israel has usually tried to shift the onus for such questionable transactions onto the shoulders of others: "We would be willing to release such and such if the United States were to ask us."[24] It is foreseeable that Pollard might, at some future date, be thrown into such a deal as a useful "sweetener." While this would do nothing by way of redemption for his crimes, he would have served a more useful purpose than mere decoration in the trophy room.

One point is clearly illustrated by the foregoing. In the taking of spies, the greatest of care should be exercised in order not to diminish their trophy value. Any good hunter will appreciate what is involved here. Again, practical rather than humanitarian considerations dictate this course. This precept was clearly acknowledged by Donovan in the Rudolf Abel trial, when he pleaded with the court to spare his client's life on the grounds, essentially, that he would be more valuable to the United States alive than dead.[25] It was just as clearly ignored by Syria in the case of Eli Cohen, and the contrast speaks greatly to the relative political stability of the two systems in question. Had the Abel case been before the United States courts at the time the Rosenbergs were tried, as it might well have been, Donovan's plea could well have fallen upon deaf ears. In any particular historical context, the emotional issues cannot be overlooked. What is sometimes desired is neither a practical morsel to supplement the national diet, nor a trophy of which to boast, but rather a blood sacrifice, pure and simple.

It is of interest to interject here an item for speculation. How would the United States have reacted to a discreet Soviet approach to have ransomed the Rosenbergs? With, perhaps, Harry Gold thrown in for good measure? There were many interesting items of exchange around at that time that could have been cobbled into a deal of some profit to the United States. Kruschev's Russia (nor for that matter Gorbachev's, though he has a much slighter lien on the property) could hardly have offered (as did Israel) to return the product of its agents' useful activities, but some sort of acceptable deal might have been struck. The Rosenbergs, even in the enormity of all they were held to have done, were hardly so very different from the "Krogers," so willingly exchanged at a later time by the United Kingdom; if anything, the "Krogers" were very much more professional and, hence, of greater potential menace. The United States foreclosed any possibility of a deal by executing the Rosenbergs, an option it was certainly allowed by law, but one which it has been severely criticized for having exercised, even by friendly powers.

The parallel with the case of Syria and Eli Cohen is again worth noting. It is also worth observing that the Rosenbergs, also Jews,[26] acted like Pollard in defense of something in which they too passionately believed, though the religion in their case was not Judaism but Communism, a much less appealing proposition for the United States in those Cold War years. But they did believe they were acting on behalf of an ally of the United States, however questionable that belief might have been at that time. They presented themselves on grounds curiously similar to those which motivated Pollard in that they felt the United States was wrong to withhold such important knowledge from a nation with which it was associated in the course of the great struggle against the Axis powers.

No addition is offered here to the judgment of history and the handling of the Rosenberg case,[27] but it is pertinent, in the present context, to consider the alternative outcome and what would have been necessary, by way of preserving the trophy, to provide for taking that different path. What does seem clear in the Rosenberg case is that despite the time available to those responsible for designing the tapestry that has eventually come to grace the walls of law enforcement and jurisprudence, the lemon was very far from being squeezed dry. This is perhaps another prudent reason for avoiding undue haste in tacking up the trophy. Time might yet show up a few damp spots in need of attention. A detached, almost cold-blooded attitude is necessary in these matters. The principle of utility should be the guiding light. These matters should preferably not be handled in an overheated atmosphere and never during feverish bouts of spy mania if the best interests of the nation's counterespionage policies are to be served. There is not only the tendency on the part of the professionals to want to get the trophy upon the wall before they are robbed of it, but also an unhealthy desire on the part of the lay segment of the body politic to irretrievably splatter over the floor what has been taken in an unbridled spirit of vengeance. In consequence, what might later be useful is lost, and little save a momentary animal satisfaction is gained.

The spy-catcher is primarily concerned with catching spies, but their disposition is of vital concern to him because it has a very real impact upon his work. Let us consider, for a moment, the "turning" of agents, that subtle, delicate process whereby they are reoriented, literally turned around, and their talents employed against those for whom they had formerly worked. In the first place, the spy has to be brought in from the cold, trawled up from the depths, or whatever. In short, he has to be well and truly taken, to be held in a viselike grip from which no reasonable prospect of unaided escape to his own side seems possible. The fact of being caught is usually manifest enough whether the outward signs are the dreaded stage props of the Gestapo, the numbing cheerlessness of Lefortovo, or the unsmiling visages of the special agents of the FBI.

Getting caught requires some adjustment, even if no more than the sucking in of breath before the bone-crushing begins. Once acceptance has sunk in, and this is often a matter of moments, the big question for the spy is, what now? Even the most heroic and most dedicated fire up the survival instincts at this time, be it in the interests of staying alive or buying enough time to bite on the cyanide capsule. If the route to long-term survival is sought, the spy needs to know, as soon as possible, where the real power so obviously ranged against him lies. Who calls the shots? Who will determine his fate? With whom can he strike a deal? Unless he is very much the Big Chief,[28] he can hardly expect to see anyone very important, certainly in the initial phases of the proceeding. If he is a professional entrusted with an important mission, a certain amount of his training will have been devoted to instructing him how the other side's counterespionage services function. He will know something of the rules, written and unwritten, that prescribe how his case shall be handled. He will have been apprised of where, notionally, the power to dispose of him lies.

The rule of thumb governing these things is: the larger the organization, the greater the division of labor and the greater the complexity of the division. Hence, in the large organizations, those who do the catching rarely have much to say directly about the final disposition. The longer the chain of responsibilities, the more likely it is that there will be both kinks and strains in the system. This offers a number of possibilities that the system will turn upon itself and tends to give a somewhat reticent character to the actions of those who actually do the catching. They know all too well that what they have done is, in a sense, provisional, being subject to a process of perfection by those farther along the chain of power.[29] Such diffidence makes its mark upon the system these men serve. The institution acquires an anonymity, a color-lessness that shifts attention away from itself.

In its most developed form, the counterespionage agency becomes something of a mystery, and its personnel become faceless servants of some larger organ that takes the credit and fends off inquiry. Ultimately, spy-catchers are made and molded by the political systems they serve and of which they are a part. The system decrees what prominence they and their work shall receive, whether they are identified, spot-lighted, even, or whether they shall remain silently in the shadows. The early *Cheka* was very different from its mod-ern, lineal descendant, the KGB, and this is very different, in its turn from, say, MI5. Each is a distinctive product of its own times and of the system it serves. What is certain is that the early *Cheka*[30] was capable not only of taking those consid-ered spies and saboteurs, but, under Dherzhinsky was di-rectly responsible for arranging and carrying out their final disposition. Even in those early chaotic days, larger political considerations sometimes overrode the limited views of the organization.[31] These political considerations are very impor-tant and influential in the area of trophy taking. The late J. Edgar Hoover was an extremely political animal. He under-stood as well as any other American public servant, if not better, the meaning of personal power and the use of politics as a source of energy for the institution he headed for nearly fifty years. It is therefore of no little significance that Hoover personally took charge of the operation against Dillinger and took pains to be seen to be in at the kill. The arrest of Abel, perhaps the most important professional spy ever taken in the United States, was left to underlings.

Image is very important to a counterespionage service, but it is more than mere Madison Avenue chic. It is built on solid, appropriately advertised achievement. Consistency must be carefully maintained, even if this means being consistently inconsistent to keep the other side off balance. In practice, different parts of the same system may develop different reputations.[32] While this imparts a desirable flexibility to the system as a whole, it can sometimes produce an undesirable kind of competition for the right to the trophy. The sum of the parts should never be greater than the whole in these matters.

Spy-catching triumphs ought not to be paraded to the discomfiture of the other parts of the system. It is inevitable that different parts of the system will suffer disproportionately from the espionage of the opposition. Certain targets will be perceived as more desirable and more vulnerable than others. Some parts of the system will necessarily be more exposed and will function with a slighter attention to the strict dictates of security than will others. Some departments of human activity invite spies as certain varieties of flowers attract insects. This may be very aggravating for those entrusted with security and counterespionage, but the fact should be treated with a certain quality of understanding rather than the studied contempt it too often receives. The spy-catcher will often enough have to minister to the needs of these tender sisters.

The spy-catcher's trophies will on occasion be of a somewhat embarrassing nature. This can give rise to some prickly situations and, if they are mishandled, lasting enmities. In the worst of cases, it can even spell the consumption of the weaker organ by the stronger as happened when the Sicherheitsdienst was able to gobble up the Abwehr after many years of intense rivalry and a scoring of points at each other's expense rather than that of the opposition.[33] Here again we see the need for a balanced overview of what is required. It is easy for one part of the system, with the best of motives originally, to begin an unrestrained witchhunt against another in the name of security. These abuses are encouraged by the undoubted fact that the performance of those against whom these actions are directed has been less than satisfactory, thereby inviting some sort of housecleaning. Every action produces its own reaction, and the standard reaction to perceived threats such as those we are considering here is to close ranks against outsiders. Genuine security risks are hidden rather than recognized in the interests of institutional survival. The universal plea is to be allowed to do one's housecleaning and, moreover, to be left unsupervised in the process. The sincerity of those making such appeals is often unimpeachable, but the results of these exercises leave much to be desired.

The rot has sometimes spread too far, penetrating through the organization like a cancer. Those with an all-encompassing, nonpartisan view of the affair should recognize when this is the case. If radical surgery is necessary, it should be taken without hesitation, but the greatest care should be exercised so as to do as little harm as possible to the healthy organs. Between the two extremes, that which produces a Philby on the one hand and that which leads to a Canaris on the other, there lie a great many alternative possibilities. These must be carefully measured by those who have the general health of the body politic in their care. There are many applications to be considered. It is important throughout to remember that we are not talking here about inefficiency, however gross, or even common criminality that has brought an organization into disrepute. The issue is the penetration of the organization by enemy agents, of the subversion of its purposes, of treachery that must be rooted out and corrected. In short, work for the professional spy-catcher.

These matters are most effectively highlighted by the 1987 discovery of a variety of serious breaches of security at the United States embassy in Moscow.[34] It is not without relevance to point out that the whole issue of what had occurred and what might usefully be done by way of corrective action took place in a blinding light of publicity such as few counterespionage agencies elsewhere in the world would have the misfortune to work under. A free press, acting responsibly, is a great force for good, and its actions have probably done more than any other sociopolitical process to shape the United States and give direction to those who serve its interests. Excesses there are bound to be, and questionable uses of this formidable power, too, but without the pressure of these constant probings and publications, it is certain that the country would be very different and the locus of power might be shielded in ways tending to produce a tyranny that would have to generate a less wholesome reaction by way of counter. But all this does make it very difficult for spy-catchers who, like stage magicians, do not work too effectively in a well-lighted environment. What we saw initially was a focus of attention upon the United States Marine Corps, some of the personnel of which assigned to the embassy in Moscow as security guards were suspected of dereliction of duty and, worse, facilitating the penetration of supposedly secure embassy areas by Soviet agents.[35] These were very serious matters in themselves and clearly required the closest, most expert investigations to determine what had happened, when, how, and why. The affair had all the right ingredients for a media spectacular descending into low comedy, with beautiful female agents[36] and naive, young embassy guards in a state of rut. Emphasis soon shifted to the physical structure of the embassy buildings themselves, both old and new and—surprise! surprise!—their security was discovered to have been heavily compromised by the Soviet intelligence services which were alleged to have taken advantage, in most undiplomatic fashion, of construction, renovations, and any other opportunity that might have presented itself to implant monitoring devices of all kinds among the hapless Americans already exposed to heavy dosages of well-directed radiation and surveillance spy-dust.[37] The USSR quickly retaliated against the media exposure of its efforts with a very well-orchestrated campaign designed to demonstrate that the Americans were doing the same sorts of things against the poor innocents of the Soviet diplomatic corps having the misfortune to serve their country in the United States. That these very necessary counterespionage methods of great sophistication, but rather questionable effectiveness, should have been employed by both sides will surprise no professional.

That the revelations should have been so cynically received by the general public is a correct measure of the temper of our times. Even presidential hopefuls have come to expect to be spied upon, perhaps even to lose their briefing books, as well as their reputations. Diplomats, whose business it is to traffic in secret matters, can certainly expect no more benign treatment. Once the bandwagon had begun to roll, however, it soon picked up speed and a host of passengers scrambled aboard along the way. Thus we were treated to the inevitable Congressional Mission to Moscow with the equally inevitable, solemn pronouncements on matters of security following a very brief visit (during which children's writing tablets were used for communication purposes for fear the itinerant legislators might let slip state secrets to the omnipresent Russians). Suggestions, ill-informed, silly, and bordering on the irresponsible, projected new and creative ways of wasting the

American taxpayer's dollar with little prospect of achieving a higher level of future security.[38] Naturally, all this focused attention upon how the investigations of these matters ought, in the United States context, to proceed. The entire matter raises some very interesting issues within the purview of what we are considering here.[39]

The United States Marine Corps, a crack fighting unit with a proud reputation stretching back into the distant past, has quite incidentally had formal embassy security duties assigned to it. In terms of smartness and symbolism, the idea seems a good one, and the Corps has hitherto discharged its responsibilities on these counts with adequate dispatch. In terms of security, however, the whole concept must have given any true security professional cause for misgivings.[40] These are key positions (literally in some instances), and the training of a fighting man is not adequate preparation for what is involved here, supplemented though it may be with courses designed to provide a proper security orientation. The Corps has maintained its reputation through rigid, military-style discipline and any reflection upon it, such as that produced by these recent events, is resented and dealt with strictly inside the family. It is easy to see the horror with which the intrusion of outsiders might be viewed.

In common with so many other United States agencies and institutions, the Marine Corps has its own intelligence arm, designed in this case to serve its particular combat needs. But, naturally, this is not a specialized counterespionage unit with the expertise and experience needed to meet the threat from the Soviet intelligence services working upon their home ground. Marines are not spy-catchers by profession (any more than they are really security guards), and any attempt to keep what has occurred strictly within the family is both unhelpful and potentially dangerous. But, and this is the big question here, who should move in at this stage? Where is the specialist spy-catching outfit upon which the Marines might call with confidence and to which the Corps might turn not only for expertise it does not have, but which might be expected to show the proper respect and a degree of understanding rather than glee at the trophy-hunting opportunity opened up by these misadventures? We must return to this in due course.

The primary responsibility for the representation of United

States interests in foreign parts pertains to the Department of State. It is there, too, that responsibilities for security of all kinds ultimately lie. This agency is also extremely sensitive to criticism and understandably protective of its prerogatives and personnel. It is just as inclined as the Marine Corps, if not more so, to dig in under fire and to try to clean up its problems in-house without recourse to unwelcome outside assistance.

In recent years, the Department of State has branched out into a surprising array of extracurricular activities to meet the demands it has felt imposed on it by the pressure of world events.[41] In particular, it has moved heavily, and with an impressive lack of success, into the area of security, principally in response to the threats posed worldwide by international terrorism. Again, this is a case of the unfamiliar chasing the unattainable. The preparation of a diplomat, at whatever level of responsibility, is most unsuitable training for a security assignment, however this may be operationally defined. Neither the organization of the United States Department of State nor the training and assignments offered its personnel are suitable for the serious professional discharge of security responsibilities. There is a certain observable departmental arrogance that impedes the sensible and timely recognition of this, but the agency's record and the level of its expenditures in this provide mute testimony to the fact that it is hopelessly miscast in a security role. But whether it undertakes the security obligations itself or whether it contracts them out to others with a more specialized ability to undertake them, there can be no doubt about where the responsibilities for seeing that these duties are adequately carried out lie. And this includes responsibility for seeing that the security functions specifically assigned to the Marine guards are properly executed.

If there are breaches of security in, say, the Moscow embassy, it is the ambassador who is responsible, and it ought to be the Secretary of State who should shoulder the ultimate responsibility of answering for any failings. Here we come again to the vexing question: who is going to investigate whom? Is the State Department, by reason of these responsibilities, to investigate the shortcomings of the Marine Corps? Is it to be allowed to investigate its own? For, again, we must underline the point: we are dealing with matters relating to spies and spying. What special competence does the State Department have in this area? More important still, what ought it properly to claim on the basis of training, functions, skills, and experience?

It is not difficult to see how the Department of State might well embark with glee on a trophy hunt in this case to protect its own hide. It is evident to even the most poorly informed and the least charitably inclined alike that responsibility for the security malaise in Moscow cannot have rested solely with a handful of unfortunate Marines. If there are significant penetrations, and, on the evidence, this is a matter requiring deep and serious investigation, it is pertinent to inquire how many State Department personnel may have been affected in some degree by these Soviet espionage efforts and to what level of responsibility they might have ascended. Such inquiries cannot be allowed to become the subject of unhealthy interservice rivalry. Again, we have a very simple point to make. The United States Department of State, like the United States Marine Corps, is an elite and, consequently, to some extent, an elitist organization. Like the foreign service agencies of many nations, it tends to recruit from the best and brightest of the classes to which it appeals and it is infused with a certain hubris that is professionally of some utility provided it is kept sensibly under control by those who recognize its potential for harm.

In their worst form, these tendencies produce an insularity that resists all forms of outside criticism and a holier-than-thou attitude born of an ability to transfer the blame for anything that might go wrong onto lesser mortals from less favored services. There is nothing unique or even unusual about such attitudes. They are merely prone to show their worst side under stress. Nor is the desire to be allowed to undertake reasonable maintenance and repair to be frowned upon; in the interests of efficiency alone, every organization must have some self-policing mechanism. How else could it reward merit, encourage effort, put the whip to the sluggard?

The real question that concerns us here is its competence to hunt down spies in its own ranks. This, as we have repeatedly stressed, is a very specialized business. It is not a matter to be undertaken lightly, along with all the other daily chores or in temporary substitution for them. A great deal more than the conventional, self-policing capability is called for if the job is to be done efficiently and with the prospect of satisfactory results.

If no specialized spy-hunting capacity exists in-house, the only excuse for resisting outside assistance for the purpose must be with a view to stifling inconvenient disclosures that might reflect unfavorably upon the organization and its administration. This is tantamount to a conspiracy to hide the spy in the supposedly higher interests of the health or even the survival of the organization. Even those entrusted with a more generous oversight of the whole are not entirely free from such notions at times, but they can hardly be accused of thwarting inquiry while lacking the means to carry it out. Only one thing is worse perhaps than amateur trophy hunting on another's preserves, and that is a refusal to allow properly qualified professionals to hunt dangerous vermin on your own territory, when you clearly lack the ability and the means to do the job satisfactorily. It must be seriously questioned whether the State Department's own relatively fledgling security organization is up to the demands of this task. The possession of a general intelligence capability, however efficient and well organized in other respects, is of no value whatsoever here. We would insist, therefore, that it is no more appropriate for the Department of State to be hunting spies in its own ranks—or, indeed, those of any others—than it would be for, say, the Department of Energy to undertake a similar exercise. This is not to say that no organization has any role in these matters when a spy is suspected of having been at work in its ranks, but there must be some clear understanding of the limitations upon that role and a certain humility in its exercise.

We are forced therefore to consider which agency ought to be responsible for investigating not whether there have been shortcomings with respect to the security arrangements in the United States diplomatic establishments in the Soviet Union or even actual breaches of security, *but whether there are spies in the ranks of those serving the United States in that area of the world*.

The principal counterespionage agency of the United States is the Federal Bureau of Investigation. Under the long directorship of J. Edgar Hoover, this agency grew from small beginnings into an exceedingly powerful and controversial arm of law enforcement. It has weathered massive assaults

upon its credibility, both under Mr. Hoover and his successors. While its rather glamorized image has been somewhat
tarnished in its later years, the public retains a high degree of
confidence in its ability to perform the duties assigned to it.
The contributions of the FBI to improving standards throughout the United States law-enforcement community, as well as
the operational assistance it lends in areas of special competence, are well acknowledged.[42] The FBI has considerable
resources in both human and institutional terms. It has a
formidable and readily accessible collective memory. It is
endowed with many attributes, including powers of arrest,
that might be envied by other less-favored counterespionage
agencies. The legacy of Mr. Hoover has made the FBI a very
trophy-conscious organization. This propensity, more than
any other perhaps, has earned it a rather glory-seeking reputation among law-enforcement agencies that has inhibited
cooperation to some degree. The FBI's function as a counterespionage organization must be seen and understood in this
wider context. *The FBI has a great deal more to do than
pursue spies*. Indeed, its work as a counterespionage agency
is a comparatively small part of its overall law-enforcement
responsibilities. However much some of its earlier, anti-
subversive programs might have irked civil libertarians and
others, these too were but a part of a much larger area of
activity. It is not that the dangers of foreign and domestic
espionage are shrugged off but, rather, that these precious
specialist resources are spread dangerously thin.

Moreover, the FBI has never been very keen on specialization, preferring good generalists, except in technical areas,
who could be readily moved through and up the hierarchy
with a certain regularity. This policy prevents the formation
of the highest standards of expertise. While it makes a certain
amount of organizational sense, it does have a number of
serious drawbacks, especially in matters such as counterespionage. This type of arrangement does not favor the acquisition
of specialist skills over a long period of career development
for, frankly, there is no career in it; it may even entail
considerable personal sacrifice.[43] This tends to reflect seriously upon the Bureau's commitment to its role in this area as
opposed to others against which it must also allocate resources.

There is, however, a much more serious restriction placed
upon the Bureau's utility as a comprehensive counterespio-

nage agency: it is primarily a *domestic* law-enforcement entity. It is organized and directed, with limited exceptions, to the fulfillment of its role at home rather than abroad. Traditionally, Mr. Hoover's FBI had a somewhat paternalistic intelligence role throughout Latin America. While vestiges of this remain,[44] its bruising conflicts with the CIA greatly attenuated the value of these outreaches which, in any event, have comparatively little value (save in the case of Mexico) as stations for a serious counterespionage campaign. Elsewhere in the world, the FBI's presence by virtue of its legal attachés in selected embassies has a useful liaison purpose, but only limited operational value. It is clear that the FBI lacks a world view of its mission in the way that both the Department of State and the Central Intelligence Agency can be said to have. This puts the Bureau at a distinct disadvantage in dealing with an agency like the Department of State over the matter of Soviet penetrations abroad, and it is easy to see how the latter might assume an air of superiority and a certain condescension as to the parochial attitude of a law-enforcement agency, the ordinary sphere of which is considerably more circumscribed than its own.

On the available evidence, the Soviets seem to have shown a healthy respect for the FBI operating on its own ground. Clearly, the Soviet intelligence agencies have made an intensive study of the FBI, its capabilities, and operational modalities. The Russians are fully aware of the limitations upon the FBI to handle an espionage problem outside its own familiar territory. Hunting for spies away from home is always an exceedingly difficult task. Hunting for them in a foreign country as security conscious as the Soviet Union, even within the artificial confines of an internationally recognized (if not always respected) sovereign enclave such as one's own embassy, requires beyond ordinary skills. This is not a propitious time or place to begin a trophy hunt. To mix metaphors but slightly, it would be better to find other ways of skinning the cat. Damage control, yes. Scapegoating, no. This is a good time to review the adequacy of our spy-hunting agencies to handle situations like this; Congress might more profitably turn its attentions in these directions than indulging in grandiose schemes and fantasies to pull down the "old" new embassy and replace it with a new, yet to be built, perfectly secure one. Such an endeavor would be a criminal waste of the taxpayers' dollars.

Trophy hunting can easily become an obsession. It is not merely an exercise in self-aggrandizement. It often takes on a more morbid, Moby-Dick-like character. It haunts the dreams and shapes men's lives in strange ways. Old spy-hunters never die nor, it seems, do they fade peacefully away. These restless Nimrods carry with them into uneasy retirements nagging memories of the big one that got away or, more usually, after their own position of thinking about these things, got away with it. These elusive trophies were not so much at large and unspotted, or unspotted for what they really were. Rather, something—or someone—at some point interposed itself or himself between the spy-catcher and his quarry, preventing it from being taken. The spy-catcher then spends the rest of his natural life, and sometimes an extension of it by proxy, trying to nail the trophy to the wall. This is a very frustrating business for all concerned. When you have seen the unicorn with your own eyes, it is difficult to reconcile yourself to the ukase of others that the beast does not exist, especially when those others, in self-defense, begin to cast aspersions upon your eyesight.

An excellent illustration of these observations is afforded by the ongoing saga of Mr. Peter Wright,[45] a former officer of Britain's MI5. Mr. Wright, like many another spy-catcher of that phlegmatic breed so characteristic of the island race and of its distinctive security service, might well have expected to live out his life in anonymous retirement far from the triumphs and disappointments of yesteryear. He had, after all, been a part of the service when these things were the norm and when little was known publicly of its workings and even less of those privileged to serve the Crown in these unreported ways. Fate and his own nature, however, decreed otherwise, for the most productive period of his service coincided with a curious cusp in the fortunes of the service of which he was once a part. Pre-war obscurity was suddenly overtaken by a wave of post-war revelations that were to have a markedly unsettling effect upon all parts of the British intelligence community for the next four decades and into the future. Despite such setbacks as Venlo[46] and Scapa Flow,[47] British intelligence retained much of the mystique through World

War II that it had acquired during the first four decades of the present century.

By any standards, MI5 can be said to have had a good war and it succeeded, even better than it recognized at the time, in keeping Great Britain free of Nazi spies. But, it seems, another maggot was already eating this unblemished apple from within. The 1950s and early 1960s brought an unprecedented crisis in the British intelligence community as tales of Soviet penetrations dating back to the years between the wars began to unfold in substantive fashion. After the first shattering blows had been absorbed, a hasty housecleaning effort was organized. But, where to start? Who had been infected and affected by this insidious disease? How high had it spread? MI5 was in no condition to investigate anyone (its proper role in this mess) until it was sure its own ranks were squeaky clean. It was soon clear to the unbiased observer that this could not be taken for granted, and considerable unhappiness ensued, as it must when all feel the cloud of suspicion hanging over them. Morale was affected, but, most difficult of all, there was a growing uncertainty about how to approach the emerging possibility of a high-level Soviet penetration still active within the organization. Even the possibility had a stultifying effect upon the business of housecleaning. There was very much an *Upstairs, Downstairs* flavor to all this that only those familiar with the peculiarities of the British pre- and post-World War II societies might appreciate in all its richness.

In the first bleak, drab, post-war years, a new class had begun to enter the cloistered ranks of MI5, less fettered by Old School Tie obligations and refreshingly free from any forelock-tugging tendencies.[48] A new breed of spy-catcher was in the making, and some of its early targets were philosophically and practically appealing. No one has ever effectively captured how MI5 felt about itself, or even saw itself, in these interesting times, but attitudes were perhaps not so very different from those which pervaded the highly structured castes of the great British Civil Service as a whole. Enthusiastic new blood, of a different group from that which had coursed in the veins of this sclerotic organization hitherto, had been infused by changing times and changing social needs. It would have been a poor spy-catcher indeed who did not at this time entertain thoughts of exciting trophies and perhaps even a place of his own in the carefully guarded annals of the service.

Top management, as we would style it in our own, present-day terms, was of an earlier vintage—cautious, conservative, and wise in the way things were (and perhaps are) done in the hallowed corridors of power. Mandarins are Mandarins the world over, but those who inhabited the warrens of Whitehall had an inscrutability that would have challenged Charlie Chan. The Administrative Class of the Civil Service, at the time of which we speak, was a closed Oxbridge society with inflexible rules of entrance and an etiquette all its own. An MI5 investigation of any portion of it had some of the character of those episodes of Masterpiece Theater with which United States viewers of PBS television have become increasingly familiar. They knew how to defend their own, and the close-ranks maneuver had been learned to perfection. Lippizaner stallions could hardly have been more disciplined or entertaining for the professional to watch. Nor were these stalwarts all bad, egocentric, or bent on the preservation of the power of their caste. They were simply wise in the ways of their world and most fervently desired to pass it on intact to their successors.

Mr. Peter Wright inherited a small portion of that world at a time when the depth of its tarnish still remained unsuspected even by some of its more knowledgeable inhabitants. But the pressure to find out had become irresistible. Along with all the other creatures of the Brave New World had come one of remarkable utility, providing, on both sides of the Atlantic, a special kind of social stimulus. The investigative journalist, long waiting in the wings, came splendidly into his own with a vengeance. These diligent bloodhounds proved to be remarkably responsible (to the surprise of many), accurate, articulate, shrewd, and highly readable. With the advent of television as a truly popular medium, their impact was greatly broadened and strengthened. They threw open doors that had been closed to the common man for centuries and let in a much needed breath of fresh air to the frosty cloisters of government. Many who had struggled alone to no avail even to open a window but slightly from within were mightily encouraged and no little in awe. The power of the press has always been much respected by those unaware of the limitations under which it works, but these "new" journalists were fearless about where they trod, being neither fools nor angels. They did not delude themselves, in the main, that they were in pursuit of "the truth;" rather, they were pursuing "the story," and with an unerring market sense they realized that there was an audience out there waiting for it to be told. People love to be told secrets; the concealed history of their own times holds a peculiar fascination for most. To the common folk, the mighty have always been a race apart. Their mortality is hard to credit; that they eat, drink, sleep, love, hate, laugh, and cry ought not to surprise—but it does. There is a fascination with their failings, at seeing them reduced to truly human proportions.

The first precept for rule by the plebeians must surely be: Keep your private life truly private. Yuri Andropov may well have been the last, in our times, to have appreciated the wisdom and forcefulness of this maxim.[49] It is not that the heads of espionage and counterespionage services cannot stand up under scrutiny. It is, rather, that the glare of publicity upon them and their doings is corrosive of their power, if not their authority. They lurk in the shadows from choice, and the cover this gives them filters down through the services they control, cloaking all with the most useful shelter from behind which many different, not always scrupulous, activities might be conducted.

Well-founded suspicions had arisen concerning MI5 as to the extent to which it might have been penetrated by the intelligence agencies of the USSR. Too many things seemed to be going wrong in ways which suggested that the problem lay very close to the top of the pile. Various inconclusive internal investigations took place and some, at least among the middle-level officers, involved in inquiring into these delicate matters had begun to form their own quite strong views about the locus of the problem. Three separate camps seem to have existed, both within and without the security service. There were those, seemingly in a shrinking minority, who remained unpersuaded that there had ever been a Soviet penetration of MI5, much less that it had reached the top echelons of the service. Among the rest, who had or were entitled to have serious, professional opinions on the matter, two substantial groupings were to be found: those who believed that Sir Roger Hollis, director general of MI5 from 1956 through 1965 and a long-serving permanent officer of that organization before that, was a Soviet agent for most of his career;[50] and those who inclined to the view that while he was not, his deputy director, Mr. Graham Mitchell, was.[51]

Mr. Peter Wright, like many other officers of his time and responsibilities, found himself in the thick of the fray. He carried out his own assigned part in the investigations with all the zeal of a confirmed trophy hunter and concluded, roundly, and, perhaps not too diplomatically, that his director general, Sir Roger Hollis, was indeed the culprit. Mr. Wright's concern can be appreciated, and it could be fairly argued on his behalf that where a viper is discovered in the nest, there is no place for diplomatic niceties. Against this might be argued the fact that many important parties were yet to be persuaded of the presence of a serpent and other less-destructive means than public exposure of all this dirty linen were in the best interests of the service and the country in general. Sir Roger was due to retire (he was to die not long afterward in retirement), and the difficulties of proving the matter one way or another cautioned fairness to Sir Roger and a certain prudence to avoid shooting the country in general and the service in particular metaphorically in the foot. But Mr. Wright (how appropriate-sounding a name for one so convinced of his own correctness in the matter!) had something of the crusader in his makeup and was simply not persuaded to bury his case. Sir Roger was investigated briefly in his retirement, but again the matter was put inconclusively to rest.

Mr. Wright was determined to nail the trophy to the wall, if not that of the service of which he was still a part, then one of his own choosing. Mr. Wright's progress in this ticklish business could have been accurately predicted by anyone familiar with Marilyn Moats Kennedy's admirable *Office Warfare*,[52] but this officer, though carrying the baggage of his earlier formation, was a true creation of our times. He had seen the blossoming of the Profumo scandal in the United Kingdom and the consummation of Watergate on this side of the Atlantic. For whatever reason, he felt himself less bound than others by outmoded shibboleths and even the Official Secrets Acts, more ready to pursue his quarry even as death had claimed the carcass for its own. Such conduct was a relative rarity in the United Kingdom, even in the 1970s, although it had become common enough as an adjunct to good government in the United States. Some countries can still say "publish and be damned," but even *Samizdat* has its devoted readers if the content is sufficiently juicy. In fact, Mr. Wright's position in the earliest moments of his resolution to come out from the shadows must have been not unlike that of Boris Pasternak. While he might have expected reasonably to escape the Gulag, professional banishment must have seemed a near certainty once the cat was out of the bag.

Mr. Wright must have been under no illusions as to the size and strength of the windmill against which he was tilting. Being of the Establishment and no novice to its ways, he would have been well aware of the consequences of telling tales out of school. He felt nevertheless that he had a most persuasive case and that his own verdict in the matter would be vindicated provided he could take it before the right audience. There were many eager (perhaps overeager) to write about these things; while themselves having the literary-skills and the necessary outlets for the product, they lacked an authoritative source to supply the materials upon which such writings might be based. Peter Wright was recognizably such a source, and all he had to do was to select his collaborators from among the potential field with the requisite degree of care. He must initially have hoped to remain, for a time at least, in the shadows, but he would have known that this would not have been possible once the ordure had struck the fan. In the event, he made what was probably as wise a choice as was available to him at the time. He chose a competent, well-informed professional writer, who had the additional indispensable merit of personal courage that would sustain him throughout the row which had inevitably to follow upon publication of these matters. Mr. Harry Chapman Pincher's opening salvo in 1981, loaded for him by Peter Wright, was a very workmanlike book entitled *Their Trade Was Treachery*,[53] and embedded therein was the grapeshot it was confidently hoped would turn the tide of battle and enable Mr. Wright to at last claim, albeit quite modestly, the trophy he had been seeking for so long. The battle could have gone either way, for a change in political fortunes had brought to power a Conservative government under the Iron Lady. Perhaps Mrs. Thatcher's temper on this matter had not been accurately gauged with anticipation? In the event, speaking as Prime Minister in the House of Commons, she roundly denounced the tale, in terms most unfavorable to Mr. Chapman Pincher, and stood firmly by the findings of her predecessors. It is clear from her pronouncements that she felt the matter had been put firmly to rest, and she clearly had no intention of allowing it to be officially reopened. Here, Mr. Chapman Pincher was to prove himself at least as prideful as his fellow in waiting. A second mighty broadside was fired in 1984, entitled *Too Secret Too Long*,[54] devoted strictly to the Hollis affair. This massive well-reasoned tome is too substantial to be ignored and is, at the time of writing, still in the process of being digested.

But the aging, indefatigable Peter Wright, now retired to far-off Australia, evidently feeling the press of Anno Domini and having some of the assurance of authorship behind him, embarked upon the publication of his own memoirs; these had a potentially embarrassing content over and above the Hollis business.[55] This move unleashed an extraordinary storm that is highly instructive in its own way. The British government, still under the sway of Mrs. Thatcher, decided to take all steps legally open to it to prevent the publication of these memoirs. It sought, in the Australian courts, a ban on publication, and having lost the first round seems determined to go through the appeal procedures to the bitter end.[56] The tide of history is running strongly against the British government, which now seems to have as little possibility of silencing Mr. Wright as the Soviets had of corking up Solzhenitsyn once he had escaped from the bottle. It is really almost as pointless. Mr. Wright may have been guilty of *lese majesté* in his disregard of the appeals to refrain from publishing certain matters. There are doubtless others within his knowledge upon which the British government, any British government, would like to keep a tight lid. In the hope of taking home the trophy, his persistent pursuit of Sir Roger Hollis had little enough steam left in it long before others began to take the reader down yet another inviting path. The outcome hardly affects the point we are making here. The issue of who does what with the trophy does not necessarily depend upon the age of the hide or who fired the fatal shot. It has everything to do with power and where that resides.[57]

Here we come to the crux of the matter. The subtle connections between spy-catching and politics must be thoroughly understood in their general, as well as specific, senses.

Everything of which we have treated throughout this book is in some way or another informed by politics, from spy mania to the collection or noncollection of trophies. Politics is all about power: generating it, acquiring it, wielding it, allocating it, managing it, curbing it—even perverting it. Every social being is, to a greater or lesser degree, a politician. Human survival, in the last resort, depends upon politics, whether it be the politics of the war on famine or the politics of the nuclear bomb. Nuclear arsenals are not found in a state of nature but are the product of conscious, political decisions.

Power is in a constant state of flux, sometimes violent, but more usually moving around in less turbulent fashion. Those who have power constantly seek to enlarge it for fear of losing what they already hold. Those who have comparatively little seek to gain what it is they desire by finding ways of exploiting the inherent and functional weaknesses of their stronger opponents. This is the genesis and sustenance of small-group, anti-establishment terrorism. It works when the force applied at a particular point in the system is greater than the force that can be mustered against it. All spy-catchers have power, but some have more power than others. They all have their own peculiar notions of duty, a personal sense of what is right and wrong in the exercise of their functions, and a personal stake in the trophy they seek to take. Most are persuaded to subordinate their own beliefs in these matters to the dictates of those they are obliged to recognize as their political masters. A few are not.

Whether it is a case of exceptional circumstances or overweening arrogance, the actors in these out-of-the-ordinary events all seek to substitute their own decisions for the decisions of those in whom the power to ordain things is usually vested. It is immaterial to which higher authority they appeal for the right to do what they do. Those who have the power, *de facto* or *de jure*, make the rules by reference to which the trophy is nailed to the wall—or consigned to the attic. Those who challenge these rules, seeking some other disposition, are usurpers of power.

The rights and wrongs of this matter do not concern us here; the only material issue is whether they will get away with it. In a well-adjusted system, there is no struggle over these things. It cannot be, for example, sensibly laid down in advance that *all* spies will *always* be executed after they have been caught. They *may* have a greater utility alive than dead as future collaborators for those who have apprehended them, or as items of future exchange. Those who have the power must necessarily have the discretion.

The power to catch and declare people to be spies can obviously be abused. The spy-catching function is used as a terrible tool of oppression in some cases. The "spy as trophy" takes on a symbolic character as part of the display of might. Whole institutions are perverted to this end, and organizations like the early *Cheka* perfectly exemplify the dangers and the distortions. There are spies, and spies are caught, but the whole exercise has an exemplary rather than an instrumental purpose, showy rather than practical. Espionage show trials certainly have their place in the panoply of power. They serve notice upon enemies and are instructive affirmations of those in control. They also serve to show the limits of power in particular instances. A powerful, totalitarian state like Nazi Germany may have practically no limitations upon it in these matters. Its power to dispose of those it declares to be spies was constrained only by the course of the world conflict in which it was engaged. The ultimate arbiter of these matters is war, and the propriety of what is done is dictated by the result. These are matters of continuing, practical importance, though their meaning may sometimes be screened. Countries very rarely go to war over their spies, but their reactions are instructive in terms of power and how it is measured.

Most embassies, as we have said, can, not improperly in our times, be regarded as nests of spies. If you do not like a particular nest in your hedgerow, it is open to you to eject the birds through the appropriate diplomatic action. Breaking off diplomatic relations has its price, but it does, fairly pacifically, get rid of the problem. When Iran's surrogates overran the United States embassy in Tehran, evidence was found, not surprisingly, that supported the claim that the embassy and certain of its personnel had engaged in activities that could be characterized as espionage. Under the circumstances, the United States had no alternative but to tolerate these undiplomatic accusations, though it would hardly have admitted to their accuracy. But, at one point, Iran threatened to put certain United States embassy personnel on trial as spies. Such a show trial was clearly in conception a challenge to the United States and its power; the merits of the matter were really of secondary importance. Iran had its trophies; but there were clear limitations upon its ability to display or exploit them. It is evident that the United States could not have countenanced a show trial of its diplomats,[58] and it would have had to take military action to prevent this. In the final analysis, Iran recognized the limits upon its own freedom of action in the case. What all this means in practice is that powerful countries will sometimes acquiesce in their spies being nailed to the wall—provided they are not nailed too hard.

From the foregoing, it is clear that the spy per se is not the trophy; *the real prize is the right of disposal over the spy, what is done with him or to him in any particular case*. While this has an important effect upon the spy-catcher's work, this is only contributing to the final result. Nevertheless, it should be noted that without the spy being actually caught, all the rest is academic. Too much disdain for the "rights" of the spy-catcher to some say in the disposal of his kill can have serious effects upon the efficiency of the organization and the morale of personnel. The great struggle between the Sicherheitsdienst and the Gestapo on the one hand and the Abwehr on the other should be seen in this light. The latter became demoralized by being robbed, in effect, of its kills to the point where its efficiency was seriously threatened. As a counterespionage organization, it had begun to give up the ghost long before it actually expired. As we have seen, the apprehension of the spy gives rise to many possible consequences. The kill may be consumed on the spot; that is, the spy is liquidated forthwith in practical fashion without fuss or ceremony as part, in effect, of the fortunes of war. In times of great conflict, where spies are numerous and many are of but slight professional consequence, this is a common enough course of action. For all concerned, trophies in such cases amount to little more than notches upon the gun belt. The kill may be placed in cold storage while its ultimate disposal is decided. The item taken may be so evidently valuable as to suggest its future utility as an item of exchange. It is accordingly put away until the time its true worth might be realized. Alternatively, time may be needed to squeeze the spy dry of the knowledge he is presumed to have on matters of interest to the counterespionage service into the hands of which he has fallen. The time is spent in a kind of cat-and-mouse game in which a number of different final scenarios are sketched out dependent upon the degree of cooperation offered by the spy to his captors. Again, the time may simply be used in turning the spy around us as in the Double Cross System or Operation North Pole[59] and using him against his former masters. In all these cases, final disposition is deferred, and the management of these efforts has to be entrusted to persons whose skills and functions may be very different from those leading to the spy's apprehension. The utility of the spy as such may be subordinated to the use that might be made of the fact of his capture and the use to which this might be put. Focus here is upon the disposition for example's sake; the event itself is shaped by the ends to which it is put. Thus, it was of lesser importance to the Soviet Union whether Scharansky was really a spy for the CIA (or any other foreign intelligence service) than that he should be irremediably depicted as such through a public process that would so label him and he be given a punishment commensurate with the finding in that process. In none of these cases does the issue of credit for the capture of the spy amount to much; what credit there is accrues to the spy-catcher—if matters turn out well. But in these cases, his unquestioned triumph is of slight overall importance, for it is soon eclipsed and begins to take a backseat as other considerations connected with what to do with the prize come to the fore. Thus, the spy-catcher is allowed the triumph, however hollow, but the trophy is whisked away for other uses. Thus, the number of cases in which the spy-catcher is actually robbed of his trophy is necessarily quite small. In most of the others, the trophy is duly acknowledged and recorded, although the carcass may be rapidly passed to others who will carve it up as circumstances and the system dictate.

For the spy-catcher, the truly galling cases are those in which *something* has been caught, without doubt, but the system denies the spy-catcher the triumph and satisfaction of the recognition that it was a spy. This may be the result of the working of what we like to call due process of law, or it may be by reason of an exercise of pure political fiat. Thus, Gennady Zakharov,[60] who was exchanged for Nicholas Daniloff in 1986, was arrested by the FBI, an arrest that held the premise of an enlightening trial, a vindication of the FBI's charges, and a trophy of some magnitude for the Bureau in its ongoing war against Soviet espionage in the United States.

Instead, this Soviet citizen was returned to his own country following a short, formal procedure in which the accused offered a perfunctory, almost derisory no-contest plea. The proper workings of the law, which might well have resulted in a substantial case being made against Zakharov, followed by a commensurate prison sentence, were truncated by the release of an accused American citizen in the Soviet Union. No doubt some in the Soviet Union felt robbed of *their* trophy as a result of what transpired. No spy-catcher on either side would really fault the result from the perspective of his own work. But—and it requires but slight alteration of the facts for the purpose—suppose the political result had demanded returning Zakharov to his native land without a stain on his character?

More serious questions are raised where political convenience of another kind dictates concealment of the case that the spy really was a spy. Such cases (Hollis among them) can only really be appealed to the Court of History. This is a somewhat unsatisfactory tribunal, rendering tardy and often contradictory verdicts, although it is one to which quite spectacular and controversial cases such as that of Mata Hari[61] have been elevated. Few spy-catchers can wait that long for vindication of their labors. The case lives on, tantalizing, long after the poor spy-catcher is forgotten. Most spy-catchers become hard-headed politicians and bow to the inevitable, reserving to themselves only the right to say, "I told you so" should a suitable, future opportunity arise.

What does all this amount to for the business of spy-catching? It is evident that we are left with some ragged edges in this part of the process. It might well be argued that the business of the spy-catcher is to *catch* spies *point final*. Once he has succeeded in this, he retires from the case; some would even deny him powers of arrest as being unnecessary to the fulfillment of his mission.[62] There is something to be said for this in theory, for it does lend an air of professional detachment, if not purity, to his role that frees him from some of the more political aspects that must necessarily come into play once his quarry is well and truly in the net. This presumes, of course, a fairly concrete set of guidelines of an operational kind within the parameters of which *all* the work must take place. This reduces all discretion to a bare minimum, which might, in practice, make it very difficult to conduct any useful business at all. The spy-catcher may march to the tune of a different drummer, but all he is doing is marking time. In practice, such a degree of detachment is quite impossible, even leaving human nature out of account. Spy-catching has far too many imponderables for the working future to be legislated with such exactitude. But where does the business really end? At what point can the spy-catcher conclude his task is accomplished? At what point can he be properly told by others that what follows is none of his business? These, as we have seen, are not easy questions to answer in consistent and convincing fashion. The answers will, quite properly, vary from age to age and system to system. The real difficulty in delineating the functions we have been discussing lies in something to which we earlier drew attention.

Before the business of spy-catching can in any sense be regarded as at an end, the spy-catcher necessarily requires some organ to officially certify that what he has caught is indeed a spy. He cannot sensibly rest content upon his own claim that what he has caught is of that genus. He cannot certify his own catch; he can only make the case for such certification. In practice, in all save the most totalitarian of regimes, this means some sort of court system regularly organized to hear cases brought before it and to pronounce upon them in accordance with some pre-established substantive and adjectival law as guidance. All countries respectful of the Rule of Law would insist on the complete independence of the courts; this indeed is what principally distinguishes them from totalitarianism. Once a case is before such courts, its outcome cannot be affected by anything the spy-catcher may do save insofar as he might be able to produce additional evidence for consideration before the verdict is in. Again, in nontotalitarian societies, detention without trial is the grave exception rather than the accustomed rule. The presumptive spy must usually, within a relatively short period, be charged and brought before the courts or turned loose. "I know he is a spy, but I can't prove it" may be the lament of the frustrated spy-catcher, but it is not allowed to hang too long upon the air of our own kind of society. Moreover, the same strict rules that seek to promote a framework of fairness in other cases are held to govern the trial of spies: the presumption of innocence, the protections against coerced self-incrimination, the onus of proof, etc. Clearly, under such a system, if the spy-catcher wants certification of his labors, he must, in the words of the Smith Barney commercial, get it the old-fashioned way—he must earn it. The United States is not only a land of laws and regulations, but a land of lawyers, all eager to earn a living by making sure all the "T"s of others are properly crossed and all the "I"s punctiliously dotted. Most, especially the innocent, would rather live under such a system than that of many other, present-day countries such as that of, for example, Iran where even the suspicion of being a spy might land one in prison for months, without representation, guarantees of a fair trial, or even contact with the outside world.[63]

What is to be observed is that all this does not necessarily make for better spy-catching. The reverse is often nearer the mark. Yet, even in the most law-abiding of societies, the spy-catcher's work does not end at the courtroom door. He will be involved throughout the case, at least in an advisory capacity; he may himself have to give evidence and subject himself to examination. This forces him, however unwillingly and guardedly, out of the shadows, more than a slight professional inconvenience in itself for some. He will continue in an advisory role throughout the appeal process and perhaps even beyond where, if his efforts are crowned with success, his input may be sought on matters of disposition where this affects his own functions. Playing within the rules presents few problems for the diligent, conscientious spy-catcher— until the spy *he* knows to be a spy walks away a free man because political expediency or the courts have undone all the spy-catcher's labors. In theory, he should accept the verdict like a gentleman—the umpire's work is final for those of the Old School. It is easy to see why there are some gentlemen who find it very hard, if not impossible, to play the game as gentlemen. After all, are we not told often enough that nice guys finish last?

Is this not what Irangate[64] (as well as Watergate) were really all about? How many revolutions have been inspired by a genuine, patriotic desire to "save" the Constitution? Before nailing the trophy to any wall in our society, the spy-catcher had better make sure that it *is* his to do that with, to have it well prepared and suitably cured, to make sure it is tacked upon the correct wall, and to have all the right tools on hand for the purpose. Perhaps the only true trophies of which the spy-catcher can ever be really sure are his own memories—and even these, like those of all hunters or fishermen, are known to play tricks at times. If he is very lucky, he may (like Giskes of Nordpol fame) be able to keep a few substantiating reminders as mementos for the mantleshelf of old age.[65] Or he can always write a book!

POINTS TO REMEMBER

1. Spy-catchers are professionals who hunt in the pay of others. The quarry is not theirs to keep. What is done with the quarry and indeed how and with what means the hunt is conducted, are often political questions—questions concerning who has the power to make the decisions and their overt and hidden agendas.

2. Captured spies should be viewed in terms of their potential value or utility in satisfying needs. They can be utilized as double agents. Spy agencies and services generally, for institutional interests, must attempt to retrieve their agents which greatly aids in establishing a market for captured spies. Thus, captured spies can be traded. They can also be put on public display and "nailed to the wall."

NOTES

1. *The Red Orchestra,* New York: Simon & Schuster, 1969, page 62. This excellent, oft-cited book is a gold mine of information about the subjects treated here and deserves a thorough, unbiased reading by all intelligence professionals. Whatever view is taken regarding the importance of this Soviet spy organization and the reliability of the information offered concerning it, what is written in this book about the efforts of the German spy-catchers is hardly to be impeached.

2. *The Double-Cross System in the War of 1939 to 1945,* New Haven, CT: Yale University Press, 1972, page 2.

3. "Spying between Friends," *Time,* 16 March 1987, pages 44–49, page 49.

4. See, for example, *The New KGB,* William R. Corson and

Robert T. Crowley, New York: William Morrow, 1986, page 204.

5. One can always get a drop more juice from a squeezed lemon. A very experienced counterintelligence officer has observed: "Even the true defector will have some secrets that for private reasons—shame, loyalty to old comrades, plans for his own use of the information—he will never give, and sometimes these secrets are important ones." William R. Johnson, "The Ambivalent Polygraph," *International Journal of Intelligence and Counterintelligence*, Volume 1, No. 3, 1986, pages 71–83, page 79. On occasion, information will be held back not because it is considered important, but for the very opposite reason.

6. On this generally, see *Spy/Counterspy*, Dusko Popov, New York: Grosset and Dunlap, 1974. "Tricycle" was a remarkable agent by any standards, and the latitude he was given by both sides was a tribute to the confidence he was able to inspire.

7. Ancient history can mean just that in the face of a truly determined attempt to bury the past. In the epilogue to his excellent novel, *Fall from Grace*, New York: Simon and Schuster, 1985, Larry Collins writes: "*Fortitude* was long one of the Second World War's best-kept secrets. The existence of the London Controlling Section, which conceived it, was not even acknowledged until the early 1970s. All the American files bearing upon the plan, held in Joint Security Council, were destroyed by Executive Order in 1946. Those of the London Controlling Section—an organization notoriously frugal in committing words to paper—have never been opened."

8. See, for example, *Spy Trade*, E. H. Cookridge, New York: Walker and Co., 1971.

The Economist, 30 September 1972, page 41, reported: "The West German view is that East Germany stacks up political hostages against a rainy day and to secure the release of specific spies. The east looks after its own. Indeed, Fran Lindres is said to have fretted to her jailers after a couple of years that 'they should have exchanged me by now.' "

9. For a full account of this extraordinary spy, his exploits, capture, trial, and Israel's attempts to secure his release, see *The Shattered Silence*, Zwy Aldouby and Jerrold Ballinger, New York: Coward, McCann and Geoghegan, 1971. While

there are certain unanswered questions in this case, none touch upon Israel's efforts to trade for Cohen's release.

10. This seems to have been universally the case in the USSR in Stalin's time and has a certain crude realism about it. Post-Stalin practices seem to be much more sensibly discriminating.

11. See the authoritative and very informative *The Case of Richard Sorge*, Frederick W. Deakin and G. Richard Storry, New York: Harper and Row, 1966. For additional useful insights on the Sorge case, see *A Short History of Espionage*, Allison Ind, New York: David McKay, 1963.

12. A leader who could summarily dispose of Yezhov and Yagoda, who had themselves disposed of countless victims at Stalin's behest, would have hardly awaited Sorge's return to the Soviet Union with fear and trepidation.

13. For a good account of this, see *The Springing of George Blake*, Sean Bourke, New York: Viking Press, 1970.

14. The definitive account of the Pollard case (perhaps by Pollard, himself?) has yet to be written, but there is ample material for study in the popular media. Worth reading are *Time*, 16 March 1987, "Spying between Friends," pages 44–49, where it is observed that "Co-workers finally noted that Pollard was taking classified papers home with him and notified the FBI."

See also "Brothers with Blood in Their Eyes," *Time*, 30 March 1987, page 40.

15. This CBS television program aired a lengthy segment on 1 March 1987, following Pollard's life sentence.

16. Larry Wu Tai Chin, a CIA employee, admitted in November 1985 to having sold United States secrets to China over a period of thirty years. He apparently committed suicide shortly after being sentenced.

17. See *The Falcon and the Snowman*, Robert Lindsey, New York: Simon & Schuster, 1979.

18. See *Operation Portland*, Harry Houghton, London: Hart-Davis, 1972.

19. We are reminded here of an old Sufi saying: "The rose thrown by a friend hurts more than any stone."

20. The holy Koran enjoins: "Do not spy on one another." *The Chambers*, Sura 49: 12.

21. Scharansky, who had been convicted of spying for the West, was released on February 11, 1986, in a complicated

East-West prisoner deal after serving eight years of his sentence. The redoubtable Wolfgang Vogel, an East German lawyer, played his usual effective role in the arrangements. Scharansky flew promptly to Israel on his release.

22. Okamoto, a member of the United Japanese Red Army who was originally identified as Daisuke Namba, was captured at Lod International Airport Tel Aviv on May 30, 1972, following an attack in the terminal which killed twenty-four and wounded seventy-six. He was released without fanfare in 1985, his mental condition having seriously deteriorated during his long detention.

23. Archbishop Capucci had been convicted of certain illicit associations with Arab extremist organizations in 1974. He was released on November 6, 1977, following a personal appeal to the Israeli president by Pope Paul VI.

24. This was particularly the case during the June 1985 TWA sky-jacking crisis. "Israel until the end insisted it could not free the Lebanese until Washington made an official request." *U.S. News and World Report,* 8 July 1985, page 21.

25. See *Strangers on a Bridge,* James B. Donovan, New York: Atheneum, 1964, page 4.

26. This very fact may have worked against them, for Khruschev appears to have had no greater liking for Jews than did Stalin, although he took greater pains to conceal his feelings.

27. For the most balanced and scholarly account, see *The Rosenberg File,* Ronald Radosh and Joyce Milton, New York: Holt, Rinehart and Winston, 1983.

28. Leopold Trepper's title. See Perrault, op. cit., supra note 1, passim for details of Trepper's arrest. See also Leopold Trepper, *The Great Game,* New York: McGraw-Hill, 1977.

29. This is particularly the case with Britain's MI5, which lacks powers of arrest. The security service must turn over those it has caught to the Special Branch of the Metropolitan Police, a force which is bound to act in strict compliance with the law in the matter of evidence, warrents, arrest, and charge, as well as bringing the arrested person before the courts in due time.

30. See Corson and Crowley, op. cit., supra note 4, pages 31–80.

31. As in the case of Kalamatiano, a United States citizen in

the hands of the Cheka during its most grisly period. Kalamatiano was released through Lenin's intervention after the American Relief Administration made its humanitarian efforts contingent upon the release of Kalamatiano and other Americans in Russian hands. On this see Corson and Crowley, op. cit., supra note 4, pages 55–56. A different account, with a strikingly different ending, is to be found in *The Conspirators,* Geoffrey Bailey, New York: Harper & Row, 1960. Bailey did not appear to be aware that Kalamatiano's life had been spared.

32. Among many instances which might have been cited is one that touches us personally. The Palestine police was feared but not respected by the Jewish underground organizations. The Field Security Branch of the Intelligence Corps was hated but not overly feared (hence the hanging of two Field Security sergeants as a reprisal by Jewish terrorists). But the Special Investigation branch seems to have evoked some admiration in its opponents. See *The Revolt,* Menachem Begin, New York: Nash Publishing, 1977, page 212.

33. See *The Game of the Foxes,* Ladislas Farago, New York: David McKay, 1971, passim.

34. This, too, is an unfolding story at the time we went to press, but the original, current media reports convey the outlines of the matter in sufficient form. See, for example, "Marine Spy Scandal: It's a Biggie," *Time,* 6 April, pages 21–22. See also *Time,* 13 April, page 20.

35. See *Time,* 20 April, pages 14–18.

36. Those inclined to dismiss the expression as a conventional exaggeration employed in these cases may like to consider the photograph of the "seductress Violetta" in *The Economist,* 4–10 April 1987, page 26.

37. "State Department spokesman Charles Redman accuses Soviet Union of using mysterious powdery substance as aid to tracking movements of Americans [Nitrophenylpentadienal]," *New York Times,* 22 August 1986, page 1.

38. "The State Department vowed Monday to take whatever action is necessary to make the new U.S. Embassy in Moscow spy-proof but stopped short of endorsing congressional suggestions that the building be torn down out of fear that it was bugged." "U.S. Promises Spy-Proof Embassy," *Dallas Morning News,* 7 April 1987, International.

"We seldom ventured into the garden—except when we

wanted to hold an extremely secret conference away from the listening devices which we assumed the U.S. had planted inside the House." *Spy in the U.S.*, Daniel Monat with John Dille, New York: Harper & Row, 1962, page 53.

39. Many of these issues had been foreshadowed in a perceptive piece by Charles R. Babcock, "Spy vs. Spy: How Good is U.S. Counterintelligence," *The Washington Post*, National Weekly Edition, 19 August 1985, pages 32–35. We shall return to these important matters in our conclusion.

40. Anyone interested in making a small evaluation of his own might profitably commence with an article, "How to Select a Guard Company" by Thomas J. Seth, *Security World*, 1983, and measure the criteria set out therein against the arrangements for using Marine Guards. A security professional on a specific assignment would use even more detailed and exacting requirements against which he would measure these things.

41. See, for example, "The Importance of Being Earnest," Edward L. Lee II, *Security Management*, September 1983, pages 149–151.

42. A very good overview of the range and depth of the involvement is provided by the address of Judge William H. Webster, then Director, Federal Bureau of Investigation, to the Annual Conference of the International Association of Chiefs of Police (1983), published in *The Police Chief*, March 1984, pages 26–31. The Director of the FBI, an IACP member, traditionally addresses the Annual Conference on issues of general concern to law enforcement.

43. See, for example, Babcock, op. cit., supra note 39, page 32. "A theme in much of the criticism is that counterintelligence is not viewed as a path to career promotion at the CIA or FBI, or at the State Department, where security has long been a low priority."

44. For a comparatively modern instance where these responsibilities yielded valuable dividends, see *Labyrinth*, Taylor Branch and Eugene Propper, New York: Viking Press, 1982.

45. See, "MI5: Mountains and Molehills," *The Economist*, 21 March 1987, pages 57–58, and 9 May 1987, pages 17–18.

46. Two important SIS officers were kidnapped in 1939 at Venlo on the border of Holland and Germany by a Sicherheitsdienst group led by Walter Schellenberg. Not only was

this demoralizing for the service and highly disruptive of its work, but it also put the Nazis in possession of important information concerning the organization and workings of the British secret intelligence services. Of even greater import was the exposure of some of the prevalent amateurism and poor security. On this generally, see *MI6: British Secret Intelligence Service 1909–1945*, Nigel West, New York: Random House, 1983.

47. Shortly after the outbreak of World War II, a German submarine effected a daring penetration of the British naval base at Scapa Flow, north of Scotland, sinking the battleship *Royal Oak* at her moorings. It was widely believed that the enterprise had been facilitated by a German spy in place which, on the best evidence, does not seem to have been the case. MI5 was, however, under a cloud as a result, and the event contributed substantially to the retirement of longtime director Sir Vernon Kell.

48. The British Labour Party, which came to power in 1945, had a deep suspicion of MI5 which dated back to 1924, the first Labour administration, and the affair of the Zinoview letter. For a good short account, see Corson and Crowley, op. cit., supra note 4, pages 86–89. The appointment of Sir Percy Sillitoe, a professional police officer, to Director General, MI5 reflects these feelings. These have not abated over the years, and some of Mr. Wright's threatened disclosures involve supposed plots to destabilize the Labour governments of the 1970s. See also "Was Wilson Bugged?" *Newsweek*, 15 August 1977, page 31.

49. In a biography of the head of the KGB on his elevation to General Secretary, CPSU, Zhores Medvedev wrote: "It is almost impossible to write anything about Andropov, the man." *Andropov*, New York: W. W. Norton, 1983, page 27. His successor may well regret the entry of *glasnost* into his private life.

50. See "A Mole in MI5," *Time*, 6 April 1981, page 37.

51. See *Molehunt*, Nigel West, London: Weidenfeld and Nicolson, 1987. There are others who incline to the view that while Sir Roger Hollis was not a mole, Guy Lidell, Sir Percy Sillitoe's deputy, was. *"C": A Biography of Sir Maurice Oldfield*, Richard Deacon, London: Future, 1985, page 86.

52. New York: Macmillan, 1986. We would strongly rec-

ommend this book, which we have cited elsewhere, to all
aspiring spies and spy-catchers.

53. London: Sedgwick and Jackson, 1981.

54. New York: St. Martin's Press, 1984.

55. These would include matters connected with the Profumo
affair and allegations concerning Lord Wilson and the Labour
administrations of the 1970s. Doubtless, Mr. Wright has knowledge of other matters that might be politically embarrassing
were they revealed at this time.

56. The seriousness with which the British government
viewed this matter is to be seen from the fact that the
Cabinet Secretary, Sir Robert Armstrong, was sent to Australia where he faced what *The Economist* described as a
"bruising cross-examination" (21 March 1987, page 57).

57. For a singularly interesting and pertinent reflection
upon this in an American context, see "Knifing of the OSS,"
Thomas F. Troy, *International Journal of Intelligence and
Counterintelligence*, No. 3, 1986, pages 95–108. It should be
studied in conjunction with that author's masterly *Donovan
and the CIA: A History of the Establishment of the Central
Intelligence Agency*, Frederick, MD: University Publications,
1981. There are many relevant lessons here in regard to the
present topic.

58. In March 1980, influential voices in Iran, including that
of Ayatollais Beheshti, joined those of the militants in urging
public travel of at least some of the U.S. embassy personnel.
Although dismissed as rhetoric by the Carter Administration,
the clamor cannot altogether have been lacking influence.
The abortive military rescue attempt took place less than a
month later. ". . . just before Arafat had flown to Tehran, he
was quoted as having told a Paris-based Arab newspaper: 'We
dismantled the biggest spy centre of the United States in
Iran.' " *The Canadian Caper*, Jean Pelletier and Claude Adams, New York: William Morrow, 1981, page 103.

59. See *London Calling North Pole*, Herman J. Giskes,
New York: Bantam Books, 1982.

60. Zavaron was taken into custody by the FBI in New
York on August 22, 1986, after allegedly paying an employee
of a U.S. defense contractor to turn over classified documents. He was accused of espionage and faced life imprisonment if convicted. He did not enjoy diplomatic immunity.
Nicholas Daniloff, a Moscow-based journalist for *U.S. News*

and World Report, a U.S. citizen, was arrested on August 30, 1986, and accused of espionage.

61. For the latest addition to the voluminous literature concerning this tragic woman, see *Mata Hari: The True Story*, New York: Dodd and Mead, 1986. One is reminded here of the slyly chauvinistic observation of Gunter Grass: "Though only a woman, she made history." *The Flounder*, New York: Harcourt Brace Jovanovich, 1978, page 16.

62. This point can be overemphasized. Giving ordinary police forces powers of arrest as necessary adjuncts to their ordinary functions does not politicize them. There is a real question whether other government agencies, such as those concerned with fiscal matters, for example, should have powers of arrest in a democratic society. The problem so far as espionage is concerned, is that without appropriate powers of arrest, a suspect might have time for flight.

63. Clearly, Iran is an important target for Western intelligence agencies, especially those of the United States, which have been criticized for failure to provide reliable, prompt information in the past. Iranian sensitivities are therefore understandable. A number of cases are worth study, notably those of Jon Pattis, arrested in mid-1986 in possession of a false Italian passport and accused of spying for Iraq, and Philip Enes, a Canadian oil engineer arrested in December 1986 and released on February 8, 1987. Gerald W. Seib, a *Wall Street Journal* reporter, officially invited by Iran, was arrested on January 31, 1987, and accused of being an Israeli spy. He was released on February 4, 1987.

64. Anyone listening to the testimony of former National Security Adviser Robert MacFarlane before the Joint Congressional Committee must have been struck by how far that conscientious public servant had been affected in his views and actions by these sentiments.

65. Perrault tells of his visit to Giskes in connection with his researches into the Red Orchestra, and seeing on Giskes' mantlepiece the miniature whisky bottles with which the unfortunate SOE agents had been supplied for their comfort on their journey from London into occupied Holland. Op. cit., supra note 1, page 59.

8

CONCLUDING
OBSERVATIONS

. . . the readiness is all . . .

William Shakespeare[1]

*I keep six honest serving men
They taught me all I knew;
Their names are What & Why & When
And How & Where & Who.*

Rudyard Kipling[2]

I always considered highly efficient and skilled technicians the most important part of a good secret service.

Walter Schellenberg[3]

In this business, as in so many other aspects of life, the difference between success and failure often lies in the preparation. Preparation puts us in a necessary condition of readiness. It is more than a state of mind; it is a statement of the ability to respond. In the business of spy-catching, preparation involves much more than a recognition that there may be spies among us actively working to gain access to our secrets and to communicate them to others from whom we would wish to keep them. It means the creation and maintenance of the means to frustrate their designs and bring them to book. This is an expensive business, but not as costly as failure to take those measures might prove to be.

Everybody has secrets, and some of these are more valuable than others. Some secrets are literally priceless; their value cannot be sensibly measured in economic terms. The secrets connected with what has come to be called the Strategic Defense Initiative (Star Wars) come readily to mind in this regard. Their commercial value would be difficult enough to estimate, but their military value might well determine who rules the world in the early part of the twenty-first century. This is a prize for the spy surely of no lesser value than the secrets of the atomic bomb (we shall return to this shortly). Unless we are prepared to defend these secrets, they will be stolen from us as surely as those earlier secrets, the loss of which robbed the United States and her allies of their hard-won preeminence in the early days following the close of World War II. The economic and military leadership of the United States at this juncture in history are precariously balanced upon the knife edge of modern technology. A slight nudge either way, by friend or foe, and that leadership may be irretrievably lost. The consequences of this are too terrible to ignore. There are extraordinary opportunities for the daring here. Our lead is slim enough to make this a decisive contest.

At this historical juncture, the well-prepared spy can do what whole armies cannot. Indeed, there is no role for armies here. This is truly the War of the Spies, perhaps the greatest that has ever been fought (to this too we shall return before closing). The well-prepared spy and his purposes can be defeated only by the equally well prepared and supported spy-catcher. To use those metaphors we have employed throughout, if the hunt is not properly organized and outfitted, there will be no trophy at its end. But that may well be the least of our troubles. We may be led away on a wild goose chase by *desinformatsya* only to discover, on our return, that the entire camp has gone, as well as the means to find our way safely back to civilization. Our conclusion on this is crystal clear: spy-catching is serious business. It had better be taken seriously in terms of organization and support, or it may cost us not an afternoon's sport, but our all. There is presently little indication that these verities have been perceived by those who must pay the piper on our account. There is even less indication of such perceptions being translated into deeds.

There is a dreadful feeling of déjà vu about all this. We feel an urge to cry: Wake up, America! For it appears that the United States is as unprepared to fight this War of the Spies as it was to defend itself from a different kind of aggression on December 7, 1941. We have been almost criminally complacent. We are in deadly danger of losing this war by default. Moreover, we have elected to enter this struggle under the gravest of self-imposed handicaps, for we have made the larceny of our secrets all too easy for those who would abuse the openness and generosity of our system. Against such predators, cosmetic measures are of no avail. We have more to lose than our Star Wars technology. When the candy jar stands invitingly ever open, it is hardly surprising that many will dip into it. Eventually, it will be empty, however often and however generously we may replenish it. It is good to enjoy a reputation for openhandedness and generosity—but not for being a sucker. Those whose patent inferiority destines them to follow rather than lead, want, like Whitaker Chambers, to be on the winning side. We cannot afford to present an image of being soft on spies or soft about spies. If we do little else for the moment, let us not be seen to encourage the pests. The world is watching us as carefully in the matter of spies as it is observing our vacillating policies for meeting the terrorist challenge.

The master strategist, Frederick the Great, instructed that when you defend everything, you defend nothing. One spy can do more harm than many armies, yet that single spy may take armies of spy-catchers and a logistical war effort of immense proportions before he is put out of action. We must face the fact that we do not have and never will have armies of spy-catchers at our disposal. Unlike those totalitarian societies we are wont to contrast so unfavorably with our own, we cannot even count upon the enthusiastic assistance of local defense volunteers to supplement our personnel deficiencies.

The climate, generally, in the United States is antithetical to the work of the spy-catcher. The national character tends to favor the underdog, even where that individual is a decidedly antisocial person. The criminal classes as a whole tend to benefit from these incongruous, often misplaced, sympathies, and the spy has a free ride on their coattails. The spy is shielded by cloying layers of privacy protection intended for other purposes entirely than the shielding of subversive activities. But the collective mind has not shown itself able or willing to make distinctions in these matters. From an espionage perspective, the United States must be accounted an exceptionally porous society. It is worth listing some of its weaknesses here.

1) Over the last two decades, it has absorbed huge numbers of aliens into its social structures, many of whom cannot be satisfactorily accounted for by the authorities. Their true histories and true sympathies are unknown. The basic loyalties of such persons and their commitment to the United States and its interests cannot be the subject of any satisfactory appreciation.

2) Any attempt to study these matters, even academically, would be greeted with cries of outrage from the general populace, and all sorts of sinister interpretations would be placed upon such efforts. On ideological rather than practical grounds, we elect to remain in ignorance.

3) It is extremely easy to introduce trained agents from abroad into the United States. They have little difficulty in achieving full acceptance in our multi-ethnic, multi-racial society, and any deficiencies of a linguistic kind, for example, are tolerated by a population whose own language idiosyncrasies are widespread and substantial.

4) The United States is still seen as a land of opportunity for the poor but talented immigrant. The Southeast Asian with an imperfect command of English, but with an extraordinary technical competence, is common enough in senior positions in our burgeoning telecommunications industry. Soviet Jews are becoming familiar in key positions on Wall Street and arouse as little curiosity. The security implications of all this are profound and disturbing. Again there is reticence bordering on reluctance even to raise the matter.

5) In the absence of some discernible hostile activity, we have no reliable means of distinguishing friend from foe. This greatly favors carefully planned long-term penetrations. Provided the long view is taken, the ease with which integration can be effected allows those who in other, more homogenous societies might be suspect (if not automatically excluded) to attain positions of great influence and authority. Once there, they cannot readily be smoked out.

6) The bias against discrimination on grounds of ethnic origin produces a strong disinclination against any action which might be construed as proceeding from racial prejudice. In practice, this tends to inhibit the crystallization of suspicions and the timely reporting of those suspicious to the authorities. Americans are inclined to make allowances for behavior

and attitudes which, elsewhere, would alert the authorities to take preventive measures.

7) Language represents a substantial cultural barrier behind which many can be sheltered. Very few native English-speaking Americans are truly proficient in a foreign language, especially the languages spoken by Southeast Asians, Arabs, or Iranians. Law-enforcement agencies are a microcosm of the community in this respect and very few have at their command a reliable capability of "listening in" to the different ethnic components that make up their jurisdictions. The truly multilingual individual enjoys immense advantages that he can employ to good effect in the business of espionage.

8) The assumption of new identities in the United States is extremely easy for the knowledgeable. It is even easier when the ethnic factors we have been considering are thrown into the scale. The authorities lack the means to keep an effective check on these changes of identity, especially when they are undertaken with illicit purposes in view. The United States is still, in many ways, a very private society. The stranger is readily accepted without too many embarrassing questions concerning his past.[4]

9) There is a ready acceptance of the idea of mobility in the United States. People are expected to travel about. The only real restrictions are economic. It is possible for the person with the means to sustain himself to live, without difficulty or too much enquiry into his affairs, almost anywhere in this vast hospitable land. And once he has made a home somewhere therein, he is sure to find a welcome. His previous residence, if he chooses to employ it for the purpose, authenticates him among his new neighbors. It may not be literally true that money gets you anything in our society, but in judiciously measured portions it will greatly facilitate the spy establishing himself wherever he might need to be.

10) Given a reasonable helping of luck, this is a society in which one's misdeeds might well take a fair amount of time to catch up with the miscreant. The horrendous burden of common crime taxes the criminal justice system to the full. In large urban areas, quite serious violations of law go unreported or are overlooked in the interests of a more useful disposition of scarce resources in other, more needy directions.

The practical difficulties in changing any of these matters must be realistically faced. What cannot be altered must be accepted. These obstacles have to be factored into the spy-catcher's plans; when they cannot be overcome, a way must be found around them. This comes down to the best ways of providing security in a basically insecure environment. These problems must be viewed without sentimentality, trepidation, or resignation. It is too easy to become complacent and accepting, overly fearful—or just inclined to give up the case as hopeless. None of these attitudes is conducive to the establishment of a satisfactory climate of security. At this time, the United States stands at a most dangerous crossroads. Decisive choices have to be made with regard to economic, military, and technological matters that will determine whether the country will retain its world leadership in these areas or whether this will be wrested away by any one of a number of rivals.[5]

We must be prepared to think the unthinkable. It would require but the slightest of losses, measured overall, in the technological field, for example, for the United States to be relegated to second or even third place at a time when the advances of mankind are becoming increasingly gauged in these terms. Were that to occur, an economic decline of commensurate or even greater proportions could rapidly follow. Effective leadership of the free world would pass quickly from the United States, and the social and political consequences of this at home and abroad have hardly received any serious consideration, none certainly of the order these matters would merit. From a counterespionage perspective, there has been altogether too much emphasis on the contest with the USSR and its satellites and supporters. We in no way make light of that contest here or even suggest that the Soviet Union is not the main enemy; any good student of Marx can see the implications of what is suggested by what is set out above.[6] Our point here is simply that the United States should not hold the illusion that these particular ideological opponents are the *only* enemy in this war.

While there are many who have basked in the favors that a prosperous and powerful United States has been able to dispense, it would be a grave mistake to assume that this also betokens a support for or even acceptance of the leadership role of the United States in the world. There are too many contradictions, resentments, jealousies, and plain disagreements to be able to confidently proceed from such assumptions of support. There has been ample evidence over the last few years of the speed with which such support can evaporate in moments of crisis and real need, leaving the United States alone, without effective allies. In the clandestine field, it cannot prudently be supposed that such lukewarm support for the leadership role that the United States does enjoy altogether precludes these supposed friends from engaging in espionage against the United States they feel might or should be undertaken in their own self-interest. Politics and secret service work both make for some mighty strange bedfellows.

The European powers, in particular, have long doubted the experience, maturity, and judgment of the United States in matters of foreign policy, and recent events have strengthened rather than moderated these beliefs. They regret only that their own relative weaknesses, economic and military, prevent them from reasserting the traditional role they believe rightfully to be theirs by virtue of historical and geopolitical considerations. The Japanese challenge to the United States in the economic and technological spheres is too serious to be ignored. More than image is at stake here. The United States cannot afford to take, or be seen to take, second place in either of these vital areas. The character and dimension of Japanese espionage should not be mistaken, nor should its dangers for the United States be underestimated, because it is not at the moment focused primarily upon matters touching the national defense. Japan gained her current economic ascendancy because she was too long regarded as a beaten enemy; she has even been seen by some as a grateful client of those who had brought her to her knees. While Japanese prowess in the field of industrial espionage has long been acknowledged, there has been a tendency to regard this as a private matter that does not touch national security. There has been altogether too much complacency about these matters. How long do we have to bleed before an attempt is made to bind up the wounds?

Counterespionage is an integral part of the overall security process. Like that process itself, it has its preventive as well as its remedial aspects. The spy-catcher has a prophylactic as well as a therapeutic role. It is the former function that has been so sadly neglected in our own times in our own society. The system has become infected through a history of benign neglect. Any curative measures now initiated must therefore have the appearance of a retrogressive action and seem more severe and antagonistic than necessary; curing the budget deficit has much the same underlying problems for those who have to undertake it. This is not an atmosphere in which anything which might be interpreted or misinterpreted as an assault upon civil liberties should be essayed; it is unlikely to prosper. Nevertheless, the adequacy of our security arrangements should be subjected to the most rigorous review, and we should be prepared to make far-reaching changes where these appear necessary or desirable.

"If it ain't broke, don't fix it" is a sound principle by which to live and work.[7] In our view, there is presently sufficient evidence in the espionage field to suggest that our own countermeasures leave much to be desired; certainly some things are broken while others are outmoded. Our counter-espionage arrangements are not functioning as efficiently or as productively as required to combat the massive onslaught engineered by our enemies on our patrimony, not to mention the predatory forays undertaken from time to time by our friends.

We have here, in view, the most comprehensive notion of security. By it we mean everything which may be required organizationally and functionally to protect those things we wish to keep safe from harm. The loss of our secrets can be just as devastating a blow to action as a loss of the will to act. Both demand special kinds of protection which require the development of distinctive skills and applications. The organization and direction of these skills calls for different qualities from those to be found among the general ranks of security professionals.

We must never lose sight, however, of the fact that all this is nevertheless security work. Methods may differ widely, but the objectives remain the same. We need a clear idea of what constitutes a security function, who is responsible for its performance, and the means by which this function can be effectively performed. These tasks are shared among men and machines, but the ultimate responsibility is always that of some human being to whom the accomplishment of certain undertakings is assigned.

In our own scheme of things, *a security function* is one requiring the person entrusted with it to take some predetermined action to safeguard life or property by interposing authority or some other capability to that end. While varying amounts of discretion will be conferred upon those entrusted with such functions, there is always a clearly defined sense of mission or purpose. It is clear what has to be done even though there may be room for argument as to how this has to be accomplished. Designing spy traps is a security function. Setting, monitoring, adjusting, and maintaining them are others. In yet another sense, security is a state or condition brought about by the presence of someone or something that inhibits the development of its counter-state, namely that in which the protected being, entity, or thing is threatened or is perceived to be threatened with harm.

A *security presence* may be represented by a human being or by an artificial construct having certain capabilities. The presence does not necessarily *provide* security, but it creates the conditions whereunder it can develop and thrive. Knowing that identity documents are frequently and randomly inspected acts as an inhibitor to unauthorized intruders and obliges them to take measures of their own to meet the requirements imposed by the system. The security presence acts as a deterrent, a modifier of human behavior. It is important in designing and employing such a presence to envisage the impact it is likely to have on those whose behavior it is intended to affect. What methods will those affected employ in order to reduce or avoid its impact upon them? How might that presence be extended or modified to meet these possibilities? A dummy surveillance camera may ward off intruders, but it is not much use in trapping the disloyal employee abstracting secret papers from the office filing cabinet.

A *security device* is a process or an artifact or other instrument designed to supplement or substitute for a human presence in the safeguarding of life or property. A surveillance camera is a security device. So is a coded, card-key access system. Such devices can never supplant altogether the human being and, in consequence, ought not to be viewed in a competitive light. Whether traffic lights generally are better than policemen at busy intersections is not in our times a useful topic of discussion; there are simply not enough policemen for traffic control. Whether, *at a particular point*, it might not be better to have a policeman is another more useful question. Security systems are many, spy-catchers are few. Their strength must be husbanded wisely and applied where it can be most effective.

The counterespionage services of the United States appear to be in urgent need of reorganization and, to a certain extent, revitalization. Our security presence is too thin in some places, and wholly absent in others. In truth, counterespionage has always been the poor sister of the American intelligence community and many another as well. It tends to receive the least attention and the smallest share of the cake. It is the first to suffer in times of budgetary constraint, and the last to be reinforced in times of need. As long as *some* spies are occasionally caught, there is a tendency to believe that all is well and that nothing further by way of personnel or resources is required. A satisfactory counterespionage capability cannot be created overnight.

Another point that we need most forcefully to emphasize is that counterespionage is not simply espionage in reverse. A good spy does not necessarily make a good counterspy. Counterespionage is a distinct and distinctive area of specialization. Its organization and employment must reflect the differences. In practice, unfortunately, spy-catchers are often treated after the fashion of marines, being regarded as neither "fleshe nor fowle nor good red herringe." There is an ambivalence about where they fit into the scheme of things. Are they policemen or intelligence officers? Or something in between?

In what we are pleased to call democratic societies, there is an understandable fear and dislike of anything that smacks of a secret police and even more so of a secret, political police. These sentiments extend in the United States even to the private sector; many directors of security have, at some time in their careers, had to endure half-humorous allusions to the Gestapo in reference to their persons or work. These underlying sentiments, whether articulated or not, cannot help but affect the approach to the work. There is a diffidence about the United States approach to security, an apologetic attitude almost, that markedly contrasts with what is to be observed, for example, in the Soviet Union.

We make the point here merely to underline the difficulties under which the American spy-catcher labors. The climate and the difficulties it creates have simply to be accepted as necessary conditions of employment. It is as unprofitable to waste time trying to change them as it is in apologizing for one's labors. The job has to be done, despite the seeming ingratitude of those on whose behalf these tasks are undertaken. If it is to be done well, the right amount of effort and resources must be committed to it, and their employment must be efficiently organized. There is a real need for leadership in this area. The pieces will not fall into place of their own accord.

In our view, the most pressing question is who shall have overall responsibility for counterespionage? It is imperative to recognize that spies operate against United States interests worldwide. It is therefore unrealistic to divide the responsibilities for counterespionage by reference to domestic and foreign considerations. A counterespionage arm that is restricted to spy-catching on its own territory is crippled from the outset. An agency that has worldwide responsibilities, but which is forbidden to conduct its activities on its own soil, operates under a similar incongruous handicap. The upheaval such a reorganization must cause is frankly acknowledged here. But the task must be carried out, and it is better to do it now than later. Postponement can only lead to further resistance and entrenchment.

If it be objected that the present moment of heightened espionage activity worldwide against the United States is an inauspicious time to embark upon so far-reaching an undertaking, we would counter with the following points. It is overly sanguine to suppose that there will be a speedy amelioration of the situation, giving the United States a breathing space in which to get its act together. Vulnerability itself produces a cumulative reaction on the part of those who wish to take advantage of it. The endeavors to exploit the perceived weaknesses are thus likely to increase rather than diminish, and the prospects for an abatement of espionage against the United States as we move toward the twenty-first century are illusory at best. Moreover, we should remind ourselves that our opponents have shown themselves willing to undertake the most drastic and far-reaching reorganizations of their own espionage and security services in times of greater crises than those we are now facing; Nazi Germany, for example, undertook a radical reorganization during what were the darkest days of World War II for that country.

It is our view that to function effectively, the entire counterespionage capability of the United States should be brought under a single authority. That authority should extend worldwide, without limitations. It is logical, having regard to the present arrangements and organization of the United States intelligence services, that a specialized counterespionage capability, with the appropriate recognition of its distinctiveness and importance in the overall scheme of things, be lodged within the Central Intelligence Agency and report through a suitable hierarchy to the DCI. The charter legislation governing the powers and responsibilities of the Central Intelligence Agency should be amended accordingly so as to permit that agency to exercise these functions at home as well as abroad.

The domestic counterespionage functions of the Federal Bureau of Investigation should be absorbed into this expanded Central Intelligence Agency, and such personnel realignments as may be essential or desirable between the two agencies should take place. The necessary legislation giving all those employed on counterespionage duties the same powers of arrest as those presently enjoyed by the Federal Bureau of Investigation in the domestic arena should be enacted. The distinct nature of the counterespionage specialty should be recognized by allocating the necessary resources to its performance and ensuring a regular career path for those engaged in it.

Specialization should be encouraged rather than the reverse, and the need for the long-term view should be practically acknowledged. Catching spies does not sit well with other jobs; it is not something that can be taken up and put down on a whim. The skills needed for effective performance are acquired over a long period of dedicated service. Career prospects should be commensurate with what is involved.

We are under no illusions as to the difficulties in the way of effecting the changes we have proposed. We believe they are essential, for we can envisage no other way of achieving the type of counterespionage service we feel this country requires in order to protect its secrets from ruthless, unscrupulous adversaries whose dedication and commitment to their task are of the highest order. We believe, too, that this is a singularly propitious time to initiate such a reorganization. In the first place, the sociopolitical climate is not averse to such a move; it does not have threatening overtones as might be the case in a time of great political instability or incipient spy mania. Second, the spate of espionage-related news has produced a raising of consciousness among the informed classes and, especially, has piqued the indispensable interest of the Congress. There is a growing awareness of the need to do something about the problem of espionage even though there is a lack of agreement on what concrete steps are needed.

Third, the appointment of Judge William Webster as DCI opens up a singular opportunity in this connection, which may not present itself again. William H. Webster came to his post directly from the directorship of the Federal Bureau of Investigation, and his leadership of the agency following a most difficult period of transition won him a general vote of confidence from a badly shaken public, as well as the approbation of those who served under him. Were the new DCI seeking to diminish the work and importance of the CIA by favoring the enlargement and strengthening of the agency he had formerly directed, he might have expected to encounter opposition. What he would be doing, however, by bringing the United States counterespionage capability under one roof, his own new one, would be the very opposite of this, and such an enhancement can only stimulate support in his present position. Logic and timing dictate such a move. It should be taken as expeditiously as possible.

Despite all we have written, it is neither superfluous nor naive to inquire as to whether the United States really *needs* to improve its spy-catching capabilities. Some spies, at least, are being caught under existing arrangements, and it is possible that others are being frightened off; nobody is suggesting that these arrangements are wholly inadequate or that they have totally broken down. We could, obviously, continue to plod along, making improvements here and there on an ad hoc basis as circumstances suggest. We could, in short, not take the spy problem too seriously. Or we can be realistic.

Those who have nothing—absolutely nothing—to hide have nothing to fear from spies. All they have is on display for all to admire or criticize as they choose. The shelves are open to all to ransack, as in the wonderful communist utopia envisaged by that poor, delusioned sponger, Karl Marx. There will still, of course, be those who, in the guise of fair and equit-able consumers, will enter with the concealed purpose of taking over the shop as did the immensely realistic and resourceful Lenin in 1917. Then we stand to lose all the goodies in one fell swoop. If the study of espionage teaches nothing else, it is most instructive with respect to the busi-ness of human nature and the incurable character of human avarice. Had Gary Hart been properly mindful of these pre-cepts, the course of the 1988 presidential election in the United States might well have figured differently in the his-tory books. Few enterprises of any real importance can today be successfully conducted with complete openness; too much *glasnost* can be bad for your health. The realization that this is the case is a standing challenge to the other party or parties to discover what is being withheld from them. And, in the nature of things, this is not something they can do openly. So we see the inevitable entry on the stage of the spy.

Nations must conduct some of their business secretly if it is to be successfully concluded. It goes almost without saying that in all areas of intensely competitive business, he who can keep his affairs secret from his rivals enjoys an invaluable edge. Why else do we speak of trade secrets? Security, in this sense, keeping those secrets from being raided by others who would make use of them at our expense, has sensibly to be seen as a high-priority item. It must increase proportionately to the endeavors of the other side to steal the secrets. It must be conceived, organized, and executed at the highest intel-lectual level if it is to meet with the success demanded by the undertaking.

Security, even poor security, never comes cheaply—but poor security is really no security at all. While the full extent of the Soviet espionage effort against United States interests worldwide can only be accurately estimated by those respon-sible for the mischief, it can be reliably opined that it has reached unprecedented dimensions and has expanded both quantitatively and qualitatively on an enormous scale during the last decade.[8] What is quite evident, on even the most superficial examination of the available evidence, is that it has not been met with a commensurate counterespionage com-mitment. And, as we have argued, Soviet bloc espionage by no means represents the totality of the problem.

The current climate, as we have indicated, greatly favors espionage. It is antithetical to security. In a very real sense, the store is wide open, and it is being looted every day. The fact that we are carrying on business as usual despite these very heavy depredations and depletions of stock has lulled us into a *false sense of security;* if we *can* still carry on, things cannot be all that bad. This is a very dangerous attitude to take. Even the most prodigal come sooner or later to realize that the cornucopia can run dry. We would urge that there are sound, practical reasons for sounding the tocsin now. We have already lost too much. A great deal remains that we simply cannot afford to lose.

Between 1945 and 1949, the balance of global power was dramatically shifted as a result of the herculean efforts of the Soviet espionage services. The long years of preparation paid off as the USSR was able to steal the secrets of the atomic bomb. The splines were adroitly filched from the American nuclear umbrella. It has never, since that time, offered the same degree of protection to those who have sought shelter beneath it. From the point of view of the United States, the loss of the technological and military edge afforded by the unique possession of a fearful, decisive weapon of war has resulted in a steadily escalating arms race, in itself an astronomical drain upon the nation's resources and unfortunate accommodations with other powers designed to prop up the country's vital strategic interests.[9]

As the Soviet bloc moved toward parity and beyond, the United States was forced to spend more and more of its patrimony on retaining an edge of diminishing utility and to enter into a frantic search for a twenty-first-century solution to a twentieth-century problem. Since the early 1980s, the still-vast resources of the United States have been committed on a substantial scale to addressing these matters. This enormously complex project, in which government and the private sector share, has come to be subsumed under the title of the Strategic Defense Initiative or, popularly, Star Wars. Unlike the research and development leading to the production, testing, and use of the atomic bomb, which had from the outset an acknowledgedly offensive aim, the Strategic Defense Initiative is itself eminently defensive in character, although its deployment would have the effect of enhancing offensive systems. Its real purpose is simply to restore the initiative that the United States enjoyed when it alone among the powers possessed the secret of the atomic bomb and the capacity to manufacture and deliver it against its enemies. There is still substantial debate as to how all this is to be accomplished. There remain many who are not persuaded that it can be accomplished at all—at least, not in the lifetimes of those who might be expected to be interested, in a practical sense, in the outcome.

But it is a fact that substantial resources have already been committed to the project and it has taken on a life of its own in terms of learning, personnel, finance, and other resources. It exists; it is a reality in its own right, whether or not viable weapons systems, offensive or defensive, are ever developed as a result of what has been started. Its value, militarily, can be assessed to some extent by reference to the degree of concern it appears to have engendered in the opposition. They cannot afford to take a gamble on the project failing to produce useful military results. There were, after all, those who sincerely believed, from a basis of experience and specialist knowledge, that an atomic device could not be exploded in 1945.[10] Had the Soviet Union, then, based its espionage strategy upon such a premise, its own atomic program would have been retarded by at least a decade. That it does not intend to make any such error with respect to the SDI is already manifest. The Soviet bloc intends to get in on the ground floor and to keep abreast of all developments in the most detailed way while pursuing its own research programs to similar ends.

In a world where pure theoretical science were king, there would be no room for vulgar espionage efforts directed at discovering and monitoring the other side's progress and achievements. These advances, and the disappointments, too, would be shared by all as the work proceeded. There are those naive souls who believe that this should indeed be the case, and who are ready to lend their good offices to that end. Similar sentiments prevailed in the realms of atomic research before, during, and after World War II.[11] Such attitudes greatly favor and assist those who are bent on acquiring by any means the fruits of the research being undertaken in those countries with open systems. There are thus considerable similarities existing between those times when the United States was robbed of its advantages in the field of nuclear weaponry and our own age in which the United States is striving to regain its lost primacy through a new scientific and technological initiative in which it has made a very substantial investment of human and material resources. As we declared above, not since 1945 have the espionage prizes been so alluring nor the perils for the United States and its interests so great. On this account alone, a realistic approach is demanded of us.

The Secrets of the Strategic Defense Initiative are very insecurely held.[12] Despite the immense sums of money involved in this project, in the comprehensive sense, there is little evidence that the security aspects have been taken seriously. It is almost ludicrously simple to follow ongoing research in even its most sensitive stages. It is almost as though the value to a prospective competitor or potential opponent of what we are engaged in has not been appreciated or taken into account. Historically, the United States is simply not a very security-conscious nation. The security implications of the SDI cannot therefore be expected to intrude obviously on the minds of those engaged in this work. Even during times of war or acute national crisis, security leaves much to be desired. At all other times, almost anything imposed in the name of security is positively resented. Civilians especially are irked by the restrictions and infringements on their privacy that security obliges them to accept. And much, if not most, of the work of the SDI rests necessarily in civilian hands. Such attitudes are the proud privilege of a freedom-loving people, but it must be recognized that they have their price. Under such conditions, the protection of secrets becomes very difficult, if not impossible. The catching of spies becomes a haphazard, uncertain business dependent more upon luck than method.

Again, we ask, does it really matter? Is improved security really worth the cost, not only in economic terms, but by reference to the hassles it must inevitably produce as its requirements become clear? What will be the collective answer to these questions? The matter may be reduced very simply to this: How much do we really care about the assumed final product of the SDI? Enough to make sure it does not fall into the wrong hands? If we truly believe that it is vital to the national security of this country and the security of our allies, it surely behooves us to take better care of what we now have and of what we hope to discover in the near future. If we are indeed resigned to having it all stolen from us by spies, why bother in the first place? We are only laboring to strengthen our enemy's hand. We make an example of this because it is of paramount and immediate importance, yet the very same arguments can be used in any field that is subject to depredation through espionage.

How much of America's current economic ills can be traced to the door of espionage can only be a matter for conjecture. Even proven losses are difficult to translate into concrete, market terms. Yet even impressionistically, the evidence is frightening. We can only keep our competitive lead by effecting marketable technological improvements, by producing new and better things that consumers will want to buy in preference to those produced by our trade rivals. We can no longer rely on outproducing the competition, producing more cheaply, or offering a recognizably better product.

American know-how and inventiveness are still prized in many areas of endeavor. This is especially true of the developing sectors of high technology, which are going to be the leading edge of progress in the early years of the next century. It is precisely here that secret knowledge is at a premium. It is knowledge per se, rather than the ability to put that knowledge to valuable use (which is now comparatively widespread), that will be the key to the dominance of future markets. The importance of keeping certain knowledge tightly held is growing rather than the reverse. The capacity to do so, meanwhile, is diminishing, at least in the United States.

Once the knowledge of how to do certain things is lost, the United States will find itself at a considerable disadvantage. For there are now many countries in a position to make as good or better use of that knowledge than is the United States, once the information is in their possession. The military and economic implications of this march hand in hand. The next great battle may well be fought not in the steaming jungles of Southeast Asia, or Central Africa, or amidst the hot arid lands of the Near East but, rather, on the more familiar terrain of Wall Street,[13] Silicon Valley, and Route 128. It is not too early to begin seeking out the infiltrators.

Counterespionage requires the development of good individual skills as well as the institutional mechanism to bring them to bear on the problem of finding and catching spies. Effective counterespionage combines all that is best in the work of the detective with the craft and skills of the intelligence operative. Performance is impaired when the work is undertaken hurriedly or haphazardly. Above all, this work requires the patient, methodical approach.

As in so many other fields of investigation, the basic tools of inquiry are organized along the lines of who, what, when, where, why, and how. As the pieces fall into place, the larger picture begins to emerge. To do his job well, the spy-catcher needs a crystal-clear picture with the most exquisite focus. He needs detail if he is to conclude the matter satisfactorily. Nothing that is acquired in the course of this work should ever be lightly discarded, for there is no telling how and when it might become useful. There is no substitute in this business for an efficient central registry of data, a repository in which everything that is collected can be stored and which is so organized as to permit rapid and easy retrieval by those entitled to make use of it. A primary concern of any counterespionage agency is the maintenance of the integrity of its own system of records. If these are lost or contaminated in any way so that they cannot be relied upon, the efficiency of the operation is immediately impaired. In an age when virtually all data is processed, stored, and retrieved electronically, and is susceptible to being accessed at a distance, the importance of this cannot be overemphasized.

Security begins very much at home, and the security of vital records must be priority number one for the spy-catcher. As record keeping becomes ever more technical, the spy-catcher must keep abreast of these developments. He must never allow himself or the system to become a prisoner of the technician.[14] The integrity of the system and all who work with and within it must be frequently and randomly tested. Nothing must ever be taken for granted, least of all the loyalty of those—all those—who serve that system. It is easy to overlook the lower orders, the toiler ants, anonymous in the bowels of the heap. This is perhaps the greatest mistake of all from a security perspective. Such creatures see and hear much and often have the capacity to lay their hands upon even more. The disgruntled secretary can often come across abstract vital information concerning the organization and its personnel; moreover, that secretary will often know, more exactly than others, what *is* vital and what is not. It is the likes of these that will be sought out by the spies and spy masters of the opposition. Purely quantitative caution can in itself be counterproductive. If everyone from the queen down is under some sort of surveillance by an army of counterespionage agents, the ant heap will soon grind to a halt; its productive energies will be turned in upon itself.

A sensible balance has to be struck. Quality rather than quantity must be the guiding rule for the spy-catcher. He needs expertise rather than numbers, technique rather than the all-encompassing approach likely to alienate those who would otherwise be helpful. The spy-catcher needs to know how to create a climate favorable to his endeavors rather than the reverse. He needs information and the skills to make what he learns work for him. A small, closely knit, wholly trustworthy team *can* accomplish more than armies on this battlefield.

The new technologies, like the jungle, are neutral.[15] They inspire their own brand of fear and mistrust. They favor those who have best learned to employ them and profit from what they have of their own nature to offer. All is grist to the spy-catcher's mill, but in the end it is the quality of the loaves he bakes that will determine customer satisfaction and whether he stays in business. We would conclude with this thought. The spy-catcher has only one job: keeping the system free from the other side's spies. His product is a spy-free system. The spy-catcher who can acceptably and consistently deliver is truly in business.

NOTES

1. *Hamlet, Prince of Denmark,* Act V, Scene II.
2. *The Elephant's Child.*
3. *The Labyrinth,* New York: Harper and Brothers, 1956, page 361.
4. An excellent illustration of this is provided by a study of the lives and fortunes of the many former servants of the Third Reich, including a number of prominent war criminals, who were able to find refuge in the United States and lead the lives of exemplary citizens. See, for example, *Aftermath,*

Ladislas Farago, New York: Simon & Schuster, 1974, page 12–15.

5. Japan's Toshiba cooperated with the Soviet Union to find and provide a technological application that would make that country's submarines more difficult to detect by the sophisticated listening devices employed by the United States. The economic cost of redressing the imbalance is estimated at $30 billion. The military and security cost is incalculable.

6. For those interested in a good, unbiased beginning, we would recommend *Communism: The Story of the Idea and Its Implementation*, James R. Ozinga, Englewood Cliffs, NJ: Prentice Hall, 1987.

7. Fixing it poorly or inappropriately can be very expensive, as any car owner will attest, and Mr. Goodwrench will endorse. We have the most serious reservations about some of the expensive solutions, including those recommended by Mr. James Schlessinger to "fix" the security deficiencies that have impaired the functioning of the United States embassy in Moscow. While this is obviously not the forum to argue for solutions, we do feel it worthwhile to go on record with our belief that most of what is suggested proceeds from faulty premises and that there are indeed better and cheaper ways of "fixing" the problem.

8. For a good overview, see *The New KGB*, William R. Corson and Robert T. Crowley, New York: William Morrow, 1986, especially pages 339–411.

9. Such, for example, as those entered into with Iran under the late Shah, Reza Pahlavi.

10. Even those who believed it could be done had little knowledge of the awful, awesome potentiality of the atomic bomb or its decisive character as a weapon of war. Can anyone doubt that had Hitler (whose mind and plans were filled with thoughts of secret weapons) enjoyed such an appreciation, the full might of the German war effort would not have been bent to producing an atom bomb? Failure to make a correct calculation, as much as anything else, cost Nazi Germany mastery of the world and brought the Thousand Year Reich to a close after a mere twelve years.

11. See *The New Meaning of Treason*, Rebecca West, New York: Viking Press, 1964, passim.

12. It is worth observing that no comprehensive security planning has been undertaken in this regard. Presumably,

everybody is just being trusted to look after his own secrets as best he can. There is no comprehensive government and private sector oversight of the entire project in this regard.

13. On this, see the fascinating and informative novel, *The Ropespinner Conspiracy*, Michael Thomas, New York: Warner, 1987.

14. It has been perceptively observed that "EDP people tend to identify with their technology to a far greater degree than with their employer or the business activity." *Crime by Computer*, Donn B. Parker, New York: Charles Scribner's Sons, 1976, page 49.

15. For the relevance of this reference, see *The Jungle Is Neutral*, F. Spencer Chapman, New York: W. W. Norton, 1949.

BIBLIOGRAPHY

Our own researches have not led us to anything in the nature of a bibliography devoted exclusively to works on counterespionage. In the nature of things, spy-catchers are interested in all matters relating to spies and spying, and works having a particular interest for them are to be found in general bibliographies on espionage, of which the excellent *Bibliography of Intelligence Literature,* Eighth Edition, 1985, edited by Walter Pforzheimer for the Defense Intelligence College, is a most useful, annotated example. We have included below a number of works that we believe to have special significance for those to whom our own book is addressed.

The diligent spy-catcher will canvass the whole field of literature or, at any rate, as much of it as his professional labors will permit. He would do well to begin with George C. Constantinides' *Intelligence and Espionage: An Analytical Bibliography,* Boulder, CO: Westview Press, 1983. We have included a few carefully chosen works of fiction which we believe have more than entertainment value. In addition, there are some interesting listings in the notes at the end of each chapter.

Accoce, Pierre, and Pierre Quet. *A Man Called Lucy.* New York: Coward-McCann, 1967.

Adams, Ian. *A Portrait of a Spy.* New York: Ticknor & Fields, 1982.

Akhmedov, Ismail G. *In and Out of Stalin's GRU.* Frederick, MD: University Publications of America, 1984.

Aldouby, Zwy, and Jerrold Ballinger. *The Shattered Silence.* New York: Coward-McCann, 1971.

Andrew, Christopher. *Her Majesty's Secret Service.* New York: Viking Press, 1986.

Bailey, Geoffrey. *The Conspirators*. New York: Harper and Brothers, 1960.

Barber, Bernard. *The Logic and Limits of Trust*. New Brunswick, NJ: Rutgers University Press, 1983.

Bargghoorn, Frederick C. *The Security Police: Interest Groups in Soviet Politics*. Princeton, NJ: University Press, 1971.

Barron, John. *Breaking the Ring*. Boston: Houghton Mifflin, 1987.

Barron, John. *KGB Today: The Hidden Hand*. New York: Reader's Digest Press, 1983.

Bernikov, Louise. *Abel*. New York: Trident, 1970.

Bethell, Nicholas. *The Great Betrayal*. London: Hodder and Stoughton, 1984.

Bothwell, Robert, and J. L. Granatstein. *The Gouzenko Transcripts*. Montreal: Deneau, 1982.

Bourke, Sean. *The Springing of George Blake*. New York: Viking Press, 1970.

Boyle, Andrew. *The Fourth Man*. New York: Dial Press, 1979.

Bulloch, John. *MI5*. London: A. Barker, 1963.

Carr, Barbara. *Spy in the Sun*. Capetown: Timmins, 1969.

Carritt, Michael. *A Mole in the Crown*. London: Carritt, 1985.

Cockerill, A. W. *Sir Percy Sillitoe*. London: W. H. Allen, 1975.

Connolly, Cyril. *The Missing Diplomats*. London: Queen Anne Press, 1952.

Cookridge, E. H. *Gehlen, Spy of the Century*. New York: Random House, 1971.

Cookridge, E. H. *The Many Sides of George Blake*. Princeton: Vertex, 1970.

Cooper, H. H. A. and Lawrence J. Redlinger. *Making Spies*. Boulder, CO: Paladin Press, 1986.

Corson, William R. and Robert T. Crowley. *The New KGB*. New York: William Morrow, 1986.

Courtney, Anthony. *Sailor in a Russian Frame*. London: Johnson, 1968.

Crankshaw, Edward. *Gestapo*. New York: Putnam, 1956.

Currey, Cecil B. *Code Number 72: Ben Franklin Patriot or Spy?* Englewood Cliffs, NJ: Prentice Hall, 1972.

Dallin, David. *Soviet Espionage*. New Haven: Yale University Press, 1955.

Deacon, Richard. *The British Connection*. London: Hamish & Hamilton, 1979.

Deacon, Richard. *The Israeli Secret Service*. London: Hamish & Hamilton, 1977.

Deakin, F. W., and G. R. Storry. *The Case of Richard Sorge*. London: Chatto and Windus, 1966.

Delarue, Jacques. *History of the Gestapo*. New York: Morrow, 1964.

Delmer, Sefton. *The Counterfeit Spy*. New York: Harper & Row, 1971.

Deriabin, Pyotr, with Frank Gibney. *The Secret World*. New York: Doubleday, 1959.

Donner, Frank J. *The Age of Surveillance*. New York: Alfred A. Knopf, 1980.

Donovan, James B. *Strangers on a Bridge*. New York: Atheneum, 1964.

Driberg, Tom. *Guy Burgess: A Portrait with Background*. London: Weidenfeld and Nicolson, 1956.

Eisenberg, Dennis, Dan Uri, and Elim Landau. *The Mossad*. New York: Paddington Press, 1978.

El-Ad, Avri. *Decline of Honor*. Chicago: Henry Regnery, 1976.

Faligot, Roger, and Krop Pascal. *La Picine: Les Services Secrets Francais 1944–1984*. Sevil Paris, 1985.

Farago, Ladislas. *The Game of the Foxes*. New York: David McKay, 1971.

Foote, Alexander. *Handbook for Spies*. London: Museum Press, 1964.

Frolik, Josef. *The Frolik Defection*. London: Cooper, 1975.

Gehlen, Reinhard. *The Service: The Memoirs of General Reinhard Gehlen*. New York: Popular Library, 1972.

Giskes, Herman. *London Calling North Pole*. New York: British Book Centre, 1953.

Golitsin, Anatoly. *New Lies for Old*. Oxford: Bodley Head, 1984.

Gouzenko, Igor. *This Was My Choice*. Montreal: Palm, 1968.

Gramont, Sanche de. *The Secret War: The Story of International Espionage*. London, 1962.

Granovski, Anatoli. *I Was an NKVD Agent*. New York: Devin-Adair, 1962.

Harel, Isser. *The House on Garibaldi Street*. New York: Viking Press, 1975.

Heilbrunn, Otto. *The Soviet Secret Services*. London: Allen and Unwin, 1956.

Hohne, Heinz. *Codeword: Direktop*. New York: Coward, McCann and Geoghegan, 1971.

Hohne, Heinz, and Hermann Zolling. *Network, The Truth about General Gehlen and His Spy Ring*. London: Secker & Warburg, 1972.

Hood, William. *Mole*. New York: W. W. Norton, 1982.

Houghton, Harry. *Operation Portland*. London: Hart-Davis, 1972.

Hyde, Montgomery. *The Atom Bomb Spies*. London: Hamish & Hamilton, 1980.

Hyde, Montgomery. *Secret Intelligence Agent*. New York: St. Martin's Press, 1983.

Johns, Otto. *Twice Through the Lines*. New York: Harper & Row, 1972.

Kimche, John. *Spying for Peace*. London: Weidenfeld and Nicolson, 1961.

Knightley, Phillip. *The Second Oldest Profession*. New York: W. W. Norton, 1986.

Knightley, Phillip, and Caroline Kennedy. *An Affair of State*. New York: Atheneum, 1987.

Lamphere, Robert J., and Tom Schachtman. *The FBI-KGB War*. New York: Random House, 1986.

Le Carré, John. *Smiley's People*. New York: Alfred A. Knopf, 1980.

Le Carré, John. *Tinker, Tailor, Soldier, Spy*. New York: Alfred A. Knopf, 1980.

Lindsey, Robert. *The Falcon and the Snowman*. New York: Simon & Schuster, 1979.

Lonsdale, Gordon. *Spy*. New York: Hawthorn Books, 1966.

Lotz, Wolfgang. *The Champagne Spy*. New York: St. Martin's Press, 1972.

Mann, Wilfrid. *Was There a Fifth Man?* London: Pergamon Press, 1982.

Masterman, Sir John. *The Double Cross System*. New York: Avon Books, 1972.

Monat, Pawel, with John Dille. *Spy in the U.S.* Harper & Row, 1961.

Moorehead, Alan. *The Traitors*. New York: Harper & Row, 1963.

Moravec, Frantisek. *Master of Spies*. New York: Doubleday, 1975.

Morros, Boris. *My Ten Years as a Counterspy*. New York: Viking Press, 1959.

Mygakov, Aleksei. *Inside the KGB*. New Rochelle, NY: Arlington House, 1977.

Orlov, Alex. *Handbook of Intelligence and Guerrilla Warfare*. University of Michigan Press, 1963.

Payne-Best, S. *The Venlo Incident*. London: Hutchinson, 1950.

Penrose, Barrie, and Simon Freeman. *Conspiracy of Silence*, New York: Farrar, Straus & Giroux, 1987.

Perrault, Gilles. *The Red Orchestra*. New York: Simon & Schuster, 1969.

Persico, Joseph E. *Piercing the Reigh: The Penetration of Nazi Germany by American Secret Agents During World War II*. New York: Viking Press, 1979.

Philby, Kim. *My Silent War*. London: Macgibbon and Kee, 1968.

Pincher, Chapman. *Their Trade Is Treachery*. London: Sedgwick and Jackson, 1981.

Pincher, Chapman. *Too Secret Too Long*. New York: St. Martin's Press, 1984.

Pinto, Oreste. *Spycatcher*. New York: Harper & Row, 1952.

Popov, Dusko. *Spy Counter-Spy*. London: Weidenfeld and Nicolson, 1974.

Powers, Francis Gary, and Curt Gentry. *Operation Overflight*. New York: Holt, Rinehart & Winston, 1970.

Powers Thomas. *The Man Who Kept the Secrets: Richard Helms & the CIA*. New York: Alfred A. Knopf, 1979.

Radosh, Ronald, and Joyce Milton. *The Rosenberg File*. New York: Holt, Rinehart & Winston, 1983.

Read, Anthony, and David Fisher. *Operation Lucy*. New York: Coward, McCann and Geoghegan, 1981.

Rees, Goronwy. *A Chapter of Accidents*. London: Chatto and Windus, 1972.

Rositzke, Harry A. *The KGB: The Eyes of Russia*. New York: Doubleday, 1981.

Sansom, A. W. *I Spied Spies*. London: 1964.

Sawatsky, John. *For Services Rendered*. New York: Doubleday, 1982.

Sawatsky, John. *Men in the Shadows*. New York: Doubleday, 1980

Schellenberg, Walter. *Memoirs*. London: Andre Deutsch, 1956.

Seale, Patrick, and Maureen McConville. *Philby: The Long Road to Moscow*. New York: Simon & Schuster, 1973.

Sigl, Rupert. *In the Claws of the KGB*. Ardmore, PA: Dorrance, 1978.

Straight, Michael. *After Long Silence*. New York: W. W. Norton, 1983.

Sullivan, William C., with Bill Brown. *The Bureau*. New York: W. W. Norton, 1979.

Sutherland, Douglas. *The Fourth Man*. London: Secker and Warburg, 1980.

Thomson, Sir Basil. *My Experiences at Scotland Yard*. London: 1923.

Trepper, Leopold. *The Great Game*. New York: McGraw-Hill, 1977.

Ungar, Sanford J. *FBI*. Boston: Little, Brown, 1976.

Volkoff, Vladimir. *The Turn-Around*. New York: Doubleday, 1981.

Werner, Ruth. *Sonia's Rapport*. Berlin: Verlag Neues Leben, 1982.

West, Nigel. *Molehunt*. London: Weidenfeld and Nicolson, 1987.

Whiteside, Thomas. *An Agent in Place: The Wennerstrom Affair*. New York: Viking Press, 1967.

Whiting, Charles. *The Spymasters*. New York: E. P. Dutton, 1976.

Wittlin, Thaddeus. *Commissar*. New York: Macmillan, 1972.

Young, Gordon. *The Cat with Two Faces*. New York: Coward-McCann, 1957.

Abel, Colonel Rudolph 12,
24, 32, 228, 277, 297,
300
Abu Nidal 46–48, 49, 108
Access 5–6
Access code 138, 139
Access control 150
Accessing electronic storage
facilities 241
Advantages 337
Agca, Mehmet Ali 42
Agent in place 175–176, 181,
182, 192, 198, 202,
205, 208, 211, 212, 253,
254
Agent, penetration 254
Agents, "turning" of 299
Allegiance 292
Alterations of appearance
and speech 249

Anastasia 98, 108
Andropov, Yuri 313
Antiespionage 55
Antiestablishment terrorism
317
Appearance and reality,
disparity between 251
Area of security 305
Assumed vulnerability 160
Automation, programmed
180
Avoidance and disguise
243–244

Background 72
Background check 6–7, 9,
29, 152
as a passive trap 152
Backgrounding 65–66, 80,
81, 90, 91, 92, 101

Backtracking 202–203
Being there 173
Big Brother 2
Biographies 272–273
Birth 7
Birth certification process 7
Birth record 8
Blake, George 291
Bormann, Martin 96, 107
Boyce 294
Built-in advantage 121–122
Burgess, Guy 212–213, 291
Burnout 117

Capucci, Hilarion 296
Catch 321
Catch-all description 182
Censorship 125
Central registry 351
Certification 322–323
Chain of evidence 78, 101
Change, indicators of 156
Cheka 300, 318, 328
Chin, Wu Tai 2, 294, 326
CIA mail-cover operation
    125
Close ranks 301
Closed elite 200
Codes and ciphers 259
Codes and passwords 138
Cohen, Eli 26, 106,
    287–288, 297, 298
Collective paranoia 35
Communications,
    diplomatic, 128–129
    speeding up 113–114
Compartmentalization 202
Computer 235–237

investigation of records
    235–236
magnifiers of human
    mistakes 236
record keeping 351
Computer state, the 119
Concealment
    of person 247
    of purpose 247, 249
Confrontation 145
Connections 255
Conqueror's problem 208
Conspirators 190–191
Contacts between skilled
    professionals 255
Conversion 175
Cordon sanitaire 209
Counterespionage 18–19, 24,
    33, 37, 43, 45, 49,
    54–56, 88, 91, 110, 129,
    130, 149, 299, 339,
    340, 342–344
Couriers 257
Courier system 114–115
Cover stories 145–146

Daniloff, Nicholas 25, 49,
    289, 320
Data 238
    correct interpretation 238
    electronically stored 241
    retrieval systems 237
    security 274
Dead drops 116
Debriefing 204
Deceptions 146, 176
Decoy ducks 193
Defectors in place 175, 210

Defectors in place (*cont.*)
(*See also* agents in place.)
Delays in the ordinary mails
130
Denunciation 145
Department of State, U.S.
305–307
Dictionary entries 184
Diplomatic mails 126
Disinformation 51, 139
Disposition for example's
sake 320
Distrust, highly destructive
197
Double Cross System 26,
320

Educational efforts 54–55
Eichmann, Adolph 96–97,
107–108
Electronic transmissions 132
Elements of identity 68
Elimination of the spy 285
Elitist organization 306
Elizabethan England 188
Elizabethan or Stuart origins
193
Embassy 309–310, 318
nest of spies 253
Encounters, inconsequential
231–232
Encryption 114, 115
Endangered species 183
Entrapment process 145
Equipment, sophisticated
communications 113
selection of 110
Escape hatch 158

Espionage 1–2, 4–6, 11–12,
16–17, 18–20, 21, 25,
27, 28–29, 39, 40,
41–43, 45, 50, 52, 54,
88, 110, 111, 126, 128,
153, 165, 171, 230
organizations 12–13
related functions 256
time devoted to business
250
Experts, right kind of
274–275

False electronic identity 241
False identity option 247
False sense of security 347
Farago, Ladislas 109
Father/confessor 157
FBI 307–309
Fear, climate of 39
Feeling of being trapped
147
Fifth Column 214–215
Fire sale 266
Fisher, David 109
Footprint 231, 232, 235,
238–240, 244
paradigm 235
Footprints 4, 16, 29,
209–210, 228, 231–235,
237, 240–241, 243,
247–248, 249, 254–255,
257, 260, 262, 275–276
Foreign policy, United
States 49
Free lamb and rice 57
Friends, striking a bargain
between 295

Gambit of uncertainty 145
Gamekeeper 154
Garb of personality 93
Geting caught 299
Giskes of Nordpol 324
Glasnost 346
Goniometry 133
Good manager 123
Grivas's cats 40

Histrionic ability 88
Hollis, Sir Roger 20–21,
    313–316, 330
Honey trap 143
Hoover, J. Edgar 25, 33,
    307–309
Hostage-taking games 24
Household, Geoffrey 1
Howard, Lee 2
Human memory 149–150,
    244–247
Hunt, E. Howard 245
Hunting procedures, stan-
    dardized 111
Hypnosis 261

Idea of mobility 337
Identifiers 83, 85, 137
Identities 8–9, 66–67, 234,
    247–248, 337
  historical 76–77
  multiple 234, 248
  serial 248
Identity 6, 8–9, 21, 29, 59,
    65–67, 68–69, 73–77,
    94–95, 96, 100, 101,
    103, 105, 107, 108,
    150, 234, 239, 337

check 65, 78
checking 80–81, 89
creation of 67
crisis of 292
detached 69
document 81
dormant 69, 70
elements of 68
false 276
false facade of 248–249
holder, the ultimate 78
ingredients of 82–83
life of its own 248
original human 78
removal of 69
sense of 180
separateness of human
    being and identity
    68–69, 234
social sheet anchor 77
socially constructed, ex-
    tension of 234
socially constructed, manu-
    factured 77
socially constructed, na-
    ture of 69–76
standing for 73
verification procedures 88
Illusion of Safe Haven 146,
    148
Impersonation 88, 137
Imposters 6
Incriminating elements 258
Incrimination 144
Indiscretions 109
Infiltrator 242, 243, 254, 276
Information, perishable
    commodity 268

Informers, enthusiastic 273
Insertion, technique of 206
Insider syndrome 155
Insiders 152–153
Intelligence services 202
Intermediaries 256–257
Interrogation 144, 261–264,
    268, 271–273, 277
  art of 261–262
  choice of methods of 268
Interrogator, limits of
    267–268
  reputation of 267
Irangate 323
Item of identification 74–75

Japanese challenge, eco-
    nomic and technologi-
    cal 339
Job, politics of 11–13

Kennedy, Marilyn Moats 11,
    109
Kleenex terrorists 45, 47,
    48
Knowing 71–72, 92

Language 137–138
  inaccuracies in 211
  within languages 138
Legend 92, 93, 265
Lie detector 6
Life, periods in 233
Lines of communication
    113
Lonsdale, Gordon 12, 105,
    231, 291
Luck 117–118, 121–124, 125

Maclean, Donald 291
Mails 125, 128, 129
  inspection of 129–130
Making the right connec-
    tions 251
Management tool 75
Man Who Never Was, The
    239, 278
Mandarins 312
Mass belief 44
Masterman, J.C. 284
Mata Hari 321
McCarthyism 3, 50
Memories, block out vivid
    246
Memory,
  content of 246–247
  most sensitive instrument
    247
  retentive 11
  tool of convenience 247
Mengele, Josef 96, 97
M15 311–312
Miller, Richard, FBI special
    agent 2
Mind, last refuge of hunted
    spy 262
Mind-altering substances
    261
Mole 19–22, 29, 149, 187,
    178, 180, 181–211,
    213–225
Molehunt 182, 201–202
Moravec, Frantisek 109
Moscow 302
Multilingual individual 337
Multiple footprints 234
Mystique 46

Native English 183
Need to believe 89, 101
New blood 311
Newman, Oscar 210

Obsession 310
Okamato, Kozo 296
One-time trap 132
Operation North Pole 320
Oyster Paradigm 27

Palestine Liberation Organi-
    zation 44–45
Paper trail 80, 86, 244
Paranoia 34–35, 39
Passive penetration 179
Passwords 138–139
Pelton, Ronald 2, 231, 278
Penetration 177–179
    agents 177–179, 184, 186,
        191, 193, 196, 210,
        211, 222
    operations 215
    point of 199
Pensioners 191
People-intensive 4
Pforzheimer, Walter 189
Philby, Kim 20–21, 31–32,
        212–213, 214, 223,
        224, 225, 291, 302
Philosophy of disposal 25–26
Pit of ignorance 137
Pollard, Jonathan 2, 202,
        231, 277–278, 284,
        291–298
Pope John Paul II 42
Population control 150, 209
Porous society 335

Positive vetting 153
Power to dispose 299
    where resides 316
Powers, Francis Gary
        242–243, 278
Preemployment screening
    142
Preparation 333
Princip, Gavrilo 42
Privacy 127–128
Profumo scandal 314

Rado 289
Rainbow Warrior 40
Reaction 301
Read, Anthony 109
Record,
    of birth 68
    of death 68
Record keeping, 236, 351
Reference check 78
Registered in the remem-
    brance 244
Relationship to the organiza-
    tion 12–13
Reorganization, need of 342
Rosenberg Solution 26
Rosenbergs, the 297–298

Scharansky, Anatoly 296,
        320, 326–327
Scouts 242–243, 254, 276
Sealed knot 220
Search 144, 258–260
    avoiding loss of or damage
        to delicate items 259
    intensive 258–259
Secret agent 42

Secret ingredient 149
Security 27, 29
  chief 27–28
  device 341
  function 340–341
  obligations 305
  presence 341
  service counterparts 202
Sender of message 121
Sensitive enterprises 209
Sensitivity of the system 238
Sensitized environment 239
Show trial of diplomats
  318–319
Signature 133
Significance 246
Sillitoe, Sir Percy 27
Situational incongruity 72
Sleeper 22, 23, 179–181,
  206–208, 210, 213,
  226
SMERSH 15
Smert Shpionem 285
Smoke screens 242
Smoking gun 257
Sorge, Richard 12, 26,
  288–290, 294
Soviet penetration 311
Specialization 308, 344
Spies, bartering of 287–288
  nest of 318
  playing at 171–172
Spookspeak 186, 189
Spy,
  as trophy 318
  colloquialism for 182
  communications 112–114
  discontented 13–14

  elimination of 285–286
  inchoate 201
  item of exchange 287
  lookalikes 15
  mania 3, 34, 35–37, 39, 41,
    49, 50, 51, 52–54, 56–59
  margin of safety 133
  master 192
  of action 41
  right of disposal over 319
  trapping 150
  traps 17, 109–110, 111,
    119, 120, 125, 129,
    134–137, 160–161
Spy-catcher 154–155, 157–158
Spy-catcher's motto 275
Spy-catching 333
Spying, basic vulnerability of
  112
Spy-proof system 229
Squirt transmission 133
Strategic Defense Initiative
  (SDI; Star Wars)
  333–334, 347–350
Striking a bargain 143, 203
Sun Tzu 42
Surface creature 196
Surreptitious search 258
Surveillance 252–257, 260
  name for observation 254
  of the individual 136, 144
  spy dust 303
  tactics 253
  twenty-four hour regiment
    of 252

Temptation 142, 143, 156
Term *mole* 183

Terrorism 39–40, 44–46, 49,
    126, 305
  mania 39–41, 43, 44, 49,
    50, 51, 58
Terrorists 15, 224
Theory of assumed vulnera-
    bility 111
Thurloe, John 192, 220–222
Tichborne, Sir Roger 98
Time constraints 272–273
Torture 269–272, 280, 281
  basis of 271
  defined 269
  effectiveness of 270
  subtle forms of 271
  threat or apprehension of
    270
  use of to make spies talk
    269
Trading undertaken 290
Trained observer 254–255
Transactions 79–81, 89, 101,
    231, 232, 235,
    238–239, 244, 278
Transformation 178
Transmissions 132, 133
Trapped rather than hunted
    197
Traps 17, 29–30
  ideas for 117, 135–136
  multiple-choice 141–142
Traven, B. 99–100, 103,
    104, 105

Trepper, Leopold 289
Trophy hunting 310
Trust 27, 37–39, 52, 58, 80,
    89, 134, 135, 146,
    153, 176
Trusted 81, 153
Turned spy 286

Unfriendly environment 56
United States embassy
    302

Vacuum cleaner principle
    274
Venus spy trap 142
Vulnerability 343

Walker John, et al. 2,
    26
Walkers 295–296
War of the Spies 23,
    334–335
Watch the watchers 52
Watergate 17, 119
Weakness, succumbing to
    157
Webster, William H. 345
Whitworth 26, 32
Witch-hunting 3
Wright, Peter 314–316

Zakharov, Gennady 48,
    320–321

H.H.A. Cooper is the president of Nuevevidas International, Inc., a Texas corporation specializing in the study of safety and survival. He was also Staff Director of the National Advisory Committee Task Force on Disorders and Terrorism of the U.S. Department of Justice. Additionally, he has been the Director of the Criminal Law Education and Research Center (CLEAR) of New York University, and Deputy Director of NYU's Center of Forensic Psychiatry. He lectures at the University of Texas at Dallas on disorders and terrorism; sociological and political aspects of assassination; and espionage and terrorism.

Lawrence J. Redlinger is Director of the Graduate Program in Political Economy at the University of Texas at Dallas. He has been widely published in the areas of illicit markets, corruption, and police narcotics control. At the University of Texas at Dallas, he teaches courses on social control; strategic planning and organization; politics and markets; and illicit markets.

We Deliver!
And So Do These Bestsellers.

Now there are two great ways to catch up with your favorite thrillers

Audio:

☐ 45066 **Suspects** *by William J. Caunitz*
Performance by Edward Asner
180 mins. Double Cassette $14.95

☐ 45116 **Final Flight** *by Stephen Coonts*
Performance by George Kennedy
180 mins. Double Cassette $14.95

☐ 45170 **The Negotiator** *by Frederick Forsyth*
Performance by Anthony Zerbe
180 mins. Double Cassette $14.95

☐ 45138 **When the Bough Breaks** *by Jonathan Kellerman*
Performance by John Rubinstein
180 mins. Double Cassette $14.95

☐ 45207 **Black Sand** *by William J. Caunitz*
Performance by Tony Roberts
180 mins. Double Cassette $14.95

Paperbacks:

☐ 26705 **Suspects** *by William J. Caunitz* $4.95
☐ 27430 **Secrets of Harry Bright** *by Joseph Wambaugh* $4.95
☐ 27510 **Butcher's Theater** *by Jonathan Kellerman* $4.95
☐ 28063 **The Rhineman Exchange** *by Robert Ludlum* $5.95
☐ 26757 **The Little Drummer Girl** *by John le Carre* $5.95
☐ 28359 **Black Sand** *by William J. Caunitz* $5.95
☐ 27523 **One Police Plaza** *by William J. Caunitz* $4.95